This book is dedicated to

CRESCENT D., my daughter
*who whispers  and makes small laughter*

and

CLANCY I., my sponsor
*whose air indifferent and imperious*
*at a stroke our mad poetics confutes*

# CONTENTS

vii

*A 32-page photo insert appears
between pages 214-215.*

# SHOOTING STAR

# 1

## The Prairie and the Desert

John Wayne, also called Duke, was playing a saloon scene in *Rio Lobo* on Soundstage 18 at Cinema Center Films studio.

*Rio Lobo* was his one hundred and forty-fourth movie. Wayne was Colonel McNally, an officer in the Union Army during the Civil War. The story was about his relentless search for some traitors who had leaked information to Confederate spies. The scene was to show Wayne questioning two young rebel soldiers just released from a Northern prison camp. The scene is rehearsed. The three men sit at a table. Wayne orders up a bottle of whiskey. He pours three drinks. They drink and talk. You are in the same basic saloon you have seen in every western you ever saw. There is the long bar and the bartenders. There are cardplayers and drinkers and whores, and the men are bearded and dirty and smoke cigars. There is noise and movement and scuffling. The Civil War is over but Colonel McNally is still pursuing the traitors.

How many frontier movie saloons has Wayne known during his career? He has stalked outlaws in saloons. He has protected decent women from lecherous drunks at the bar. He has exposed claim jumpers and cattle rustlers, risked his life dozens of times, and has shot it out while drunks and poker players clambered for safety under the tables. Yes, he knows it backwards and forwards. He should be bored to death by it all. Another take in the same old saloon.

He shifts his enormous hulk of a body in the wooden chair, waiting for the signal. He waits. The extras—about forty, forty-five—mope around waiting. Cinematographer William Clothier is lighting the setup. It takes a long time. He puts another mask on another klieg light. It is one of those interminable pauses between one take and the next. Most of Wayne's hours as a star consist of waiting around. Killing time. Smoking. Pacing. Conversing. Playing cards or chess. Waiting. He is on a set eight hours and maybe there will be two or three minutes of usable film to show for it all.

Wayne does not seem to give a damn about it. He appears to be blasé. He ignores the enormous camera hanging almost directly over his head and the operator perched on it. He doesn't seem to see Bill Clothier. A boom microphone is swaying close and it does not bother him. He does not seem to be here at this moment. He does not seem to be involved. Howard Hawks, the director, whispers a change in a line to him.

"Yeah," Wayne mutters. He covers a yawn.

And then a miracle takes place.

Ten feet from the set is the console. The sound engineer is sitting there, earphones clamped to his ears, fingers pushing switches and twirling knobs. He has pressed a buzzer and it emits a loud rasping blast.

The sound man says, "Talk."

Hawks says, "Camera."

And Wayne goes into action.

When he hears that buzzer, he reacts like Dr. Pavlov's dog salivating at the bell. At once, he becomes Colonel McNally, in 1866. His blue eyes harden. His jaw stiffens. His muscles tense. He speaks his lines perfectly. He sits where he has to sit. He does not forget lines. He never stands or sits in the wrong position and he never moves out of the range of the camera eye. He enters completely into the dramatic moment. This saloon becomes a real saloon outside a Union prison camp. He plays the interrogation scene with gusto. There are five takes. The young actors he is interrogating do not always remember the words.

Wayne plays it as spontaneously on the fifth take as he did on the first one.

Motion pictures are made out of pieces of action which are filmed in a disconnected way and then spliced together. It seems impossible to sustain a mood, or create a character, in the sense in which an actor can do it on the stage in a theater. In shooting a movie, the work is forever being interrupted for another take, another change of lighting, a new camera setup.

Hence, the technique of movie acting depends on mastery of one's body and emotions and imagination to such a degree that one can instantaneously turn oneself on like a light switch. Wayne has mastered this most difficult of human actions in such a way that, at the sound of a buzzer, he can instantly come alive for the camera eye and the sound boom.

Wayne's longevity as a superstar, as well as his continuing box-office appeal, is one of the most astonishing phenomena in the movie industry. On a *Variety* list of the one hundred highest-grossing films of all time, he had starred in seventeen. Joyce Haber, *Los Angeles Times* movie gossiper, once estimated that his pictures "had grossed more collectively than those of any other star in history. The total is now well over four hundred million dollars."

And his artistic achievements are as significant as his financial power. His relationship with John Ford, one of the world's greatest cinema directors, is the longest and most enduring collaboration between a star and director in the history of movies. It has spanned a lifetime: both men pictorially and dramatically went through youth and manhood and maturity and middle age and the twilight of life in a succession of now classic films of great beauty and great truth. Long taken for granted, Wayne began to come into his own during the 1960's and to be regarded by such newer American and European critics as Andrew Sarris, Henri Agel, John Baxter, and Peter Bogdanovich as one of the most powerful and gifted movie actors of all time. As the achievements of such hitherto bypassed directors as Howard Hawks and Henry Hathaway began to be recognized, so did John Wayne's glory come more and more into the critical focus, for they had made many of their best films with Wayne.

In his art and in his life, Wayne is in the American grain. He is a pure product of the American movie industry. He is Iowa. He is the high desert of Southern California. He is Glendale. He is Hollywood. His entire career has been structured within the Hollywood system. He never went to New York to appear in plays. He never aspired to tour with Broadway road companies as other movie stars have done. He has not made a series for television. He does not yearn to play in obscure and symbolic films and be directed by European directors. Not once has he been directed by a French, British, Italian, or Swedish director. He plays an American hero. He plays an American man. Sometimes he plays an American superman. In his personality are the virtues and the vices, the strengths and the weaknesses of the American. And he is complicated as Americans are complicated. He is a complex and contradictory person, and the characters he has portrayed express his own contrariness, his own fears and romanticism, his own courage and idealism, and, yes, his own madness.

He was born Marion Robert Morrison in 1907 in his parents' home at 404 East Court Street in Winterset, Iowa (pop. 2,956). Winterset is forty-five miles southwest of Des Moines. It is the county seat of Madison County. He was the firstborn son of Clyde L. Morrison and the former Mary A. Brown. Miss Brown hailed from Des Moines. She had been a telephone operator when she met her future husband at a Methodist supper-and-social in Des Moines. Morrison was a druggist. He was a graduate of Simpson College in Indianola, Iowa. He had been a football player. He had made All-State fullback during his Simpson years on the varsity. He was possessed of a fine baritone voice and was frequently called upon to regale friends with selections from light opera. On that enchanted evening in Des Moines, whither Morrison had journeyed to find employment as a pharmacist's clerk, he sang several ballads. Miss Brown fell in love with his deep voice, his handsome face, and his sturdy physique. She at once determined to marry him. Morrison, who was already known as Doc, was a shy person but she encouraged him, and after a violent and romantic courtship they were married in Knoxville, Iowa, on September 29, 1905. Marion was born on May 26, 1907.

The exact site of Wayne's birthplace is still argued by Winterset old-timers. Lloyd H. Smith, secretary of the Madison County Historical Society, informs me that "there is a lot of disagreement around here as to which spot should have the honor of the birth of John Wayne. Some say it was just southwest across the corner of the intersection at Monumental Park, just back of the Arcade Hotel at that spot. Some say just straight south across the street. Some say a block south. They do all agree that the birthplace was from a few feet south across the street to up as much as a block or two. Just say in the vicinity of a block east and a little south of the southeast corner of the courthouse square, and that ought to please 'em all. The house where John Wayne was born has long since been torn down or moved. The drugstore where his father worked has been changed. A partition between it and another building has been removed, and the two buildings together now compose a variety store."

In a monograph published in 1961, entitled "Scenic Madison County, Iowa, Historical Significance," Dr. Smith has given 404 East Court as the correct address of the nativity. I am not inclined to cavil with the historian even if other Winterset citizens may have their doubts.

As of this writing, there is no plaque or marker to indicate the place.

There is a minor mystery connected with Duke's name. All published references to his birth name, all school records, publicity releases, and Duke's own statements refer to it as Marion *Michael* Morrison. Yet his birth certificate, a transcript of which I have before me, gives his name as Marion *Robert* Morrison. One may surmise that Mr. or Mrs. Morrison was fond of the name Robert, for when they had a second son they named him Robert

Emmett Morrison, and perhaps it was then that they changed Marion's middle name to Michael.

In most respects the Winterset of today is not so different from the Winterset of 1907. The population is still fairly small—3,710 at the last count. There were once sixteen covered bridges and there are seven remaining. The landscape is green and fertile in the summer. The town and its environs have not been overwhelmed by monotonous tract houses and factories. The air and waters are not polluted. The primary occupation is farming. The cash crops are corn and soybeans. Hogs, cattle, poultry, and horses are raised. On the outskirts of town is a rich limestone quarry, hacked at for a hundred years, which yields a light gray limestone. There are private homes, built a century ago of limestone bricks, which remain standing and occupied. The handsome courthouse on the square is made of this limestone. Almost one hundred years old, it is a simple but elegant structure in the style of a Greek cross—with four equal flanges, four entrances, four porticos, four stone staircases on the four sides of the building. An imposing domed Byzantine tower with four clock faces lends an exotic touch to the surrounding white clapboard houses.

The streets of the village quickly merge into farmland; there are large farmhouses and barns and livestock, and there are still the acres of many vegetables, especially corn. Oceans of tasseled cornstalks sway in the wind in autumn.

Growing up in Iowa, Marion Michael (or Robert) Morrison absorbed the values of the American heartland. On both sides, he came of pioneer stock—English, Irish, and Scottish. His grandparents had settled in the Midwest before the Civil War. Western movies involving Indians and outlaws were not fables but factual stories, like those told to him by friends and relatives. He grew up on tales of Jesse James and his gang—they had robbed many trains and banks in Iowa. Once, in 1873, they hid out in a now dilapidated stone house, near the Clark Tower in Winterset. The hideout is still there. Marion's mother and father could remember the pioneers trekking through Iowa in their covered wagons. In 1894, a Winterset native noted that he had seen "no less than twenty-five prairie schooners loaded down with human freight. Never a day passes but there are from five to twenty-five teams on the move, going somewhere, many of them having to stop and beg for food, which sometimes was refused. This looked hard but it was all in a lifetime and one had to get used to the idea, for if everyone was fed, one would go broke trying to feed them all."

The Sioux Indians were still going on the warpath in northwestern Iowa, "scaring the natives out of their wits," said the *Earlham Echo*. Even in the early years of the twentieth century, federal troops were fighting Indians in Iowa.

The Civil War, also, was an important part of Marion's consciousness. Marion had uncles and one grandparent who had fought for the Union. A block from where he was born stood the Civil War Monument in Monumental Park. It is a fourteen-foot shaft of white marble surrounded by four cannons. Iowans assert that it was the first Civil War memorial in the country. The idea of "the Union," the belief that "these dead did not die in vain," was part of an intense love of country which became part of the landscape of his heart.

Unfortunately, his mother and his father fought another war, and some of it took place on this land in his heart. Mary and Doc were very different people. He was quiet and serious and laconic. She was petite, vivacious, with sharp blue eyes and red hair. She had a hot temper and a rich Irish vocabulary. She told stories well. She loved mimicking people and making fun of them. Her older son says she looked and behaved like Billie Burke. She was hard to get along with, and Doc never did get along with her. In terms of power, she was the stronger. She dominated him. She dominated the family. She even had to run her husband's business affairs.

Doc's first important job was as a clerk and pill-pounder in M. E. Smith's Drugstore in Winterset. Mary saved enough money to buy a pharmacy in Earlham, and in 1910 the family moved there. They had four prosperous years. The pharmacy was successful and Doc was making good money. They built a fine two-story Victorian frame house with gables and a tower. Doc drove a one-horse carriage. His horse, Sadie, was a familiar sight to Earlham folks.

Doc was crazy about football. He had gone to Simpson College on a football scholarship. He knew in his bones that his son Marion would get to be tall and strong and be a football player. Doc was always interested in working out with his son and other boys. He took part in helping the Earlham Academy get a good football team. He coached the boys. His 1911-1912 Earlham team was the best high school team in Iowa that season. He dreamed of Marion going to Annapolis and playing on the Navy team. Then he would become a civil engineer.

Mary thought he should be a lawyer.

Mary and Doc were not happy together. They quarreled often. She made fun of him and criticized his lack of business acumen. He was too kind to customers. He would allow them credit for too long. Sometimes, Mary got after Doc so hard and so bitingly that he would be driven to the wall and turn on her and explode. Then he would walk out of the house, slam the door, hitch up Sadie, and go for a ride by himself.

In working hours, Doc drove the horse and wagon to his drugstore. He tied Sadie up during the day. An old man, still living in Earlham, remembers how "that little boy often requested me to go see if his daddy's horse was still tied back of the store."

Marion had begun to live in daily anxiety. There was no emotional security in his home.

But there were good memories also. There were times when Doc showed him how to hold a pigskin and throw a pass, how to block, how to tackle. Doc said that football was a game which built character into a man. A man had to have character. A good character, that was more important than money or success. He told Marion that there were three rules in life.

1. Always keep your word.
2. A gentleman never insults anybody unintentionally.

3. Do not go around looking for trouble. But if you ever get into a fight, make sure you win it.

Marion worshiped his father and wanted to be like him. He could not understand why there was no peace at home. His father was just about a perfect man. He was more than a druggist. He was the town's philosopher and medical adviser. He helped people with their emotional problems. He did not have an enemy in the world, with the exception of his wife. He never argued with her in public. He was afraid of her.

In December, 1912, Marion was suddenly taken away to stay at Doc Holmes' house. Doc was a dentist. The young boy was terrified. Nobody told him what was happening. He did not see his father and his mother for three days. It was a cold time of year. The snow lay over the countryside.

On December 8, not long after supper, a woman friend of Mrs. Morrison's rushed into the house.

"God has sent you a baby brother," she informed Marion. "Isn't that just what you prayed for, Marion, dear?"

"I didn't pray for no brothers," he muttered.

"Don't you talk like that," the lady said.

"Well, I didn't."

"He's incorrigible," the lady said to the dentist. "He's a bad boy, always has been, always will be. Well, I'm supposed to fetch him over so's he can see little Robert. That's what they're going to christen him. Isn't that a nice name, Marion?"

"I dunno," Marion said.

She started to get him dressed for outdoors. He still remembers the hateful expression on her face when she yanked on his leggings and how she seemed to take savage delight in hurting him as she buttoned the many buttons on the leggings and the overcoat. She grabbed him by the hand and they strode the few blocks to the Morrison house.

Mama lay in bed. She smiled. Doc was sitting on the bed beside her. There was a new bed in the room, a small crib with brass footboard. Marion was nervously scuffing his shoes on the carpet.

Doc took him over to the crib. "Meet your new brother," he said jovially.

Marion regarded the wrinkled face of his brother. He kept rubbing his shoes on the carpet. Then he put out his hand and his fingers made contact with the brass footboard. He had stored up so much static electricity that at the contact a shower of sparks appeared.

"See," Marion cried to Mama and Papa, "I can make lightning."

Subsequently, he found out that Benjamin Franklin had anticipated his discovery.

Marion hated his brother. He felt things at home were getting worse all the time. One day he slunk into the kitchen. He had a pet at the time, an Airedale named Schnickelfritz. He huddled with his dog in the kitchen until both of them fell asleep.

In childhood, Marion manifested several peculiarities of behavior. He had trouble going to sleep. Neighbors were often called in to rock little Marion when he was having one of his tantrums and Mama was busy with brother Bob.

Marion was unable to sit still. He was a fidgeter. When the family went to church on Sunday, he frequently embarrassed them. He "was a lively boy and kept his mother busy during services as he preferred running between the seats."

He hated getting his hair cut. He screamed when he was put in the barber's chair. The barber had to lather his face and then pretend to give him a shave with the smooth side of a straight razor in order to calm him down.

He was also given to running away from home, which was understandable. The Morrisons then lived at 328 Ohio Street, which was near the railroad depot. Marion would often sneak into the freight yard and hide in a freight car. Sometimes it would start moving and he would wake up in another city. Blanche Powell Neff, telephone operator in Earlham and now living in Tujunga,

California, recalls that many times Mrs. Morrison would call her hysterically. Marion had disappeared again! She couldn't find him anywhere. She couldn't leave the house. Would Miss Neff phone around town and see if anybody had noticed Marion?

After Bob was born, Doc Morrison came down with tuberculosis. He was coughing up blood all the time. He got very sick and weak. A doctor in Des Moines told him he had to get out of Iowa. He had to get into a warm climate or he would die. He sold the drugstore in Earlham, and Mary and the boys went to live with her folks in Des Moines. Doc went out to buy land in California. He bought eighty acres of land on the rim of the Mojave Desert in Palmdale. He was going to homestead it. The land was cheap since nobody had ever farmed it before. A ditch for irrigation ran through the property. It was a bleak and barren desert, but Doc felt good in the sun. His health improved and his strength came back. The other farmers around Palmdale and Lancaster grew alfalfa and fruit, but Doc planned to get rich by raising corn. He would show them you could grow corn in the desert. He would show all of them. He would show Mary.

He went to work and put up a ramshackle bungalow with two bedrooms and a kitchen and a small parlor. He built a little shack for the horses and farm implements. He knew about farming; his father and grandfather had been farmers.

In 1914, he sent for his family. Mary and the boys took the Rock Island from Des Moines to Chicago and then the Southern Pacific all the way, directly to Palmdale, where the train stopped on demand. Palmdale was on the main line of the Southern Pacific. Doc was there to meet them, driving a horse and buggy. His wife thought he looked marvelous but she was horrified when she saw her new home. Was this Doc's idea of a home?

"Guess you'd have to call it a miserable little shanty," Wayne says today, shivering slightly. "Didn't have gas nor electricity nor water. None of the public utilities ran out that far. Evenings we lit kerosene lamps to read by. Mother cooked on a woodburnin' stove. No telephone lines out our way, of course. Went to bed an hour after supper and got up at dawn. You wouldn't believe we were less'n seventy miles from downtown Los Angeles. By car, in those days, you could make it in three, four hours if there had been an asphalt road. You gotta realize that was before the freeways. But we didn't even have paved roads. Even the old Ford Model T's had trouble navigatin' some of those caked mud roads with the rocks in 'em. Anyways, we didn't have a car. No phone. No gas, no electricity. We were cut off from the world.

"We had these two horses. They lived in a sort of barn. Dad was not much of a handyman. But he had the real pioneer spirit. He was determined to show Mother he could grow corn. You see, she got it into her mind he was a failure. Anyway, to get to Los Angeles from Palmdale by horse-and-wagon was a real trip. Took a day and a half. We never left Palmdale except to go to Lancaster. Our nearest neighbors were a mile away. It was a hard life. A stranger visitin' from Iowa wouldn't have believed he was in the twentieth century. Hell, we didn't have runnin' water. Or toilets."

The village consisted of a livery stable, a blacksmith shop, a post office, a land office, two churches, a general store, a men's clothing and supply store, and a shoe store (which made shoes as well as repaired them). There was a small hotel which boasted the town's only restaurant and saloon. Palmdale's two blocks of "Main Street" could have been the set for any western shootout, except there was no sheriff's office and no dance hall girls and no bordello.

The Morrison property teemed with rabbits and snakes. "And I don't mean just a few," says Wayne. "Seems to me like there musta been millions. The more you killed—the more they kept on comin'."

With the help of his older son, Doc cleared the land. He hitched one of his horses to a spring-tooth harrow, which he drove up and down, ripping out the brush, cacti, and mesquite. He also dug up the boulders. These activities flushed out the rabbits and the rattlesnakes. Duke followed his father, a rifle in his hand. As soon as a reptile or a rodent came into sight, the boy got a bead on the varmint and shot to kill. He didn't like to kill rabbits—he was sentimental about rabbits. And the snakes —he was scared of the snakes. But he didn't tell anybody about his feelings.

He had been a good shot for several years, though in Iowa he had only shot at stationary targets, tin cans on fenceposts and the like. Aiming for rattlers was different. And rabbits ran fast. But those snakes—they always seemed to be coming at him.

Duke was sure that if he didn't get the rattlers fast enough they'd strike him in the legs and sink their poison fangs into him and he'd swell up and die before they could get him to a doctor. He couldn't sleep well because he had nightmares about hordes of slithering snakes advancing on him, rattling their tails, some of them just disembodied heads with flickering snake tongues. He'd wake up at night in a cold sweat, knowing he had to face more rattlers in the morning.

He learned two lessons.

*One:* No matter how scared you were about something, you would still have to get through that lonely night by yourself. And then you'd wake up when it was still dark and there were still more jackrabbits and rattlers to shoot and you would have to go through another day and live through another night. *But you survived just the same.*

*Two:* It was possible to exterminate, or at least discourage, rattlers—but jackrabbits were always there.

These lessons, imprinted on his young mind, may have been valuable to him in coping with the traumas of making movies. They may have been just as important to him as becoming familiar with guns and horses.

"I never recall bein' taught how to ride," he reveals. "I was ridin' as soon's I could walk. Never was afraid of horses. I just felt natural when I mounted one. But I don't particularly love ridin' and horses the way some people do, like John Ford or John Huston. I never felt about horses the way I have about certain dogs. I wouldn't make a pet of any horse. To me, a horse is something you use, on a farm or in a movie."

The Palmdale public school was located on 8th Street and Palmdale Boulevard and was about four miles from the Morrison farm. It was near the Southern Pacific railroad tracks and not far from the two-lane dirt road which ran through Antelope Valley and was extravagantly named Mint Canyon Highway. It was not paved until 1921. Marion got up at five in the morning and had some breakfast and did some chores. Then he walked the four miles to school, attended school for five hours, then trudged home. He was miserable at school. He was tall for his age and had a skinny, awkward body. He was shy and insecure and talked with a Midwestern accent, which made the other kids in school laugh at him. He quickly became the prey of the other boys and was often beaten up and ridiculed. He didn't complain about his troubles but swallowed his misery.

Sometimes he escaped by means of fantasy.

Several times a week he was sent into town to pick up mail or supplies. He rode Jenny, one of the horses. He would pack the supplies and mail into a gunnysack, which he slung over his shoulder. After his errands were done, he mounted Jenny and hit the Mint Canyon Highway for home. There was a certain place where the road curved around a pile of rocks. You couldn't see what was lurking behind the rocks. The closer he got to this cliff, the more he frightened himself. In his mind's eye, he was a frontier scout or a paymaster carrying a load of gold bullion in his gunnysack, and around the bend in the road were lurking outlaws or Indians, waiting there to ambush him.

And sure enough they were there when he turned the curve. He played out the scene with all his heart. He took them one by one with his Winchester rifle, digging his imaginary spurs into Jenny's flanks and dodging imaginary bullets. Just the same, his heart was pounding as if he were in real danger. Even though there was nothing there, there was everything there and it was real to him. At this stage of his life, he had never seen a western movie or indeed any movie. However, he didn't need to see western movies to know about the dangers of frontier life. He'd grown up in Iowa hearing stories about covered wagons and train robbers and stagecoach bandits.

We think of the West nowadays as most western movies think of the West, the geography being Texas or Utah or Arizona or New Mexico. But, for most of the nineteenth century, Iowa was frontier territory and homesteading was still dangerous. This was also true of the other prairie states—Kansas, Missouri, Nebraska, and the Dakotas.

The boy's imagination drew upon stories he had heard from participants in the opening of the West. His retreat into fantasy was also a reaction to the discomfort in his life at home. Mrs. Morrison regretted ever having gone away from Iowa, leaving her friends and family. More and more she talked about going back there, without her husband if he insisted on remaining here in Palmdale. She couldn't stand living here. It was killing her. Doc didn't know how to meet the responsibilities of fatherhood. They never should have had children. He was always promising this or that, but he never made good on any promises, and those damned jackrabbits came out during the night and ate up all the shoots of the green vegetables she had planted. It was an accursed barren ground on which nothing would grow, and it was getting to the point where even if they got a good price for the corn, they'd have hardly enough to carry them through another year. They were living on credit for the staples, and they never had meat or chicken on the table. It was potatoes, potatoes all the time, as bad as Ireland in the 1840's it was. And awful killing heat in the daytime, sometimes 110° in the summer, and always freezing cold at night. Wasn't a natural climate, was it? She had been out of her mind to let him talk her into moving out to the desert. She didn't have any friends here. She sure missed her folks and the neighbors.

"I tell you, Doc," she'd sometimes yell, "one of these days, mark my words, one of these days, I'm just going to pack up and go back to Des Moines, kit and kaboodle. You'll see, this wife of yours will just vamoose."

To placate her, he invited her parents to come out

and live with them. The idea was that Grandpa would help with the farming. But Grandpa did not like the idea of working. He had his Civil War pension and he had a little money saved up besides and he just liked to laze around and play with young Marion. Marion loved him. He remembered back in Iowa how he and Grandpa would build snowmen. Once, Doc Holmes—that was that dentist friend of Clyde Morrison's—had built a really monster snowman and little Marion started talking to the snowman. Then Doc Holmes started throwing snowballs at the snowman's face. This got Marion nervous. He started crying and he blocked the snowman. Doc Holmes was laughing and throwing snowballs, hitting Marion. Marion remembered one of Grandpa's pet phrases and he started calling Doc Holmes a mean son-of-a-bitch. When Papa heard about it, he got out his strap and started tanning Marion's backside. But Grandpa intervened and stood up for him. It was a fierce and glorious argument and Mama, naturally, took his side, on the assumption that anything her husband was doing had to be wrong.

Yes, he really loved Grandpa Brown. He loved to drink something that was colored amber and smelled terrible and came out of a bottle. He was always taking walks with Marion, out past the fields of corn, out among the sagebrush, where he had many pint bottles stashed away. He would first look about him and, seeing that the coast was clear, he would uncork a bottle and take a long swig. Then he would dance a little jig and sing a song. Marion was told that this business of the hidden bottles was a deep secret between the two of them. Marion never told about the bottles.

They had to leave Schnickelfritz in Iowa but they got a collie in Palmdale. Once they were clearing some land and they heard the dog barking. Marion and Papa rushed out to see that brother Bob, about three years old, was sitting on the back porch and throwing sand at a nine-button rattlesnake. The collie was barking at the rattler, which made him keep his distance. Marion ran into the house and got out his shotgun and killed the snake.

They were so poor at one stage of the game that a dairy farmer nearby gave Marion a gallon of milk on the pretext that the boy had to have some milk for his cat and that anyway the milk was going to waste. The Morrisons were able to save face and at least the children got milk regularly.

Mary never went home to Iowa, though she kept threatening to do so. They lived on the farm and things got worse. The first year they had a fine corn crop but the market was down and they didn't make enough to live on for another year. Even though there was no money, that Hallowe'en Mary wanted to give the family a treat. She had scrounged a dozen frankfurters from the grocer in town. She baked a cake. There was sauerkraut and mashed potatoes. They sat down at the table —Mama, Marion and Bob, Grandma, Grandpa. Doc was out in back washing up. Ma brought in the huge bowl of boiled frankfurters.

Suddenly, Marion heard a mysterious scratch-scratch at the door. And then an eerie high-pitched whistling *moan!* Could it be a coyote? A mountain lion?

He leaped up and went to the door. His nerves were strained. He slowly opened the door. Great jumping jehosophat—there was a real ghost out there, looking about ten feet high, a white ghost, a creature in a ghastly shroud.

He screeched. And then ran back to the table. He seized the bowl of frankfurters and, running to the door, hurled the bowl and its steaming contents at the ghost.

The ghost screamed in pain. The ghost was, of course, the unfortunate Doc Morrison, who couldn't do anything right.

"The frankfurters were ruined," Wayne recalls, a rueful scowl on his face. "So it was back to mashed potatoes for dinner again. Ma cussed me out. Doc didn't say much. He had a black and blue mark on his face where the bowl hit him."

Doc finally got rid of the land and the horses and the farm equipment. He bought a secondhand Model T Ford.

And they moved to Glendale.

Mary Morrison had decided it would be all right to remain in Southern California as long as they lived in a nice little town, a town like Earlham or Winterset. She had discovered Glendale, a respectable suburb of Los Angeles, just a few minutes from downtown Los Angeles and all those big drugstores where Doc could get himself a real job and maybe work himself up to be manager of a store—just ten minutes it was, on the Pacific Electric surface cars from Glendale to City Hall and the business district of L.A. Mrs. Morrison had scouted around in Glendale and it seemed like it was composed of neighborly small-town folks; it had nice little white shingled and frame houses and it wasn't too big, just right for them.

They moved to Glendale in 1916. Duke was nine years old. It was in Glendale that the shy, underweight, gangling, awkward, frightened, neurotic Marion Michael (or Robert) Morrison began to assume the shape of a man and began to become Duke Morrison, actor, football player, and big man on the Glendale Union High School campus.

## 2

## A Glendale Person

Marion Morrison arrived in Glendale when he was nine years old. He was more equipped to be a western movie actor than a boy in a small town. He could shoot and ride horses and he knew mountains and deserts and prairies. On the other hand, he was a shy, withdrawn child, given to introspection, subject to spells of terror, a victim of nameless dreads. Already ridiculed by his Palmdale classmates because of his height and flat Midwestern speech, he came to the Doran Elementary School feeling alienated. His family was a poor one. He wore old clothes, though they were always clean. He was afraid of fighting with the other boys. He was constantly being terrorized and beaten up. He did not know what to do about it. Glendale, now a densely populated Los Angeles bedroom community of 200,000, was then a sparsely inhabited rural community with large cattle and horse ranches, and with many vineyards and orchards bearing oranges, grapefruit, avocadoes, and walnuts. It was only ten minutes away from downtown Los Angeles. After World War I, it went through a revolution and became a small city, with one-family houses, row after row, taking over the farmland. Glendale, James M. Cain noted in *Mildred Pierce,* was "on the verge of the real estate boom of the 1920's, such a boom as has rarely been seen on this earth." Glendale is most celebrated for being the home of the original Forest Lawn Memorial Park. The natives like to crack that "no real Glendale person would be caught dead at Forest Lawn." Grandview Memorial Park is where the died-in-the-wood Glendalian is buried.

During the nine years the Morrisons were Glendalians, they lived in eight different houses, all of which they rented. The homes became shabbier with the years. Some of them are still standing, though the city has grown around them. It was a mute chronicle of steady financial deterioration, this packing up every year and moving out and starting over again. The family lived in small cottages on Reynolds Street and Louise Street, now gone, and also at 315 South Geneva, 443 West Colorado, 815 South Central, 129 South Kenwood, 237 South Orange, 207 West Windsor. The house on Kenwood was a comfortable two-story place with plenty of grounds. It was near the imposing Glendale library, which Marion had begun to frequent as he became an intense, omnivorous, and devoted reader of novels and history, starting at the age of ten or eleven. Alone with a novel by Richard Harding Davis or Conrad, or with the short stories of Kipling and O. Henry, he could escape from the family bickering and the arguments over money; he could flee from the pressures of living in a world of schoolmates and rivals. He became a good student, a teacher's pet type of boy, almost a sissy type. He could not seemingly take the heat.

In 1919 he transferred, on the eighth-grade level, to the Glendale Intermediate Junior High School. Vera Brinn, now eighty-four years old, was a mathematics teacher who taught young Marion. She remembers him as a very tall and thin and handsome boy. She says he was attentive and intelligent. His complexion was pale; he seemed to be nervous and awfully tired. She often wondered whether he was sickly.

"I'll never forget his first day in class," recalls Mrs. Brinn. "He was a transfer from Doran Elementary. I used to tell the students to choose their own seats. New students always take seats way back. Not Marion. He sat down in the very front row of seats, close to my desk. He was a quiet boy. He was clean and nicely dressed. He came to school in a blue serge suit, white shirt, and tie. It was like going to church. He never raised his hand in class. I taught him algebra and geometry two years. When I called on him, he always knew the answer. His eyes followed me around. A teacher can feel it, even when she's at the blackboard. He had sharp bright eyes. He was a good student. He did his homework on time. His homework was neat. He did not appear to me to be well. I spoke to Marion about it and he said he was fine. So I sent for his mother. Mrs. Morrison was a fine lady. She was embarrassed about Marion's health. She said the reason he was tired was because he worked mornings before school. I had no realization that the family was poor, for young Marion looked so well got up in class. Marion did not tell me about the job. He was a reserved young man."

Some of the reserve was neurotic withdrawal. There was also physical fatigue, which sometimes seemed to be reserve. He was tired out because he had to work before and after school. When he was ten, he overheard a terrible argument between Doc and Mama. She wanted to buy her sons new clothes and there was no money. Marion had been outside, sitting on the back steps, when

Ma called him into the house. She was enraged.

"Looks like you will have to go out and make some money yourself, Marion, if you expect to look decent in class."

"The Lord will provide, Mother," Doc Morrison said.

"The Lord helps those that help themselves," his wife answered.

Marion acquired a beat-up bicycle. He got a paper route and delivered the Los Angeles *Examiner*. From the age of twelve he had to partly or wholly support himself. He was already contributing money at home as well as buying his own clothes and his brother's. The *Examiner* was a morning paper. He had to get up at five-thirty to collect his bundle and make the rounds. In the afternoons, he delivered prescriptions at whatever pharmacy his father was working. He also worked on Saturday at the Palace Grand movie theater. When he got stronger, he worked as a helper on an ice truck and on produce farms.

"I had to hustle all the time," he says. "I had to make it on my own. I had to keep moving all the time."

His grandparents were now living on Valencia Street in downtown L.A. Sometimes Marion and Bob were sent there for a weekend so that their mother and father would be able to fight without having to be polite in front of the children. He remembers his grandfather, who was of course still imbibing, showing him how to catch bees and tie a loop around their abdomens. Then the bees were released. Marion held them to a long string—they were living kites. He thought Grandpa was a marvelous man. He never told a soul about Grandpa's habit of drinking from the secret bottles on Valencia Street. It began to dawn upon him, as he noticed the improvement in Grandpa's moods whenever he imbibed, that whiskey was a miraculous elixir.

In one respect, Glendale was an ideal place for a future movie star to live. Because of the unspoiled terrain and the rugged Verdugo Mountains, Fox and Vitagraph shot many westerns in and around Glendale. Colonel Selig and his famous studio and zoo were located nearby in Avondale, and Tom Mix had his studio there also. The

Kalem Motion Picture Company—one of the earliest
and most successful of the silent movie studios—had
moved to Glendale from New York in 1909. It was the
first movie studio to shift operations to Southern California. Kalem was named from the initials of its three
owners—Kleine, Long, and Marion. Kalem was located
on Verdugo Boulevard, at the present site of Pike's Verdugo Restaurant. Kalem put up a replica of a frontier
street and had several large stages for interior scenes.
Kalem specialized in one-reel and two-reel action pictures. They did not make romantic pictures or comedies.
Kalem's biggest success was the series of Helen Holmes
two-reelers, released under the rubric *The Hazards of
Helen*. Miss Holmes, a dark-haired girl with gorgeous
eyes, had been a model and then wrote a scenario about
a girl telegrapher who saves a train from a wreck. Kalem
bought her screenplay and starred her in it, and she
became the leading competitor of Pearl White, who was
doing a series *The Perils of Pauline*. Miss Holmes' hazardous adventures almost always involved railroading
—there was a special genre of serial known as the "railroad serial."

With the presence of Helen Holmes on his consciousness, fantasy and reality came together for young Marion.
At this time, about 1917 or so, Marion's folks lived in
a rundown bungalow on West Colorado. About five
blocks away, on West Lomita, was the luxurious Spanish-
California-style mansion in which lived Miss Holmes.
Marion fell in love with her. He took to skulking about
the vicinity of her house in the early morning. Every day
she came out from her walled hacienda about eight A.M.,
mounted on a palomino. She galloped away like a princess,
her auburn hair flying in the wind. Marion not only fell
madly in love with her but he fell madly in love with
the movies and the making of movies.

During his adolescence, Duke once told me, he went
to the movies four or five times a week. His father was
a pharmacist at the Jensen drugstore on Brand Boulevard, and Jensen also owned the Palace Grand flicker-
ama. Jensen's son managed the theater. Doc was a friend

of Bob Jensen or Jense, as Marion called him, and Jense gave the boy a part-time job distributing handbills around town announcing the change of bill. He had a change three times a week. And Marion had an unlimited pass to the Palace Grand. He became starstruck and movie-crazy. When *Four Horsemen of the Apocalypse* played Glendale it ran for seven days. (This was the movie that made the name Valentino a household word.) Marion was overwhelmed by it. He saw it every day of its Glendale run, twice a day. He still remembers it almost in its entirety, frame by frame. Even so, he still managed to deliver the *Examiner,* deliver prescriptions, hold down odd jobs, and be a good student.

But the movies were his primary passion—the movies and his dreams about the men and women in them were the real heart of his existence. There was no real girl in class who was like Helen Holmes, for Helen Holmes was a goddess to him.

He saw Helen Holmes when she was working on the Kalem lot. He saw the process of contriving illusions. He saw the tricks and the gimmicks at first hand. Yet he believed in the illusions when he saw the picture in the theater.

Frequently, Marion trudged several miles north to the Kalem studio. He would hang around and watch them shooting.

He has a vivid memory of a scene showing Helen tied up on the railroad tracks. A spur of the Southern Pacific went to Glendale, and Kalem directors used real SP rolling stock and tracks. In this scene, she was supposed to be killed by an oncoming train. She was really laid across the tracks. They did not fake it. They had a real locomotive and freight train bearing down on her. The director had the camera focused on her body and you could see the locomotive getting closer and closer. Helen was wriggling her body until she rolled off the rails and lay between them. You could see the train passing completely over her body. And you could not be sure until the train passed whether she had been crushed or not.

"You see," Duke says, "what they did was dig a pit

between the tracks and she crawled into this hole before the train passed over her. She didn't use a double. It was a dangerous stunt."

Another time he watched Miss Holmes as she was held captive in a remote farmhouse. She started to telephone for help. The outlaw went up a telephone pole. He was about to cut the wire when the hero came. He shot him dead. The man hurtled down and was caught—out of camera—by a net stretched below.

Young Morrison had a universal taste in movies. He liked every kind of movie. He was movie-crazy. He liked western pictures, but not any more than he liked any other kind. He had watched Hoot Gibson and Harry Carey being filmed on locations in Glendale. He admired Dustin Farnum and William Farnum. He admired William S. Hart, who was the first western star to play a dust-begrimed, realistic, whiskey-drinking, hard-nosed hero. He was a real man of flesh and blood. He often played an outlaw on the run from a sheriff. But Marion's favorite westerner was Harry Carey, who had become more authentic than the actors who had grown up in the Wild West. Carey had grown up in the Bronx. He had gone to Fordham Law School and had practiced law. Then he had become an actor and, one thing leading to another, he came to Hollywood in 1915 and soon became one of the finest western heroes in the business. Marion felt a mysterious affinity with Carey from the first time he saw him. He had a strength there and a kindly smile. And he wore his costumes like he belonged in them. Only his boots and Stetson were new. The rest of his clothes— shirt, bandanna, Levi's—were soiled and dirty. Carey moved and bore himself like an authentic cowhand. And when sound pictures came in, he talked like one.

However, the movie star whom young Morrison really worshiped was Douglas Fairbanks, the All-American hero, who did incredible acrobatic stunts himself. He was a handsome and sinewy man who projected an irresistible charm from the screen.

"I think I can describe every interestin' scene Doug Fairbanks ever played," Wayne once said. "He could handle a blade like a master swordsman. In *Three Mus-keteers,* he dueled a dozen opponents up and down a staircase. Sure, it's been done a thousand times since then, but nobody ever did it like Fairbanks. And he always had this beautiful grin on his face as he was doin' these impossible tricks. God, how I wanted to be like him. I dreamed of being like him. I remember him in *The Mark of Zorro.* He did some fantastic leaps from balcony to balcony. I tried a balcony transfer with some of these new friends, the Louise Street gang we used to call ourselves, when we would play movin' pictures."

Marion's love of pictures and his daredevil nerve helped him to make his first real friends in Glendale. His closest friend was Bob Bradbury. Bob's father was William Bradbury, a movie director. The Louise Street gang went through rigorous imitations of a real movie being made by Kalem. Bob's father brought home old empty jars of makeup from the studio, and the kids pretended to rub makeup on their faces. They borrowed clothes from their parents for costumes. Bob Bradbury played the director—he knew how to do it from having watched his daddy on the set. The camera was a cigar box with holes, mounted on a broomstick tripod. The kids went through detailed imitations of making a western movie or shooting a love sequence, with Bob shouting "Action" and "Cut," and everybody playing his assigned part. Bob Bradbury went to college with Marion. Later he changed his name to Bob Steele and became a successful western star during the 1930's.

Determined to emulate his ideal, Marion attempted a leap from a second-story window. He planned to grab hold of the grapevines on a trellis, swing on the vines, enter another window, and rescue a damsel in distress. He did this successfully, while the Louise Street cinéastes gasped in fear, "but I sure ruined Mrs. Perkins' grape arbor. Another time, I climbed a roof. I hung there, gettin' ready to leap to another building, two-story building. I was holdin' on to a chimney for support. The chimney collapsed. I fell. I did have the presence of mind to grab onto a fence as I was comin' down. It was a barbed wire fence. I didn't break my neck—but I sure ripped up my hands something terrible. I still have the scars on the palm of my left hand."

In one of their many residence changes, Marion's family moved near a firehouse. Marion liked to come by and look at the engines and talk to the firemen. At this time he had an Airedale named Duke, and the firemen started calling the boy Duke, too. One of the volunteer firemen was athletic director of the Vernon Country Club in Pasadena. He had been a professional boxer. One day, Duke, on his way home from school, dropped over at the firehouse. He had black eyes and a bloody nose and his lips were cut. He didn't want to tell the firemen about it. Finally they got it out of him. There was a boy in the eighth grade who had been bullying him for a long time. Duke had been bullied by everybody who had a bullying nature, but this guy in particular was out to get his scalp. He started fights with him and then beat him up. Usually Duke ran away. Everybody laughed at him. Even his friends in the Louise Street gang thought he was a big coward. The ex-boxer said he would give Duke lessons in the manly art of self-defense. He did, and Duke became handy with his fists.

One day the bully started pushing him around on the handball court. Suddenly, Duke turned on him and began punching. They swung wildly toe to toe. Duke beat up his enemy. His knuckles were bruised. His heart was pounding. His mouth was dry. He had been scared to death of this kid. He was still scared when the fight was over. But during the fight he had been taken out of himself. He had felt supremely confident. After that, he went after anybody who called him "Marion" and sneered at him for being a sissy with a funny way of talking. They started calling him Duke about 1919 and they haven't stopped since.

Sometime later, while he was playing sandlot baseball on Sunday, he got into an argument about a close play with a tough kid, a different one, who was older and heavier. Doc Morrison was watching the game. He didn't want to disgrace Doc. When the older kid started taking a punch at him, Duke suddenly swung back and the boys went at it furiously. Duke kept getting knocked down and arising. Down and up. He kept coming back and striking at the big guy until he gave up.

Later, returning home alongside his father, he felt warm when Doc praised him for standing up for his rights, for being willing to give as good as he got. After this, Duke had more confidence in his strength. He had passed a test. He was a man. He began dividing himself into different people. There was the serious side of him, the side who was a reader of books and an assiduous student who got high marks. There was the dreamer, the fantasist of the movies, the imitator of Douglas Fairbanks and Rudolph Valentino, the daredevil of the Louise Street gang. And there was a third Duke Morrison. A tough guy. He told me that he started running around with "probably the toughest roughest gang of guys in the Glendale High School."

People began showing respect for Duke.

"Once I was invited to some girl's birthday party," Wayne says. "My mother was busy that afternoon and I had to bring Bob along. The party was a fancy party, out on the back patio of this big house. The place was decorated with Japanese lanterns and balloons hanging from trees. After the cake and ice cream and punch was served, they started to play games like spin-the-bottle and post-office, and some wise guy said, 'Get that little jerk out of here.' Meanin' Bob. I took umbrage at this remark. I took a poke at this character and the party almost broke up in a free-for-all. The girl's mother bawled me out. I said I had punched him because he insulted my brother. She ordered me *and* my brother out of the house. I was awful sore.

"I had a friend by the name of Walter Cruckow. He lived next door. I went over to Walter's. I got an air-rifle, climbed a ladder to the roof of Cruckow's garage. I started pepperin' the party next door with BB's. I busted every balloon on the patio and punctured the lanterns. I sure scared the hell out of the guests. The girl's mother reported me to Doc. I figured he was going to give me a beating I'd never forget. But he said I had done the right thing. I stuck up for my younger brother. I defended the family honor."

If you knew what was good for you, you just didn't go messing around with Duke Morrison any more. There was the time some of the boys thought it was amusing to spray Duke with some cheap perfume. Duke got revenge by stealing a vial of asafetida from a drugstore where his father worked. The next one who tried the cheap perfume caper got a shot of the asafetida, which "made him smell like a barn. A friend of mine took the asafetida and spilled it on a girl. She took it to the principal's office. Dr. George U. Moyse, the principal, took the bottle to all the stores in town and finally traced it to Baird & Echols, and my father. My father told me to confess if I had stolen it. I did confess, but I would not tell Dr. Moyse who had thrown the asafetida on the girl. Neither would she."

Dr. Moyse was quite stern with young Morrison.

"Do you realize what a serious act you have done?" he said. "It might have been a poison. Suppose somebody had put some poison in that girl's food and seriously harmed her?"

"I certainly wouldn't have taken any poison bottles out, sir," Duke said.

"What is the name of the boy to whom you gave this bottle?"

"I cannot tell you but I will try to make the boy come and tell you himself."

Duke leaned on his friend. His friend came to Dr. Moyse and confessed.

By his junior year in Glendale High School, the formerly quiet boy, the shy and scared Marion, had become one of the school "big shots." Duke was one of the most popular students in school. Though he still fermented inside with anxieties and uncertainties, he was outgoing and active. He was elected president of the class of 1925. He was a good journalist and was on the staff of the weekly student paper, *The Glendale Explosion*. He was chairman of the Senior Dance. He was the chairman of the Ring Committee. He was president of the Comites Club, which was the honor society of Latin students. He was a member of the Honor Club, whose requirements were character and scholarship; you had to have a B+ average to qualify, and Duke Morrison had been getting straight A's. In the light of his interest in movies and girls and his many hours working at one occupation or another, this was a remarkable achievement. He had learned to discipline himself. He had learned to separate the many areas of his life in compartments and to perform each task well.

And the most amazing feat was that he was also a member of the varsity football team.

That Glendale team of 1924-25! They still talk about it. It was the most glorious football team in Glendale history. Physical education instructor Normal Hayhurst was the coach.

Duke played running guard on that Glendale eleven.

It was undefeated in its league.

It was unscored upon that season.

Glendale triumphed over Covina, Pasadena, Van Nuys, Citrus, Colton, Monrovia, Alhambra, Orange, and Compton.

MORRISON BATTERED GREAT HOLES THROUGH THE LINE reported the *Glendale Explosion* in its account of the Alhambra-Glendale game.

He was a hard-driving, ruthless competitor. He had to win. He would not give up an inch to the opponents. That is how Cecil Zaun describes Duke in Glendale. Zaun still lives there. He was captain of that historic team of 1924.

"He just would not give away any territory," Zaun recalls. "They never gained any yardage through him. And when one of our backs was carrying the ball, that's when Duke looked great, on the offense, knocking holes through the opposition. He was a real killer, all right.

"That team, now, you see, in regards to weight and height we had men who were above average for high schools at that time. Most of us were well over six feet. I was six foot three, Duke was six foot four, the Elliott brothers, Howard and Bud, over six, also Les Lovell and

Babe Herman. Babe later played major league baseball.
He's still around in Glendale. Oh, it was a team, I tell
you. There wasn't one of us that weighed less than one
seventy-five and we were solid muscle."

There are many photographs of Marion Morrison in
*Stylus,* the Glendale High School yearbook for 1925. In
them, we see a curly-topped, high-cheekboned face, with
penetrating eyes that capture you. He was still exceedingly slim. He did not look like a football player. He
had a poetic look about him.

I went to Glendale to interview Normal Hayhurst, who
has risen in the world. He became a banker during the
Glendale boom years and is now chairman of the board
of a chain of savings and loan banks. When I mentioned
the name John Wayne he bridled.

"I don't know any John Wayne," he said sharply. "I
do know Marion Morrison. I do know Duke Morrison.
I don't know John Wayne. Last I saw of him was in
1925 and he was Marion Michael Morrison. Never seen
him since. He never came back. I've had many students,
stars of my teams, men who have gone on to make All-
American, compete in the Olympics, play major league
baseball, outstanding men in business or professional life
—they're always coming back to see me. If they have
moved away they still write and keep in touch, and always look me up when they are visiting Los Angeles.
*They* aren't ashamed of Glendale. They're proud of our
town. *Why is Duke Morrison ashamed of Glendale?"*

I waited as he looked at me. I changed the subject.

"Did you know Clyde L. Morrison?" I asked. "Also
known as Doc Morrison? Duke says he owned a drugstore
in Glendale and later got into the ice cream business and
finally had a paint store."

"To the best of my knowledge, Clyde L. Morrison
never owned a drugstore in Glendale," Hayhurst said in
a chilly tone. "I never heard of the ice cream business or
the paint store."

And it was so. I had to believe it was a fantasy which
Duke Morrison invented to protect his image of his
father. He could not accept the idea of his father as a

failure. He could not live with his mother's assessment of Doc's failure in life. A careful search of the Glendale city directories during the years between 1915 and 1930 disclosed no record of any pharmacy, ice cream factory, or paint shop owned by Doc Morrison. For one year he was a partner in the Baird & Morrison Pharmacy. In other years he clerked or made up prescriptions in other men's drugstores. The directory lists his occupation over the years as "drug clerk" or "pharmacist."

Duke Morrison returned to Glendale only once in later years. It is true—as banker Hayhurst pointed out, and other Glendale old-timers as well—that he has never come back as a conquering hero, or to accept any of the civic tributes which have been laid before him. But it is not out of a sense of snobbery. He is not haughty about Glendale. It is just that the decade in Glendale was a time of great pain in his personal life. He had learned to live, as I said, on many levels at once. At the deepest level, as the son of Mary and Clyde Morrison, he lived in an anguish so strong and so unremitting that he cannot go back to Glendale, for almost every street and many of the old buildings, which still stand, bring back the terrors of the parental hatreds.

On May 1, 1926, the Morrisons were legally separated, after a marriage that had lasted twenty years, seven months and one day. According to the records of the Superior Court of Los Angeles there was no community property to be divided between the parties. Mrs. Morrison alleged that her spouse had "deserted and abandoned" her. She sued for divorce, and an interlocutory decree was granted to her on February 13, 1929; the divorce became final on February 20, 1930. After a short time, Doc Morrison married a Glendale person who was a gentler soul. She worked as a buyer of lingerie in a small department store in Glendale. They had several good years together until he died. Duke supported his stepmother until she died. There was one child—a daughter—but Duke has never spoken of his half-sister.

Duke has come back to Glendale only once, and that was when his half-sister was graduated from Glendale

High School in 1949. She lives in Scottsdale, Arizona, now, and she does not wish to talk about her famous half-brother.

Mary Morrison moved to Long Beach, where she began a new life. She was always glad that she and Doc stayed together long enough for Duke to finish at the high school and make a start on his college career. She always thought she had done the right thing. There was nothing else a decent person could do, was there?

Even his closest high school friends, such as Don Williams, Bob Bradbury, and Cecil Zaun, were not aware of Duke's love life, any more than they were aware of the trouble between Duke's parents. Several Glendale informants assured me that Duke had never romanced any girls in high school. He did not have the time nor the money to date, they say. They never saw him at Baird & Echols, where the younger set went for ice cream sodas. He was going around for a while with Polly Richmond, whom he met in his sophomore year. She was the daughter of a retired colonel in the U.S. Cavalry. She was a lively dark-haired girl who flirted with every eligible man. She had a tremendous crush on Duke. He had the tiny gold football, with a "G" on it, given to every varsity man. He is said to have pinned her and then she returned the pin because they had an argument about certain "bad companions."

He recalls, "I used to take her to dances, school affairs, and then to the Tam-O-Shanter on Los Feliz Boulevard, it was a hamburger joint, the first one I remember. Hamburgers were a nickel at the time. So were hot dogs. I liked to drag. Every time we had a heavy rain, I'd get the loan of Dad's car, he was driving a Reo at the time, and I'd head out to Chevy Chase Boulevard and race in the mud. I started serious drinking when I was in high school. Polly did not like my drinking and the guys I drank with. They were the rough crowd at Glendale. I didn't usually hang around with them, except for drinking and drag-racing and picking up a certain type of girl on Saturday nights."

Like a Victorian rake, Duke Morrison was having his own secret life on a small scale.

"There was one time," Duke says, "six of us bought six pints of bootleg whiskey. We got into the one car. We were going on an overnight camping trip. We planned to get drunk. It was just something you did then. It made you feel like a man. To violate the Prohibition law and to get drunk. We did not pick up any girls. There was no room in the car for any. We went over to Pasadena and up the trail to Mt. Lowe. We started drinkin' this terrible hooch and some of the kids started getting high and one passed out. We were climbin' and laughin' and having a high old time. Then some kid got so drunk he fell off the trail and down a hill—about fifty feet. There was only one other guy and myself who could still walk. We crawled down and rescued him. That was my first real drunk. I loved it. Didn't have a hangover. After that I would drink almost every weekend and I didn't like dating girls who were against my drinking. I just kept my drinking companions separated from my refined Glendale friends. Well, that was all right as I figured I knew how to handle it. I was getting much confidence in myself, though still shy with girls, but the whiskey was good in that department. But it didn't help much when I was speaking in public. I was good at it—but afraid."

Duke made his debut as an orator in June, 1919. He had won a prize of twenty-five dollars offered by the Shriners for the best composition on World War I. He was asked to read his essay at the grammar school graduation. He was scared. His voice was still in that unpredictable phase of puberty when it was liable to crack and squeak suddenly. He was also wearing his first pair of long pants. And he was worried about a line in his speech which was, "And the worst thing the Germans had done was . . ." This sentence was hard for him. He kept leaving out the "had" and saying, "the worst thing the Germans done was . . ." He rehearsed himself faithfully before a mirror and made sure he would remember that troublesome phrase correctly.

When he got to the fatal sentence, he shouted it. "And the worst thing the Germans had done was . . ."

He felt so happy about having remembered the "had" that he completely forgot the rest of the speech.

But everybody else was impressed. They thought it was so dramatic. And Marion Morrison—why he had such a fine voice, and was a splendid looking young man. Mrs. Morrison told her friends that she prayed he would become an attorney-at-law.

He started debating at Intermediate Junior High School, and later in Glendale High. He debated *mano a mano* as well as on the team. He remembers winning a debate on which the topic was: *Resolved:* that the airplane has made the battleship outmoded. He took the affirmative. He won the debate. In high school, he became an active member of the Stage Society—but not as an actor. He was a prop man. He helped to build the settings. He went out to borrow lamps and tables for drawing-room comedies. Once, he was supposed to ring a bell offstage. This would be the ringing of a telephone which a character would answer. He deliberately did not put the phone on the table as he was supposed to do. He wanted to pull a fast one on the boy playing the character. He didn't like this student. At the cue for the offstage ring, Duke rang the bell. There was no phone on the stage. Duke got a bawling out from the faculty adviser—he never did anything like this again. He played several roles in school versions of current Broadway shows, such as *Dulcy*. He played a foppish English duke in one of these plays, which reinforced his nickname.

In his senior year, he won the Southern California Shakespeare Oratory Contest, reciting Cardinal Wolsey's farewell speech. He then went on to compete in the state-wide finals, which were held at the Pasadena Playhouse.

Backstage, he found himself surrounded by young men and women who were well dressed and spoke in refined diction and had learned professional mannerisms. Some had already been playing child parts in the movies. Duke felt self-conscious. He was still wearing the old blue serge suit. His shoes were not in style. He felt gawky and

stupid. He remembers the other students gossiping knowl-
edgeably about the Broadway stage and talking of famous
New York personalities such as Ina Claire and Wilton
Lackaye and Frank Craven and Lunt and Fontanne.

He felt he did not belong with these sophisticated boys
and girls. Sometimes the feeling had come to him that it
would be marvelous to be an actor, to be like Douglas
Fairbanks and Rudolph Valentino, to go before a real
camera, as he had done in make-believe with the Louise
Street gang. Now, all at once, he did not feel that he
belonged with actors.

"I was out of my class," he says. "When it was my
turn to do the speech, I went up in my lines. I mumbled.
I coughed. I sweated. I was plain frightened to death.
The audience was snickering. And when I finally got
through it and went backstage, the looks that fancy young
actors and actresses gave me were contemptuous.

"As I left the theater that day, I said to myself, *acting
is sheer hell. One thing you're never going to be, Duke,
is an actor. Never.*"

3

## The Rectitude of Howard Jones

In 1924, Howard Harding Jones, who was to become one
of the legendary football coaches of the golden age of
sports, was made head coach at the University of Southern
California. His first season would begin in the autumn of
1925. The USC Trojans had been losing games for many
years. Their ancient rivals, the Stanford Indians, under
Pop Warner, were the leading team in the Pacific Coast
Conference. Jones was a man of austere morals, high

seriousness, and a master of the running attack in football.

Jones at once began investigating the promising players in Southern California. Since the 1924 Glendale team had beaten every team in their league, from San Diego to Bakersfield, he wanted them to become Trojans. Jumbo Pierce, a Glendale boy and a varsity tackle, said he would find out the plans of several Glendale athletes, including Marion Morrison. Pierce reported that he planned to become a Navy officer. He had been nominated as an alternate for the U.S. Naval Academy in Annapolis. In the event that he did not make Annapolis, Duke Morrison was already weighing offers for football scholarships from nine universities, including the hated Stanford. Jumbo Pierce further explained that the student's father wanted him to enter the Navy and the mother wanted him to be a lawyer.

Hardy Elliott, another member of the varsity, another Glendalian, and a personal friend of the Morrisons, happened to be taking pre-law at USC. USC had a first-rate law school. Elliott was ordered to do everything possible to induce Duke Morrison to matriculate at USC. He was a member of Sigma Chi, one of the most prestigious fraternities of the period. There was even a song about a co-ed who was "The Sweetheart of Sigma Chi."

The USC administration and a committee of affluent alumni were collaborating with Howard Jones.

Elliott went out to see Doc and Mary and talk up USC to Duke, who respected him. He arrived a few days after the family had learned that there was no opening at Annapolis. Elliott did a masterful selling job on the Morrisons. Duke agreed to enroll at USC, which would pay his tuition and fees on a scholarship. He also got him interested in possibly pledging Sigma Chi. He knew the Morrisons were having hard times. He said Duke would get free room and board by working in the house. He invited Duke to go out the next Saturday on a Catalina Island cruise and meet the brothers. He made sure that Mary Morrison knew what a fine law school USC had.

Duke went on the cruise. He was accepted by USC.

He pledged the Alpha Upsilon chapter of Sigma Chi. He got a job washing dishes at the Sigma Chi house. An alumnus found him a position as a map plotter with Pacific Telephone. He plotted the route of old telephone lines on new maps. He did not know the purpose of this. He worked during the summer hiatus and then part time when school started. He was paid sixty cents an hour.

On September 10, 1925, his freshman year started with orientation week. Hazing was a traditional on the USC campus at that time. And a group of sadistic sophomores, wearing black sweaters with a white figure, disciplined the freshman; the sophs carried out the orders of a secret society, the Trojan Knights, who wore red sweaters with white figures. Collegiate, collegiate, yes they were collegiate, rah rah rah. Duke had to wear a red beanie for one week. His behind was frequently paddled when he forgot to say "sir" to upperclassmen. He had to walk around with his trouser legs rolled up, wear his shirt with tails out, wear his suitcoat inside out, and push pennies with his nose along the sidewalk.

He loved it.

And he loved fraternity life. He still speaks warmly and affectionately of the Sigma Chi brothers. For he was completely accepted by them in a way he had never been accepted before. Most of them were the sons of rich— very rich—fathers. Most of them were playboys, flask-toting rah-rah men, who came to college to pass a few years enjoying themselves before going into the old man's oil business or bank. Yet the Sigma Chi chapter respected scholarship and character and seems to have been a successful democracy. Among the members was another freshman, the great football hero Jesse Hibbs, from Chicago, who was a good student as well as a good player. Marshall Duffield was another Sigma Chi and also played on the varsity. He won a Rhodes scholarship and became a historian.

"The fact that I washed dishes didn't make them treat me like an inferior," Duke says. "There was no snobbishness in the house. We were all equal."

Duke, who already was a first-rate chess player and

bridge player, made himself a place in the brotherhood, because he could do what had to be done and do it well. He was handsome and amusing and was a champion at the card table. He could hold his gin like a real man. They taught him how to wear clothes and polished his manners and mannerisms until he had attained a degree of finesse. He was a good companion. He had the ability to listen, as well as to talk, and he did more listening than talking, but they learned that he had a hot temper, and that when he was crossed he exploded, and that he could fight like Jack Dempsey. And he was bright, a good student. He was an all-around great guy to be with and all his qualities were making an impression on them. He was getting a *carte d'identité* which could have carried him into the world of finance, banking, corporate law, into an upward-mobile marriage to one of the daughters of the old Los Angeles families.

During his freshman year he dated Polly Ann Young. Polly Ann was the oldest of three daughters of Gladys Royal Young. Abandoned by her husband, Mrs. Young, a Utah lady, had migrated to Los Angeles in 1916 and opened a theatrical boarding house. The three girls became, in time, movie actresses. Besides Polly Ann, there was Betty Jane (who changed her name to Sally Blane when she went into the movies) and the youngest, Gretchen. Gretchen became the most successful of the Young *soeurs*. She is known to history as Loretta Young.

Besides showing he had an eye for loveliness, Duke proved himself on the freshman football team.

The freshman squad numbered sixty players—including a future All-American, Jesse Hibbs, and Don Williams, from Anaheim High School, who became a good friend, and two Glendale buddies, Bob Bradbury and Scotty Lavelle. Assistant coach Cliff Herd, with three helpers no less, was coaching the frosh!

Every afternoon at Bovard Field there were gruelling drills and practice sessions. Then they started playing. His pads and crash helmet became a part of his body. He learned to live with cracked bones, sprained ligaments, and bruises. He thrilled to the sound of the crowds roaring out the USC cheers, like the one they called the Double T.

     T-T-T-R-O
     J-J-J-A-N
     T-R-O
     J-A-N
     TRRRROOOOOOOOOH—*JAN*

And he was an integral part of the miracle machine being created by Howard Jones which was setting the whole of Los Angeles on its ear. The running attack of Jones' men was getting attention all over. They were now known as the "Thundering Herd" and the amount of yardage they gained was so incredible that some of their games were described by sportswriters as "track meets," and so they seemed, in contrast to the slow trench-warfare kind of football that most teams played. Herd's freshmen had a beautiful season. They did not lose a game, either against other college frosh or against high school varsity teams. It was usually a lopsided score, something like 47 to 0. Typical of the comments about Morrison was this one, made during his freshman year: "Morrison, Thomas, and Phillips were towers of strength."

In their first season under Jones, the Trojans cracked the coast conference wide open. They ended in third place. Morton "Devil May" Kaer made All-American quarterback. The running attack, Jones' clever and original formations, and his intuitive powers became famous. Grantland Rice wrote, "There is no coach in the game who can throw three men at one spot ahead of the runner with deadlier effect than Howard Jones."

Jones imposed strict training rules on his men. They had to be as puritanical as he was. "No smoking, no liquor, and no women—and of the three, women are the worst," he asserted.

Jones was a man of "numbing rectitude," wrote columnist Edwin Pope.

His character and his strength made a strong impression on Duke, who idolized him and sometimes fancied he might mold himself along those noble lines. Jones was a soft-speaking coach who trained his players to use their intelligence on the field. He did not weep or orate between halves. He was not the "Win one for the Gipper" type of coach. He got results by being the personification of honesty, decency, and an inward serenity which assumed that he was always in the right and that it would be of benefit to the rest of humanity if they saw life in his way.

Doc Morrison was proud of his son. One of his dreams had come true. He knew that Duke was having hard sledding, and whenever he could spare some money he sent him a five-dollar bill. Like other members of the squad, Duke got two tickets for every home game on the fifty-yard line. He always gave them to his father. As the Trojans played one great game after another, almost beating Stanford, the tickets were in demand, bringing fifty dollars a pair and even more, but Duke always gave them to his father, who never suspected how much they were really worth.

The Trojans had set Los Angeles on its ear. The town had become hysterical as the season continued. To get a box for the home games was a mark of status. Among those who decided he had to have a box for the season was Tom Mix, who was now the *número uno* of the western heroes. He was paid seventeen thousand five hundred dollars a week by the Fox Film Corporation. He asked Jones for a box. Jones got him a box. In return, Mix said he would give summer jobs to any members of the football squad.

In June, when the semester ended, Jones sent Duke and Don Williams over to see Tom Mix. They found him on a frontier street setup on the old Fox lot at Western and Sunset. He read the letter, his face deadpan. He rarely smiled. He had a big beak and soulful gray eyes. He was wearing an ivory-white ten-gallon hat "that was the biggest of its kind I ever saw," Duke recalled.

Mix took the men to his private bungalow and showed them his personal gymnasium and steam room. He was enthusiastic about physical culture and kept himself in excellent condition.

"Men," he said to Duke and Don, "I believe a star owes it to his public to keep in physical condition. You fellows will be my trainers. You will be on full salary and be able to keep in condition yourselves so that our great Trojan team will benefit from your condition when you make the varsity next season. Do you think you boys will beat Stanford next season?"

They nodded.

"I say that Howard Jones is a great American."

They would drink to that.

"You are both splendid-looking men, and I think there is a future in pictures for both of you. I'm shooting a movie about a train robbery this summer and I'm going to see that you men get good parts in my movie, while we're all keeping in condition."

He said to report to him personally in three weeks.

Duke did. He gave his name to the gateman, who looked it up on a sheet and said he was to report to George Marshall. Marshall, later a director, was in charge of personnel. Marshall assigned Duke to work on the "swing gang," which went from one set to another, moving furniture and props around.

"Couple of days later," Duke recalls, his bitterness still intact, "I was haulin' a lamp and a chair across the lot to one of the interior stages and who do I see but Mr. Tom Mix being driven in his big black Locomobile, which was about two blocks long. It had red leather seats and the initials T and M engraved in gold on the doors. The limo stopped. I went over and told him my name and story. He looked sideways and nodded and that, so help me, was the last I saw of Tom Mix, the last. Still I was gettin' thirty-five dollars a week—good money for a student. He *did* keep his promise to get me a job. But what happened to trainin' him? And the part in his movie? He had fooled me, all right. I was hurt."

# 4

# To Meet John Ford

One morning, Duke was told to work on the set of *Mother Machree,* being directed by John Ford. At thirty-one, Ford was already a veteran director, having made fifty-five silent pictures. He had started out in 1917 as a director of two-reel westerns at Universal. He came to the Fox studio in 1921 to make full-length features. *The Iron Horse,* an epic about the building of the transcontinental railroad, was Ford's most important picture to date.

Duke went over to the set. It was a replica of a country road in a little Irish village. There were to be chickens, ducks, and geese in the scene. Duke's job was to ride herd on the poultry. He was to release them from their pens when Ford gave the signal. He was to sequester them when Ford said "cut." Duke was given a large pole. Assistant director Lefty Huff would give him his orders.

At a signal, Duke opened the gates. He whacked the birds until they scurried up the dirt road as the actors acted. Ford wanted another take. Duke had to chase the birds back into the pens and then chase them out again. It was maddening work. He could prod the chickens and ducks, but the geese were stubborn. They persisted in squatting under the cottages. They kept on honking, and the honking got on Ford's nerves.

"So I started in pictures as a goose herder," Duke says. "I wasn't worried about handlin' the birds. I'd been around poultry before. I knew a little about farmin'. I was just takin' my time roundin' up the geese from where they

were settin' under the houses. Guess I was too slow to
suit Mr. Ford, but geese are stubborn. Time I finally
chased the last one from under the houses and into the
pen, he'd be yellin' *action* and I'd have to release them
again. Kept on chasin' geese back and forth all day.
Everybody was laughin' at me. I didn't like that. I didn't
like their being so intimidated by Ford. They were all
scared shitless of him, all except me and the geese. I
think he was pissed off with me *and* the geese.

"Hell, it was just a summer job to me.

"Not that I didn't admire some of the pictures he
made. Guess I had seen every one he did with Harry
Carey over at Universal.

"But I wasn't lookin' to be in pictures. That was a
kid's idea which I figured I had outgrown in high school.
I was finished with the dream of bein' another Douglas
Fairbanks."

It was a hot morning, in the nineties, and Duke was
perspiring profusely. Ford looked cool, as he always did
under pressure. He was a tall, strong, and energetic party,
was Ford. He strode between the camera and the actors,
adjusting this, changing that, barking to the camera operator, murmuring softly to an actress to evoke a facial mood,
always moving restlessly, demanding instant obedience
with a frown or a curse, always completely in command
of his set.

Wayne remembers him as being attired in dirty brown
khaki pants, an old white shirt, an old crumpled black
fedora. Ford didn't belong to the jodhpurs, boots, and
riding crop category of Hollywood directors. His black
eyes focused through thick glasses, and he looked like
an angry eagle. He was smoking a pipe.

On Duke's first day, Ford didn't speak to him. On the
second, just before the noon break, Ford yelled, "Hey,
Morrison."

"Yes?"

"You one of these football players?"

He nodded.

"What position do you play?"

"Running guard."

"Take your position, will you?"

Duke crouched down on one knee and braced his palms on the ground.

When Ford liked a person it was his curious habit to try to goad him into an explosion so that his customary civilized mask cracked and he could observe what was behind the mask. Years later, Ford confided to a *Photoplay* reporter that he had tried to "get Wayne's goat a million times but I only succeeded in doing it on a few occasions."

This was one.

As Duke crouched, Ford charged him. He couldn't knock him over. Duke was in prime condition, one hundred eighty-five pounds of hard muscle and sinew. He was conditioned to be immovable, and he was, though Ford pushed and heaved with all his might.

Then Ford lunged and, without warning, he kicked Duke's arms from under. Duke collapsed on his face. He ate dirt. Ford thought this was very funny, and the cast and crew laughed happily.

"Think you could take me out?" Ford sneered.

Duke nodded.

"Let's pretend I'm a quarterback. I've got the ball. I'm going for a touchdown." He stood forty feet away. "I've passed all the guards except you. Now take me out—if you can."

Ford started a broken field run. Duke streaked for him. Ford swerved as Duke closed in. He weaved, halted, changed direction. Duke moved with him and then, for a moment, it seemed like Ford would break free.

Duke caught him. Not with a tackle. With a kick. He kicked him square in the chest. A real dirty business. None of your clean honest college football. He didn't know Ford liked a dirty player when he was fighting for his honor. Duke had been kicked, and he was kicking back.

The kick took the breath out of Ford. But he didn't go down. He had just been stopped. Duke now went for his legs and caught them and shoved his shoulders against Ford, and Ford's body hit dirt with a nasty thud.

Everybody was quiet.

Ford slowly raised himself to a sitting position. He cleared his brain with a few shakes.

Then he walked over to Duke and growled, "I'm hungry, kid. Let's go eat something."

From then on their friendship slowly ripened into a deep relationship. Yet, close as they were to become, they always remained master and disciple.

The next day, Ford gave him a new pipe and asked him to smoke it. He did. Ford gave him another pipe. Duke felt honored. Then he suddenly realized that "the son-of-a-bitch was usin' me to break in all his pipes. He wasn't smoking cigars then. For a while I took up pipe smokin' but went back to cigarettes."

Duke Morrison had come to the movies during the talking picture revolution. Ford was still shooting films without voices—but now they were dubbing in sound effects and adding musical scores to the soundtrack. With an eye to the future, Ford was now seeking interesting voices as well as faces. He saw something in Duke Morrison that intrigued him. He saw a lean and bony face, a vulnerable look in the eyes, a certain awkwardness of youth in the body, and a marvelous trembling vibrato in the baritone voice. Duke had inherited his father's rich voice. He did not know, nor care, if Duke could "act," in the usual sense of the word, for he knew that film acting, in its truest form, is not like acting for the theater. Ford was one of those men who did not have to look into a camera's finder, or see the rushes, to know what was on the acetate film. His eyes looked at reality with the eyes of a camera. He did not have to screen-test Morrison to know that he would have something for the screen. He did not suspect how much he would eventually have to give to film. Who could suspect this in 1926?

Ford was already gathering around him a band of actors who appeared in all his films, the ones who would be known as the John Ford Stock Company, and Duke

Morrison was one of its original members, along with Ward Bond, Victor McLaglen, John Qualen, Paul Fix, Yakima Canutt, Grant Withers, Harry Carey, J. Farrell MacDonald . . .

*Mother Machree* was about a suffering Irish mother. After this, Ford went right into production on *Four Sons,* another suffering mother picture, a German mother in this case. This sentimental melodrama was one of the highest-grossing films of the decade, netting Fox a profit of over ten million dollars.

It is indeed curious that, of all the events that occurred during the making of *Four Sons,* both Duke and Ford remember only one incident. However, they remember it differently.

Here is Duke's version:

"There was a scene where Margaret Mann gets the news that her third son died. She's on the porch of her home. It's autumn. Lots of dead leaves are blowin'. My job was pilin' up leaves in front of this big fan and turnin' on the fan and the leaves would blow around the porch while she's readin' this letter. After each break, I swept up the leaves and got them ready for the fan. Ford didn't like something about either the setup or how Miss Mann was playin', and he kept rehearsin' the scene many times. After a while I got to sweepin' up the leaves automatically. Then it seems she began cryin' just how she was supposed to and it was a good take, so I just picked up the rake and started sweepin' and Ford screamed I was an idiot and I had ruined the only good take.

"I didn't realize the cameras were goin' when I did it.

"Ford came over and told me to march. I marched. One of the extras was playing a German officer who had an Iron Cross on his uniform. Ford told him to pin it on me. Then he said, 'Assume your position.' I kneeled and he gave a swift kick in the butt."

Now we cut to 1966 and Peter Bogdanovich is interviewing John Ford for his monograph on the Master. The subject of *Four Sons* arises and Ford speaks only of the dead leaves and the young prop man:

"I remember we had one very dramatic scene in which the mother had just received notice that one of her sons had died, and she had to break down and cry. It was autumn, the leaves were falling, the woman sitting on a bench in the foreground—a very beautiful scene. We did it two or three times and finally we were getting the perfect take when suddenly in the background comes Wayne, sweeping the leaves up. After a moment he stopped and looked up with horror. He saw the camera going, dropped the broom, and started running for the gate. We were laughing so damn hard—I said, 'Go get him, bring him back.' Fortunately they finally caught up with him, and he came back so sheep-faced. I said, 'All right, it was just an accident.' We were all laughing so much we couldn't work the rest of the day. It was so funny—beautiful scene and this big oaf comes in sweeping the leaves up."

Duke Morrison made his debut in Ford's next film, another Irish drama, based on a novel by Donn Byrne, *Hangman's House*. It was a small role. He played an Irish peasant lad who was tried and found guilty of a murder he hadn't committed. All he had to do was stand in the prisoner's box and bow his head as the judge said, "You shall hang by the neck until dead, dead, dead." (Actors spoke their lines in the silent movie period and this was still a silent, though made during the transition period.)

The first time they did it, the judge's solemn look made Duke giggle. The second time, he got an uncontrollable fit of hysteria and couldn't stop his laughing. Ford finally screamed, "Get that son-of-a-bitch out of here and don't let me set eyes upon his idiot face again!"

Duke skulked away, feeling humiliated. In the dressing room, he got out of the costume and looked at himself in a mirror despondently. A.D. Lefty Huff quietly came over and said it was all right and reassured him that Ford really liked him and knew he could act.

"You just keep out of sight for a while and I'll bring you over to the Old Man when he's in a better mood," said Huff.

Later, Ford forgave him and they went back to the same scene.

How could he possibly keep himself from breaking up? Duke closed his eyes and tried to imagine himself being sentenced to death. He pictured Mr. Ford glowering at him from a judge's bench and passing sentence of death on him.

And now, when the actor said, "You shall hang by the neck until dead, dead, dead," Duke did not laugh.

He felt an emotion vibrating in him. The emotion was reflected in his facial muscles and in his eyes.

Ford said quietly, "Print it."

Now the moral of this event is not that Duke, out of necessity, suddenly learned to use his emotions as an actor, for what he had done was accidental. Many years later, Ford told him that it was precisely at the moment when Duke seemed so maladroit, while he was in a fit of giggling, so adolescent and unprofessional—it was then that Ford first got that feeling in his guts that Duke had something vital inside of him that could be exposed by the camera.

Another director might have forgotten this gawky youth.

It was fortunate for him that it was John Ford who was directing *Hangman's House*.

In the fall Duke Morrison went back to college.

Fox had paid him thirty-five dollars a week. He had saved five hundred dollars. He was now a sophomore. He was a member of the varsity football team. He had his number—24!

Twenty-four.

There were thirty-three men on that history-making team of 1926-27. Duke Morrison played right guard, running guard. He was sent in frequently during the third quarter to substitute for Hibbs at right tackle when USC was ahead. USC was usually ahead. Whittier went down 74 to 0. Santa Clara was beaten 42-0. Duke was in the starting lineup against Oregon State on November 11, 1926. He played a fine game. The crowd roared. The cheerleaders led the cheering. *Gimme a T, gimme an R, gimme an O, gimme a J . . .* There were beer busts and gin parties after the games. Los Angeles football is playing in hot sun, the spectators wearing light clothes. The bands play and the cheerleaders jump up and down. It was a very good time to be young and a football hero. Duke Morrison did not think about John Ford. He was thinking much about women. He had been dating a USC flapper, Polly Ann Young, a gloriously skinny bleached blond. She had a kid sister, Loretta. Loretta Young was starting to play little parts in the movies. She admired Duke Morrison. He thought she was swell. Yeah, he had the world by the tail, and the cheers would never end. He was one of the Trojans. He was part of the Howard Jones machine. They were going to beat Notre Dame someday. He smelled greatness and glory in the liniment sweat smells of the locker room. They were sure to play in the Rose Bowl next season or the one after that. Duke says he and the other players were supremely confident that Howard Jones would lead them to the Rose Bowl.

Jones was the first citizen of Los Angeles now. He was not flamboyant. He was not rhetorical. Jim Murray, *Los Angeles Times* sports columnist, summed him up in 1972: "Howard Jones was an austere man. You didn't know whether to kiss his ring or cover your eyes when you were ushered into his presence. He didn't talk to you. He gave audiences. They did everything but carry him around in a sedan chair . . . [He] won 121 games as coach of those glorious teams in an era when L.A. was considered that quaint little city on the other end of the Santa Fe Super Chief . . . The only thing [about Los Angeles] to be taken seriously was that football team. The Trojans all seemed to be six feet tall and able to run the 100 in 9.6."

They came close to beating Notre Dame in 1927. Jesse Hibbs made All-American. In 1928, they finally put down Notre Dame by a score of 27-14. They won the Rose Bowl game. In 1929, Duke's fraternity brother Marshall Duffield, quarterback, made history when he faked a run, whirled, threw a long forward pass to Francis Tappan for a touchdown, which beat Stanford, after the conversion, 7 to 0.

But the Oregon State game in 1926 was to be the last game Duke began and finished. His future was not in the Rose Bowl.

# 5

# Appointment in Balboa

Balboa is fifty miles south of Los Angeles. In 1926, it was a remote and sparsely inhabited beach village. Some of the rich old families owned summer homes there. The fishing was good. The body-surfing was good. Duke had become a body-surfer. Some of his Sigma Chi brothers lived there during the summers. They would go also in holiday periods when the houses were opened. There were many roadhouses and country clubs where liquor was served illegally.

In November, the USC chapter threw a Thanksgiving dance at the Balboa Inn. There was a six-piece jazz band playing in a pavilion lighted by lanterns. Duke had broken up with Polly Ann Young. He had a blind date with Carmen Saenz. Her family had a second home at Balboa. Their Los Angeles home was in the Hancock Park quarter, which was fashionable, and where lived the *ancien régime*. Carmen was the daughter of Dr. José Sainte Saenz, a Spaniard of royal blood, who had come to the United States in 1880. He had fought with this country in the Spanish-American War. At this time, he had become a very rich businessman. He owned a chain of drugstores catering to the Mexican-American market in San Antonio and Los Angeles. Besides his *farmacias,* Dr. Saenz practiced medicine and was also the consul of the Dominican Republic. His wife was a French lady from Lyons. They had four daughters—Carmen, Josephine, Violetta, and Zoraida.

So Duke took Miss Carmen Saenz from Hancock Park out to the dinner and the dance in Balboa and she was a good dancer. It was a pleasant evening. He didn't say very much in the way of repartee, but it was fine because they were sitting at a circular table with four other couples. And then he walked Carmen Saenz to her home by the beach. When they got to her house, they found another couple, also returned from an evening on the town, sitting around the front parlor. It was Josephine Saenz, Carmen's younger sister, and her date.

Both couples decided to go for supper. There was an all-night diner on the pier. They sat down in a booth and ordered hamburgers and coffee.

"We were sitting around in this joint and just talking," Duke recalls, "the crazy kind of conversation kids make. I kind of liked Josephine when I first saw her back in their house, and then I happened to catch her eyes while we were talking."

Their glances came together. He felt those sensations which are a symptom of early love. Marion Morrison fell in love at first sight. And Josie Saenz fell in love with him at first sight.

She was a beautiful creature, small and perfectly fashioned in form. Her skin was a smooth white alabaster and her lovely face was framed by her jet black hair combed into a bun over the nape of her neck. A small diamond tiara was fixed in her coiffure.

And her eyes. Deep enormous black eyes, long lashes, and curving brows.

She seemed like something carved out of ivory and ebony. Duke fell under her influence as if "a hypnotist had put me into a trance." He stared at her, lost in her look of serene repose. She had been educated, by her French mother and the nuns at the Sacred Heart Academy, to be a woman of the aristocracy. Even so, her skin flushed as unspoken messages passed between her soul and the young man's sitting across the table.

Duke once told me he stared at her so long that finally Carmen was amused and said, "Duke, are you going to put in the sugar or not?"

He looked at his hands. He became aware his right paw held a spoonful of sugar. He didn't know how long he'd been holding it. He was so confused he put the sugar in his mouth. He didn't know what he was doing. He chewed up the sugar.

Josephine Saenz watched him. She fell in love with him. What an absurd, darling, big, awkward thing he was, chewing his sugar up like that. He had a case on her, there was no doubt of it, and she was glad about that, because she had fallen for him.

There was a change of partners in the quadrille. Josie became his date the rest of the evening. After they had finished supper, he and she went out to the end of the pier and sat on a wooden bench there. The air was cool now and smelled of the salt spray. The waves cracked on the beach. The sky was deep purple and the moon was hanging in there for all the lovers of the world. Here is how it was in his own words, which he told me many years later:

"I was looking out at the ocean. I was full of feelings I never had felt before. I was so hypnotized I don't think I said more than two words that night. I remember opening the door of the car for her, and my fingers happened to graze her arm as she was standing on the running board, kind of pulling this black coat around her. A shiver went through me. I knew I must be in love. I had read about it in stories, seen love scenes in the movies, read love poems about feelings like this, so I knew this was what it had to be. It was my first time. But they don't tell you it hurts. They never tell you how much it hurts. They don't tell you it hurts from the start and I guess it never stops hurting, but it sure is a beautiful feeling to have and it wasn't long after that we started keeping company and she was my steady girl, and it was beautiful but it hurt a lot. Why don't they tell you how much it hurts?"

The courtship was long and nerve-wracking, and it hurt Josephine Saenz as well as Duke, and maybe the pain is part of the beauty of their kind of love. For each love is unique, as well as being fundamentally the same old story of a man and a woman. For Josie, it was the first and the only romantic experience of her life. There was to be no other lover in her life but Duke Morrison.

The next weekend Duke drove down to see Josie Saenz. On Sunday morning, after they came back from church, they went out on the beach. She watched as Duke was towed out by a motorboat. He was out a mile, it seemed. He waited for a big wave building up. He dived in and took his position on the roller. He swam into it and rode it like a bucking bronco. It was a big wave. It raced faster and faster as it closed on the sands. He was in control of his body, flat on the crest of the wave. Closer to the shoreline. This was it, now. The moment of truth. You have to control it so you don't get sucked into the concave underside of the wave. If you get sucked into that maelstrom of foam and terror, you are out of control. You are like a piece of wood in a typhoon.

He lost it. He lost his body. You never know how it happens. Something goes wrong and then the wave beats you. It pulls you into itself and you flounder and flail your arms and legs but you have had it. He was hurled on the beach by the wave crashing down on the beach. It was like being shot out of a cannon, he says. Josie ran over and some of the men watching pulled his body backwards so the next wave wouldn't float him back out into the ocean. Then they pumped the water out of his lungs. And he vomited. There was a bad pain in his right shoulder. He could hardly move his neck and arms. He felt awful.

The next morning it was worse. His shoulder was swelled up. He went to the doctor. He had ripped his muscles. It would take several months until they were healed. He had to take it easy. He would have to write and eat with his left hand. Football? No more football

this season. No more swimming or surfing or tennis playing. No more sports, for at least three months.

Duke did not accept the verdict.

He did not tell Howard Jones about the accident.

He came to football practice every afternoon. He was
playing as hard as he could, throwing that rotten shoulder
into the tackles as if nothing happened. But one day,
while he was practicing tackles on the dummy, he smeared
the dummy. Again he felt that searing pain in the
shoulder. He had ripped it up again. He played with a
harness strapped around his shoulder. He had substituted
for Hibbs in the Stanford game when they lost by one
point and also played against Oregon on November 11
and against Idaho on November 20. They beat Idaho
28 to 6 and that was the last game he ever played for
USC, but he did not know it at the time. Jones had no
intention of putting him in any future games. He did not
release him because he wanted him to get his football
letter. He knew how much it meant to Duke. Duke got
his letter in December, 1926. He did not play in the
Montana game or against Notre Dame.

He felt it like a rejection of himself. His ego was all
tied up with football. He wanted to run away. He was
ashamed of telling Doc what happened. He didn't want to
face Josie. It was like he was some kind of coward. He
had always been a runner since his childhood. He wanted
to run away again. He sulked around the Sigma Chi house.
He could not share his humiliation even with his closest
friends, Jesse Hibbs and Don Williams. Finally he drove
out from the campus to where John Ford lived in an old
Spanish-style stucco house on North Highland Avenue in
the Hollywood hills.

He opened himself up to Mr. Ford.

Ford said, "Duke, you wait until your shoulder is back
in shape. That is all there is to the matter. And no use
making a tragedy out of it. Football—why it is just a
child's game. The skin of an animal being kicked around
by twenty-two grown men. A year from now you'll be
wondering why you felt so terrible. You've earned your
football letter. You're in love with a fine Catholic girl,

though you don't deserve her, being the atheist that you are. So you go back to school and finish out the damned term. Come back and work for me next summer. Now stop your blathering and let's have a glass of genuine Scotch, or so my bootlegger swears."

In about a year, the muscles had knitted together. He never played football again, but he surfed again. He swam and rode and hunted. Physically, he was as strong as ever. He maintained his condition by strenuous workouts at the Hollywood Athletic Club on Hollywood Boulevard, near Wilcox.

6

## Sometimes You Simply Can Do Nothing

He had a rotten sophomore year. He lost interest in studying. His grades were down to C's and D's. He drank too much. He brooded too much. He thought about Josie Saenz all the time. She said she loved him, but she treated him strangely. What kind of a love was this? Why did she do what her mother and father said? Her parents did not approve of him. They frowned on her going steady with a young man of no social status or good family. He had no money and no prospects of a career. He was not of their faith.

You could not blame Dr. and Mrs. Saenz if you knew their values. Duke Morrison did not suggest security. He suggested a dashing and irresponsible gallant in white linen slacks and navy blue blazer. They knew their daughter had lost her head to a football player. She would get over this adolescent crush, they were sure of that. She was too inexperienced in the ways of the world. They reminded her, over and over, of Duke Morrison's faults. She was forbidden to see him more than two times a week.

She was a dutiful daughter, and did what they said.

They arranged for her to see other men at dances and parties. She was torn between her lover and her parents, between love and duty. She wanted to try to make Duke understand how fine her parents were. She wanted them to see what a sensitive and idealistic young man Duke was. She failed on both sides.

They were two confused children. Duke loved and respected her. Suddenly, he would get angry at her chastity. He would boil over in tears and rejection. Yet some part of him was assured by her high morals. She was a good girl. He respected her. He could not have given her his heart so entirely if he had not respected her. And she, on her part, did her best to sympathize with him, but it was very hard for her. There was no way in which she was able to understand the forces that pulsated in him.

So they danced the courtship dance, sometimes literally at dancing places like the Ambassador, and sometimes walking in Griffith Park or going to a movie on Wilshire. During the week, she had to be home by eleven, and on Saturday she was allowed to be out until one A.M. They were not accompanied by a flesh-and-blood duenna on their meetings, but a metaphysical duenna hovered over Josie. Her virtue was going to be intact in the best Hispanic tradition. She felt intensely the poetry of the Catholic church.

It was hard for her because she was also human. She found herself feeling passion when they were together and were silent and looked at each other's faces. But she went to confession and made novenas and said her Hail Marys while counting beads. He had given her his pin but she was not allowed to wear it before her parents. It was the first dishonest thing she had done. She felt guilty about it, knowing it was hidden in her change purse when she was at home. She tried to feel contrite about it during confession, but she found it hard to summon up genuine contrition.

When they parted after a date, Duke wanted to be alone; sometimes he drank heavily and cursed his fate. He saw now—or thought he saw—that the one thing he had going for him was football, and he had lost football. They had taken it away. In his black despair, he sometimes thought he could never go back to college again. He could never be part of the Sigma Chi circle. He didn't want to get drunk with the guys again. He did not want to have imaginary wild dates with promiscuous flappers. He did not want to be with any girl but Josephine.

And her, he could not be with most of the time, and he wanted to be with her continuously, eternally. He read sad poems of love by Poe, Shelley, Byron, and Keats, and memorized many, and tried to write poems, which he sent to her. He would phone her and hang up when the maid or her mother or one of her sisters answered.

When the second semester was over, he and Josie got into a series of arguments which culminated in a dramatic climax. He told her he wasn't going back to school for he had the promise of work at Fox. He could make forty dollars a week and they could live on that—and he wanted to get married right away. She cried and said she loved him and wanted to marry him soon, but she could not until her parents consented. And they were opposed to her taking this step now.

He got angry and his voice rose. They sat in the Bungalow Sweet Shop on West Jefferson. It was near the campus. He told her that she did not really love him. She had never loved him. She loved her parents. She loved the Catholic priests and nuns. It was over, all over between them. He could not abide her cruelty to him any longer. She was deliberately torturing him. He was going insane. He drove her home and didn't get out of the car to open the door on her side. She went to the church on Rossmore to pray for guidance.

He decided to chuck it all. He went up to San Francisco. He was going to have one hell of a wild drunken time up there and then he would ship out to sea and nobody would ever hear of him again. A lover of Richard Harding Davis, Joseph Conrad. and Rudyard Kipling, Duke always had these imaginings of a wanderer's life available to his mind when reality became intolerable. He had always been an avid reader of both fiction and nonfiction, and particularly doted on stories involving the ocean and sailors because he was deeply attracted to the sea.

George O'Brien, one of the leading men at Fox, was from San Francisco, and he gave Duke some addresses. He also told him to look up his father. His father was police chief. Duke also had several fraternity brothers up there. He sold everything he owned—the Chevy tourer, a tennis racket, the textbooks. most of his clothes. He had a good run at a bridge club and amassed about two hundred dollars. He was feeling free and extravagant. He felt as if he had cut himself loose from everything bad when he cut himself loose from Jo. He was certainly glad he had not given in to his desire to kill himself on her front lawn by swallowing poison. She wasn't worth it, damn her to hell. No woman was worth it. Yes, he was going to play the field, have a good time with some real jazz babies instead of that inhibited virgin of his. Yes, it had not taken him long to get her out of his system. God, what a sap he had been. a twenty-four-carat sap, letting some dame make a fool of him. Yeah, he'd slick down his hair, wear bow ties, give them the old razzle-dazzle, fornicate like a lover who knew the ways of the world.

Given the shape of his character, he was as likely to do this as he was to embark on a career of armed robbery.

He tried the game in San Francisco for a time. He just didn't have it in him to be a rake. He didn't perform as he was supposed to perform. And Josie had a way of suddenly clicking on in his brain, like a dark room when it suddenly gets illuminated and you feel blinded for a moment. He couldn't get her out of his brain except when he passed out while drinking. He was drinking and partying and necking and petting and seeing the sights, and all he felt was emptiness and a guilty conscience. He spent an interesting afternoon with George O'Brien's father, who showed him the newly constructed jail. Later, Duke gave a big party at the St. Francis Hotel and invited the local girls he had romanced and all his friends, and bootleg champagne flowed. When he settled the bill, he found he had no more money. For a time, he boarded with his friends while he was planning his next move. He went around to the shipping companies, but there was no work, not even on the freighters. And he still had not gotten Miss Saenz out of his mind. He had to get on a boat. He had to get out of the United States of America.

He was enthralled by his romantic misery and his magnificent frustration. He was twenty years old. He acted out his customary fantasy of reckless adventure. He would stow away on a cruise ship. He was Lord Jim and Axel Heyst and young Marlow on the not-so-good ship *Judea*. He chose a Matson steamship going to Hawaii, the S.S. *Malolo*. It sailed at noon and he wandered aboard and mingled with the passengers and their visitors. All he had were the clothes on his back, a toothbrush, a comb, a nail file. But he looked like a rich young man in his Harris tweed coat and striped flannel slacks and a striped repp tie and the narrow-toed black shoes with inserts of gray suede. He wore a tweed cap set on his head at a jaunty angle.

He did not know how you went about hiding on a boat. He had planned to secrete himself in a lifeboat or in a coiled-up hive of rope as he had seen it done in pictures. He sauntered out of the saloons and pretended he belonged. The last call for going ashore sounded. The gangplank was pulled up. The ship eventually moved into the Pacific, into the unknown, and the voices of the revelers became softer; you heard sudden bursts of laughter. He felt like it was the start of a new life. He walked out to the open deck and looked at the cloudy sky and watched the gulls turning and screaming and felt the motion of the ship under him, creaking strangely.

He said silent farewells to Josie Saenz and John Ford, to his mom and to Doc and brother Bob, and Jesse Hibbs and the guys at Sigma Chi and old Bob Bradbury and the whole U.S.A. with its rotten women—he hated love and would never be a sucker again. He looked forward to a future with some half-caste mistress in Samoa or Singapore.

He lingered on deck until the last of the seagulls had given up and ceased wheeling and returned to shore. He experienced for the first time the immensity and loneliness of the ocean and the sense of the smallness of a man, which he had often read about.

He conceived a melodramatic touch. To start out clean, from scratch, he drew out all the money he had remaining—less than a dollar in silver coins and a few nickels. He knotted them in his fist and then scattered them into the sea.

He went looking for a convenient lifeboat or a coil of rope. The lifeboats were out of reach and he could not find any rope.

Stealthily he loped in and out of the public rooms. It was time for dinner and everybody was now drinking legal martinis and wine and Scotch because the ship had passed the twelve-mile limit. He smelled the odors from the dining room and he could see the happy travelers gorging themselves. He was hungry. But what the hell. It was part of the adventure. Starvation was good for the soul. He had put his whole life on the line, and the hell with dinner. Later he found an unoccupied stateroom in the forward section of first class and he hid out in there on the first night.

In the morning, he brushed his teeth and washed his face. Outside, he roamed around and inhaled the air of the ocean. His poor stomach was growling with a great hunger. He was on the way now to unknown places and to a new life.

But if only we studied the tales of Conrad more carefully! We read them when we are young with the distortions of youth. It was like Lord Jim. *After two years of training he went to sea, and entering the regions so well known to his imagination, found them strangely barren of adventure.*

It does not turn out the way it is supposed to turn

out—the traditional bitter disillusionment of youth. Like the girl in the Hemingway story when she says that everything turns out to taste like licorice, Duke's first voyage was a little like Marlow's first one.

> . . . *there are those voyages that seem ordered for the illustration of life, that might stand for a symbol of existence. You fight, work, sweat, nearly kill yourself, sometimes do kill yourself, trying to accomplish something and you can't. Not from any fault of yours. You simply can do nothing, neither great nor little—not a thing in the world—not even marry an old maid, or get a wretched six-hundred-ton cargo of coal to its port of destination.*

It was quite a wretched voyage for young Morrison. If it symbolized anything about existence, it was simply that you couldn't run away to Honolulu if you had an appointment in Balboa.

He was getting to know one of the problems of an adventurer: how to survive. An adventurer instinctively knows how to survive by his wits or his fists. Duke lacked this basic ingredient of the adventurer. He was getting famished to the point of madness, and he did not know how to get food.

At eleven A.M. he was happy to find out they served beef bouillon and melba toast on deck. He had several cups and much toast but it did not satisfy his appetite. But he was determined to hold out. He searched outside cabins looking for trays of half-eaten food. A good buttered roll and a pot of coffee? Nothing. Eventually he found his way to the bar lounge. He would have sold his soul for a stiff drink. Three men were playing bridge and asked him to make a fourth. (This was before Harold Vanderbilt invented contract bridge, and the game was auction bridge, which had swept the land during the early 1920's.) They were playing penny a point—an expensive game. Duke said he would play, but not for money.

His partner was as good as he, and it was a successful game for the latter.

Recalling the event, Duke says, "They let me sit in

until somebody came along who'd play for stakes. They said the three would pay each other off. Well, my partner and I made a fortune. We had a fantastic run of cards and we played well and our opponents were potzers. For a while, it was game. slam. game, game, set, slam, set two doubled and redoubled. It was wild. I would have made a hundred dollars if I was in for money. Christ, I would have paid for my trip if I'd played bridge and had luck like that every day. I never had a run of cards like that before or since. The losers didn't want to stop for dinner. Nobody bought me a drink. Jesus but I felt rotten with those good hands, incredible, and my pockets empty. Then I couldn't stand the hunger. I went back and sneaked into that room and fell dead asleep. I didn't know they served sandwiches and coffee in the bar lounge around half-past ten, and if I'd only played bridge longer I could have lived on sandwiches until we made port. It was a ten-day voyage.

"I was finally going out of my mind after seventy-two hours without food. Finally there was this cabin boy who was younger than me. We had gotten to be friends. I told him the situation. He said he would speak to the room steward.

"I looked bad. Hadn't shaved in three days. The room steward was a little Irish character with rusty hair—looked like a dishonest Barry Fitzgerald or Donald Meek. I confessed my crime to him and he said that stowing away was heinous—he pronounced it *heinious*—and unlawful but he was taking pity on me as I was so young and innocent. He would bring me food."

He would also bring a razor. brush, and shaving cream. Once in Honolulu he said it would be simple for Duke to slip away and lose himself on shore without being apprehended.

In return, he asked for little enough—a mere bagatelle. One hundred dollars. Duke said he would gladly write an I.O.U. for a hundred and pay him as soon as he was established on a copra plantation, or maybe it would be rubber, out in Singapore or Tahiti.

Well, said Barry Fitzgerald or Donald Meek, unctuously rolling his eyes to heaven, would it be possible for him then to disgorge seventy-five dollars? No? Then maybe fifty simoleons?

Duke revealed he was literally penniless.

Meek-Fitzgerald whistled ominously. He spat into a spittoon. He said one didn't take markers from stowaways. He wanted cash on the line.

"My advice to you, young feller, is turn yourself in to the captain, makin' a full confession of your heinious and evil deeds and throwin' yourself on the mercy of the court. Stowin' away, that's a serious business on a ship, believe you me, though not as heinious as mutiny to be sure."

Duke trudged to the top deck and the bridge. In the captain's quarters, the steward turned him over to an executive officer, saying that this miscreant had been guilty of a most "heinious" deed.

Duke was handcuffed. Then he was marched down to a lower deck and placed in a barred room without portholes.

"I haven't had a thing to eat for three days," he moaned. "For the love of God, get me some food."

The officer coldly told the steward to tell the bar steward to make up a tray of sandwiches and milk and bring them to the prisoner when he made up the evening collation for the cardplayers. That was when Duke found out about the free supper.

He cursed himself and his hard luck.

In Honolulu, he was transferred, still in irons, to a Matson liner going east. He remained in the brig on the return voyage. He was handed over to the harbor police in San Francisco, then taken to the same jail which he had last examined as a tourist, the newly constructed jail.

He was jailed on Sunday. They did not believe him when he said he was a friend of the chief of police. He was allowed to make two telephone calls to Los Angeles. He called John Ford. He called his mother. Nobody was home. He spent the night in prison.

On Monday he got through to George O'Brien at Fox. O'Brien thought the whole adventure was rather amusing, but he did call his father. The chief straightened matters out with the District Attorney's office. He reported that Marion Morrison was a USC student and a friend of his son's, and an honest person who had made a small mistake. The Matson Navigation Company decided not to press charges. Duke was released on Tuesday. Chief O'Brien bought him a return ticket home.

Home?

Where was that?

Didn't they know he was a missing person who had been found? He didn't have a home.

Now it may occur to you that Morrison didn't have to go back to L.A. Why didn't he hang on in San Francisco, work at some menial labor, get up a stake, ship out on a freighter to Asia? Or surely he could have made it to Chicago and New York?

He was fleeing from Josephine Saenz, wasn't he?

But you see he had appointments to keep. An elemental force, as powerful as a storm at sea, returned him to L.A. and to her. These matters are beyond scientific analysis. He had to be with her, whatever the cost. He had to look at her. He had to hear her gentle voice. All his pain and resentment, all his frustration and wish to be free of her—these were quite irrelevant. He was held by love. He needed her presence—just her presence —in any way.

And he came back and told her he loved her and could not live without her. She looked pale and frightened. She had been sick while he was gone. She thought he would never come back. She had been very sick. Her mother had become shaken by the sight of her, knowing also now that she was witnessing a force which she could not control. Yet Mrs. Saenz was determined to postpone and delay the marriage, hoping against hope that her daughter's love would prove to be a passing infatuation.

Poor Josephine Saenz! She couldn't resolve the opposing parties. She could temporize. She could pray. Dr. Saenz came to terms with the inevitable before his wife did. They all finally worked out a compromise which was that Morrison would go back to college in the fall and take up his studies and then go on to law school. If he and Josie still wanted to get married when he was graduated, then they would consent. During the next year, the lovers would agree not to see each other more than two nights a week.

She went often to the Christ the King Church on Rossmore Avenue. It is a beautiful church. She made many devotions and lighted many candles.

And Duke got a summer job at Fox Film Studio.

# 7

# Propping, Juicing, Gaffing, Stunting, Doubling, and Acting

In July, 1927, Duke Morrison came back to Fox. He planned to work only until college opened in the fall. He never went back to school. He could see no means of supporting himself in school. His father had no money. He had lost the football scholarship. He could not raise tuition and living expenses. He had a good job in pictures. He liked working in the studio. He was somebody. At USC, he was a failure. He wouldn't go back to washing dishes at the Sigma Chi house. In some ways, he had become a man. He was doing a man's job. He was earning a man's pay. Josie did not like it. Her parents said it proved that her sweetheart was a man without ambition and culture. There was no future with Morrison, they said. She loved him. He loved her.

For three years, Duke was a property man. He performed other functions at the studio, but his specialty was the objects and artifacts of a setting, the things an actor had to carry on his person to suggest his personality or to use in the action. Having to choose and place properties gives one a unique slant on a screenplay. Duke's mind, as an actor, has been conditioned by his training as a prop man.

"As anyone who has ever been connected with the manufacture of a motion picture will tell you, it may take a certain minor talent to write, direct, produce, or star in a movie, but it takes genius to be a good prop man," George Axelrod once facetiously wrote.

Duke propped for Fox directors Frank Borzage and Raoul Walsh and, of course. John Ford. George O'Brien, who was one of the important romantic leading players on the lot, always insisted on having Duke prop on his pictures.

While propping, Duke learned the importance of details. Such pieces of flotsam as cigarettes, handkerchiefs, hats, coats, chairs and tables and flowerpots, lamps and hitching posts and decks of playing cards, all these and so many more of the tools of daily living are of no concern to an actor except when he has to use one of them in a scene. He is concerned with his lines and his readings and his moods and his camera angles. If there is an eating scene, for instance, he takes it for granted that the prop man will keep on supplying him with the identical meal for each retake. Propping is an art, a minor art but an art, and not one that is easy to master. Even those of us who are fascinated by movies have relatively little awareness of the importance of properties and the role of the prop men. Often it is the props that make one film more authentic than another film.

Duke, because of his propping years, will read a script in a special way. He will read the sentences enclosed in parentheses. (HE LIGHTS HER CIGARETTE AND THEN CROSSES TO BAY WINDOW. THROWS MATCH INTO FLOWERPOT.)

Duke would not only ask himself what would be his motivation for the action, but he would also instinctively think: Cigarettes. What brand? Should I have a cigarette case? What kind of flowerpot? Plant? Cut flowers? What kind of flowers? Table in bay window?

Even when he is not playing a scene, Duke cannot help but be conscious of the props. When he watches a film, he enjoys seeing how the props have been handled and how cleverly they have been chosen and arranged by the chief property man and his assistants. He learned every craft in moviemaking. He learned it as an apprentice. In those days stars and directors made three and four pictures a year. They worked fast. One month to prepare a scenario and two months—or less—to get it in the can. There were no unions and no union hours. You worked at night, sometimes, and on Saturdays and Sundays.

Duke says: "In those days, you could operate in every department of pictures. You didn't need a union card. I was a carpenter. I was a juicer. I rigged lights. I helped build sets. Carried props. Hauled furniture. I got to know the nuts and bolts of making pictures. That is why I know what a scene is going to look like on the film. I don't have to look at the daily rushes. I never do. At this time, I had no ambition beyond becoming the best property man on the Fox lot. A chief property man was getting a hundred and fifty a week. That was what I wanted to be, at first. Then a stuntman. But acting—hell, no. I was embarrassed seeing my face on the screen. I thought I looked ugly. I did not have the ego which enjoys seeing itself as a star. But I knew there was a place for me in the movie business, behind the scenes. And that was fine. I had a permanent position at Fox. I thought that there would be no obstacle to my marrying Josie now. Through my friendship with George O'Brien, I was made to feel I belonged on the lot. I loved going to work at the studio. I felt this was my life, my future."

Duke became part of the Fox studio population. His best friend was Hughing Scott, a young assistant director. Duke, as a citizen of the special world of a film studio, became known to the other directors, to the stars, the supporting players, the extras, the technicians. He didn't consciously set out to learn the art of making films. He didn't set out to be an actor. He was doing a job with people he liked. He ran with Hughing Scott. They drank and played with men and women who were immersed in the frantic existence of filmmaking.

Duke was also an extra in mob scenes. When he did a walk-on or a bit part, he got five dollars a day extra, sometimes seven-fifty. He appeared in many obscure films playing just a face in a crowd. He was an undergraduate, a dancing body in a dancing crowd in a musical comedy with a fraternity and sorority love story: *Words and Music* (1929). He got his first screen credit as "Duke Morrison." He got to wear a tuxedo and dance the foxtrot with Lois Moran, with whom F. Scott Fitzgerald fell in love and whom Zelda suspected of having an affair with her husband.

He went on location for a northwestern with George O'Brien—*Rough Romance* (1930). He played a bit in *Cheer Up and Smile* (1930). starring Arthur Lake and Dixie Lee. Lake subsequently played Dagwood Bumstead in a series of comedies and Dixie Lee married Bing Crosby.

In 1928, *Four Sons* and *Hangman's House* were released—the actors silent, the dialogue still in subtitles, but with musical soundtrack, songs. and sound effects of bells and rolling wheels. Duke was surprised to see that the scene in which Mother Bernle fingers the fatal letter while autumn leaves fly about her had been cut by Ford. All that aggravation about his clumsiness—and it had been edited out in the end.

And that difficult moment before the judge, in which he had been told he would hang by the neck until dead, was printed as a special effect. What one sees is a silhouette, just a black figure appearing in the fireplace as the judge stares into it and remembers the past. Yet there is a clearly visible shot of Duke Morrison toward the end of *Hangman's House,* during an exciting steeplechase race across open country.

It was an auspicious debut for the future John Wayne. Ford made the sequence by alternating long shots of the horses and riders with closeups of the Irish peasants behind a white picket fence. The peasants are cheering. And now we see John Wayne vividly. Three times. Three breathtaking glimpses of his first exposure on film. In our last glimpse, taking off his cap, we know that exuberant splendor in him, shining on the screen, as he breaks through the fence excitedly, runs out on the field.

Duke Morrison is on his way to becoming John Wayne.

He was photogenic. This seems to be a rare quality that is given. It cannot be taught. It cannot be copied. There are persons of charm and vivaciousness in a room who are uninteresting on the screen. And there are other persons, who seem reserved and plain, who become luminous for the camera's eye. Where does it come from? Is it some emanation from the eyes? Is it a radiation from the rhythm of the body? Is there a glow in some human souls and not in others?

The Irish peasant boy of *Hangman's House,* this walk-on part, this nothing, was everything in the eyes of John Ford. Duke had it. Right from the start, he was a movie face. It was a face of innocence, and not because he was young. There are some young movie faces that suggest sophistication and corruption. Duke's face always conveyed innocence, even when he got old and fat and wrinkled. This innocence made even his most revolting scenes of violence, of cruelty, less degrading. Duke's innocence on screen is like Marilyn Monroe's naïveté, which she always retained so that even when she played unwholesome characters doing wretched things, she was lovely and sweet.

Not all the suffering he was to experience, not all his dissipation, nor the spiritual ravages of fighting for his place in Hollywood, nor his intense dedication to his work, ever took away his innocence. It remained. It shines through every role he has ever played.

His next role, also a small one, was in Ford's *Salute,* a film of rivalry in love and football between the Army and the Navy. Ford shrewdly wanted to hire real football players to work in the picture. Specifically, he wanted the members of Howard Jones' famous Trojans. After John Ford himself, and several Fox executives, had failed to get permission from USC president Rufus E. von Kleinschmidt, Duke was assigned to persuade President von Kleinschmidt that this would be a splendid thing for USC and for the students. He talked to the president for two hours and made a good case. He even agreed to let the football players take their final exams in April. *Salute* was to start filming in Annapolis at the end of April. Sol M. Wurtzel, head of production at Fox, told him that Duke decided to let the Sigma Chi gridiron heroes monopolize the action. He told them about the deal, but in order to make points at the studio he said they would only get fifty dollars a week. They accepted gleefully. Now Duke figured Wurtzel would raise his salary or give him a bonus. Wurtzel complimented him on his shrewdness.

Duke wanted to know about his salary. Wurtzel said he was getting the same thirty-five dollars a week as before.

Now he knew what they meant around the studio when they said things were going from bad to Wurtzel. Wurtzel was a tight-fisted businessman. His brother Ben, equally parsimonious, was in charge of the technical crews at Fox.

Duke indignantly said that the least the studio could do was pay him the same fifty dollars as the other football players.

He was granted his favor. He went away, kicking himself for having maneuvered himself out of twenty-five dollars a week.

Ford wanted about twenty athletes to go on the trip— it was to be all-expenses-paid in addition to the salary. Duke knew there were enough Sigma Chi's to fill the bill. He went over to the house one morning. He had a bus. Word had gotten around about the casting call, and several rugged characters who were not Sigma Chi's showed up and tried to get into the bus. Among them was a USC running tackle, a huge hulking man with thick lips and big ears.

Duke knew him, of course. When he saw him in the crowd, he motioned to him to go away. The man said that he had as much right as any other Trojan to get into the movies. He had always wanted to be an actor. He was going to school but he would rather be an actor. Duke hooted at the idea of a human being as ugly as a gorilla expecting to become an actor. Duke and he got into a pushing and shoving melee, but the big man forced his way into the bus.

At the studio, they lined up. Duke stood beside Ford with a list of students and prepared to check them off. Ford looked over the men.

"Who's that big ugly galoot over there?" he asked.

"Who?" replied Duke, who knew damn well.

"That one," Ford pointed.

"He just came along for the buggy ride, Mr. Ford. You wouldn't want him. He's just an overgrown loud-mouth. Now over there, that's Scotty Lavelle, and Don Williams, Don worked here last summer—"

"I'll take Williams, you can check him off. I also want that other one, that ugly one."

"Mr. Ford, if it's ugly guys you want, I know a couple of them over at the house much uglier, much much uglier."

"Yeah, but he's lovable as well as ugly. What's he called?"

"Wardell Bond," Duke said.

"Hire him," Ford said.

Duke checked off his name. Bond had watched it all.

"Too damn bad, Duke," he said, grinning, "but it seems like all the passengers on your gravy train ain't going to be sweethearts of Sigma Chi!"

Bond played a heavy in *Salute*. Duke played a West Point cadet. After graduating from USC in 1929, Bond soon established himself as one of the most intriguing character players of the 1930's. He was the bus driver in *It Happened One Night*, a small town sheriff in *The Grapes of Wrath*, a homicide squad detective in *The Maltese Falcon*.

Duke and Bond were assigned to the same Pullman bedroom on the Washington-bound train. They were enemies at first. They did not talk to each other. The students were to sign their meal checks. Bond signed his dinner tab. He had had a full course steak dinner. A front-office auditor, going over the checks, did not like Bond's expensive collation. He told Duke to inform the students they were to live on ten dollars a day. Duke said the original bonus condition was unlimited expenses for meals. He said football players had to eat more steaks than other people. Most of them had steaks three times a day. Duke told the players to ignore the book-keeper and order what they wished.

The following day the auditor told Duke that he was fired from the production.

Bond now suddenly saw Duke in a new light. He organized a players' strike. He told Ford about the injustice. Ford's tactic was to eat a twenty-dollar breakfast and sign the auditor's name.

The whole matter was dropped then and there.

*Salute* was Ward Bond's first movie.

In later years, when Bond got disgusted with Hollywood and said he wished he were a doctor living a normal life, Duke would always reply, "I did my damnedest to keep you the hell out of the picture business. But you had to shove your fat butt into the bus, so you got only yourself to blame."

Duke's next assignment was propping on John Ford's *Submarine*, his second talking picture. *Salute* had been the first. Dudley Nichols wrote the screenplay for *Submarine*. It was his first job for Ford. The movie was released as *Men Without Women* in 1930, without apologies to Ernest Hemingway. The plot dealt with a submarine en route from Shanghai to San Diego. After an engine room explosion, the men are trapped underwater. There was a race against death, as the U.S. Navy attempts to rescue the fourteen doomed men. The climactic scene was one in which the sailors are expelled through the torpedo hatch one by one. They surface above water in a maelstrom of bubbles and froth.

Duke's job was to produce the bubbles. It took many days to complete the sequence because the water around Catalina Island, where they were shooting, was rough that week.

Day after day, Duke took his position on a yacht anchored in the channel. He pushed an air pump which churned up the bubbles at the place where the men would surface. Two stuntmen had been hired to double the actors. They had to leap into the Pacific and then emerge. They were paid seventy-five dollars for each dive. Four days they had been waiting for the waters to subside. The waves were still high and risky. They refused to dive. The filming schedule was thrown off badly.

Ford was desperate. He was in his place on the top deck. The churning seas heaved the ship from side to side. Most of the actors were in San Diego. J. Farrell MacDonald had gone to Mexico for two days. George O'Brien was the star. He stood beside the director, shaking his head.

O'Brien and Ford debated whether they shouldn't pack it in and just do the rescue scene on the ranch and back lot in the new Beverly Hills studio of Fox, the one on Pico Boulevard. There was a good-sized man-made lake out there on the back lot. Goddammit, Ford thought, it wouldn't look right, it wouldn't feel right, I don't like it, I want to do it this way and no other way; I got the whole goddam U.S. Navy out there and I want them in the background, and I'm going to do this come hell or high water.

Of high water there certainly was no paucity.

Ford happened to see Duke Morrison heaving away at the pump. He laughed. He remarked to O'Brien that somebody had forgotten to tell Duke that the camera wasn't going and that they didn't need any bubbles today. Then he decided to see if Duke wanted to risk his life. He knew that Duke was a body-surfer and a genuine water rat, a fine swimmer, and a guy with *cojones*.

What he did not know was that at this time Duke was in desperate need of money. He owed a few hundred dollars to some bookmakers. He had bet on USC against Notre Dame the previous Saturday, and USC had lost by one point. The way Wayne recalls it, "I bet everything I could beg or borrow. I didn't know where I could get the cash to pay off. I had to pay off or they wouldn't let me make any more bets. I wasn't afraid of being beaten up. I was afraid of losing my credit. Ford called me up to the top deck. He saw I was down in the dumps and he asked me why. I told him I was in this situation where I needed to make some money to pay off these markers. He said, well if you're a guy who's not afraid and you're willing to take a few dives, you could change costume and double the actors. The studio was paying seventy-five a dive, he said. I wasn't afraid of the water. I was more afraid of being hit by one of the small Navy boats which were shooting around in the channel. I made six dives."

George O'Brien also needed some extra money. He was courting a beautiful young actress, Marguerite Churchill. The courtship of Miss Churchill was as prolonged and as difficult as the courtship of Miss Saenz. O'Brien had enlisted in the Navy during World War I, when he was only seventeen years old. He. like Bond, had planned to become a doctor. He earned the rating of Pharmacist's Mate Third Class. He was not one of those fragile sensitive actors—he was a tough man. He was a good amateur boxer and had been light-heavyweight champion of the Pacific fleet. Like Duke, he was a good swimmer and surfer. He volunteered to do some diving too.

O'Brien did his own emergence from the water and then doubled five other actors—six dives in all. While this was going on, J. Farrell MacDonald returned from Tijuana, "drunker than a fiddler's bitch," in Ford's words, "and nobody would speak to him. So J. Farrell came staggering out on the top deck and looked down. 'What're you doing?' he says. I said, 'I'm supposed to be shooting.' He says, 'The camera going?' I said, 'Yes.' He said, 'I don't want anyone doubling me!' and he did a beautiful dive—forty feet—hit the water, swam out there, he must have been sixty years old at the time. He came back sober . . ."

When Duke signed his work sheet at six o'clock, he saw he was credited with only seven dollars and fifty cents' bonus, instead of four hundred fifty. He said there had been a terrible mistake. Not at all, said a Wurtzel minion. He was listed as a property man and he could not be paid a stuntman's rates.

"So what about this seven dollars and fifty cents? What the hell's that for?"

"That is for your day's pay as an extra, which you are entitled to, Morrison."

Duke should have gone to Ford. He didn't. Ford didn't like whiners. Duke has carried this bitterness about being cheated out of his stuntman's pay for a long, long time— up till this day. He bears his resentments on the same grand scale that he upholds his admirations.

At least, he had found out one thing. He had the nerve and recklessness to be a good stuntman, and he liked the money. From now on, he was a stuntman as well as a prop man. And just as his mind became conditioned to seeing a movie in terms of its artifacts, he gradually became accustomed to thinking in terms of actions, stunt actions, gag actions, as he made a film. For a long time, for over a decade, he thought of himself as a stuntman rather than an actor—he was a stuntman playing the part of an actor playing the part of a fictional hero . . .

He even lucked into the money to pay his gambling debts. On the yacht, riding back to the San Diego harbor that fateful day, Duke got into a high-stakes poker game and won six hundred dollars.

Ford shot some of the interior scenes in the doomed submarine on the Fox Hills lot. There was one involving a naval lieutenant and a mate. Ford didn't like the performance of the actor doing the lieutenant. He told Duke to play the part.

This was Duke's first interesting role, a few minutes in length, but some closeups and some dialogue. It is not impressive in itself. It confirmed Ford's estimate that he had a rich, interesting voice, and could speak his lines with some flair.

# 8

# The Making of John Wayne

Raoul Walsh acted in two-reelers for D. W. Griffith in 1910. He played John Wilkes Booth in *The Birth of a Nation.* He started directing in 1918. Eventually he became one of the most versatile directors in Hollywood. He directed Douglas Fairbanks and Victor McLaglen, Marlene Dietrich, Mae West, Pola Negri, Gloria Swanson, Errol Flynn. Many of his films—*What Price Glory? The Thief of Bagdad, Sadie Thompson, The Roaring Twenties, Battle Cry, High Sierra,* and *White Heat*—are classics.

He made Morrison over into Wayne. He made him into a shooting star.

Walsh is alive and jaunty at the age of eighty-seven. He saw Griffith plain. He learned camera tricks from Billy Bitzer. And there he sits, across from you at a table in the Sheraton-Universal coffee shop. He sips iced tea and remembers. He drove over by himself from his Simi Valley ranch, seventy-five miles away. He had some business at Universal. He stands erect and tall in a western outfit, with high boots, and a broad-brimmed Stetson hat.

He remembers the sound revolution and Hollywood in 1927. They all said that the big outdoor western was finished. In those days microphones had to be concealed in fixed positions. Cameras had to be put in heavy soundproofed booths so their noise wouldn't be recorded. You had no mobility. You couldn't get the action of a western any more, they all said. Walsh said it was possible. His studio put out the Fox Movietone Newsreel.

76

He used a Movietone News sound-truck and a lightweight mobile camera and he shot the first western talkie for one hundred thousand dollars: *In Old Arizona.* He made history. The quality of recording was rough, but it was real. He concealed mikes in sagebrush and mesquite. You heard horses clattering and guns shooting and bacon sizzling.

*In Old Arizona,* with Warner Baxter as the Cisco Kid, was a smash, so the studio bought a story about the Oregon trail and they said he should go ahead and make a spectacle movie, *The Big Trail.* A million-dollar movie. William Fox, the most powerful man in Hollywood, was going to make the biggest western of all time. And they weren't going to risk it with silent movie stars, because they really did not know how to enunciate. They engaged leading Broadway stars: Tyrone Power, Sr., Ian Keith, Tully Marshall. There was still the part of the frontier scout to be cast. They couldn't find one on Broadway. Walsh wanted Gary Cooper for the part. Cooper had started making aviation pictures in 1925; he was now under contract to Sam Goldwyn. Goldwyn agreed on the loan-out. Then he changed his mind. He decided, instead, to do *The Winning of Barbara Worth* with Cooper.

By now, the studio had laid out one hundred thousand dollars on story and treatment, and the leads were on salary. Winfield Sheehan, the new head of production, was riding Walsh hard. Walsh auditioned every cowboy actor in town. He did not think of Duke Morrison. Duke had propped for him several times, but he was just a faceless member of the crew. He could not find a frontier scout. The cinema cowboys could ride and shoot but they could not talk worth a damn.

The director's bungalow was over at the Fox Hills Ranch on Pico Boulevard. Walsh went over, one day, to the administration building at the Fox lot on Western. He passed a studio warehouse and saw a man carrying furniture out and setting pieces on a truck. It was very hot. The young man wasn't wearing a shirt. He was sweating. He had rippling muscles. Walsh was so desperate for an actor that, just like in all those legends, he decided to test this stranger. He watched him. He watched the way he strode. Walsh says that "he had a western hang to his shoulders and a way of holding himself and moving which is typical of a westerner."

He struck up a conversation and learned that his prospect was Duke Morrison, a prop man on the lot. He liked the sound of his voice. Walsh asked his assistant Eddie Goulding—later a producer—if he knew this kid. Goulding said that he did. Walsh sent Goulding over to talk to Duke.

"Duke," he said, "don't take any more haircuts."

"What for?"

"Let your hair grow long a couple of days."

"I wasn't figurin' to be a musician, Eddie."

"Duke, keep this under your hat. Raoul Walsh is getting ready to make a big western. He is going to test you."

"I'm no movie actor, Eddie."

"You never know, Duke, you just never know."

On Friday, Duke was informed that Mr. Walsh wanted him to go to a quiet place on a mountaintop and "yell out your lungs for a couple of hours." He was to yell himself hoarse over the weekend. "Mr. Walsh wants you to bring down your voice."

Besides screaming on a mountain, Walsh instructed him to "practice reading aloud. He says you get the Sunday paper and read the editorial page out loud to yourself. Idea is to practice speech and get used to your own voice, Duke. Next week, you'll be taken off Ford's picture. But you'll be on salary while Mr. Walsh works with you. Yes, we've cleared it with Mr. Ford and Ben Wurtzel."

"One of us is crazy, Eddie, and it ain't me."

"What's your size, Duke?"

"It's a thirty-eight long."

"Mr. Walsh is choosing a western costume for you."

On Monday he was fitted with buckskin pants, fringed jacket, denim shirt, and dark cowboy hat with wide brim. Walsh said they were testing tomorrow afternoon on Stage 4. He explained the scene to Duke.

"You're going to be a scout. Your job is to lead this

train of wagons from Independence, Missouri, to Salem, Oregon. You've grown up in the West. You're an Indian fighter, hunter, lived outdoors. But your wagon people are mostly settlers, going out to be farmers. They're not sure what's ahead for them. Most of them don't know what wild country is like. They're going to ask you many questions. That's the scene I'm making for this test. You just answer their questions."

"What should I say?"

"Anything that comes into your mind. Don't think about words. Just try to express your feelings. Listen to their questions and respond."

The other actors knew their lines cold. Duke was not given a script. He confronted Tyrone Power, Sr., and Ian Keith on a bare soundstage. Keith looked at him disdainfully, with the lofty air of an experienced stage veteran facing a Hollywood primitive. Duke looked to be about sixteen years old. He was scared. He was perspiring. Art Edison, cinematographer, lit the scene. Walsh told them to roll. The three actors started throwing the questions at Duke. How long would the trek last? Were there dangerous animals? How about the Indians? He could not think of what to say. He was stammering and scared. There seemed to be a deliberately nasty ring to Keith's voice. He got on Duke's nerves. He was his old enemy, the bully in the school playground. Suddenly Duke turned on Keith and started firing questions, one after another. Could he handle a gun? Could he ride a horse? Was he scared of Indians? Had he ever killed a man?

He kept hammering at Ian Keith, until the man broke down, stammering and then speechless.

Walsh ran the test for Wurtzel and Sheehan.

"How do we know he can talk?" Sheehan asked.

"You just heard him talk, didn't you? It was a hard scene and he talked damn good, Winnie."

"We're taking an awful chance," Sol Wurtzel said.

"You'll not find anyone better," Walsh said. "He's the best one we got. He's the *only* one we got."

"He's no Gary Cooper," Sheehan said.

"We haven't got Cooper."

"I don't like this name, Duke Morrison, it's no name for a leading man," Sheehan said.

So Walsh knew the decision was in favor of Duke Morrison.

"We got to have a good American name," Sol Wurtzel said.

Walsh admired Mad Anthony Wayne, a general of the American Revolution.

"How about Anthony Wayne?" he asked.

They mulled it over.

"It sounds too Italian," Sheehan said.

"Then let's make it Tony Wayne." Walsh said.

"Then it sounds like a girl," Wurtzel said.

"What's the matter with just plain John? John Wayne," Sheehan said thoughtfully.

"John Wayne," repeated Wurtzel. "It's American."

"You betcha," Walsh said.

"Send him to my office tomorrow," Sheehan said. "Now, Sol, how much we going to pay John Wayne?"

"We ought to give him a raise. He's getting thirty-five now. Let's give him forty-five."

"Forty-five? Forty-five? Are you gentlemen serious?" Walsh sighed.

"He should pay *us* for this chance," Wurtzel said.

"If it ever gets out we're paying our leading man forty-five and Tully Marshall five hundred, we'll be the laughingstock of the industry."

"Five hundred? You're crazy, Raoul."

"We can't afford it, Raoul. We've got to hold the budget down."

"You guys are breaking my heart. At least give him two-fifty."

They finally went as high as seventy-five and not a penny more.

Sheehan presented Duke with a five-year contract, starting at seventy-five dollars a week, with renewable options every six months, which would bring him to a five-hundred-dollar level in five years. He had no lawyer or agent to advise him. It was strictly a one-way contract in the studio's favor. He signed the deal without a murmur.

But he balked at changing his name. He told Sheehan he was proud of being a Morrison. Sheehan pressured him, wheedled him, threatened him—until he acceded. He resented then, and still resents, the arrogant attitude of studio bosses. They did not care about his feelings. How do you go and suddenly inform your father that you are not bearing the name he gave you?

Until the name was firmly established on the scene, the John Wayne cognomen proved to be a constant source of trouble because he was always getting mixed up with John Payne and Wayne Morris. They got each other's mail. They got each other's phone calls and romantic propositions. Their activities were erroneously reported in Jimmie Fidler's column or Hedda Hopper's because some informant had mistakenly said "Wayne" when he meant "Payne." Once John Wayne had attended a party, and it was only when he arrived there that he realized they were expecting John Payne. And John Payne once flew down to Mexico and was the guest of honor at a film industry soirée. As he heard the speeches, he realized that they had John Wayne in mind. The two men resembled each other vaguely. Payne made believe he was Wayne. He made a gracious acceptance speech and praised Mexico. He took back a sterling silver statue with "John Wayne" engraved on it. He told Duke about it.

"It's in my den," he said. "I'll be damned if I'm going to give it to you. I had to listen to those damned speeches about what a fine actor and great human being you are."

To get "John Wayne" in condition for *The Big Trail,* he was sent to stuntman Steve Clemente for lessons in knife throwing. He was sent to Jack Padgin, Fox's best western stuntman, for lessons in throwing a lariat, handling a gun, riding like a movie westerner rides. And, alas, he was also sent to a certain Lumsden Hare for speech lessons. Duke had first run into Hare while he was propping for Ford on Victor McLaglen's *The Black*

*Watch* (the movie version of Talbot Mundy's *King of the Khyber Rifles*).

So great was the apprehension of studio executives as to the ability of silent-movie directors and silent actors to give a good account of themselves in the new kind of cinema that they were hiring actors and acting coaches from England and New York. Hare was a British Shakespearean actor and play director. He was a pet of Sheehan's. Sheehan assigned him to every Fox movie. Hare was one of the most hated men on the lot. He played a British officer in *The Black Watch*. He also directed several scenes with McLaglen and Myrna Loy, who was rendering an Indian girl. (This was the first, and last, time anybody else ever directed a scene in a John Ford movie.) Wayne remembers that Hare had no feeling for the imagery of movies and he made them "just talk, talk, talk—empty words."

How one goes about directing a movie and manipulating movie actors was illustrated by one of Ford's capers during the making of *The Black Watch*. There was a scene in which McLaglen fights with an Indian wrestler inside a ring of fire. They kept doing one retake after another. Ford always had trouble getting Vic worked up to an emotional pitch. He was a gentle soul. The scene demanded him to be vicious. A real wrestler had been hired. He was a light-skinned Negro, costumed as an East Indian. Ford took Duke aside.

He whispered, "Kid, you can make yourself an extra piece of change. I want you to go in there and give that black wrestler the works. I want you to shame Vic into giving a good performance."

Duke got into the fiery ring. He and the wrestler started going at each other. Duke put everything he had into the struggle. He finally threw the black actor down on the ground and pinned him there.

Ford cast some aspersions on McLaglen's strength. McLaglen got mad. He jumped into the ring. He grabbed the black man by the waist, heaved him up high, and then hurled him clear out of the ring . . .

Lumsden Hare would watch such matters with a curled lip.

He went to work to try to make a Clive Brook or a Ronald Colman out of John Wayne. He tutored him three hours each afternoon. He showed him how to mince properly, how to posture, how to roll the eyes, how to elongate a vowel. Wayne could not stand it after the first week. Neither could Hare. He told Wayne that he had little or no talent as a thespian.

In September, 1929, Wayne and the company went out on location in Yuma, Arizona. Walsh had erected a replica of a frontier settlement on the Indian reservation there. Some of *The Big Trail* was shot here, and the rest in Yellowstone National Park, the Grand Tetons, Sequoia National Park, Jackson Hole, and the Grand Canyon!

Wayne did his own stunts. Walsh was impressed by Duke's seriousness and his sobriety. But he will never forget the first month of filming, during which Duke was suffering from diarrhea. He had come down with a bad case of the *turistas*. He had been in bed the first week of shooting. He had been weak and almost useless for two weeks after that. At least, this had kept Wayne away from the bottle. Everybody else, it seemed to Walsh, was drunk most of the time.

"That picture should have been called *The Big Drunk*," he says morosely.

The screenwriter—a famous *Saturday Evening Post* author of western serials—was taken on location to rewrite old scenes and invent new stunts. He was plastered most of the time and Walsh had to improvise on the set. The New York actors were going crazy. They were not used to desert heat and the intense, parching blaze of the Arizona sun. They were not accustomed to arising at dawn, breakfasting, reporting for makeup at seven, and being on the set at eight. On a desert location, you do most of the filming before ten A.M. and after three P.M. When the sun is straight overhead, you get washed-up results, flat lighting. The New York actors generally went to bed at dawn, after a night on the town. Many had not seen a sunrise in twenty years. They were miserable on the desert. And they were utterly confused by the filming process, in which a lengthy sequence—ten minutes, five minutes being a very long time in film—is filmed in brief takes, dismembered fragments. They were unable to respond emotionally to the fact of repetitive takes and of shooting the same lines of dialogue from different camera angles.

They hated the desert. They hated the hot sun. They hated the movies. They hated Walsh. The only thing that made life bearable was whiskey, and they had a runner going back and forth, from Yuma to the location and back to Yuma, bringing bottles of bootleg whiskey.

For three weeks, Walsh had to shoot around Wayne, who was deathly sick. And for three weeks he had to hurriedly indoctrinate the New York crowd into the science of cinema. As if that were not enough, *The Big Trail* was being shot in a new wide-screen process, known as Fox Grandeur. *The Big Trail* was the first 70 mm. film —antedating by two decades those films made in Cinema, Panavision, Warnerscope, Cinemascope, and Todd A-O.

William Fox, a megalomaniac and a genius, actually foresaw the threat of television as long ago as 1928. He told Upton Sinclair—who reported it in his book about Fox published in 1932—that just as radio had taken audiences away from silent movies, so television would someday steal the audiences for talking pictures.

"I reached the conclusion that the one thing that would make it possible to compete with television was to use a screen ten times larger than the present," he said away back in 1932!

Fox bought the Mitchell Camera Company, which made most movie cameras. They developed a 70 mm. camera. He also bought International Projector, and they developed a projector and a screen capable of showing Grandeur process pictures.

*The Big Trail* would revolutionize the size and scope of movies and make millions for Fox, as *The Jazz Singer* had done for Warner Brothers.

It was a dangerous dream. At the same time that Fox

was scheming to revolutionize movies, he was also plotting to take over M-G-M by means of stock manipulation. He would merge Fox and Metro and would be the emperor of the greatest domain in Hollywood. In 1928, Fox Film Corporation stock sold for one hundred twenty dollars a share and paid a four-dollar dividend on earnings of eleven dollars. Fox owned and controlled eight hundred theaters. He was planning to equip each of his theaters with the Grandeur screen and projector and show *The Big Trail* in all its spectacular and gargantuan beauty. Every theater in the U.S. would have to follow his example in order to compete.

And John Wayne would ride to glory on Fox Grandeur films.

In 1929, even before the stock market collapsed, William Fox was in financial trouble because of his Wall Street manipulations. He now had to race against time. He had to get *The Big Trail* made quickly and released quickly and he would be saved.

Walsh did not know he was to shoot *The Big Trail* in Grandeur Screen until he got to Yuma. Sheehan and Wurtzel were there with this enormous camera. They broke the news to him. At that time, there was no way of squeezing 70 mm. film into 35 mm. Since American theaters were equipped only for 35 mm., every take had to be done twice over—once in 35 mm. and once in 70 mm.

Walsh got to work and somehow, "though I felt like I was up to my ass in drunks, and those geezers who weren't drunk were down with Montezuma's revenge or just goddam stupid," he started shooting some of the stunts and action scenes.

There were many Indian extras on the picture. They also liked to drink a little firewater now and then. And when they got stoned on hooch, they would set fire to the false-front houses on the frontier set. Walsh remembers that the night before the cast and crew departed from Yuma for the next location, the one in Wyoming, the Apaches set fire to the baggage cars on the train! They were having a hell of a fine time. They had not removed their makeup for a scene they had done that morning, the usual Indian-attack-on-a-wagon-train scene, and they were still in war-paint and headdresses. They rode around the train, screeching and screaming their war cries, and firing burning arrows into the railroad cars. Cochise and Geronimo would have been proud of them.

Remembering the Yuma location, Wayne told interviewer Richard Warren Lewis recently that he had lost eighteen pounds from the *turistas,* and that they threatened to replace him if he didn't get to work. "So . . . I returned to work. My first scene was carrying in an actor named Tully Marshall. who was known to booze it up quite a bit. He had a big jug in his hand in this scene, and I set him down and we have a drink with another guy. They passed the jug to me first, and I dug back into it; it was straight rotgut bootleg whiskey. I'd been puking and crapping blood for a week, and now I just poured that raw stuff right down my throat. After the scene, you can bet I called him every kind of an old bastard."

Walsh still remembers the hard luck that beset *The Big Trail.* "There must have been a curse on *The Big Trail,*" he says. "Most of that New York crowd, the actors, were dead, heart attacks. within a year, two years. The worst thing happened was William Fox went bust and none of his houses had the Grandeur Screen. Nor would other theaters spend the fifty thousand for the equipment. Aside from the Roxy and Grauman's Chinese, *The Big Trail* was only shown in the 35 mm. version. Damn shame. It was a beautiful picture and Wayne did a fine job. He asked me to hire his friend Ward Bond. I believe it was one of Bond's first pictures. He had a nice part. He was one of the settlers. He had to grow a beard. But he was out getting drunk with the other drunks every night. Oh, I tell you, it was the worst experience ever, and I don't know how we ever got it in the can."

When he returned to Hollywood, Wayne had his first interview with a fan magazine writer. Miriam Hughes profiled him for *Photoplay Magazine* in December, 1930.

She described him as "shy and boyish, with that same appeal that made Charles Farrell a delight to fans. Yet he has more energy and virility and less of whimsy than Charlie has."

Farrell was one of the leading Fox stars. He was a romantic leading-man type, the kind that exists in a pair situation. He had been paired with Janet Gaynor in several films. Their *Seventh Heaven* was one of the great hits of that period.

*The Big Trail* was two hours and five minutes long. It had its world premiere at Grauman's Chinese on October 24, 1930. It was one of those Hollywood grand openings, with searchlights sweeping the sky, famous stars arriving in Hispano-Suizas and Duesenbergs, masses of spectators on tiers of benches cheering. There were gold tickets of admission and thick souvenir programs bound with red cords. California Governor James Rolph hailed the movie in a speech he made before the showing.

Governor Rolph praised the Grandeur Screen and the genius and vision of William Fox He spoke of how much the movie industry had contributed to the growth of California. He ended with a flourish:

"And now, ladies and gentlemen, let us sit back in our chairs and watch the most spectacular motion picture ever made in this great country of ours—" He paused for effect. *"The Big Parade."*

The audience sat stunned. Governor Rolph had mistakenly promised them M-G-M's famous World War I movie with John Gilbert and Renee Adoree. Nobody applauded. There was nervous tittering. The house lights were dimmed at last and the film began.

Visually, when seen on the wide screen, *The Big Trail* overwhelmed audiences. Its broad sweep of landscape—the rushing of men and horses and wagons across the land—has rarely been equalled in any western. The vastness of our country became a vivid experience. The pioneers looked real. They were dusty and unshaven. The women's dresses were ragged and used. The men wore torn pants and patched shirts. They went through real pangs of hunger and fear. The prairie schooners weren't those bright shining covered wagons of James Cruze's epic. They looked old and worn out. This was what Walsh had wanted.

Several of the action sequences were superb. The fording of the Colorado River. The lowering of the wagons down a gorge. The hunt for buffaloes. The attack of the Indians. William K. Everson, film historian and scholar of western films, has said that the Indian attack "is still the most spectacular such sequence ever filmed . . . In terms of size and action, *The Big Trail* is still one of the most impressive of all super-westerns."

Wayne received excellent notices. Mordaunt Hall's review in the New York *Times* was typical: "Mr. Wayne acquits himself with no little distinction. His performance is pleasingly natural." Nobody hailed him, however, as a glorious new star. Those were not the days of overnight sensations. One had to slowly earn one's reputation.

Winnie Sheehan believed in Wayne's future. Duke went out on a personal appearance tour to the Northeast and the Middle West. He was now given the intensive buildup treatment. He already had a new name. Now he was given a new personal history. The studio flacks devised a fanciful biography of Wayne—former USC All-American football hero. He had been born on a Montana ranch. He had been a wrangler and a sheriff. He had joined the Texas Rangers. He had killed several outlaws and hunted down criminals. He was having a beautiful romance with Marguerite Churchill. He was given a speech to memorize for interviews and at theater appearances. He was outfitted with a weird costume: yellow boots with elaborate designs, a green plaid shirt, a beaded jacket, draped leather chaps, and a white ten-gallon hat. They gave him "a goddam squirrel gun" for a rifle. He was to carry it at all times. He had two guns in a belt holster and a Bowie knife.

"I can't wear these clothes," Wayne protested. "Don't make me do this. It's like puttin' a red dress on an elephant."

They made him do it. Sheehan told him to put himself in the hands of the studio. They would handle his career.

He tried to tell Sheehan the canned speech was ridiculous. There was a passage in it about the thirteen thousand horses used in filming *The Big Trail*. He said he would gag whenever he had to say it.

He was photographed descending from the Twentieth Century Limited in New York. The papers printed pictures of him in the cowboy regalia with captions making fun of him; one had an arrow pointing to his wristwatch, and the caption was: "This frontiersman never has to worry about the right time."

There was a press conference in a suite at the Astor Hotel. A woman reporter asked, "Mr. Wayne, do you normally wear these clothes?"

"What do *you* think, sister?" he replied, flushing. He felt humiliated.

"Answer the question," another reporter said.

"I wear what I wear."

"What kind of an answer is that?"

"No," he said softly, "no, I don't wear these clothes ordinarily."

"Did you ever kill anybody while you were a Texas Ranger?"

"I never killed anybody."

"How many years were you with the Rangers?"

"I wasn't."

"Mr. Wayne is just being modest," the publicity man said. "He doesn't like to talk about his personal life."

"How about your experiences as a cowboy, Mr. Wayne?"

"I'd like to say that I am not a cowboy and never have been. I never was with the Texas Rangers, either."

"How did you feel when you were named All-American?"

"I wasn't ever named All-American," he said. "I only completed two years at the University of Southern California."

"What's going on here anyway, Mr. Wayne?"

The questions were coming from all sides of the room. One after the other. Bang bang bang. He couldn't field them all.

"I'll tell you what it is, folks. The Fox movie company is tryin' to make a goddam Buffalo Bill character out of me and I'm no Buffalo Bill. They won't even let me get a haircut."

(Wayne's candor went unreported in the press. Nowadays an actor speaking out like this would be the toast of the town.)

"John Wayne can throw knives," the press agent said. "He's one of the best knife throwers in pictures."

Skeptical laughter.

"Yeah?" said one reporter. "Let's see you throw a knife."

Wayne took a knife out of the sheath and threw it expertly a few feet above the reporter's head.

It was agreed that he was an excellent knife thrower.

The studio had set up a session with dozens of police officers outside the precinct station in Central Park. It would be filmed by the Fox Movietone Newsreel crew. Wayne chose a handsome white stallion at a riding stable on West 63rd Street. They didn't have a western saddle. The press agent said he had to wear a red bandanna and that oversized Stetson. The owner of the stable warned Wayne not to ride this horse, as he had a nasty temper. Wayne mounted him anyway and the horse shot out of the stable and crossed Central Park West, charging in and out of the automobiles and Fifth Avenue buses, the double-deckers.

In the park, they got ready for the demonstration of Wayne showing big-city law officers how a western sheriff operated. (It was just like an episode of the television series *McCloud* with Dennis Weaver.) The newsreel crew had set up reflectors to control and focus the light. The reflectors hit the horse's eyes and he started bucking and whinnying nervously. A platoon of mounted policemen sneered at Wayne's discomfiture. He borrowed a club and slapped the horse across the flanks. This calmed him down.

A police lieutenant dashed over and grabbed for the stick. "Gimme that billy club, you dumb bastard," he shouted. "We don't hurt animals in New York."

"I wasn't hurting him," Wayne said.

"For a westerner, you don't know how to handle horses very well," the officer said.

"Think you can do better?"

"You just step down and I'll show you."

Wayne dismounted. He threw the reins to the officer, who started mounting, but the horse snapped his head sharply. The reins slipped out. The horse was free. He galloped away over the hills of Central Park.

So Wayne gave a demonstration of knife-throwing for the newsreel. He gave demonstrations in Washington and Philadelphia and Baltimore and Boston and Hartford and New Haven and was ridiculed by the students at a matinee because he wore long hair to his shoulders. *Get a haircut!* they cried. And the *Yale Daily News* ridiculed his costume and hair in a feature story.

In Chicago, he eluded his publicity man, and got a haircut. And after that he called quits to the tour and returned to Los Angeles.

9

# The Unmaking of John Wayne

*The Big Trail* was a disaster at the box office. Wayne was ignored by Winfield Sheehan and Sol Wurtzel. The publicity department did not ship out still photographs of him. There were no items about him in the columns. He was just another seventy-five-a-week contract player. In the world outside, such a salary during this time of the Depression was enviable. Wayne did not envy himself. For a moment, he had allowed himself to dream fantasies of glory. He had seen himself married to Josephine at last, and living in grandeur. He had seen himself impressing her parents. He blamed the studio for everything. They had taken away his name. They had robbed him of his dignity. He did not feel like an actor. He did not want to act. He wanted to carry props and maybe do stunt work and doubling. Life was a rotten mess. Life was dealing him one yarborough after another. As a gambler, he was resigned to losing. He knew that you win one, you lose one. But it seemed that he was consistently losing.

After *The Big Trail* fiasco, the Fox executives decided that he was not cut out to be a western hero. He would be a clean-cut collegiate character. He was put into the lead of *Girls Demand Excitement,* a 1930 filmusical directed by Seymour Felix, a Broadway choreographer who had never made a film previously. Set in a mythical university, the "weenie" of the story concerned the rivalry between the men's basketball team, captained by Duke, and the women's basketball team, captained by Virginia Cherrill. She had played the blind girl in Chaplin's *City Lights.* She subsequently improved her life by marrying Cary Grant, divorcing him, and marrying an English duke. The movie with Wayne was a bad dream.

One evening, as Duke was disconsolately trudging to the Fox parking lot, he ran into Will Rogers. Rogers had become a successful movie comedian. He observed Wayne's melancholia and inquired about it. Wayne complained about the front office, the movie with Miss Cherrill, and the director's ignorance.

"Waal, I'll tell you something, young feller," Rogers said, "you're workin', ain't you?"

"Yes."

"Just keep on workin'," Rogers advised, "just you keep right on workin', young feller."

Once Rogers and Wayne went out to visit Leo Carrillo, who lived on a fifteen-acre ranch in Santa Monica. Most of the land was uphill. The cowboy philosopher surveyed the terrain and remarked, "Leo, I got to say one thing about your place—it's the only ranch I ever saw that you could lean against."

Wayne co-starred with Loretta Young in his next Fox film, *Three Girls Lost.* Three girls came to Chicago to seek husbands and money. It might have been called *How to Marry a Millionaire,* which was the title of a similar 20th Century-Fox comedy with Lauren Bacall, Marilyn Monroe, and Betty Grable. Duke impersonated a struggling young architect. Loretta Young was in love with him. He was in love with the blonde Joan Marsh. Lew Cody, villain of many a film of that time, played a gangster, one of those suave Chicago racketeers. One of Cody's henchmen was played by a former New York director and playwright turned actor—Paul Fix. Fix was to become an important man in Duke's life.

Sidney Lanfield, a Fox veteran, directed *Three Girls Lost.* In one scene, Loretta Young was supposed to be forced into a black car by some hoodlums as Wayne stands by watching.

This was not right, Wayne objected. "I should hit those men," he said.

"Duke," Lanfield explained, "you cannot get into a fight with those heavies. You are supposed to be a college graduate and a gentleman."

"You don't know what the hell a gentleman is," Wayne said.

*Three Girls Lost* opened at the Roxy on May 1, 1931. The New York *Times* said, "It is all rather silly."

John Wayne heartily agreed.

Fox did not pick up his option.

Harry Cohn, head of Columbia Pictures, immediately put him under contract. He had had his eye on Wayne. Columbia was changing its image from a manufacturer of action westerns and low comedies to a maker of sophisticated pictures. Wayne looked good in a dinner jacket. He was smooth when he played a dancing scene. He had the romantic look of a Charles Farrell—but a debonair Charles Farrell. Cohn at once put him in *Men Are Like That,* a military picture in which Wayne did not get to wear evening clothes. He played opposite Laura La Plante, who had a great reputation in silent pictures. Miss La Plante was now going downhill fast, and this movie did nothing to halt her slide toward oblivion. The screenplay was written by a young newspaperman making his first flight into screenwriting: Robert Riskin. He was to become one of the best high-comedy screenwriters in Hollywood, and later wrote the scripts for many of Frank Capra's classics. Riskin married Fay Wray, not long after she had that unpleasantness with King Kong.

The New York *Times,* which was losing patience with Wayne, disparaged the movie, concluding, "Miss La Plante is not convincing in the role, any more than John Wayne is in the part of Denton."

But the film started making money. And fans started writing in for handsome John Wayne's autographed picture. Harry Cohn, aware that Wayne was moping around the lot, called him in one day, expressed his love for Duke, clapped him on the back, and assured him, with what now seems like amazing prescience, "You are a money actor, Duke."

He said he was having Riskin write a high-class comedy tailored to Duke's personality. This was on Friday.

On Monday, Wayne came to the Columbia gate on Beachwood Street.

The gateman refused him admittance—on Harry Cohn's orders.

For a week he brooded. He got his salary. He did not know why he was barred from the lot. Then Cohn summoned him.

He accused Wayne of being drunk on the set and of playing around with Columbia actresses.

Since Wayne had been both chaste and sober during his working hours, he was bewildered by these accusations thrown at him with Cohn's earthy vulgarity of speech.

"I've had reports you go into women's dressing rooms," he said, "and I don't want you doing this. Y'understand? The rule at this studio is—keep your fly buttoned up."

Duke could not understand what was happening. He went out in a daze.

Though he was twenty-four, he was innocent in matters of sexual chicanery. He had not shared in the libidinous intrigues of the Hollywood studio, neither at Fox nor at Columbia. He was never the sort who makes passes at every comely female. He was not in the habit of going into dressing rooms and playing around.

A prop man on the lot cleared up the mystery. He said Cohn thought Wayne was making a play for a starlet in *Men Are Like That*. She was Cohn's girl—that month, at least.

This was the master's way of punishing him.

Later, he found out that the starlet was making up stories about herself and Duke in order to make Cohn jealous.

Cohn was not satisfied with just locking out his imaginary rival. He figured out an exquisite and humiliating revenge. At option time, he renewed Duke's contract for six months, raising him to three hundred fifty a week. Columbia was still making two series of low-budget westerns, one starring Buck Jones and one starring Tim McCoy.

So he put Wayne into several McCoys and Joneses as a supporting player—as a junvenile. He relished humbling the star of *The Big Trail*. But Cohn's thirst for revenge was still unsatisfied. He now conceived the neatest sadistic ploy you can imagine. Columbia was doing a football movie with Jack Holt and Richard Cromwell in the leads. Wayne played a bit part. That was humiliating enough. But the part he played—it was a dishonest football player who sells out his college to gamblers!

Cohn had remembered that Wayne had once been Marion Morrison of the USC Trojans!

Wayne never forgave him. When Duke became a box-office attraction, Cohn tried many times to become his friend. He tempted Wayne with screenplays of good quality and with first-rank directors.

Duke would not work for Harry Cohn.

Twenty years after he had insulted Wayne, Cohn thought he knew how to get him on the Columbia roster. Bill Bowers, one of the best writers of westerns, had completed an original story and screenplay about an aging frontier hero who is tired of killing. Bowers showed it to Wayne. Wayne wanted to buy it for fifty thousand. He loved it. Cohn bought it for a hundred thousand. Now he was sure that Wayne would make peace with him.

Wayne would not do it. He told Cohn that he would not work for him if Columbia was the only studio in town.

Fox later took over the property and hired Gregory Peck. The movie was one of the best westerns ever made, Henry King's *The Gunfighter*.

Wayne loves the screenplay so much that he can tell you, giving specific details, how he would have played the great scenes in this film. He hated to turn down *The Gunfighter,* but he had to. His honor was more important to him than this movie.

Wayne made movies for every studio in town after he became a star, with one exception—Columbia Pictures Corporation.


Al Kingston, a former movie trade paper reporter, was now an agent with the Leo Morrison Agency, located in a suite of the Hollywood Roosevelt Hotel on Hollywood near Highland. One day, without an appointment, John Wayne dropped in to see him. It was in the latter part of 1931. He had been out of work since June.

Kingston recalls him as a shy and nervous young man. He was handsome and clean-cut, another Charlie Farrell. He did not present himself as a cowboy actor. Kingston had been impressed by his acting in *The Big Trail*. Wayne had a natural easygoing quality on the screen. But in a room he was jumpy. He broke down during his interview. He suddenly confided that he desperately needed work. He was madly in love with a girl. They had been engaged for many years. He had to get some work, any work, so he could marry her. Fox had dropped him. Columbia had dropped him. George O'Brien told him to get an agent.

Kingston signed Wayne to an agency contract. He then took him over to see Nat Levine, known as the King of the Serials. Levine owned Mascot Films. He was one of innumerable hole-in-the-wall movie entrepreneurs who operated in a stretch of Hollywood around Gower and

Beachwood, between Sunset and Santa Monica. They called it "Poverty Row." Columbia had risen out of the depths of Poverty Row. The RKO studio was still on Gower. Further east, on Melrose, was the realm of Paramount Pictures.

The real Poverty Row hustlers had no capital and owned no equipment or soundstages. They specialized in the kind of movies major studios had largely abandoned when talkies came in—serials, cheap westerns, action-adventures. They rented cameras and sound equipment, usually from Disney. Their films were processed by Horsley's Gower Street lab, which did fast work at cut prices. There were warehouses where they could rent properties and costumes in the neighborhood. Dozens of "producers" came and went, the sweatshops of the dream factory, names long forgotten: Tiffany, Resolute, Puritan, Beacon, Majestic, Crescent, Superior, Victory . . .

Nat Levine was a fat little man wearing thick glasses. He looked like a wholesale butcher. He talked through a cigar. He looked like a caricature of a Hollywood tycoon. He made money on animal serials. He was the original producer of the Rin-Tin-Tin pictures. Another one of his animal stars was Rex, the Wonder Horse. Rex played a brave kindly horse in pictures; in real life, as often happens with movie stars, he was a horse of another color. He was a vicious beast who loved to kick human actors and bite directors. He had bitten Levine often.

"Shake hands with John Wayne," Kingston said.

"It's a pleasure," Levine said.

"He was a star of *The Big Trail* and he just finished out a contract with Columbia. He's got a little time between jobs while I'm firming up a deal with a major. So, Nat, you got a chance to grab a real talent before somebody else does."

"He looks younger than I expected," Levine said.

"You could age him," the agent said.

"We got a story here about a flier, a serial, you know, a Lindbergh type."

"Did you ever see anybody who was more the spit'n' image of Charles A. Lindbergh than this fellow here,

Nat? He's an All-American type and you are a very fortunate man."

Lindbergh's solo flight in a monoplane had stirred the nation. And, led by writer John Monk Saunders and director William Wellman, both of whom had been fighter pilots during World War I, the studios were making aviation war films such as *Wings* and *The Dawn Patrol*. In April, 1929, James Quirk, editor of *Photoplay*, the most widely read movie fan magazine, had consigned the western hero to oblivion. He wrote, "Lindbergh has put the cowboy into the discard . . . the western novel and motion picture heroes have slunk away into the sagebrush never to return. The cow ponies have retired to the pasture with the old fire horses. Tom Mix, Hoot Gibson, and Ken Maynard must swap horses for airplanes or go to the old actor's home."

A Mascot serial consisted of twelve episodes, two reels to an episode. A one-reel trailer was also shot. All serials were now continuing stories, rather than self-contained episodes. The formula was standard who-done-it. Crimes occurred. Suspicion fell on various persons. The villain was not disclosed until the last installment. Each episode had to end with the hero or heroine, or both, trapped in an impossible situation.

A serial was a long film chopped into little parts. A Nat Levine serial equaled five hours of playing time—the equivalent of three or four feature pictures. Wayne's first deal paid him a thousand dollars—his highest salary to date.

It seems like a pittance, and it was. On the other hand, the way Levine made serials it was good pay for an unemployed young actor during the Depression. Levine ground out twenty-five cut reels in less than three weeks. Wayne averaged three hundred dollars a week.

Levine did not believe in wasting time. He said he wanted to start shooting *Shadow of the Eagle* tomorrow —if Wayne was available. He was. Very well, he would come and pick him up at his place at four A.M. He would have a location set up at once. By the time Duke was out of the office, Levine was on the phone lining up a cameraman, director, extras, stuntmen, equipment.

It was still pitch dark when Duke and his producer started out next morning, in Levine's chauffeur-driven Packard. To save time, Levine brought Duke's breakfast along. He had coffee and danish pastry while Levine outlined the story. He had a makeup kit along. No precious moments were wasted on makeup at the location. Duke patted on some pancake base and a few lines around his eyes and mouth. Then he changed into costume as they tooled along Ventura Boulevard on the long route to Antelope Valley—there was no Ventura Freeway in 1931.

Arriving at the location, about three hours' driving time from Hollywood, they started shooting as soon as the sun rose. The director was G. Reeves Eason, known as Breezy Eason, hard-nosed action director. He worked swiftly, going from one setup to another as fast as possible. He didn't worry about the lighting nuances or perfection of sound reproduction. Most of the weeks, Duke worked six days, twelve hours a day. In emergencies, the cast and crew went seven days—and some days were as long as eighteen hours!

One day during the filming of *Shadow of the Eagle* there were one hundred fourteen camera setups in a single day!

On this occasion, Wayne learned what it was like making movies on Poverty Row—which could actually be in far-distant Bakersfield or in Ojai or somewhere in the Antelope Valley, but had the spirit of Gower Gulch just the same. They had been shooting constantly until it was midnight. Breezy said they would make a sequence at an "abandoned stone quarry" the next day at six A.M.

Duke figured out that this would give him, the big star, just about time to drive home, take a catnap, and return to the location.

This did not appeal to Duke. He decided to remain on location until the morning. The crew had built a fire. It was high-desert country and it was damn near freezing by now. There were no cabins or motels to house the sufferers. There were no tents. Some of the wiser birds had brought along bedrolls. There were no commissary trucks to bring them hot meals. Bread and cheese and whiskey was the diet.

"I don't remember anybody squawking," Wayne said recently. "It was the way we made B pictures then and I was part of it and it got so I loved roughing it out there. Hell, nowadays we squawk if there's no cream in the coffee, or if the motel is not up to our high standards. Hell, we thought we were living good if the producer had tents for us and they served sandwiches and hot coffee for lunch and you were within twenty miles of a halfway decent truckdriver's cafe."

Duke did not have bread and cheese, but he did have a pint bottle of hooch to help him through the long night of filming *Shadow of the Eagle*. He sat by the fire and started swigging. He felt cold and he felt disgusted. His body was aching with pains. He was completely worn out.

A man sauntered over and crouched by the fire.

He did not speak. Duke had met him that morning. Duke did not say anything but handed him the bottle. The man uncorked it. He tilted it and then took a long swig. He wiped his mouth with one big hand and said, "Well, Duke, it don't take very long to spend the whole night here."

Wayne laughed. He took a pull at the whiskey.

"Sure don't," he said. He laughed. They both laughed. They were comrades now and remained collaborators and friends for many years. The man was Yakima Canutt. He was then a large stocky character. He had a hawk nose and mean black eyes. His real name is Enos. He was reared in the Yakima Valley of Washington state. He is part Indian. He has the Indian's straight black hair and black eyes. He became the most famous rodeo rider and bronco-busting daredevil on the circuit after World War I. He became an actor and stuntman in silent pictures. He was the greatest stuntman with horses and horses and wagons. But he had nerves of steel, and he also did stunts with planes and cars. In *Shadow of the Eagle,* he doubled Wayne on a dangerous motorcycle stunt. Duke studied Canutt's way of riding a horse. He studied Canutt's loping walk and drawling speech. Wayne played the sedulous ape to many masters during his apprentice years, to Harry Carey and Jack Padgin and Yakima Canutt.

He learned how to go without on location. He learned the tricks of cutting corners. "Once, Levine's budget was so tight that he could only afford one horse," he recalls. "So in the first scene I had to shoot the villain's horse and ride away with it. This was fine because it wasn't a western. If you use ingenuity, you don't need money. And you get used to hardships and after a while, Christ, you kind of look forward to the hardships. I have no kick comin' as far's those Mascot serials. Made three for them. The aviation one, a railroad serial, and one about the French foreign legion. We had only one set for interiors, and to show changes of scene, we changed our clothes. Some days I had to change my clothes twenty times. I began hating to change clothes. To this day, I hate to get out of what I'm already wearin' into somethin' else. Can't stand dressin' for dinner.

"The usual workin' day was twelve to twenty hours. Mascot used two shifts of directors and two writers. We didn't have a hell of a lot of dialogue. And we didn't fool around with retakes. The first take was usually the one we printed.

"I've kinda believed this is what you should do even when you're makin' a fine movie. I mean, if you've got a director that knows his business and you have good writing and professional actors and a competent guy on the camera and a lighting technician that knows his job.

"I'll tell you why. Your first take is the most natural, most spontaneous.

"We didn't worry about nuances in these serials and B pictures. Get the scene on film and get on to the next scene. They were rotten pictures, most of them. But they taught me one thing. How to work. How to take orders. How to get on with the action. You can waste an awful lot of time when you have a director and a cameraman who are fussing around with lights and shadows and shadings of interpretation. That means they haven't done their homework or they are insecure.

"And you learned never to give in to the elements. We shot *The Three Musketeers*—that was the foreign legion serial—out in the Mojave Desert, near Yuma, with the temperature hitting 120° during the day. Now when you shoot on location in the desert you usually film early in the morning and late in the afternoon, when the sun isn't too murderous. Levine would get goin' at sunup and we didn't knock off until it was dark and we were about ready to drop dead from exhaustion.

"Levine was too much of a piker to bring properly trained horses, used to workin' in movies. Would have cost him a few dollars to get 'em shipped from Hollywood with a ramrod. He didn't. He found some tired beasts in Yuma. Well, they were ready for the glue factory. Now there is this scene where I ride up on my horse through a crowd. I grab hold of a rope and haul myself hand over hand to the second story of this North African fort. We were usin' the local jail as a fort. Now I didn't use doubles much in those days, but I couldn't climb a rope fast enough, so ole Yak was doublin' me in this scene. Now the poor horse, he was scared of the light reflectors which are focusin' the sun on him and he was jumpy with all these extras standin' around in their long white Arab robes. So the horse was paralyzed. Would not budge one inch. He just stood there. Yak was spurrin' it and cursin' it and it still wouldn't move and the camera was goin', so Yak asked me to get him a club, which I did, and then he started beatin' that horse without mercy, usin' this big hunk of wood, until finally the nag is trotting and the scene is over. Later, I said to him, 'Yak, what will my fans think? They know that John Wayne is too decent a guy to ever beat a horse like that.'

"He looked at me and grinned and said, 'You just tell them that John Wayne just had to beat the horse that one time and will never do it again.'

"You know, a stuntman that is doublin' you, he gets to feel he *is* you and you get to feel you are him. He might not resemble you too much up close—neither Yak nor Chuck Roberson, who has been doubling me for many years, looks like me if you put us side by side—but when they're playin' me you couldn't tell the difference. Even I would not be sure if I am looking at an old picture I made twenty years ago whether it was me or a double.

"I remember one picture where Yak was playing the heavy and also doubling me in one of the stunts. We had a scene in which we're in a fight to the death. He is pumping a handcar on the railroad tracks, tryin' to get away from me. I'm ridin' hell for leather in pursuit of him and then I have to jump from the horse right smack onto his handcar and start wrestlin' with ole Yak. This is a very unhealthy piece of business to do. But my pride was strong and I wanted to do the stunt myself. I knew I could make the leap, though I might just miss and break my legs, both of 'em.

"I was standin' there by the setup, tryin' to make up my mind, really trying to get up enough nerve to do it, as I wanted to show Yak I was as good a stuntman as he was. I knew I wasn't and he knew I wasn't but that was just the kind of a mood I was in. I just didn't have the guts, however. But I wouldn't make up my mind. Finally Yak said, 'Well, are you gonna do it—*or would you rather double me?*' "

Yak's line may not strike anybody but stuntmen as being clever, but they think it is probably the greatest single line a stuntman ever threw a star. The idea of doubling the actor who is playing the soft side of a gag breaks them up.

In one of Duke's B westerns, Noah Beery was playing the villain and Yak was doubling Duke in a terrific fight scene with Beery and Wayne. Duke was not avoiding the scene because he was scared but he was shooting an interior scene to save time. Anyway Noah Beery had gotten into a contretemps with the producer and had cursed him violently.

The producer took Canutt aside and said, "Yak, you could do me a big favor. In this fight you and Beery are shooting, I'd like you to *really* rough him up—just beat the hell out of him, will you?"

"Sure," Canutt said, "I'd be happy to beat the living daylights out of him on one condition."

"What's that?"

"That you get Noah to call me the same names he's been calling you."

*Hurricane Express,* Wayne's second Mascot serial, was a good example of this dying genre. It combined the traditional railroad melodrama of the Helen Holmes serial with airplane and automobile stunts. Duke played a young aviator. His father, a railroad engineer, was killed in a wreck on the L & R line. "Hurricane Express" is the name of the crack train on this railroad. There has been a mysterious series of wrecks and accidents on the L & R. Who is "The Wrecker"? Duke intends to find out. As a result he is being shot at, beaten up, knocked unconscious, thrown in the path of an oncoming train (just as Miss Holmes had been thrown in a Kalem episode). Besides Wayne, various guilty-looking parties are accused of being The Wrecker, including the president of a competing airline! While committing his foul deeds, The Wrecker wears an ingeniously constructed stocking mask so that he looks like other men. There is an escape convict, who had lost his job and been railroaded to prison, so to speak, by Tully Marshall, general manager of the L & R. His daughter gets work as a secretary to Marshall to find out the identity of The Wrecker. Marshall is under suspicion, also. There is a suave lawyer for the railroad, played by Conway Tearle, one of the leading men of silent pictures who had lately come upon hard times. Tearle was finally revealed as The Wrecker in the last chapter.

There was more dialogue in *Hurricane Express* than you would have found in a serial from the golden age of serials. But every chapter had at least one good fight and several stunts—explosions, collisions, automobile chases, airplanes chasing cars, airplanes chasing trains—and there were tense sequences on board the "Hurricane Express."

Each chapter consisted of two reels of ten minutes each. The episodes were prefaced by an off-camera commentator, who spoke with a British accent and who summed up the story to this point during vivid cuts from

the previous chapters. Neither these serials nor many of
the five-reelers which Duke subsequently made were
scored. Without the subtle background of musical stings
and passages, these films seem eerie the voices like echoes
in a vast cave. We are so accustomed to the music under
the dialogue, the musical bridges and transitions, the
musical accentuations of action, of battles, of love scenes,
that we take them for granted. When we see one of the
films made during these early years without musical scoring, we realize how dead they are. How important were
the contributions of persons like Alfred Newman and
Lionel Newman, Herbert Stothart and Max Steiner, and
the ineffable Dmitri Tiomkin. I remember once watching
a rough cut of *Giant* in the company of director George
Stevens. *Giant* had not yet been scored. Knowing the
effect of the music on the film's emotional impact, he came
to the screening with records which he played at various
times, and when he couldn't find a suitable record he
would hum a little obbligato.

Wayne seemed to be quite secure and in command of
himself in these early pictures. He looked slender, almost
lanky, and spoke his lines well, for he was beginning to
extend the range of his voice. He looked awkward still
when he had to run and jump. He did all the stunts in
this picture, including several hazardous falls from roofs
and trains.

Tully Marshall looked bad. He showed the ravages of
his years of dissipation. The experience of shooting *The
Big Trail* in the desert had been, as Raoul Walsh told me,
the beginning of his end. He was about to die. He looked
like a walking corpse in this one. He looked like an old,
unshaven skid row boozer from downtown L.A. There
was death written all over his face, but the hardy old
buzzard lived on until 1943.

At this time, Sid Rogell and Leon Schlesinger, two
Warner Brothers producers, decided to remake some old
Ken Maynard silent westerns which Warners owned. They
were high quality pictures, being "in terms of excitement
and sheer size some of the best program westerns ever
made, with extensive location shooting, big action scenes,

no stinting in extras, horses or wagon power. When the script called for a mad stampede of fifty covered wagons, they got them and not just half a dozen . . ."

Rogell and Schlesinger planned to convert the Ken Maynards into talking pictures, keeping the action footage, adding sound effects to them, and shooting new scenes with a young actor who resembled Maynard as he had looked ten years before. Maynard himself was still around and making westerns. But, alas, he did not look like the old Ken Maynard.

Kingston at once brought Wayne over to be interviewed. Rogell looked him over. He shot a test with Duke to see if the substitution would be successful. It was. Closeups of Duke could be intercut with long shots of Maynard riding hell-for-leather and you wouldn't know which was Maynard and which was Wayne. He said he would sign Wayne up for the remakes as soon as he cleared it with Schlesinger.

Two days later he phoned Kingston. He said the deal was off. He had found out that Wayne was a drunk, a trouble-maker, and a woman-chaser. He didn't want to hire an unreliable actor. Kingston said that Wayne was always on time and had not missed a day with Mascot. Rogell said he was looking for another actor to play the Maynard pictures.

Duke blew his top when his agent told him the situation. He stormed into Rogell's office and shouted, "I know who told you I was drunk. I know who told you I chase broads. The man who told you that is a dirty liar. And you tell Harry Cohn if he says that about me once more in this town, I am going to knock his teeth so far back into his throat he will have to eat his meals with his neck."

He slammed the door.

Rogell, who despised Cohn, pursued Wayne.

He made a deal for fifteen hundred a picture. Wayne made six remakes of these old Ken Maynard classics.

He now, at long last, had the money to support Josephine Saenz. Dr. and Mrs. Saenz had, after almost seven years, become resigned to the inevitable. So, on June 24,

1933, Josephine and Marion Michael Morrison became man and wife in a ceremony in the patio and gardens of Loretta Young's estate in Bel-Air.

Franklin D. Roosevelt had begun to serve his first term. Prohibition had been repealed. Ten million people were unemployed. 20th Century-Fox had gone into bankruptcy and William Fox himself was sent to prison.

Robert Morrison was the best man. Dr. Saenz gave the bride away. They were able to drink imported French champagne. Josie did not like the name John Wayne. She never legally or socially called herself Mrs. Wayne. She was Mrs. Marion M. Morrison. She has always remained Mrs. Morrison—even to this day. They began married life in a small, three-room furnished apartment in a cracked yellow Spanish-style garden apartment complex on Orange Grove Avenue, between the Hancock Park area and Hollywood proper.

Several months afterward, Mrs. Morrison informed her husband that she was pregnant.

This was unfortunate because Duke had finished up the Ken Maynard remakes. Al Kingston had left the Leo Morrison Agency to go into business for himself, but Duke's contract was with the agency. And Morrison, one of the town's leading horse players and girl chasers, was living it up in the nightclubs. He was not concerned whether Duke worked or not.

Duke would join the parade of men and women shuffling along Poverty Row in the hot sun, the royal palms overhead, trudging along, sometimes knocking on the bungalows of one of the movie hustlers, looking for work. It was a restless parade of unemployed actors and actresses, former stars, of fading beauties and lovely innocent young girls from the dust bowl, of extras and bit players and stuntmen, tall men and short men, midgets and other freaks, comedians and tragedians, acrobats, old and young, some in the habiliments of their trade, for there was a big demand for cowboys on Poverty Row and a man could sometimes pick up a day's work if he were there at the right time. The cowboys walked around in their boots and Levi's. They lounged on the open porches or outside the Columbia Drugstore at Sunset and Gower. This part of town was known as Gower Gulch. There were shops which catered to the cowboy clientele. You could have boots made to order here. You could have boots repaired. You could have jodhpurs made to order and cleaned. This was where you could buy a good used white Stetson for ten dollars. You could buy guns and rifles in a gunshop. Everything a western actor needed for the act was right here on Gower Gulch. And what he needed most, the job, was also sometimes found here. You would hear the rumors about a casting call at Paramount or over at Universal or Warner's in the valley.

Duke, for a time, was working at anything he could get—bits, supporting parts, doubling, stunting. Loretta Young got him a week's work playing a prizefighter in a movie with Douglas Fairbanks, Jr.: *The Life of Jimmy Dolan.* This led to a week's work as a boxer in a George Bancroft picture for Paramount. He played a department store floorwalker in *Baby Face,* one of Barbara Stanwyck's earliest flicks. He was given a little work here and there, especially around the Warner lot.

It was impossible to support a wife and a forthcoming child on the basis of being unemployed two weeks and working two days.

He could never get Leo Morrison on the phone. He had to pay him ten percent of every salary check, yet he had an agent who did not get him any work. In desperation, Wayne sought out his former benefactor, Al Kingston.

"Wayne was in a tough situation," he says. "They did not have a Screen Actors Guild at that time. Agents would sign up an actor for seven years. An actor would be trapped as Duke was. Today an agency cannot sign you up for more than one year, and if an agent doesn't get you a job in three months, you can leave him. Well, Duke was stuck with this seven-year contract with Morrison, and Morrison wasn't doing anything for the poor guy." Morrison was well known as a high-roller and a man-about-town. He was interested in horses and broads and not in representing talent, but Leo had a million bucks' worth of charm.

"So Duke comes into my office and he's got a long face. His wife is pregnant. He hasn't got a dime. He needs a job. I told him I could get him a job provided he got a release from Morrison. Morrison wouldn't give him a release but said it was all right for me to get him a job. I liked Duke and knew where I could place him. Trem Carr and Leo Ostrow had organized a little company on Poverty Row, Monogram Pictures. On Santa Monica and Van Ness. They even had a soundstage. They were making these quickie B westerns and adventure pictures. The building's still there. It's now owned by the Lutheran church and is known as Family Pictures, Inc. They make religious films for television, I believe.

"So anyway I brought Duke over and Trem Carr liked his looks and I gave him my best sales pitch about the great job he had done for Warner Brothers. (I didn't mention the Mascot serials. Serials were a dirty word.) He signed a deal to make eight westerns in a year, at twenty-five hundred a picture, which was a terrific deal for him because Monogram could wrap up a movie in five days. Carr gave him a check for a thousand as an advance. Duke was a few months behind in the rent and owed the doctor and the phone bill and for groceries and you name it. Never could manage money, that kid. I thought Josie would have straightened him out in that department, but she was as dumb about money as he was. But he was very much in love with her and he sure had a worried look on his face.

"Incidentally, I never got a nickel's commission on the Monogram deal, though I think it's fair to say I had more than a little to do with Duke's success.

"Now Trem Carr took a big liking to Duke because Duke had learned discipline in his work. He had excellent work habits, especially for an actor, for most of them are slovenly as to being on time and doing their job. Duke got to makeup on time, he didn't loaf on the location, and he worked fast. He was a fast study. And he got better and better and better.

"Then Herbert Yates, who owned Consolidated Film Laboratories, which was the biggest processor of movie film in Hollywood, decided he wanted to get into production. He had been lending money to some of those small outfits on Poverty Row and he saw how much money there was in Nat Levine's operation and Trem Carr's; also, some of the boys owed him money because he carried several shoestring producers and made work-prints and negative-prints for them on credit. So he went out and merged Monogram, Mascot, and a slew of other Poverty Row companies, including Majestic Pictures, Liberty. This was the start of Republic Pictures. Trem Carr was the vice-president, and it was Trem Carr who brought Duke into Republic. Duke started out making five-reelers for them, and before you know it he was one of the biggest box-office attractions in the South and Southwest. Now all this time Duke is a buddy of Jack Ford's, and Ford would keep ragging him, along the lines of, 'When you learn to act someday—I'll put you in a good picture.' Ford used to make fun of these Monogram and Republic pictures of Duke's. Duke would always take insults from Jack Ford that he would have killed another man for saying."

## 10

## Hero of the Five-Reelers

Wayne made sixteen five-reel westerns for Monogram. They were released under the rubric of Lone Star Productions between September, 1933, and April, 1935. The first of them was *Riders of Destiny*. It was written and directed by Robert N. Bradbury, the old-time western

expert from Glendale, father of Duke's boyhood friend
Bob Bradbury, who was now Bob Steele. Paul Malvern,
producer of the Lone Star horse operas, decided to make
the hero a singing cowboy. Wayne had a short-lived career
as the first of the singing cowboys, preceding Gene Autry
and Roy Rogers by several years. Bradbury's gunfighter,
Sandy Saunders, was a secret agent of the U.S. Secret
Service. Malvern decided to make him Singin' Sandy. For
twenty-five dollars he bought a ballad. The idea was for
Singin' Sandy to sing the ballad while shooting the vil-
lains. It was rather avant-garde for its time. Malvern intended to make Singin' Sandy the running character of a
series, so the first time out he was called in the main
title: JOHN WAYNE as SINGIN' SANDY in *Riders of Destiny*.

The film was a fast-moving, tightly constructed, brilliantly directed western which still sustains interest. It
opens with an establishing shot of mesas and desert. A
long shot of Wayne on a white horse. On closer view we
see that his guitar is slung casually across him like a rifle.
He strums the guitar and sings:

> A cowboy sang his song of fate
> As he roamed the desert wild . . .

After several choruses, the ballad concludes with:

> There'll be guns a-blazin',
> A-blazin' with lead.
> Tonight you'll be drinkin' your drinks with the dead.

Wayne's voice was not dubbed in. He sounds flat. He
had argued against the singing, but Malvern insisted.
Malvern had also wanted him to be gotten up in white
hat and spanking-new boots and chaps and shirt. This he
would not do. He insisted on dressing Singin' Sandy in a
sweat-stained Stetson, a dirty old kerchief, a soiled checked
shirt, rumpled denims, and worn boots.

He looked like a man who had been on the trail for a
long time. He was on his way to the town of Yucca in
the Antelope Valley.

The film was photographed in the same arid country, around Palmdale and Lancaster, where Doc Morrison had gone into the corn-growing profession twenty years before.

The leading villain was the owner of the Kincaid Land & Water Company, which controls all the water around Yucca. The farmers hate him. In his spare time, Kincaid is the boss of a gang of robbers, which has been holding up stagecoaches and banks, robbing the government mailbags. Kincaid's big project is to drive all the ranchers and farmers away by shutting off their supply of water and buying up their land at distress prices.

"There were two types of heavies in a western," Wayne states. "The brain heavy and the dog heavy. The brain heavy did not do any rough work. He was the schemer. The dog heavy was the guy who had to do the dirty work. They called him a dog heavy because he sometimes kicked a dog in an early scene. He was a tough-looking hombre, mean as hell, a real dirty fighter."

Yak Canutt was the dog heavy in *Riders of Destiny*. Forrest Taylor was the brain heavy. George Hayes, to become famous as Gabby Hayes, played the heroine's father. He played straight in this film. Cecilia Parker was the heroine. Hayes, or Denton, has a small well on his property. Singin' Sandy says that they should fill a wooden tank from the well. They will drive the tank into town and slake the thirst of the citizens, who are boycotting Kincaid's high-priced water but getting dry.

Taylor tells Canutt to get some gangsters and kill the tank-car rider. Then he is to shoot holes in the water tank.

He says, "I'll own Denton's place before night . . . I have made Denton an offer he can't refuse." (They were making irresistible offers in movies long before *The Godfather*.)

The driver is killed. Wayne leaps on the water wagon. In Yucca, there is a montage of men, women, and children as they come to fill pots, pans, pitchers, and cups with the precious water. One charming shot shows a thirsty dog licking water from the bottom of the tank. Like every silent movie director, Bradbury knew how to communi-

cate emotions and events without words and by means
of significant images.

The theme of water, of irrigation, had a special meaning for Americans in 1933. It was the time of the dust
bowl, of the prairie states suffering drought, of crop disas-
ters.

Kincaid, frustrated by Wayne, looks him in the eye.
He makes the classic western movie remark: "You have
interfered with my business once too often. *I'm giving
you one minute to get out of town.*"

Singin' Sandy saunters up the street. Yak Canutt follows him. Singin' Sandy now chants his ballad about outlaws drinkin' their drinks with the dead. There is a shootout. The guns were a-blazin' with lead and Canutt was
drinkin' his drinks with the dead. This impresses the brain
heavy. He invites Wayne to join up with his gang. Wayne
does so, being an undercover government operative. He
tells Kincaid to dynamite Denton's well.

So they put the dynamite in the well. It explodes. Then
—in a montage reminiscent of the famous irrigation
sequence in King Vidor's *Our Daily Bread,* which was
made two years *later*—we see the coming of the water to
irrigate the high desert. First a small geyser breaking
through the hard desert crust, then the water bubbling
out, then more water, the trickle becomes a stream, and
the stream becomes a rushing river, and the river a raging, life-giving torrent; the Denton well, it seems, was the
headwaters of Lost Creek River.

Kincaid shoots a confederate and flees on a horse.
Wayne pursues him. The brain heavy rides over a cliff
and, with poetic justice, he and his horse fall into the
newly rushing river. He drowns, a few final bubbles of
water showing us the place of his death.

The film ends with the hero and heroine coming to a
romantic understanding, with the approval of Papa, who
tells him to be nice to her because she's brokenhearted
over having misunderstood Wayne. Singin' Sandy takes
her in his arms. They envelop each other in a passionate
embrace. They kiss for a long time.

And the running time of this well-made film was a paltry fifty minutes!

Herbert Yates signed a new contract with John Wayne on May 11, 1935. Yates did not know the first thing about motion-picture production. He was a money man. He had come from Wall Street. He had been an executive with Liggett & Myers. Then he had become a speculator and a high-risk investor. He was a shrewd gambler. Around 1912, he had loaned some money to Fatty Arbuckle to make some two-reel comedies. He had tripled his money in a year. He figured there was a fast buck or two to be made out of Hollywood. He had purchased Consolidated Film Laboratories in 1922 and he had made it the leading processor and printer of movie films. All he knew about was B pictures. He had observed that there were five thousand small-town theaters which still played westerns. As long as you could make horse operas cheaply and quickly, you could triple your money in a year. He had become compulsive about tripling his money. Yates had no love for movies and never read scripts. He was a big amiable man who did not take actors and movies seriously. He usually let Wayne have his own way, for Wayne made money for him. Yates was just happy being a millionaire and tripling his money. He was not troubled by guilt feelings about Republic pictures. He did not want to make artistic movies. He just wanted to keep right on making money.

The first Republic picture was *Westward Ho!,* directed by Robert N. Bradbury. Trem Carr produced it. It was a high-quality B western. Carr was so proud he put his name on the main title, which reads:


JOHN WAYNE
in
*Westward Ho!*
TREM CARR: VICE-PRESIDENT IN CHARGE OF PRODUCTION


As far as I know, this is the first and only time that a vice-president put his name and rank on the opening title, which followed the Republic Pictures logo, that proud eagle.

Basically, *Westward Ho!* was a story of two brothers; one grows up to be a law-and-order man and the other is an outlaw. They do not know they are siblings until the end. The time and place was California in the 1870's. Wayne organizes his vigilantes and he tells them to ride white horses and wear white bandannas so they will recognize one another on the trail. His men were known as the Singing Riders. They sang songs as they galloped in pursuit of outlaws. Wayne refused to sing. He never sang any more songs in the pictures. Nobody, not even Yates, could make him sing. Because of his refusal, Republic had to beat the bushes until they came up with other singing cowboys, who became millionaires during this period.

There was an exciting battle scene between good and evil in which the vigilantes rode seventy-five white horses and the outlaws rode seventy-five black horses. This was more horses than Wayne had seen in many years in a picture. *Westward Ho!* also boasted an Indian attack on a wagon train, leaps off buildings, hand-to-hand fights, including a spectacular saloon brawl in which Wayne took on a dozen gangsters and beat them to a fare-thee-well. He was beginning to play love scenes more smoothly. His leading lady was Sheila Manners, a lovely young brunette. It is not true, as legend has it, that the cowboy never fell in love seriously and that he only kissed his horse. For six years, Wayne drudged in the sweatshops where B pictures were ground out. He was always kissing girls. He had no relationship, erotic or otherwise, with a horse. Others such as Autry and Roy Rogers might fraternize with horses, but not Wayne. He was definitely a ladies' man. Consequently, even these hard-action B westerns had a great appeal for women. Wayne's leading ladies were well chosen, for their tender warmth, their voluptuousness, and a kind of physical flexibility. They usually portrayed frontier women of character and strength, which were more important than slinking about naked in bedrooms, though this would be hinted at in these Wayne movies. The girls were starlets, ambitious girls on the way up in the movie business.

Three of Wayne's leading ladies in these horse operas went on to later fame. In one of his Three Mesquiteers pictures, *New Horizon,* which is concerned with a land-grab scheme to cheat farmers in Texas, the girl was a slender dark-haired girl of innocent face and luminous black eyes dominating the screen during her few scenes. She was then known as Phyllis Isley. She later became Jennifer Jones. This was her first film. And Carole Landis began her bright and all-too-short career as the heroine of *Three Texas Steers,* another Mesquiteer. Ann Rutherford started her career with a sparkling performance in *The Lawless Nineties.*

Duke wanted to express desire and love for women in his westerns, though at this time it wasn't being done by his rivals. He wanted to act like a man acts. This was why he did not want to put on glistening white cowboy regalia like Roy Rogers. He has always hated white hats. Given a choice, he will wear a black Stetson, though tradition demands that the western hero be a white-hat. And he was determined to fight back when attacked. It came about that his instincts were right. He began playing the first western tough guy who was a good guy since William S. Hart. He was the B western equivalent of Jimmy Cagney and Humphrey Bogart and Clark Gable. The time was propitious for such a hero. Though he remained obscure for many years, Wayne began to win a tremendous following with these Republic pictures in the South and Southwest, because men and women could identify with the characters in the films and with the realistic stories.

"I made up my mind," Wayne once told me, "that I was going to play a real man to the best of my ability. I felt many of the western stars of the 1920's and 1930's were too goddam perfect. They never drank nor smoked. They never wanted to go to bed with a beautiful girl. They never had a fight. A heavy might throw a chair at them, and they just looked surprised and didn't fight in this spirit. They were too goddam sweet and pure to be dirty fighters. Well, I wanted to be a dirty fighter if that was the only way to fight back. If somebody throws a chair at you, hell, you pick up a chair and belt him right back. I was trying to play a man who gets dirty, who sweats sometimes, who enjoys really kissing a gal he likes, who gets angry, who fights clean whenever possible but will fight dirty if he has to. You could say, I made the western hero a roughneck. That's why I didn't want to be a singing cowboy. It was phony. My movie fights were realistic. I copied Jack Dempsey's style. As a kid, Dempsey had been my idol. He was a rough and tough street-fighting boxer, not a pink-tea type like Gene Tunney. I was being Dempsey when I traded punches with Yak Canutt or any other heavy. I loved playing these fighting scenes. I studied Dempsey in some newsreel fight movies of him training before a championship bout, and I tried to duplicate some of his moves and how he maneuvered his arms and fists. At that time, in pictures, the way they did a fight was, you and your opponent, you hit each other in the shoulders and faked it to look like real.

"Well now, here I was putting all my strength into it; I was makin' Yak Canutt and any other man with whom I fought really sore, black and blue. They didn't like it but couldn't do anything about it. Except ole Yak kept complaining and said there must be a better way to do it, but I wouldn't hold back when I felt myself gettin' all worked up with hatred for a villain—I wanted to kill the son-of-a-bitch. Matter of fact, I guess I liked these fight scenes more than any other stunts we did.

" 'Course a fight in the movies has to be different from a real fight. There are no rules. You have to stay limber. You purposely exaggerate every punch you throw. And both men have to remain in balance, while in a real bout the idea is to knock the other guy off balance.

"Well, one day, after getting sick and tired of Yak's bellyaching about his bruised shoulders, Bradbury came up with an idea. He said that he thought if he placed the camera at a certain angle it would look as if my fist was making contact with Yak's face, though my fist was passing by his face, not even grazing it. We tried it out one day, and when we saw the rushes we saw how good it looked. Bradbury invented this trick, which he called the *pass system*. Other stuntmen and directors picked up on it, and it became the established way of doing a fight. The really nice thing about it was I could hit as hard as I wanted, put all my power into a punch and not have to hold back, because there was no body contact. Remember that fight Vic McLaglen and I had in *The Quiet Man?* He didn't lay a hand on me and I didn't lay a hand on him. I was a retired American prizefighter in that one. It was the first time I played a fighter in a quality picture. We did not touch each other once, and yet we were punching away as hard as we could.

"Later when I began making pictures with Randolph Scott, I fought many fights with Allan Pomeroy, who was a stuntman who always doubled Scott. Pomeroy had been an assistant director at Republic in those days, and he learned the secrets of the pass system from Canutt and from Bradbury himself. Well, fortunately, Pomeroy looked so much like Randy Scott that we could shoot closeups of our fights and you couldn't tell it wasn't Scott. Pomeroy and I put on some of the most beautiful fights you ever saw. Fighting was not Randy's cup of tea. But I loved fights. I had plenty of fights on the screen—I've been told I've done more fighting in pictures than any other star—and I've also had a few fights off the screen."

In retrospect, those years at Republic have taken on a joyous glow for Wayne. He says:

"I didn't know how good I had it when I was makin' those quickie westerns for Republic. April to September —we worked like hell, makin' our quota of pictures, which were already sold in advance in a package to the exhibitors. And then, oh around September one, off I'd be dove shooting. Right after that it was deer season and then duck and geese, and maybe Ward Bond and Grant Withers, we might go on Mr. Ford's yacht, the *Araner,* down to Mexico for some fishin'.

"So you see, I didn't have the time to learn tennis or golf. They're games, golf and tennis, you have to give a lot of time to them, and I didn't have the time to give to them then and I don't have the leisure now because I'm still makin' pictures.

"But thinkin' back I sure had one hell of a time back there because I had these four, five months of freedom and I was out there doin' the things that keep a man physically fit. I was always in prime condition, even with my drinkin', because I was out there huntin' and fishin' in the open air. I didn't worry once I got away from Los Angeles. Yeah, it sure was a hell of a good life."

I once asked Wayne what was the most valuable lesson he had learned during these years.

His answer surprised me. It was not learning how to do horsefalls, playing a love scene, handling a Winchester .73, brawling with Yakima Canutt, or braving the heat of desert locations and the freezing weather of mountain locations. It was learning how to deliver expository lines convincingly!

"The quickie westerns taught me how to speak lines," he explained. "Straight lines. Most anybody can play anger or hysteria, but try to do a long borin' speech like *The stage from Albuquerque is due in at four and there's a shipment of silver and I hear that Joe and his gang are headin' for the Panamint so you take two men and be there to meet the stage and I'll keep an eye on Mike because he's fixin' to kidnap Maybelle because she thinks her claim is worthless but it's a silver mine* and you got trouble.

"The biggest difference between a B western and an A western is in how they tell the story. The B picture has to do it with stretches of talk, straight exposition. Every once in a while they stop the action and the hero or somebody explains the background or why somebody came to town.

"In a good picture, you get the stories and character across indirectly, and you build up characters and dramatic scenes with images and action."

John Wayne learned how to talk in these "cheapie" westerns, how to say *please pass the sugar ma'am* and *stable my horse for the night* and *what time is it?*

We were reminiscing once about the innumerable stars

of low-budget westerns during the 1930's—about his old friend Bob Steele, and Buck Jones, Bob Baker, Tim McCoy, Tex Ritter, and the others. I wondered what qualities in Wayne had made him rise above the mediocrity of cheaply made westerns.

I asked him then, "What was different about you, Duke?"

He finished smoking a cigarette. He crushed it out in the ashtray. Then he smiled crookedly and replied:

"John Ford."

# 11

# Waiting for the Stage to Lordsburg

The years after his marriage were a time in which Wayne went through many periods of deep depression about his identity as a man, as a husband, as a father. At times he became bitter about his profession. He seemed doomed to be an unimportant western movie actor. He had no sense of fulfillment in his work during these spasms of melancholia. He wanted to flee from Los Angeles. He wanted to flee from the picture business. He wanted to get away from his wife and his children. In other moods, he felt tranquil and good about himself. He loved his children. Michael came in 1934, Toni in 1936, Patrick in 1937, and Melinda in 1939. He would feel deep surges of romantic tenderness for Josie. Yet that Irish morbidity would suddenly seize him. He would tell himself that he had only become an actor in order to look important in his wife's eyes and to make enough money so they could get married. In the throes of bitterness, however, it all seemed to be a trap. Yates was now paying him four thousand for each movie and he had continued the old Monogram contract, which would run until 1936.

The Waynes bought an elegant two-story Spanish-style mansion on North Highland Avenue, between Oakwood Avenue and Beverly Boulevard. It was in the fashionable Hancock Park quarter. Set back from the sidewalk, it was framed by Italian pines and shrubbery and had a red-tiled roof. They moved in after Toni was born. Josie furnished the house in exquisite taste—antique carpets and delicate antique French furniture. Mrs. Morrison—as she called herself—began giving supper parties for her San Marino friends.

Duke felt uneasy at home. Once he plumped down on a fragile French chair and it collapsed. He had to be careful to sit down gingerly. He walked around the house as if he was in a museum. He lowered himself into chairs. Finally, an upstairs room was converted into a special den for him. It had heavy custom-made chairs, a big desk, and a long sofa on which he could stretch out in comfort.

"It was a beautiful home," Paul Fix recalls, "because Josie was and is a woman of good taste and character. She wanted to create a beautiful place for him and her children, but Duke just didn't feel he belonged there. It wasn't his kind of a place. He never was at home in his home. Josie could not comprehend this. I guess he couldn't figure out why she didn't fix up the home differently. I tell you they both really tried hard to make a good marriage but it just wasn't in the cards, because by the time they were married Duke, well, he was a changed person from when they had been courting."

As a married woman, Mrs. Morrison now began participating in the social, religious, and charitable activities of the diocese. In her mind, her social position and her religious convictions imposed certain theological responsibilities as well as benefactions to those in need. She and Loretta Young and Irene Dunne were the three leading personalities of the Catholic enclave in Hollywood. But the former Josephine Saenz was also society. Though Loretta Young was often at her house, Josie also moved in the aristocratic social strata of old Los Angeles. Several evenings a month, the Morrisons attended formal dinner parties, musicales, and other soirées.

"Duke is not a man for tuxedoes," an old friend says. It was galling to return home after a day's work—when he was working on interiors at the Republic studio—and have to bathe, get into a stiff shirt, put studs in it, tie a black tie, and don a dinner jacket.

On these occasions he had to limit his drinking to one cocktail before dinner and several glasses of wine during the meal and then a brandy afterwards. Among these rich sportsmen and third-generation scions of industry and land, he felt like a fish in strange rivers. And to them, he was just a second-rate picture actor who played in shoot-'em-ups.

And most of all Wayne was bored, bored, bored. He was restless and bored. And he was uncomfortable with himself. He felt inadequate most of the time.

What was wrong?

The marriage had not come out the way he had dreamed it would come out. From the first year it had been wretched. He felt great passion for Josie but it did not make him happy. They should never have waited so long to be married. Six years. You change in six years. She expected to live with the young awkward romantic boy whom she would gradually shape into a proper husband, but during the long engagement he had begun congealing into a different shape, worked on by sculptors like John Ford and Yakima Canutt.

Had he expected to find, once their union was legitimized by church and state, a rapturous consummation of flesh and spirit?

Did Wayne begin withdrawing from the marriage into work and drinking because of what he fancied was frigidity—or did she become cold and preoccupied with uplifting charities because he plowed his mind and energy into his westerns?

The late Beverly Barnett, who was Duke's close friend as well as press agent, once described Josie to me as a "very wonderful person," but he believed that "they should never have gotten married. They weren't right for each

other. On the surface, they were a happily married couple
—but it wasn't a real marriage." During the hearing leading to their divorce, the question of her coldness was
brought up. In response, she pointed to the fact of their
four children.

"Yeah," Wayne murmured bitterly to Barnett, "yeah,
four times in ten years."

Well, men and women do say sad things when they are
unhappy.

I believe it was the agonizing six-year delay between
falling in love and getting married which engendered such
frustration, and therefore hostility, in each of them. During these six years of postponements it became virtually
impossible for them ever to trust each other completely.
His love had come to her too soon and her postponements
propagated a fear. She had given him her heart completely, but by the time she had given it, he did not believe
in her love. He accepted it in memory only. They lived in
a strange world of reconsiderations. They did not find in
matrimony what they expected. They could not do anything about it.

Duke was not a man to escape into clandestine
romances, a universal solution in these matters in Hollywood and elsewhere. He was of course surrounded by
beautiful and eager women. But as Bev Barnett once said
to me, "Duke is not and never has been a philanderer.
He is a one-woman man. He just isn't a chaser. He needs
a woman to complete his life. He has to admire and respect a woman before he can sleep with her. And he just
isn't able to sleep with any dame because she's available.
He has to be three-quarters in love with them. I never
saw him make a pass at just anybody."

These were sad and frustrating years for Josie and
Duke. Caught in a trap, they saw no way of springing it.
So they went on performing the rituals of daily living,
drawing further and further apart from each other.

Duke's friends thought that Josie's adoration of Christ
and her devotion to the church was the primary cause
of their dissension. And it is true that she was a highly
spiritual and pious lady, who faithfully attended Mass

and took communion and made confession and participated in novenas and was active in the charities of the Los Angeles diocese. Frequently she had priests and nuns to the house for dinner and theological conversation. Duke had a strong aversion to organized religion. He also suspected that she had the priests around—some of them were bright and witty Jesuits and Dominicans—to convert him. He did not want his soul saved, even to save their marriage.

Things went along in this haphazard fashion and there was no overt talk of a divorce until 1938. Josie violently opposed a divorce—as violently as she had opposed love's consummation before marriage. Duke simply could not understand her nature; the intensity of her love for him; her seriousness about the rules of the game.

From 1939 on there was a physical and emotional gulf between them that they both accepted. Theirs was a marriage in name only—but their public reputations were never tarnished by rumors or gossip in Louella Parson's column. Soon he ceased to make more than token appearances with her at her charitable functions and society suppers. He felt he had tried hard to be a decent husband in the first five years of their marriage. He put on company manners when priests came calling, but he couldn't cope with these situations unless he had several belts of whiskey inside his body.

And this Josie Morrison wouldn't permit at home. She was the ruling power at the North Highland mansion. Duke accepted this. Having grown up under a domineering mother, he easily fell sway to a domineering wife. She hated whiskey. She hated how it altered Marion's sweet personality, coarsening him, removing his inhibitions, making him an animal, slurring his speech and blurring his gaze.

If it can be said—as Wayne's friends said for years to the press—that her obsession with Christ and the Roman Catholic church ruined the marriage, I think it can also be said—and Josie's friends said this but not to the press because she asked them to preserve her privacy—that Duke's love of alcohol turned her against him more and more. She was revolted by the sight of him intoxicated, by the smell of his breath, the grossness of his behavior, by this erosion of the romantic young man with whom she'd once fallen madly in love and defied her parents to marry. You see, she had, in a sense, given up everything for him; she had made a sacrifice for her love. He did not grasp this. She could not understand his lack of understanding. She did not respect the movies he made. She did not like the location absences. Just as he was disconcerted by her Jesuit priests, by her Catholic matrons, she could not abide the presence of John Ford, Grant Withers, Ward Bond, Paul Fix, Yakima Canutt, and the other whiskey-swilling cronies with whom her husband consorted.

"Duke," Bev Barnett told me once in 1954, "was never sure when he came home to dinner if there'd be two priests or three priests at the table. But he always knew there'd be at least one. As for her society friends—well, he couldn't stand them."

He and she found different patterns of living, and their marriage became one of those in which husband and wife are like two children playing back to back in a sandpile, each occupied with his own private game and seemingly oblivious of the other but quite conscious that another game is occurring and desperately anxious to be content with the game being played by himself.

There is a moment of pathos in *The Undefeated* (1969). Wayne, playing Colonel Thomas, a Union officer retired after the Civil War, is running three thousand wild horses into Mexico to sell to the Emperor Maximilian. En route, he and his men join up with a large party of several hundred Confederate officers and their families traveling to Mexico to make a new life. Among the group is the widow of a Confederate officer killed during the war. She and Wayne fall in love and there ensues one of those tender middle-aged romances that Wayne has been rendering with great artistry for a long time. The Confederates, now in Mexico, make a Fourth of July party. The Unionists attend. There is singing and music and food and whiskey. Wayne and Marian McCargo, the widow lady, find themselves alone, and he compliments her on her dress. She smiles and remarks that he seems to know how to please a woman, and he says no he does not. He was married once but now he is divorced. She asks about his former wife.

He tells her that they had gone out in the Oklahoma Territory and he was homesteading and ranching and his wife did not like it. And with deep feeling he speaks these lines:

"She was so busy being a lady that she forgot to be a woman. And it was Indian country—and she didn't like that. And I wanted to go huntin' and fishin'—and she didn't like that. But I guess she's happy now livin' in Philadelphia with her cat and givin' piano lessons."

He smiles wistfully.

And you want to cry at the sadness of life, so well does he express it.

These lines, which director Andrew McLaglen let him develop from a simple reference to his ex-wife's dislike of pioneer life, came as vibrations always waiting to emerge when he plucked the deepest strings of his memory, the memory not only of Josie but also of his mother, of Mary Morrison shrilly accusing Doc of dragging the family out to the Palmdale desert.

*She was so busy being a lady that she forgot to be a woman.*

Josie Saenz Morrison is neither an actress nor a writer. We cannot be certain how she vibrates when she plucks her old memories. One can imagine there are pangs. One can well imagine that.

To her intimates, Josie Saenz Morrison was one of the most gracious and lovely women in creation. Loretta Young recalls her as being lovely to look at and almost an angel in personality. She was a "divine dancer" and was vital and effervescent. Miss Young says she has the social manners of Queen Elizabeth and the wit of Clare Boothe Luce. It is almost embarrassing to quote Miss Young's praise, which is replete with such adjectives as intelligent, tactful, kind, forgiving, honest, generous, dependable, self-disciplined, tasteful, and good natured with a most "beguiling and delightful kind of laughter." She was also, in her way, a sensual and highly passionate person, according to Miss Young, and consequently appears, in this portrait, unlike the stiff and inhibited religious fanatic painted by other acquaintances sympathetic to Duke.

Duke once gave me the following explanation of his troubles with Josie:

"Well," he said thoughtfully, "Josie and I—we were just movin' in two different channels. I was part of the movie group. She was part of the society group. I found small talk boring. So we went our own ways. Josie didn't like my friends and I didn't like hers.

"I don't know exactly when a husband and wife stop lovin' each other. I can't say it was this year or that month. Maybe by our third or fourth year we both knew somethin' was not right. But we shared many good experiences together, of which our children was the best. And we did try, many times, to make our marriage work. We had many blowups and bitter arguments.

"I don't deny I'm not an easy guy to get along with, because I do have a short fuse. I have a temper. I guess I hurt Josie many times without intendin' to. Maybe we should have separated right away, but I was in love with her and when the children came, we both wanted to work it out. I felt strongly about the children.

"I didn't want to break up. I had grown up in a home of bickering and I know how children suffer when their parents fight. But I also know how hard it is for them when parents get divorced. Well, we stayed together and made the best of it and our children, thank God, came out fine. I have to give the credit to Josie."

Could they have reconciled their differences if Duke had not been a heavy drinker?

As an imbiber, Wayne is one of those rare persons whose organism is able to metabolize enormous quantities of alcohol without deranging his mind and destroying his body. Almost any other man who drank as much as he drunk over as long a period of time would long ago have killed himself in a suicidal depression or died of cirrhosis of the liver or heart stoppage. While alcohol has not made

John Wayne a better actor or a nobler person, it has not destroyed him. Yet his consumption of alcohol has averaged a quart a day for forty years.

Jim Henaghen, who often drank with him during the 1950's, says, "Duke never measured a drink in his life. He never counts drinks. He just drinks. Sometimes he stops when he gets high. Sometimes he drinks until he passes out. I remember once when he and I decided to go on the wagon. We would quit cold. Nothing. Not even a cold beer. So my wife and I were invited to Wayne's house for Thanksgiving dinner. He was then living at this big ranch he had out in Encino. Well, the table was all set and you could smell the turkeys roasting in the kitchen. The holiday spirit got to me and I told Duke, hell, I think I'm going to have a martini. Just one. I sipped mine. He said he would join me. He gulped his and started on a second and by the time I had two, he had had his fourth.

"I stopped on my second to watch him. He stirred up a big pitcher of them and started knocking them back. I counted. In about two, three hours he had sixteen martinis. Now you know that no human being on God's green earth can drink sixteen martinis and stand up. It is scientifically impossible. I fall apart after four of them. Duke held his liquor. He went through dinner eating and talking and laughing and I got so mad I started belting wine during dinner and spent the rest of the day in the toilet throwing up.

"I mean—sixteen martinis! I saw it with my own eyes.

"Now I think the answer is Duke doesn't get stoned when he has problems. He keeps a clear head. He never was an alcoholic. But most of his friends like Ward Bond and Jimmmy Grant were, and I believe Jimmy Grant even tried Alcoholics Anonymous.

"Duke can stop drinking whenever he has a mind to. He has a self-control that used to make me envious. And self-discipline. He will work come hell or high heaven, hangover or no hangover, sick or healthy. He's there on the set, the first one of the actors."

Recently, in Mexico, I witnessed an example. On a

Sunday evening in May, 1972, after a week of intensive outdoor shooting, Duke and several members of the company—including Rod Taylor, Chris George, and Bobby Vinton—went out for an evening of dining and drinking at a Greek restaurant in Torreón. Duke had some martinis and then hot shrimps and a big steak and a bottle of wine and then settled down to some serious brandy drinking, as one by one the others dropped out of the drinking, leaving only Rod and Duke matching each other drink for drink until Taylor, an Australian of stout physique and big capacity, gave up, though he's twenty years younger than Duke. They all staggered happily back to the Hotel Rio Nazas in the early morning.

And the following morning Duke was breakfasting at six A.M. He was made up and costumed, driving to the location forty miles away in his camper. He slept an hour in the camper and was ready for the first shot of the day at eight A.M.

His fellow drinkers were hollow-cheeked and exhausted.

The next day Duke came down with diverticulosis, a painful condition of the intestinal tract which is brought on by nervous tension. But this did not stop him, either. He came to the set every day—on time.

One thing, however, can be said with certainty. Wayne does not drink during the working day. This he learned years ago from John Ford. Ford, as wild a roisterer as Duke, never drank during a film and always tried to get remote locations where liquor was hard to get. One of the reasons he liked Monument Valley was that it is on a Navajo reservation and the sale of liquor is illegal. Ford stopped drinking in 1950 and he tried hard to get Wayne to live a clean and sober life.

Wayne did not always eschew drinking during the day. During the painful years of the 1930's, he found, after a night of marital arguments, that he could not get started in the morning without a few drinks. He sometimes came to the set in a drunken stupor. Sometimes they had to wire his legs to the horse so he wouldn't fall off the saddle. But these lapses were rare. His salvation was in his work and he was serious about his work, even if he hated the pictures he was making.

He saved his serious drinking for the evenings and the weekends, usually in the company of Ward Bond. When they got drunk, they got pugnacious. They started fights with each other or with anybody against whom they had a grievance. Once, at the Hollywood Athletic Club, they got into a fight and started slugging it out as the other members scurried outside. They rampaged up and down, making a shambles of the place. They had to pay the club a few hundred dollars for repairing the damage. They were suspended for a year.

When he and Bond went on their hunting trips they also drank, of course. Once the two of them were hunting quail—the kind with spotted feathers—in the San Bernardino valley. Duke admired the new 20-gauge shotgun Bond was carrying. Wayne wanted to try it and Bond did not want to lend it to him, but finally he agreed. Both men separated in search of quail. Wayne saw a covey in their cover and he opened fire and then he heard terrible screams. He went over and there was Bond, prone and bleeding. Duke took him to the car and to a doctor. He removed dozens of shotgun pellets from his back and neck and scalp.

When the wounds healed, Duke came over to pay a sick call on his amigo. He made a joke about the pattern the buckshot made on Bond's back. How he admired that shotgun, he said. He would very much like to buy it—or trade one of his own guns for it.

"I got to have it, Wardell," he said.

"Over my dead body," Ward said.

"Well," said Duke, looking him over, "if that's the only way I can get it . . ."

When they read his last will and testament years later, they found that Ward Bond had bequeathed that 20-gauge shotgun to Duke Wayne . . .

One of his favorite drinking partners was Grant Withers. He was a huge boisterous actor who played in many of Duke's pictures. He was one of the original members of the Ford Stock Company. He had been married to

Loretta Young for a few months in 1930, until her mother annulled the marriage because Miss Young was under age. Like Bond, Withers was a roistering drinker who could keep up with Duke, drink for drink.

He did many wild things with Duke. Once when they were on location in Arizona, both of them got liquored up, and Withers said he knew a couple of "beautiful broads" who lived alone in a house on the outskirts of town. They were waitresses and had truckdriver boyfriends, but the drivers were out of town on a long haul and Withers had fixed it up for him and Duke to come over and visit. "If the coast is clear," he said, "these dolls will pull their windowshades halfway down as a signal."

It all sounded too good to be true. Duke smelled a rat. He pretended to go along with the intrigue. But he armed himself with a Colt .44 loaded with blanks.

They arrived at the isolated house. Withers yelled out, "Is Annie home?" Inside the house, a prop man who was in on the joke was lying in wait. The game was that as soon as Duke opened the door, he would blast at Duke with a rifle loaded with blanks.

Duke opened the door. He got the picture. He took out his automatic and started firing at the prop man. Terrified, the latter started running through the house, broke through a rear door when he could not unlock it, and was last seen tearing through a meadow. He never returned to the set!

As time went on, Wayne got sick and tired of playing in westerns. He wished he could go back to being a master property man or a stuntman. He wished he could be anybody but who he was. He was ashamed of westerns. He hated himself during his black moods. And he finally came to detest horses. He thought they were exceedingly stupid animals. He loved dogs but he hated horses. He had to force himself to act with horses.

"I never knew him to have a horse he loved," says Henaghen, a friend and business associate for many years. "Away from the camera, he does not act friendly with horses. A horse to Duke is what a motorcycle is to a traffic cop. Part of his work. He would rather have been a stuntman like Canutt than an actor in the kind of B's he was making during the 1930's. I remember his saying once, 'If I was only as smart as Yak in doing stunts, I would not have to act anymore.'

"Duke worshiped Yak. He used to follow him around when they worked in the same picture. In those days, Canutt made more money than Duke even if Duke was the star because he got a salary as an actor and also as a stuntman. Even when he got big in the 1940's, Duke always listened respectfully when Yak started telling a story. He kind of hung on his words. Canutt was his idea of a real man."

From Canutt, Wayne learned his famous rolling walk and his slouch on a horse. He also learned several basic western stunts—the *horsefall* (floating over the horse in the air when your horse buckles or is "shot") and the *transfer* (leaping from your horse to another horse, or from horse to stagecoach, or train to horse, or horse to train). He learned *bull-dogging* (in movie stunting this denotes leaping from the horse to jump a rider on another horse) and *doing a cat* (dropping in a slump from your horse when horse is "shot" out from under you).

He was tired of westerns. He did not want to make any more. He expressed his anti-western mood to Alexander Kahn, Hollywood correspondent of the New York *World-Telegram* in 1940. Kahn reported that "if he never forks another cayuse it's all right with John Wayne. With three pictures in a row, none of which has anything to do with the range" (*Seven Sinners, A Man Betrayed, Lady from Louisiana*) "he hopes his career as a western star is left behind permanently." Wayne mournfully recounted how he had tried "to get into other things" but somehow always found himself trapped in another horse opera.

"Not that I think I'm too good for westerns," he said, "but I'm getting to be something of a veteran in this business, and if I don't progress there's not much satisfaction in the job."

In December, 1935, his old Monogram deal expired. Yates offered him a new contract: twenty-four thousand a year, to make four westerns every year over the next five years. It was the best deal he had ever received. Yates promised that he would spend more money and make a better quality Wayne western.

Wayne spurned the proposition. Dammit, this time he was going to do a man's work. He and Josie had talked about it. It was going away from his home on location that was tearing them apart. Dammit to hell, a man had to be with his wife and his family. What kind of life was that, out there in Arizona or Utah, living in shacks or tents, getting up at dawn, never seeing your own children growing up, being a stranger to the only woman you ever loved? He was going to get into a real profession of some sort. He was going to go to an office downtown from nine to five. He would come home for a dinner with the family. He and Josie would have a real life together.

Through her connections, Wayne took a flier as a customer's man in a Wilshire and Hope brokerage house. He failed. He went into real estate management. He failed.

He took up prizefighting. This was his longest experiment with a nonacting career. It is the best-kept secret of his life. He once blurted it out, apropos of a comment about Cassius Clay. Duke fought prelims and a few top of the card fights under the name of Duke Morrison in California and Nevada. For about six months. He failed. He had a good style, just like Jack Dempsey's, but he lacked Dempsey's punch. He went back to movie acting —but now he made up his mind to act in good pictures. He went to see Cecil B. De Mille. De Mille was casting *Northwest Mounted Police.* The part of the frontier scout hadn't been cast. His agent got him an appointment, and he waited outside De Mille's office on the Paramount lot at the specified time. De Mille came out an hour later and ignored Wayne. He just strode rapidly outside and into the street. Wayne trotted alongside, blurting out, "I'm Wayne, Mr. De Mille. I wanted to see you about *Northwest Mounted Police.* John Wayne."

They were moving fast now.

"You were in *The Big Trail,* weren't you?"

"Yes, sir."

"What have you done since then?"

"Westerns at Republic."

"Well, you'll hear from us if we have something."

He never did.

It was during this discouraging period that his vocal coach and bosom friend, Paul Fix, informed him that he had written a play and asked if John Wayne would like to tread the boards. Hell, yes, was Wayne's first impulse. Now he would show Josie and her elegant friends that he was a real actor, an artist. Having agreed, Wayne began to feel stagefright. He was reasonably easy when he talked before a camera and sound equipment. But speaking to a live audience from a stage! He now rediscovered something about himself he'd first found out in school, and which is still true today. He is afraid of speaking in public. He is shy and terrified, and when he has to speak he has a speech prepared in advance which he memorizes. He has a fast mind and a superb memory and can memorize a two- or three-page speech after one reading. Even then, so great is his dread of an audience that he has to have several drinks before going on.

He was sorry he had agreed to appear in the play but he had given his word and he went into rehearsal. It was a waterfront play, set on the San Francisco docks: *Red Sky at Evening*. Sally Blane was to play the co-starring role. After two weeks of rehearsal, they had a dress rehearsal in a theatre on Figueroa Street that Fix rented. Several hundred friends and professional movie people were invited to the dress rehearsal.

Fix planted himself in the rear of the audience and watched. The curtain rose upon the set, a shabby furnished room. Sally Blane enters, puts on the light. The door opens and Wayne enters. She screams. He is a stranger to her.

Fix did not know that another drama had been played out backstage. Duke's brother, Bob, had brought a bottle of Scotch to remedy the star's flutters. By the curtain's rise, Duke had taken the contents of the bottle and was feeling no pain. He came on stage somewhat unsteady, reeling a little. But that looked in character. Sally Blane screamed again and hit him with a vase. (It was a breakaway vase and it broke and Duke looked baffled.) He said, "Where am I?"

This was not precisely the line Fix had written, but it was close enough.

Fix looking on realized he had never seen such a simple and overpowering example of the actor's art. You actually believed the young sailor did not know where he was. Confusion, vague anxiety, befuddlement—all were written on the hero's face and expressed in the contortions of his body. How authentically he leaned on a chair, that glazed look in his eyes. Fix thought he was holding the moment too long but he waited.

"Where am I?" Duke blurted, weaving drunkenly. "Where the hell am I?"

Fix knew now. "I realized the son-of-a-bitch was stoned out of his mind," he remembers. "I wanted to kill him. I went back and told Gordon Oliver, the stage manager, to ring down the curtain. Duke was still on stage. I'll never forget a shrill voice in the audience yelling, 'Duke, you are a disgrace. You are just—a—disgrace.' It was Josie Wayne. The first and only time I ever heard her raise her voice."

Thus ended John Wayne's career as a stage actor.

*Red Sky at Evening* never played a single performance.

You may think this evening was the nadir of his career, but the nadir was still ahead of him. It came along in the shape of Trem Carr. Trem Carr, formerly executive producer at Republic, had just been made an executive producer at Universal.

He invited Duke to rise to better things. He promised to take John Wayne out of Levi's; he could unstrap his holster forever. He would never have to mount another horse unless he wanted to go riding in Griffith Park. Trem Carr always believed that Wayne was a distinguished movie actor of potential greatness.

Wayne heard the siren song. Between April, 1936, and May, 1937, Wayne performed in six Trem Carr productions for Universal. Carr kept his word. He cast Wayne as a coast guard commander in *The Sea Spoilers,* a prizefighter in *Conflict,* owner of a truck fleet in *California Straight Ahead,* news photographer in *I Cover the War,* hockey player in *Idol of the Crowds,* and whaler in *Adventure's End.*

These pictures were a series of artistic failures and box-office fiascos, an unbeatable combination for a career nadir to end all nadirs.

"I made a big mistake," Wayne says. "Not because they weren't westerns, but because they were cheap pictures. Trem Carr was trying to make them on a budget of about seventy-five thou. He was cutting costs and production values as if he were still making Republic cheapies. Well, this time we were not competing with other Poverty Row operators and their programmers. We were competing with quality pictures that cost five hundred thousand and up. We were bucking 20th and Warners and Paramount and we struck out.

"We were trying to sell cotton hose in a silk stocking market."

(For some peculiar reason, the hosiery metaphor is Duke's favorite to describe the movie industry. He was still using it apropos of television when we talked in 1972. Now women have not been wearing either cotton *or* silk hosiery for twenty or thirty years. Apparently, Duke heard the phrase long ago, liked it, and adopted it. If you get into a discussion of box office and grosses and movie quality with Duke, sooner or later you will hear about the cotton stockings and the silk stockings.)

Out in the backwoods, John Wayne was still a name to conjure with. But even his small-town fans did not—forgive the expression—cotton to him as a news photographer or a hockey player. They wanted the same old straight-shootin' John Wayne. They shunned these Universal pictures like the rest of the country.

"Well," Wayne says, sighing tremulously, "I lost my stature as a western star. I got nothing in return. In six months, exhibitors wouldn't touch a John Wayne with a ten-foot pole. I said adios to Trem Carr and I tried free-lancing and about the best I could get was a B at Paramount, a cattle drive, trek type of picture, terrible. Almost as bad as those Trem Carr specials.

"Finally I just had to come crawlin' back to Herbert Yates and beg for mercy. I didn't want to make these cheapies for Republic, but seemed like there was nothin' else to do. There were three children now. Yates put the screws into me. Sure he would sign a new contract with me. But no more talk about twenty-four thousand. I'd have to settle for sixteen. And I would have to go into those terrible series they had. And they wanted a five-year deal. John Ford told me not to make a long-term deal. I held out for a two-year deal. Then Yates said if I signed for five they would let me play Sam Houston in a high-budget picture they were getting ready."

Wayne had long admired Sam Houston.

He once told a friend, "If I could choose one person in American history I wish I'd been, I'd choose Sam Houston. He had a philosophy of life I've tried to live by. He always wore a ring, a ring his mother gave him. Just a plain gold ring. When he died, they took it off. It had a word inscribed inside: *honor*. They put the ring back on his finger before they buried him."

When Republic started shooting the Sam Houston story they gave the role to Richard Dix. Yates told Wayne he was not big enough at the box office for such an important picture.

Duke felt he was condemned to be just a "cheapie" actor in "cheapie" B's. The Mesquiteers were cheapies, all right. Maybe they were cotton stockings like his other B westerns—but these had holes and runs in them. He made eight Mesquiteers for Republic. They were the dreariest films he made in this decade. Shot in five days, they looked as if they had been made in one morning. They were slapped together with absurd dialogue and a paucity of action stunts. The last four were *The Night Riders, Three Texas Steers, Wyoming Outlaw* and *Frontier Horizon*.

They were released after Wayne became famous, in 1939 and 1940. He was humiliated by them. He hated Republic for sending out these terrible Mesquiteer pictures, but he couldn't stop them. Wayne's down-home fans loved the Mesquiteers and were glad that John Wayne was back in the saddle and had forsaken his tenderfoot mistakes with Universal. They did not love him as an aviator or a photographer. They loved him as a good-guy western hero. They even loved his Mesquiteer movies, pure junk, as much as or more than they loved his high-class fancy dude westerns directed by John Ford. Republic Pictures knew their audience. They were oblivious to the other American audience, but they knew their backwoods audience, for sure.

## 12

## John Wayne Reads a Screenplay

As 1937 was ending, John Wayne looked back on a dreary past and contemplated a dark future. He was now thirty years old, long past the prime when an actor should expect to play romantic leading-man parts.

In the Hollywood of that period, youth was worshiped. A leading man started establishing himself before he was twenty-five, and at thirty he was already either a star or an important character actor. Wayne was neither. He was a piece-worker in the sweatshops of Poverty Row. He had no money. He had no prestige. He had no importance in his eyes, in his wife's eyes, or in the eyes of his peers. Perhaps he had mastered the rudiments of movie acting, but what did that mean? Perhaps he had learned how to project a certain character type with simplicity, power, and grace, but it didn't pay the rent spiritually. He knew about lights, props, stunts. He knew what to do when the director said, "Action. Speak."

He had not wanted to be an actor but he was an actor.

In 1937, he was running fast in order to stay in the same place. His private life was a tragic melodrama. He alternated between sullen acceptance of Josie's rules and angry rebellion in which he exploded in drunken escapades.

Sometimes he felt like a man at the end of his lonely trail. Disillusioned, burned out, melancholy. Yet he continued to work. Work was his salvation, even though he despised the cheapie westerns, Republic, the fast-buck operators of Poverty Row. He despised himself. He was not always deterred from sadness by the drinking, the hunting, and the fishing.

In November, 1937, John Ford invited him to come for a weekend aboard his yacht, the *Araner,* named for the Irish islands of Aran where Ford's family came from. Wayne anticipated the usual drinking and gambling. Ford's favorite game was a variation of poker, High, Low, Jack, and the Game. He was good at it. Wayne was better. Wayne was the only man who could beat him at poker.

He was still beating Ford in 1972 when Denis Sanders was making a CBS documentary film about John Ford, *The West of John Ford.* Ford and Wayne went to Monument Valley, where Ford would enact his directing of Wayne in a typical western. Both men were there for a few days and they played high-stakes poker at night. Afterwards, Ford told me about it, regaling himself with the righteous indignation in which he took such pleasure, his nonpunctuating mollybloom sentences flowing from his sensual lips.

"Well I wasn't working when I went down to Monument Valley went up there to beat Wayne out of a few dollars but I didn't. There was one hand the son-of-a-bitch he beat me I had a full house kings high and I bet my ass off and he beat me four-eighty on the hand with four deuces. Says he's going to have both hands framed. Then some Mongolian idiot from the Screen Directors' Guild phoned to say my pension was stopped because I was working in a picture not that this television documentary was a picture anyway but I told her I was playing poker not working.

"No, my most thrilling stunt was not the Indian attack in *Stagecoach* don't give a damn what the experts say what do they know it was the Dakota land rush in *Three Bad Men* my God it is thrilling saw it screened for me last week they're using some cuts in this documentary my grandson's making we used over two hundred vee-hee-culls stages contestoga wagons buggies brougham every blasted vee-hee-cull there was and hundreds of men riding horses all waiting for the signal to cross over riding like hell and there's this little baby and she's right in the way of the galloping horses and goddamit we used a real child there was this stuntman Jack Padgin whom I've mentioned in connection with Duke and his wife Marcella she was in wardrobe and he was a stunt rider and she said why don't you use a real baby? they had this two-year-old kid and I said hell it's too dangerous and she said don't worry Jack will pick her up just as the stampede is coming if you'll pay us extra so goddamit I made Fox pay her two-fifty extra for the kid and that was one good stunt, in *Stagecoach* we used a real baby same name as Mrs. Padgin, Marcella, she was a couple of weeks old she played this baby Louise Platt gave birth to. Trouble I had getting Walter Wanger to take Duke as the Ringo Kid and then the bastard takes credit for discovering him well I never liked producers anyway."

So behold Wayne in the winter of his discontent, in 1937, hoping to have some escape aboard the yacht with Ward Bond and Vic McLaglen and Grant Withers and the Old Man and beat these potzers at cards.

But there was nobody aboard except himself and Ford and the crew. They sailed. Ford handed him a short story clipped from *Collier's* and a 123-page screenplay written by Dudley Nichols. The story was "Stage to Lordsburg." The screenplay was *Stagecoach*.

On April 10, 1937, *Collier's* published Ernest Haycox's "Stage to Lordsburg." It was a lean, tightly constructed tale of three thousand words, about the hazardous journey of an oddly assorted group of frontier characters through the Indian territory of New Mexico. Among the passengers on the stagecoach were a lonely gunfighter, Malpais Bill, "a slim blonde man," and Henriette, a prostitute, "small and quiet, with a touch of paleness in her cheeks."

Among the readers was John Ford. He had not made a western since talking pictures came in. For eight years, he had removed himself from what had once been his favorite genre. But the Haycox story turned him on. He bought the movie rights for four thousand dollars. Then he and Dudley Nichols elaborated the little narrative into a rich tapestry of characters.

In the same issue of *Collier's* was another short story, quite different in tone and setting: "Bringing Up Baby," by Hagar Wilde. The plot was about a sophisticated couple and a baby leopard. This story fascinated director Howard Hawks. He bought the story and not long afterwards started shooting a screwball comedy based on it, with Cary Grant and Katharine Hepburn as the screwball lovers.

It was a strange coincidence. One issue of one magazine had supplied the plot and characters of what turned out to be two of the most famous pictures of that decade.

In the screenplay of *Stagecoach,* the young gunfighter seeking revenge is not Malpais Bill. He is the Ringo Kid.

Ford said he would like to have Duke's opinion of the text. Duke immersed himself in the story and in the imaginative elaboration of it which Nichols and Ford had fashioned. At once he knew that he was natural for the Ringo Kid. He also knew Ford did not intend to cast him in the part. Ford had been gibing at him about his B westerns. Yet—was it possible?

They had dinner and many drinks. Ford did not mention *Stagecoach*. They played gin rummy until it was late. Duke got a headache from the stench of Ford's cigars.

At one moment, Ford narrowed his eyes cunningly. He puffed a cloud of smoke in Duke's face.

"I need some help from you," he said.

"Sure, Pappy," Duke said.

"You are acquainted with some of the new young

actors. I was wondering if you knew of one that could play the Ringo Kid."

Duke was so tired he didn't get mad. He just assumed Mr. Ford wouldn't want him anyway. As an actor he did not rate with him. He was a man with whom to drink and play cards and carouse. Wayne pondered over various young actors and finally suggested the name of Lloyd Nolan.

"Nolan?" said Ford with a quizzical expression. Then he suddenly arose and said good night. Duke went to bed with a bottle of cognac. He drank until he passed out. In his stupor, the present voyage recalled his erstwhile South Seas adventure when he had stowed away on a Matson liner to Hawaii and been put in irons. Ten years ago!

Ten years!

Where had they gone? How little he had accomplished. How bleak was the future. In the mind of every major studio casting director there was an unwritten label on his photograph.

JOHN WAYNE. OVER 30. BLUE EYES. BROWN HAIR. SIX FEET FOUR INCHES. WEIGHT 180 POUNDS. B WESTERNS. MONOGRAM. REPUBLIC.

Play the important romantic lead in a John Ford movie? Hell, he wasn't even good enough to play Sam Houston in a Republic picture.

He slept late the next morning. His hangover was abysmal. He drank beer. During the rest of the voyage Ford incessantly baited him with references to Republic quickies and his problem in finding a suitable young actor to impersonate the Ringo Kid.

As they were docking in San Pedro, Ford, chewing a cigar, snarled at him, "Duke, I want to tell you something. I have made up my mind. I want you to play the Ringo Kid."

Obviously, he had planned to cast Wayne as the Ringo Kid from the first. Why had he tormented him?

Henaghen's theory is that, "Ford is a genius as a director, but a rotten human being. He is sadistic. He kept Duke squirming just for the pleasure of watching him suffer. I never knew why Duke always took insults from him. Duke has always worshiped him. Even when he was up in the million-dollar-a-picture class, Duke would come running if Ford whistled and work for whatever Ford wanted to pay him."

Paul Fix has been a close friend and colleague of Duke's. He has played important parts in a score of Wayne films, including the recent ones. For many years, he would stand off-camera when Wayne was working in a scene. They had worked out a system of covert signals. Fix was Duke's unofficial acting coach. He never told anybody about this. They had these signals so Fix would let him know when he was moving too slowly or had to turn a certain way. Nobody ever guessed the system, but Ford suspected something. He couldn't decode the facial tics by means of which Fix got information across.

Fix also believes there was a cruel streak in Ford's nature. He played one scene in *Fort Apache* in which he had to fall down on some broken rocks. Fix says Ford deliberately kept doing retakes.

Fix finally said, "This granite is cutting me all to hell."

"Just you play the scene," Ford said.

"I cannot do it, Mr. Ford, this is killing me."

"If you do not play that scene you will never work in another picture for me."

"The hell with you and your pictures, Mr. Ford," said Fix and he stumbled away, never to appear in any movies directed by John Ford, or even be on the set.

Had Ford been tormenting Wayne about *Stagecoach* for sadistic amusement?

"I don't know for sure," Fix says. "Maybe it was just a cruel prank—because Ford loved pranks."

You could not be sure if he was degrading your spirit or just having some good wild Irish fun, innocent send-ups and insults. Fix thought these games usually had no purpose beyond amusement.

I do not agree. John Ford was a master of actor's psychology. What he did, he did for a deliberate artistic reason. It was, in one respect or another, a way to focus an actor's mind on the movie assignment.

Here is how he handled Wayne when he started shoot-

ing *Stagecoach* in the spring of 1938. He bullied him and
berated him every day. To a detached observer this would
seem like a stupid tactic, for Wayne felt insecure enough
playing with such experienced professionals as Thomas
Mitchell and George Bancroft. Should not the director
have handled the neophyte with particular tenderness?

But John Ford did not treat him lovingly. *Au con-
traire*. He went out of his way to criticize Wayne openly
before crew and cast. He disparaged Duke's speech.
("Chrissakes—stop slurring your lines, you dumb bastard." "I can't hear your words." "Faster—faster.") He
criticized his moves. ("I said hold your position before you
turn. Chrissakes—can't you even walk? Not skip—just
walk. Goddam fairy. Put your feet down like you were
a man.") And he was hardest when Duke was in scenes
with Claire Trevor or Donald Meek or one of the other
veterans. ("You're stepping on Claire's lines again, kid.
Just listen when she talks. Don't rush in." "You're getting
arrested. Get mad, won't you? Bancroft is your enemy.
Weren't you ever mad? You look like a baked potato.
Some expression. And listen when he's speaking.")

By the third week of shooting—*Stagecoach* was completed in ten weeks, though the editing and scoring required another three months—Ford suddenly changed his
manner with Duke. And one afternoon, he murmured
sweetly, "Would you like to see the rushes? I'm running
them at five. You look very good."

He knew when to turn the heat on an actor and when
to soothe him. Always he had a sense of the actor's inner
life and its relation to the progress of the film, to the
dynamics of the fictional character he was portraying. In
one scene, Duke was not able to look real when he was
shooting his rifle at the Indians. So Ford ordered that the
rifle be loaded with real shells! And Duke rehearsed with
live ammunition until he felt he was really pulling the
trigger of a lethal weapon. Only then was the scene shot
with blanks.

Ford permitted Wayne to do many of his own stunts,
though he took the risk of Wayne breaking a leg and
holding up production. He did it against the opposition of

Wanger, because he knew it would give Duke a better sense of reality, though he insisted on Canutt doing the most hazardous stunts.

Visiting the set one morning, out in Monument Valley, producer Wanger was shocked to see Duke playing a scene in which he leaped out of the stage and climbed on the roof.

"Jack," he said to the director, "I want you to get Wayne to stop stunting. He is too valuable to lose. From now on, I want Canutt to double him in the stunts."

"You tell it to Duke," Ford said nonchalantly.

"Duke," Wanger said, "you are going to be an outstanding star. I do not want you to do any more of these stunts. My God, if you broke a leg or an arm—it would hold up the picture for weeks. You have to learn to take care of yourself."

Wayne looked at Ford to get a cue.

Ford smiled ambiguously.

"Now, Mr. Wanger," Wayne drawled, "there is no need for you to worry. I can handle myself. I been ridin' horses and stuntin' for years. I'm not an actor. I don't act. I react. I'm just a stuntman."

Wanger was not impressed by this show of modesty. He started to get angry. Ford was now afraid that Wanger would make such a fuss that a day's shooting would be lost.

"Duke," he said, "I think our producer has got a point. From here on out, Yak is going to double you. And now let's break for lunch."

Duke laughs when you suggest to him that Ford loved cruelty for its own sake. He does not believe that there was a sadistic bone in Pappy Ford's body. It was John Ford's pursuit of artistic perfection amid the special problems of filmmaking which led him to behave in such anomalous ways.

"Sure, he got me angry," Duke says. "He would turn me inside out. I would want to murder him. But he knew what he was doing. First of all—he was makin' me feel emotions. He knew he wouldn't get a good job of work out of me unless he shook me up so damn hard I'd forget to worry about whether I was fit to be in the same picture with Thomas Mitchell. He knew how tough it was for me to be playin' with Claire Trevor. He knew I was ashamed of bein' a B western cowboy in the company of these big stars.

"And don't forget he couldn't be sure that after all these years of working in those cheapies that maybe I had not ruined my acting.

"But that wasn't all there was to his tricks. He also knew that when there's an unknown actor like me who is put in the key role of a movie, well there's an unconscious resentment on the part of the veteran against this unknown. There has to be. Now Mr. Ford, he wanted to get the veterans rootin' for me and rootin' for the picture—not resentin' me.

"Well, see how smart he was. By deliberately kickin' me around, he got the other actors on my side and hatin' him. Hell, they were doin' everything in their power to help me out.

"Mr. Ford only wanted to do one thing and that was to make good pictures, and to do this he would do anything, anything."

Wayne cited another example of a director facing a similar situation but solving it with different tactics. The director was William Wellman. The film was *The High and the Mighty* (1954). Duke played the pilot of a transpacific airliner which encounters serious problems en route to San Francisco. Almost all the action took place on board the plane. Including passengers and crew, there were twenty-two persons on board.

Just as in *Stagecoach,* the lives of diverse persons, accidentally thrown together in a vehicle, intersect in a situation of great danger. Besides Wayne, the cast included such veterans as Claire Trevor, Sidney Blackmer, Jan Sterling, Robert Newton, Paul Kelly, Paul Fix, and Laraine Day.

More experienced by then in the complications of a film of this nature, Wayne wondered how Wellman would integrate the large cast, many with long careers and all with great egos, not to mention his own. And how would

he get them to surrender themselves to the film? And
there were also several neophytes in the cast, including
Karen Sharpe and John Smith, who played a honeymoon
couple.

Perhaps John Ford would have set the newcomers
against one another—or against the old-timers. But Wellman did it another way.

"He did a smart thing," Wayne told me, shortly after
he'd finished *The High and the Mighty*. "The first scene he
shot was with these two inexperienced kids. So everybody
on the set was pullin' for them. Smart, huh? We all wanted
them to look good. Without makin' any speeches, or givin'
us orders, Bill Wellman, with one scene, made us work
together as a group, gave us this *esprit de corps*."

Ford's direction of a movie sometimes took on the
quality of a movie itself. He arrived late on the set. He
arrived in a chauffeur-driven limousine. Danny Borzage,
an accordionist who was long a part of his entourage,
would play "Bringing in the Sheaves" as he alighted. A
flunky brought him a mug of hot coffee. He preened his
feathers and strutted onto the scene as if he were General
Douglas MacArthur reviewing the troops. At once he began laying about him, distributing insults and diatribes,
setting one person against another, always looming as the
most important figure on the scene, no matter how many
stars and superstars were there.

An actor who worked for him in *The Horse Soldiers*
on location in Louisiana watched this morning ritual with
increasing disgust. He concluded that John Ford was not
only an egomaniac, which he knew every good movie
director was, but also a pompous ass.

And yet Ford's peculiar militarism, his strange exercises and rituals, the lackeys dancing attendance on him,
the musician playing his favorite songs—these were not
intended to flaunt his importance. In point of fact, Ford
was a most modest man, who eschewed personal publicity
all his life. His ego was satisfied to feed on the works of
his genius.

No, the rituals had another purpose. They made his

presence on the set significant. They made the day's work
meaningful to the cast and the technical crew. His solem-
nity, his strutting, his gibes and put-downs were all part
of the romance of his own assertion of complete control
of, and total involvement in, the film.

And he understood an actor's soul. He knew the peril
of ennui that awaits the actor on a set—the debilitating
effect of those lengthy periods of preparation between
takes, of just sitting around and waiting, and so he shouted
at them and stirred up their emotions and got them roil-
ing and moiling inside and outside and, by God, nobody
was bored on the set of a Ford movie, something was
happening all the time. You looked forward to it when
you were called to work on a new Ford movie. When
you finished one, you looked forward to the next one.

He always had music to entertain the company between takes. Borzage, always, and sometimes other musicians to make up a trio or quartet. He remembered how
music had been played on the set during the making of
silent pictures—to get performers in the right mood, to
keep them emotionally occupied. And he knew the importance of not letting them drift into this emotional
inertia.

What he succeeded in doing was to make manifest to
everybody on the set his own sense of heightened crafts-
manship. They could see only a part, sometimes a part
of a part, while he could see the great whole which would
finally be printed on 35 mm. strips of acetate film.

"There has never been enough credit given to Mr.
Ford as to how far he'd go to make an actor feel comfortable," Duke was saying recently. "Like havin' Danny
play accordion music, so we wouldn't get bored. Oh,
sometimes Ford will get you so mad. He has gotten me
so goddam mad so many times but I love him. He knows
what he's doin'. But there's one thing that's galled me
over the years, which is him takin' credit for discoverin'
Monument Valley. He's made plenty of good pictures
there, including a few with me, *Fort Apache, Yellow Ribbon, Wagon Master*. So it got to be that people saw that

dry bed and those two buttes, and they knew it was Monument Valley and how *Stagecoach* was the first movie made there and what a genius John Ford was to have found it.

"Now I'll tell you something. It's a secret I've kept for many years. I was the guy who found Monument Valley. And I told Ford about this place.

"I'll tell you how it happened. It was back in '29, and I was proppin' and stuntin' on a George O'Brien location, out in Arizona. One Sunday, I wanted to get away by myself. I took a car and went drivin'. I went out on this Navajo reservation. It was comin' on sunset. Then I came to this valley. I parked the car and got out and looked at it and, well, you know how it looks, and that evening it looked, well, kind of like it was another world. I said to myself this would be a fine location for a western because the cloud formations were fantastic in this area. Those two buttes—I guess they're over a thousand feet high—sure would frame a composition.

"I never forgot about it, and when Mr. Ford was talkin' about locations on *Stagecoach* I told him about Monument Valley and he looked at me as if I was stupid because he thought he knew the Arizona and Utah country and he never heard of the valley. I was with him on a party when he was scoutin' locations in Arizona. I remember Pardner Jones was ridin' with us. Jones was very close to Mr. Ford. He gave him advice on period details, as he had been a deputy sheriff during the days of Billy the Kid. He had known most of the famous outlaws. He was a great character.

"Well, we were drivin' along and finally came to this reservation and went down the road and came to the valley and then Mr. Ford pretended to see the buttes and said, 'I have just found the location we are going to use.'

"It was Monument Valley.

"And the old buzzard looked me straight in the eye. I said nothing. He wanted to be the one who found it. I don't know why he never wanted to give me credit for tellin' him about Monument Valley."

After the first weeks of shooting, Ford ceased tormenting John Wayne, and addressed himself to mocking the other members of the cast. Toward the closing days of shooting, he realized he had not yet made a monkey out of Andy Devine (who was playing the driver of the coach) and it was also time to give Duke a fresh comeuppance. So, one day he again invited Duke to look at the rushes with him and asked him what he thought of Devine's performance. Duke said, well, the way he held the reins, he held them too loosely. He should put a spring-arm exerciser on the reins to make them tight and this would make Devine pull harder. Would Mr. Ford like him to tell a prop man to install one of these on the stagecoach reins? He had often used this device in westerns, he had, and could vouch for its viability.

"Hold it, Duke," Ford said, "I want everybody to hear this."

He got everybody to stop working, and when they were all collected around him—even the wardrobe workers and grips and electricians—Ford said loudly, "I want you all to know that our new star, John Wayne, thinks the picture's great, that we're all doing a hell of a job—but he can't stand Devine's performance."

Wayne stood there embarrassed. He did not say a word. If he defended himself, he would only dig a deeper hole. But Devine knew the game being played. He winked at Duke. It was all right. Both of them believed that it was far better to be the victim of Mr. Ford's strange pranks than to be ignored by him. He wouldn't harass if he didn't like you. Whom the Ford loveth, he chastiseth, for it kept an actor and actress on their toes.

Wayne was always on his toes when he was working for Ford. It began with *Stagecoach*. He lived in a small cabin with Yak Canutt on Harry Goulding's Indian Trading Post, which was then a poor and primitive outpost. Today it is an up-to-date village, with a luxurious motel, shops, and fine restaurants.

Each night, Duke rehearsed his lines and thought over his bits of action and practiced walking back and forth across the room, using Canutt as a sounding board. He came to the set prepared, knowing his dialogue, prefiguring his body movements, and this freed him to release his emotions. It is a practice he follows to this day.

In the magazine story, Malpais Bill is one of the original passengers who boards the stage in Tonto. In the movie, he is now called the Ringo Kid and he appears on the outskirts of Tonto, when the stage is already full, halting it. He carries his bedroll and his rifle. Andy Devine shouts to George Bancroft, who is a marshal riding shotgun, "Hey—it's the Ringo Kid."

The stage stops. Wayne delivers a long expository speech about the fires he has seen, the fires set by Indians on the warpath. Geronimo has broken out of the reservation, and is burning and raping. He speaks simply and almost prosaically with a sure mastery of exposition, this mastery which he says he learned in the B westerns. He speaks a long block speech and, replying to the marshal, who wants to arrest him and handcuff him:

"You may need me—and this Winchester!"

But he's broken out of jail and is wanted. He is put under arrest and placed in the coach with the passengers. They regard the manacled cowboy with some trepidation.

The man at thirty-one has finally found his destiny, and his destiny has found him. He is a lone gunfighter with a Winchester rifle and he is going to Lordsburg to seek revenge, to kill the brothers who have murdered his father and brother.

With this entrance he entered our imaginations and was to remain there more than a quarter of a century. He also demonstrated his sensitiveness in a delicate scene with Claire Trevor, in the moonlight during the stop at Rosales, when he asks about her family and she says she lost her parents in an Indian massacre on Superstition Mountain. He has looked at her since he got on the stage in a special way. She has been gratified by his politeness and attentions—though to the other men she is just a common whore. And he says:

"You got no folks. Neither have I. I got a ranch across the border, there's a river and trees. A man could live there and a woman. Will you go?"

How beautiful in its Biblical simplicity; how powerfully rendered by Wayne; how subtly counterpointed by Miss Trevor's tremulous animality under which her scarred soft femininity comes alive again.

Wayne was never to forget the style of this screenplay, the laconic shorthand of the emotions which Nichols, working with Ford, used in such scenes. Duke would hereinafter always want dialogue written for him that was simple, direct, without rhetoric and verbal decorations, lines that revealed his character, opened up his emotions, and advanced the story. He became convinced, subsequently, that nobody could write for him as well as James Edward Grant.

*Stagecoach* was previewed at the Fox Westwood Theater, Los Angeles, on February 2, 1939. Duke invited several executives from Republic to see it. They were not impressed.

"Duke," Sol Siegel told him, "you better realize that when it comes to making westerns—you should leave it to us at Republic Pictures."

At this preview there was distributed an elaborately gotten up souvenir program illustrated with drawings and woodcuts. It was about the making of *Stagecoach*. It had been sent out to thousands of movie critics, movie reporters, and newspapermen. Producer Walter Wanger fancied himself an artistic producer, another Sam Goldwyn, and he liked to swathe his pictures in evening clothes. Unfortunately the text gave Wanger credit he did not deserve. He was alleged to have discovered the Haycox story, discovered John Wayne, hired John Ford, conceived just about everything in *Stagecoach*.

Ford scrutinized this bizarre concoction before it was distributed. He was so perturbed that he threatened to take Wanger and Lynn Farnol, advertising and publicity director of United Artists, to court if they did not rescind these imaginary claims.

So Wanger wrote a letter addressed to Farnol, which was reproduced and inserted in every copy of the souvenir brochure.

Dear Lynn:

I think the book on *Stagecoach* is interesting and attractive. It fails, however, to indicate the full measure of credit that is due John Ford for his part in the making of the picture.

I read the story—but after Ford had purchased it and brought it to me. Again, it was Ford who worked with Dudley Nichols in creating a fine script; and John Wayne as the Ringo Kid was also Ford's idea.

While I am proud to be the producer of *Stagecoach,* will you please do everything in your power to see that the picture is known as John Ford's achievement.

Sincerely,
Walter Wanger (signed)

Yet a few weeks later, on his way to Hanover, New Hampshire, where they were starting work on his production *Winter Carnival* (that ill-fated movie in which F. Scott Fitzgerald, collaborating on the screenplay with the young Budd Schulberg, went on a monumental drunk, which Schulberg later fictionalized in his novel *The Disinherited*), Wanger was interviewed by Regina Crewe of the New York *Journal-American.* He boasted of his discovery of John Wayne.

"The leading man is not some matinee idol all too familiar to the nation's screens," he said, "but John Wayne, whom I recruited from western and program pictures."

Wayne's performance in *Stagecoach,* sensitive and graceful and powerful though it is, did not win him any extravagant accolades. The reviews, even the favorable ones, even the enthusiastic ones, showed little awareness of both the movie's grandeur and, in particular, Wayne's achievement.

He was already making his work look too easy.

Frank S. Nugent opened his review in the New York *Times,* March 3, 1939, with a roll of the kettle drum: "In one superbly expansive gesture . . . John Ford has swept aside ten years of artifice and talkie compromise and has made a motion picture that sings a song of camera."

But from here the notice became restless, qualifying and compromising the original encomium. You see, one simply was not comfortable admiring a western film as a work of cinema perfection. Nugent went on to praise the pictorial splendors of the film. But it was not a subtle film, as Mr. Ford was "not one of your subtle directors." The characters lacked shading, it seems, and the narrative was straightforward. The characters are "stereotyped." And yet he certainly has to say that the cast Mr. Ford has assembled "have taken easily to their chores." He doesn't single out John Wayne, choosing only Donald Meek for special attention. Howard Barnes, in the New York *Herald Tribune,* patted Wayne on the head, saying he was "fine as the outlaw who shoots it out with three enemies in Lordsburg as an anticlimax to the action."

The only review I have found which saw some of John Wayne's greatness was by the British critic C. A. Lejeune, who described him as a great film actor with a haunting face that she said she would long remember.

The most unappreciative notice was in *The New Yorker,* written by John McCarten. It had a devastating effect on Wayne, because *The New Yorker* was a magazine he enjoyed reading.

Wrote McCarten in the issue of March 4, 1939:

The movies I've seen lately suggest that kind of party you get caught in out in the country, where you have to be thankful there is at least some scenery. It's the landscape that saves your life. For the sake of the view, you forgive all. In *Stagecoach* the view is certainly something, and it hardly matters at all what goes on. The credit for the valuable things in this film unquestionably belongs to the cameramen, the Messrs. Glennon and Binger, both of whom, I discover, were involved in the making of *The Hurricane,* which had its pictorial moments, you may remember, and to a Mr. Ned Scott, evidently a stranger without any recorded history, who is held responsible for the "still photography." Being an old-fashioned "western" with a story of Arizona and New Mexico, *Stagecoach* at least provides an opportunity for the camera experts to focus on handsome mountains, deserts, valleys, streams and beautiful horizons. Toward the end, for a big climax, John Ford has directed an Indian battle—arrows flying straight into the coach and missing heroes and heroines by mere inches—which must have forced the cameramen, except Mr. Scott, I assume, to whisk about with their implements. The narrative follows all the classic rules of "westerns," including the inevitable expectant mother, always present on these difficult journeys, whose great experience complicates the general scuffle and harasses the valiant. The actors and actresses are mostly familiar persons, like Claire Trevor, and some geniune Apaches, so we are told, have bolted out of the reservation to contribute their little bit toward the progress of art.

And that was the full and complete review of one of the classic American films in America's most sophisticated magazine. The patronizing tone epitomizes the snobbish attitude toward western movies common at that time.

Wayne read this notice with horror. It was the birth of his conviction that the Eastern cultural establishment was against him and his kind of acting and kind of film. Long before he incurred resentment because of his political conservatism and anti-Communist positions, he felt he was being unfairly criticized by the New York mandarins.

Well, he was taken for granted or ridiculed, yes, but not out of any effete snobbish conspiracy. Given the cultural attitudes of that period, he was doing the kind of work that did not fit the then current definitions of movie acting. Even so, it is hard to understand how Mr. McCarten's senses could have been so oblivious to the poetry of the love between Claire Trevor and John Wayne and the originality of the entire film, in concept and writing and execution, and in the gallery of superb characterizations by nine actors. His limited knowledge of moviemaking reveals itself in the reference to a still photographer, a man who takes pictures on a location for the purposes of publicity and advertising. Of course, cinematographers and their camera operators do not conceal themselves inside stagecoaches and dodge arrows.

As for "the inevitable expectant mother, always present on these difficult journeys," I have seen more than my share of westerns, good ones and bad ones, and the pregnant lady is neither inevitable nor omnipresent. One is forced to surmise that the critic went out of his way to destroy with malice what he could not comprehend with love.

And yet I must not condemn him out of hand, for he was expressing the conventional attitude of his time. Twenty-five years later, it was possible to write, as did Bob Thomas in a profile of Yakima Canutt, "The *Stagecoach* stunts, unsurpassed in the current remake, had the beauty and precision of a ballet filled with danger." What a perfect metaphor! Yes, Canutt and Wayne were like dancers, executing their movements—in and out of the stage, leaping from coach to horses, from horse to horse, falling, rising—with rhythm and elegance.

John Wayne would probably kill you if you said he had been Rudolf Nureyev to John Ford's Balanchine. What he did in *Stagecoach,* and in so many subsequent films, was an expression of bodily strength and grace—a dancer's, a bullfighter's, a prizefighter's—for he was mastering his muscles and his limbs and converting his emotions into physical movements of much naturalness and exquisite truth. But he was generally part of a film entity, and his naturalistic style of acting rarely called attention to its technique, for the technical achievements were not a combination of tricks but came out of the very heart and soul of the man, and so in that period it was not looked upon as "acting."

That year—1939—was alive with an enormous number of magnificent films and magnificent performances. Wayne wasn't nominated for an Oscar. John Ford was, and so was the picture, but it did not win. The only western that ever did was *Cimarron* (1931), directed by Wesley Ruggles, with Richard Dix and Irene Dunne. Peter Bogdanovich wrote in 1972, ". . . I saw it [*The Big Trail*] recently at the same time as I ran two critically acclaimed Oscar winners of similar vintage, *In Old Arizona* and *Cimarron,* and the Walsh-Wayne film is infinitely superior."*

The 1939 nominees for Best Picture included *The Wizard of Oz, Dark Victory,* the Laurence Olivier *Wuthering Heights, Ninotchka, Of Mice and Men,* and *Mr. Smith Goes to Washington.* But it was the year of *Gone With the Wind,* which swept all the major awards. However, Thomas Mitchell won Best Supporting Actor with his rendition of the alcoholic Doc Boone in *Stagecoach,* and the four composers and arrangers of the score also received an award.

What an *annus mirabilis* that was, for among the films that were *not* nominated there were Marlene Dietrich's *Destry Rides Again,* Carole Lombard's *Made for Each Other,* Cary Grant's *Only Angels Have Wings,* Charles Laughton's *Jamaica Inn,* Cagney and Bogart in *The Roaring Twenties.* And there were so many more.

Wayne had to outwit Republic Pictures to get permission to appear in *Stagecoach.* Wanger had objected to casting Wayne as the Ringo Kid. Ford made a clandestine screen test to persuade Wanger. Wanger invited Charles K. Feldman, who was one of the leading agents of the period, to see if he could represent Wayne and get him out of his Republic contract, which had four more years to run. Feldman's problem was that Wayne already had an agent—Leo Morrison. Feldman, who was also a playboy, had heard along the bacchanalian grapevine that Leo Morrison was "Tap City" (he was broke) as a result of some fast women and slow horses, to quote the old gag.

Al Kingston, who was still rooting for Duke, though he was now a literary agent, being part of the T. N. Swan-

---

* *In Old Arizona* was nominated but did not win the Oscar in the 1928-29 period; *The Broadway Melody* was the winner. Warner Baxter received the award as the best actor.

son Agency, told Feldman that he thought twenty-five thousand would buy Duke's contract.

Feldman bought Duke's contract. Now, for the first time, Wayne had one of the shrewdest agents in his corner. Charlie Feldman, under his mask of geniality and epicureanism, was a hard bargainer. He swung a big club in Hollywood, for he represented a glittering roster of stars and directors and screenwriters.

Feldman entered into negotiations with Yates. He told him the old contract was unfair and that it had to be changed. He said he, Feldman, was soon going to get a hundred and fifty thousand a picture for Wayne. Yates leered at the thought of such lustful sums of money. But —if Yates would be smart and give his permission in writing for Wayne to make *Stagecoach* for United Artists and also to have the right to make pictures for other studios—why then Republic could have John Wayne's services at the same old measly salary. Yates could not resist such a bargain. He changed the contract. Though Wayne had to work for Republic for many years, the quality of his pictures improved.

John Ford had taken him by the hand and led him out of the treadmill of Poverty Row.

# 13

## Ladies, Leading and Misleading

Duke had won his spurs as a star in a western. But he did not wear them during most of the pictures he made in the following years. He made eleven films in the three years after *Stagecoach*. All of them were A pictures. Four were westerns. In the other seven, Wayne played a sailor, a navy lieutenant, a farmer, a gambler, a sea captain, a gold miner, and a lawyer. In *Lady from Louisiana* he is a young reform lawyer fighting a crooked lottery in New Orleans; he falls in love with Ona Munson, whose father operates the crooked lottery. In *Wheel of Fortune,* he is a small-town attorney who comes to New York to investigate a murder and the trail leads to racketeers and a political boss who protects them; he falls in love with the statuesque Frances Dee, whose father, by one of those unfortunate coincidences Duke seemed to run into whenever he played an attorney, was none other than the corrupt political boss.

In both cases, it made his courtship unusually complicated but he won the hearts of both women. Mary Morrison Preen, Duke's mother, who had always dreamed that her son would be a lawyer, was delighted with his performances. She was one of the few persons who had a high opinion of these films.

In a mood of bitterness once, Wayne expressed some resentment over these hard-working and seemingly purposeless years.

"Well, you see," he said to me, "you have to look at my career as a long fight to get to the top—almost by my own bootstraps. Because I never had a studio behind me. I don't call Republic a studio and anyways Herbert Yates, a nice guy, but he didn't know shit about good pictures or bad pictures. I never had a studio executive like Thalberg or Zanuck who would build me up. Look for good stories for me. Find directors. Develop me. Publicize me. Yeah, sure, I did have one good break. John Ford loved me. Best director in the business was on my side and he was loyal to me. He put me in *Stagecoach* in a beautiful part and later he gave me other good parts so he showed other producers and the major studios my potential, see, and so I got other jobs."

His first non-Republic film was for RKO in 1940: *Allegheny Uprising,* a banal historical film laid in pre-Revolutionary America. Wayne played a Daniel Boone frontiersman and Claire Trevor was teamed with him again. It was a rabidly anti-Indian film. The redskins go about scalping settlers in western Pennsylvania and stealing children and women. The whites call them "barbarians," "heathens," and "murderers." The romance (in the film, that is) between Miss Trevor and Duke was a lively one, and the scenes they played together were good. The best action sequence was the one in which Wayne and a group of settlers disguise themselves as Indians and paddle up the river to attack an Indian tribe. Miss Trevor also goes on the expedition, putting on male clothes.

There were rumors around town that the Trevor-Wayne relationship lingered after the day's work was done. She was then a beautiful, lively, and witty woman. She still is. They laughed when they were together and enjoyed each other's company.

Both Duke and Josie now resigned themselves to the tragedy of the broken marriage. It was beyond repair. He hardly slept in the North Highland home now. He stayed either at one of his athletic clubs, with friends, or at the Hollywood-Knickerbocker Hotel.

*Allegheny Uprising* demonstrated Wayne's importance. Pandro Berman, RKO executive producer, treated him with respect. He was given a top-level director (William Seiter), and a fine supporting cast that included George Sanders, Brian Donlevy, and Wilfred Lawson. His first Republic picture under the new deal was Raoul Walsh's *Dark Command.* Claire Trevor was again the co-star. Yakima Canutt created some incredible stunts. And Walter Pidgeon and Roy Rogers were featured players.

Walsh was delighted with the progress of his protégé. Wayne now had poise and competence. In the decade since *The Big Trail,* Duke had learned to talk and to walk. He now looked as real in a long dialogue, in a romantic scene played on an interior set, in an expository monologue as he did riding hell-for-leather, his guns blazing.

His performance was praised in the New York *Times* by reviewer Thomas M. Pryor as one of "conviction and casual assurance."

Republic spent what for it was a handsome budget— almost two hundred thousand. The movie was a success.

Just before the release of *Dark Command,* Yates phoned Duke and said that Cecil B. De Mille had asked for a print to screen privately. He was interested in Wayne's performance. Yates was palpitating with pleasure, for he suspected that De Mille would put John Wayne into one of his epics and it would further enhance Wayne's money-making powers for Republic Pictures.

"No, Herb," Wayne said, to Yates' surprise. "I don't want you to send him a print. You just tell him if he wants to see *Dark Command,* you'll set up a screening for him on the Republic lot. Yeah—that's what I said. Otherwise, let him just wait until it's released and see it with the common people."

Duke got "a little kick to be able to refuse De Mille."

He never forgot an injury. He never forgave an injury. And just as surely he never forgot a kindness done to him.

De Mille saw *Dark Command* in a Republic projection room. He was enthralled by Wayne's screen presence. Wayne was the man he wanted for a new picture he was casting, *Reap the Wild Wind,* based on a best-selling romantic novel about ship salvagers in the Caribbean before the Civil War.

De Mille sent over to Wayne a screenplay with a letter expressing his admiration for Wayne's acting.

Wayne was not impressed. He had not forgiven De Mille for the brush-off several years before.

But just saying "no" to De Mille through Feldman would not slake Duke's thirst for revenge. Instead he sent the Master "seventeen pages of suggestions for changin' the script, as I told him the way it read, I'd be put second to Ray Milland, who was a Paramount star under contract. I figured that would just about wash it up.

"Well, I sure was surprised when he phoned me. He was damn polite and flatterin' and said he had to see me. He said he needed me. Well, I have to admit it kind of won me over. But I was still against workin' for him. Well, this time when I went over to see him, his secretary showed me right in, and he came out from his desk and walked up to meet me halfway. He had an office, well it was big, seemed like you had to walk and walk from the door to his desk."

De Mille looked up at Wayne thoughtfully. Then he said, smiling, "I read your letter, sir. It had much worth in it. But if we are to work together you must trust me."

Duke said, softly, that much as he respected De Mille, he had no desire to work for De Mille.

"Under no circumstances?"

"Well," Wayne said, "I might consider it. But I'd have to be protected. I know Paramount will protect Ray Milland. I don't want to wind up doing a supportin' role."

De Mille looked him square in the eye. He put out his hand. Wayne took his hand.

"I want you for this film, John," C.B. said. "I want you very much. I give you my word of honor that I will do you justice. You know that I was fair to Preston Foster in *Northwest Mounted Police* even though Gary Cooper is a Paramount star."

That seemed reasonable, but Duke could not resist another cut. "Mr. De Mille," he said, "I've heard how you bawl people out. I don't want to get a bawlin' out from you."

De Mille didn't smile. He said softly, "John, I never bawl anybody out that does not deserve to be bawled out. I am fair. Well, John, if you want the job—you have got it."

So he got it. De Mille did not have any trouble with Wayne. Wayne remembers the experience as one of the pleasantest in his career. He was treated with respect, and even deference, by De Mille. One incident was especially gratifying. A group of exhibitors was touring the lot and visited De Mille's set. He was shooting a scene in which a gang of salvagers boards a ship and gets into a fight with the crew. The actors fought awkwardly. De Mille glanced at the exhibitors. Then, making sure he had their full attention, he put his megaphone to his lips, and called out:

"John, I want you to show them how to play this scene."

John went on the mock-up of a ship's deck. He demonstrated how he threw punches and how he received them. He placed each man in the group in a certain place. He quickly choreographed a series of interweaving movements to create the illusion of a wild brawl.

Then De Mille called for action and sound.

John Wayne was the hero of the theater owners at the banquet which Paramount laid on afterwards. He knew it was the director's way of making amends for his seeming cruelty to Wayne before.

*Reap the Wild Wind* was the only film he ever made with De Mille. He wishes he had made more. He thought De Mille was "the best showman" in the film business. He admired De Mille's adroitness in handling mob scenes, which he thought was as good as and sometimes better that D. W. Griffith's manipulation of mobs. "Well, C.B. could give a large group a personality of its own. In spectacle, he was outstanding. Because De Mille put me in to star in this picture, I had no trouble holdin' up my head in Hollywood, even though Republic was still tryin' to mess me up with their rotten pictures. You see, Republic just couldn't make good pictures, except once in a while by sheer accident."

God knows, Republic, prodded by Charlie Feldman, wanted to make good pictures with Wayne. *Three Faces West* (1940) cost over a hundred thousand. The superior script was by F. Hugh Herbert, Samuel Ornitz, and Joseph Moncure March, all top-flight movie writers. It was a serious film about a migration to Oregon of dust-bowl farmers during the Depression of the 1930's. John Wayne played a Middle Western farmer who leads the trek to the Northwest. Charles Coburn impersonated a German refugee doctor. He had a daughter. She was done by the voluptuous Sigrid Gurie.

Like every woman into whose ken he swam, Miss Gurie was charmed by John Wayne's politeness and shyness. Most women found these good-boy qualities to be amorously irresistible because they emanated from a powerful hulk of a man. Miss Gurie fell in love with him, or as much in love as an actress ever falls in love with a leading man. Where does the make-believe end and the real thing begin? Or where does reality blend into the role? She was a strong person and made all the overtures to Duke. This was helpful because he was still quite awkward about romance. He was flattered by her attentions and they got along very well, though the actual depth of the liaison remains unknown.

But it was Duke's first intimate knowledge of the European female, specifically the erotically liberated Scandinavian woman.

Wayne has always married the same physical type—the small, delicate, dark Latin-American woman. During the 1940's, he broadened his interests to include Swedes, Danes, Germans, and Czechoslovakians. He had a not uncommon inhibition about dating American girls. He has been a hundred percent American patriot in everything except sex. Wayne felt more comfortable when he was flirting, or engaging in erotic love-play, with a foreign lady. The reason is that Wayne was never able to overcome his early conditioning as to the depravity of masculine lust. Consequently, he might be making small talk with a charming woman while sharing an intimate dinner with her. Meanwhile his brain was teeming with copulatory fantasies. Some men, like Duke, feel guilty about the disparity between their social conversation and their head-trips. When he was with a foreigner, though, he was safe. She could not suspect his fantasies because he was thinking in English and it wasn't her language. This is irrational, of course, but that is how it is with American men—and also Frenchmen and Italians and Russians with their countrywomen—and certainly that is how it was with Duke.

Now in the case of Sigrid Gurie and her successors, we have also to consider that the sort of human being who seeks a film career and risks all by traveling six thousand miles to a strange land is likely to be self-willed, self-confident, and able to take the romantic lead overtly. In the 1940's Wayne, alas, was still a tongue-tied blushing adolescent from Glendale when he found himself in a situation of physical intimacy with a woman. By that time he was thirty-three years old, but he never had the inclinations, the nature, and the development that make a man into a good womanizer—though often these are precisely the men who worship and adore women the most. But they care too much. The intensity of their feelings often provokes a paralysis of their bodies. So it was with Marion Michael Morrison, who was becoming John Wayne in everything but affairs of the heart and genitals.

Those attitudes which had been drilled into him by Iowa, and reinforced by Glendale, could only be anesthetized by alcohol, and fortunately Wayne's virility was not adversely influenced by even huge amounts of it.

His next Scandinavian experience was with the Danish actress, Osa Massen. She was not one of his leading ladies. He came to know her when John Ford cast him to play Ole Olson, the young Swedish sailor, in a beautiful film based on four Eugene O'Neill one-act plays, called *The Long Voyage Home*. Olson is a shy awkward fellow, torn between a desire to go back to his family's farm in Sweden and the lure of the sea. His shipmates plan to help him go back. They make him hold on to his money and buy a ticket, which is sewn into his coat. In a seamy Liverpool saloon, Olson is tricked by a waterfront whore, given knockout drops, shanghaied, rescued by his friends and sent home.

It was a variation of the *Stagecoach* structure, a mixed group brought together in the frame of a transportation device. The suspense is twofold—will Olson get home this time, and will the S.S. *Glencairn* make it with her cargo of munitions or will she be torpedoed by submarines? It was cast with Ford's sense of extreme, but universal, specimens of our race. Ward Bond, Thomas Mitchell, Mildred Natwick, Jack Pennick, and John Qualen gave deeply moving and simple performances. Though one thinks of John Ford and John Wayne as persons of the land, of the wide desert spaces, and they are, they are also haunted by the sea, as Eugene O'Neill was haunted by it. Mitchell played as effective a drunk in this film as he had in *Stagecoach*.

And yet, surely, it is less complicated to portray a pica-

resque and whimsical boozer than it is to play the simple
Olson.

Duke had to speak lines with a Swedish accent. This
posed a problem for Wayne. He was afraid audiences
would laugh at him if he spoke with an accent. He remembered how El Brendel, a low-comedy actor who
worked with a Swedish accent and made many Fox films,
had been a discordant note in *The Big Trail*.

"I figured they always connect a Swede accent with low
comedy," Duke once explained.

Yet the role called for it. Ford insisted on it. One did
not argue with Ford in such matters. Sure that movie
audiences would jeer, Wayne told his agent that he was
going to "sink like the freighter that's torpedoed." (The
S.S. *Aminta* got torpedoed in the movie.) Feldman's
solution was rather brilliant, if typical of this man-about-
town. He proposed that Wayne make friends with a
Swedish actress and he would get suggestions in accenting
his lines without coming out funny. Feldman stated that
he had learned the rudiments of Italian and French by
means of Italian and French mistresses. To combine lin-
guistics and love, he explained, was one of the best ways
to pick up a foreign language.

And he had just the girl in mind. Osa Massen. Well,
she was Danish, but Danish, Swedish, it's the same accent.
She was a client. She was an intelligent and good-looking
girl and all Duke was to do was take her out dining and
drinking and he was sure, especially after he, Feldman,
explained the problem to Miss Massen, she would be
cooperative. It was not every young actress who had a
chance to assist a star in a linguistic problem.

It is significant that Wayne was thinking about the
nuances of the role many days before he faced the camera.
He gradually became more and more adept at laying a
foundation of his character's speech and emotions and
thoughts, and then mastering the most important trick
of all—retaining his emotions during the long day's work
so that no matter how many takes were required, no
matter how many interruptions, he would be able to

summon up at once the emotion of the part of the sequence being shot.

His accent in *The Long Voyage Home* is a soft slight distortion of English. Wayne played the young man suffused in a halo of adolescence and, in fact, to adopt the Stanislavskian phrase, he "used" his uneasiness about the Swedish accent and converted it into the character's awkwardness about life. The scene with Mildred Natwick was sentimental in the best sense of the word, in the exquisite delicacy with which John Ford expressed feelings of tenderness.

But Wayne had to suffer the penalty of being taken for granted. Howard Barnes remarked that "his [Wayne's] casual and drawling style is nicely adapted to the part." He made his often difficult achievements seem so natural that one was not impressed by their difficulty.

Miss Massen had done her work well. They studied the dialect on many afternoons before shooting began. He read his lines over and over and she corrected his pronunciation until he got it right—or rather, wrong. Whether, like Paolo and Francesca, there came occasions when they "read no more in the script that day," I do not know. But a real fellowship arose between them. He was beginning to enjoy a woman as company, as a friend. It was an experience he was able to have only with a European woman at this period of his life.

*Long Voyage Home* was received with great pleasure by the critics, though it was a box-office failure. It is one of the loveliest-looking films Ford ever put his hand to. Wayne recently told me, "Usually, it would be Mr. Ford who helped the cinematographer get his compositions for maximum effect—bring out what was good in any setup— help him light it—but in this case it was Gregg Toland who helped Mr. Ford. *Long Voyage* is about as beautifully photographed a movie as there ever has been."

In *The New Yorker,* John Mosher called it "one of the most magnificent films in film history."

It was Eugene O'Neill's favorite movie, and he owned a print of it and ran it over and over.

Duke's next European *amie* was Marlene Dietrich.

He made three pictures with La Belle Marlene: *Seven Sinners* (1940), *The Spoilers* (1942), and *Pittsburgh* (1943). As a team, they strummed a delicious counterpoint. These three films are gems of their kind. Lusty, fast, amusing, filled with action and fights and love. The stories were primitive. The characters were raw and virile. The scenes were violent and direct.

Here we can see Wayne developing methods of being himself, being Big John in every role, and still inventing unique qualities and mannerisms for each character, so he isn't the same and yet retains a continuity as do all the superstars from one movie to the next.

After a long period during which Marlene Dietrich's career had been almost ruined by Josef von Sternberg's over-delicate direction, she was revitalized in *Destry Rides Again* (1939). *Seven Sinners* followed *Destry* and in it she again portrayed a flamboyant saloon entertainer with an appreciation of men, a sense of humor, and a delight in sexual joys, drinking, and the animal pleasures of life. Her Bijou in *Seven Sinners,* her Cherry Malotte (the Klondike whore) in *The Spoilers,* and above all her Josie in *Pittsburgh* were all manifestations of Marlene herself. In Wayne she found an actor who was an animal, an animal of honor and dignity, the sort that she always played most excitingly against, rather than the weak and helpless fools with whom she had toyed in Sternberg's pictures—which is not to detract from the splendors of *Die Blaue Engel.*

How curious that Duke did not ask the writers to change her name in *Pittsburgh* to something less personal than Josie. Dietrich's Josie is a child of the coal mines, a Hunky, who is the mistress of a rich crook and is passing as a countess. She shows who she really is during a mine cave-in when she helps Duke rescue some victims. When they meet, Duke and his bosom companion, Randolph Scott, are two coal miners. She and Duke fall in love and he decides to better himself. He becomes a rich industrialist and marries a tycoon's daughter, but he always loves her. Marlene, Randolph Scott, and Duke are a triad. There were several great fights between Scott and Duke, hand-to-hand combats, in *Pittsburgh,* and of course in *The Spoilers.* (This was the fifth remake of Rex Beach's novel about Alaskan claim jumpers and what is special about this version is not the famous fight, which is awfully good, but the camaraderie between Wayne, Dietrich, and Scott.)

*Seven Sinners* also featured a magnificent fight in which Broderick Crawford and Wayne pummeled each other and in which sailors and civilians tore apart the Seven Sinners Cafe.

*Pittsburgh* is also worth regarding from another angle, aware as we are now of Wayne's fervent patriotism. He was as patriotic about the war against the Fascists and Nazis, and for this country's victory, as he was during the Korean War and the Vietnam War. *Pittsburgh* went into production a few months after Pearl Harbor, and one purpose of it was to increase war production by citing the case of a profiteer and anti-labor industrialist (Wayne) who becomes a decent human being and a friend of labor unions (as well as getting together with Marlene Dietrich) because the war opens his eyes to his selfishness.

Wayne had tried to enlist as soon as war was declared. He had been rejected because he was thirty-four years old, was married, had four children, and a defective shoulder. He attempted to enlist twice more and once he flew to Washington to plead with Ford, by now a lieutenant commander in the Navy, to help him get a post in the Navy. He failed. This was a bitter disappointment to Wayne. He had let down his father once more, and thank God, Doc Morrison wasn't around to see him.

He was able to go to the war zones many times with the USO entertainment units, but he has always been hesitant to publicize both his rejection by the services and his USO appearances.

*Pittsburgh* was an overt act of propaganda and red-blooded Americanism, though its virtues as cinema have little to do with its message, just as Eisenstein's *Potemkin* is a beautiful film but not because the director was a Marxist-Leninist at the time. Duke Wayne believed in the emotions of his character, a ruthless, self-willed upward-striver. He also believed in the patriotic message of the movie. He followed Stephen Decatur's maxim, "Our country . . . may she always be in the right—but our country, right or wrong!"

As I've said, the everyday Marlene Dietrich resembled in many ways the three women she played in these films with Wayne. And it was a kind of woman from whom Wayne was learning to experience stimulation, intellectual and emotional. She was by far the most interesting and sensual of all the European ladies of this period in his life. She was not only his counterpoint, she was also his counterpart. The two of them were alike in so many ways that their relationship became that of two old friends.

During the three years of his friendship with Marlene they became socially intimate, to such an extent that, for the first time, Mrs. Morrison (as she still called herself) became alarmed, not because she was in danger of losing her husband, for he had been lost long before, but at the scandal that might erupt. Up to now, his previous cultural exchanges with friendly European actresses had been kept discreetly private. But now she heard from her friends, and read in the columns, items about her husband and Miss Dietrich. Now this might not have signified anything carnal, because Miss Dietrich (whose husband, Rudolph Siebert, once described her as "just a regular guy") was a good friend, without being the lover, of many married men, such as Ernest Hemingway. In fact, some persons whispered that it was not in Miss Dietrich's personality to experience romance with a male. Others, on the contrary, described her as another Catherine the Great, who devoured men with an insatiable appetite.

Judged by any standards, Miss Dietrich and Wayne did not flaunt their relationship. They went out a lot in public, but then it was natural for a star to wine and dine with his leading lady, *n'est-ce pas?* And there were often others about, friends and agents and their lady friends. Speaking of *Seven Sinners,* Dietrich's biographer, Leslie Frewin, can only suggest this. "Her leading man," he writes, "was John Wayne, in whose company Marlene was often seen outside the studios during the making of the film."

The friendship never became as public as Dietrich's

liaison with Gary Cooper when she was filming *Morocco* (1930). At that time, Lupe Velez, a hot-tempered lady, who claimed Gary as *her* man, made a great outcry about Marlene Dietrich's poaching. She threatened to tear out Marlene's eyes if she didn't leave Cooper alone.

With Marlene, Duke shared many interests, especially film-making. It is much rarer to find a shared understanding with a woman in pictures than to find a capable sex partner.

She and Wayne enjoyed attending football games and prizefights. They went fishing and hunting and took long drives up north to Santa Barbara and San Luis Obispo. Like Duke, she liked simple hearty foods—steaks and broiled fish. She drank in moderation but she was a drinker. She was a man's woman and could even have been called a man's man. It is said by those close to her that she has the mind of a man, if there be such a thing as a distinctively masculine mind.

The most absorbing aspect of life to her was the movies. Her films and other films. She was involved with the technical and artistic sides of it as well as the acting. Like Wayne she had an awareness of the parts of the whole, which is unusual in an actor. "My work is my interest in life," she once said. "I have no hobbies. I have no time for anything but my work."

And this was not far from the place at which Wayne had arrived.

While the readers of Louella Parsons and Sidney Skolsky fancied, as they read the items, that John Wayne and Marlene were locked in feverish embraces, they were probably running current movies at her Beverly Hills place and critically analyzing them. This too is a form of mutual affection, perhaps more enduring and more satisfying than sex.

*The Spoilers* was shot on location in Lake Arrowhead. An actress remembers an incident when Duke "had this idea of doing a scene where Dietrich's sitting on a wheelbarrow and she told him it was a dumb idea and she wouldn't do it and later he was tying his bandanna and made a big knot and she criticized him for the size of the knot and he socked her across the face so hard she went down and clunked on the earth. He looked real sorry. She wasn't crying. She seemed to like being manhandled. She kind of made a fist and made believe she was socking him, but it was a love punch. He hugged her and they kissed. Only time I ever saw him get personal on the set, although they seemed to be partial to each other's company, but I never was one of these persons who could tell by looking if two people were in love or just being friendly, and I guess it's been one of my problems with men, including my ex-husbands."

In 1942, the contract with Republic was up for renewal. Feldman negotiated a new contract. The best part of it was that Wayne was to be paid ten percent of the gross—an almost unheard-of proposition in Hollywood then. This was in addition to a salary of a hundred thousand. Duke's share of the profits of *Wake of the Red Witch* was two hundred sixty thousand dollars and for *Sands of Iwo Jima,* three hundred eighty thousand.

During the 1940's, Wayne worked for every major studio: Paramount, Warners, RKO, M-G-M. He was shooting three and four, even five pictures a year.

He learned another chapter in his book on the varieties and diversities of Woman when he became Paulette Goddard's friend while they were filming *Reap the Wild Wind.*

But as far as the movie was concerned, the most memorable physical relationship which he had in it was with an enormous octopus whom Wayne encounters undersea when he has gone down in a diver's outfit searching for buried treasure.

Paulette Goddard, a vibrant, strong, exciting, and intellectual woman, in addition to being unusually voluptuous and extremely angelic of face, might have had a great romance with Duke. They could even have gotten married, who knows? But at this time she had a handicap she could not overcome. She was neither a European nor a Latin-American, and consequently she drifted in and out of his life as casually as had that other protégée of Chaplin's, Virginia Cherill, with whom he had flirted during the making of *Girls Demand Excitement,* twelve years before.

But the next two ladies in his life were more suitable to his amorous ideology. One was a Czechoslovakian and the other was a Mexican.

# 14

# Appointment in Acapulco

In 1941, Bö (a Swedish name pronounced *Boo*) Christian Roos became John Wayne's business manager. He strongly influenced Duke's personal and economic life. Bö Roos was one of the most intriguing behind-the-scenes personalities in Hollywood. For five percent of the gross, he managed the incomes of Merle Oberon, Red Skelton, Johnny Weissmuller, Lupe Velez, Fred MacMurray, Joan Crawford, Ray Milland, Marlene Dietrich, and others.

Miss Dietrich, dismayed at the forlorn state of Duke's finances, advised him to put his money in Roos' hands. Roos and Duke knew each other for years at the Hollywood Athletic Club. Roos was one of the founders and committee members of the club. He disapproved of the locker-room wrangles of Wayne and Ward Bond. Wayne was just the kind of reckless, extravagant movie actor whom he viewed with distaste. Now that they met on a business basis and Wayne was getting to be a big star, they got along better. Roos was not as conservative as the other business managers of that epoch. The others had sweated through the Depression; they were timorous about investing. They put their movie clients into safe bonds and government notes. Not Roos. He believed in high-risk speculations, in Wall Street and real estate. Personally he and Duke were kindred spirits. Roos liked to drink, play poker, hunt, and fish. Roos had a forty-foot cabin cruiser. He had, for several years now, been going to Mexico. He had discovered Acapulco and believed in its future as a tourist resort. Mexico reeked with investment opportunities.

Roos expatiated on his business theories at their first meeting. He explained his modus operandi. He first showed Wayne that an actor's time of prosperity was short—usually five years. He told him doleful tales of once-famous, and formerly wealthy, movie stars now living from hand-to-mouth. He said he took over total management of the money. He sold you insurance. He planned expenses and investments in relation to income tax. He had to approve of every luxury outlay. In general, he frowned upon conspicuous consumption, to which actors, made dizzy by sudden wealth, were prone. He was opposed to furs, jewelry, swimming pools, Bel-Air mansions, custom-made European sports cars, and frequent divorces. He was a stern believer in monogamy, if only because it saved a man money in the long run.

Roos himself practiced what he preached. He had been married to the same woman for twenty years. (They are still happily married after fifty years.) He told Duke that he managed about twenty-five million worth of income, and that his clients usually had about five million invested in a typical year. He told Duke about real estate syndicates, tax shelters, oil wells, cattle ranches, and expressed an enthusiasm for common stocks which he was sure would rise when the war was over.

"He showed me," Wayne explained later, "that an actor like me can gross more'n most businesses and corporations. I had tax problems like any business. And I had to bring my expenses into line with how much I made. He wanted to put me on a strict budget, somethin' ridiculous like fifty bucks a week, but I wouldn't go for that. However, I listened to him. He made a lot of sense."

They did not sign any contracts. Just a handshake and a verbal agreement. (Roos did not hold with the opinion of Sam Goldwyn, who had once remarked that a verbal contract wasn't worth the paper it was written on.)

Duke was put on a weekly budget of one hundred dollars, which is nice walking-around money. There was a budget allotted to Josie. Trust accounts were set up for each of the children. Roos and Mrs. Morrison got along swimmingly. She followed her domestic budget. But Duke couldn't follow his. He couldn't stop patronizing expensive saloons. He always insisted on picking up the checks. He was a generous human being. Money had no meaning for him as a symbol of power. He was not a grasping person. He liked to spend his money or give it away. He was a sucker for a hard-luck story. If anybody had ever done him a favor, or been decent to him when he was struggling, Duke felt forever in his debt. Roos says that in some years a million dollars would be splurged on handouts, loans, and investments in the dubious enterprises of friends to whom Wayne felt he owed a moral debt.

"It was impossible to get Duke to stay on a budget," Roos remembers. "He just couldn't say no to a guy he liked and, hell, sometimes he wouldn't tell you, wouldn't tell me, or anybody in the office he was signing a check. However, at least we"—that is, Roos' company, Beverly Management—"did get Wayne's capital invested to some extent."

Wayne got into such things as a Culver City motel, a Catalina Island yachting marina, a beach club, a fast-freeze food-processing factory, a country club, various apartment buildings, oil wells, and common stocks.

Most significantly of all, Roos turned Wayne on to Mexico, for Bö was enamored of Mexico's climate, its people, its scenic beauty, its natural resources, and its future as a developed country.

Up till Roos' advent, Wayne had only known Mexico like any average Angeleno—the border towns, Tijuana and Ensenada, just over the line from San Diego. Now he started going south on long visits. He began putting money into Mexican businesses. (At one time, he was the principal partner in a group that owned shrimp fisheries in Central America and Mexico—and imported about sixty percent of all the shrimps eaten in the States.) He became—and still is—the proprietor of Los Flamingos, a lovely resort hotel on the cliff above the beach at Acapulco. He became so devoted to the landscape of Mexico that he began shooting many of his pictures down there.

Mexico is now his second country.

Bö Roos put Wayne into many fine Mexican ventures. And among the Mexican ventures—and adventures—into which he put Duke was a certain Esperanza Baur Diaz Ceballos, or Chata, which means "pugnose" in Spanish. Esperanza (which means "hope" in English) had a deliciously *retroussé* nasal appendage and was a dark, sultry, and voluptuous beauty with a bad skin problem, but otherwise a physically beautiful specimen. She wore makeup to cover her epidermal blemishes. Her eyes were liquid and black. Her hair was silken and long and black. She laughed crazily, showing two rows of perfect ivory teeth. She had studied a little English in school and spoke it in a confused way.

Esperanza, or Chata, Baur, was a movie actress. She used her mother's maiden name professionally. Her mother was Mexican-born of German descendants.

Señorita (or Señora) Baur (for she was married at this time, though estranged from her husband, who by a peculiar coincidence was a Mexican named Morrison, a young student, Eugenio Morrison) was one of Mexico's leading movie stars. She had just completed the Hispanic version of *The Count of Monte Cristo*.

In August, 1941, Bö Roos took a galaxy of his "kids" (as he called his clients) on a business *cum* pleasure voyage to Mexico. There was Wayne and Ward Bond, Ray Milland, Fred MacMurray and Bö. Wayne needed rest. He was physically burned out, as he had just made two demanding films, one right after the other: one with Joan Blondell, *Lady for a Night,* and De Mille's *Reap the Wild Wind*, with Paulette Goddard. And he was worn out by the endless arguments with Josie.

Duke yearned for complete escape in Mexico—sun and water and tequila and doing nothing. He certainly was not looking for entangling alliances with females. He was in a very anti-social mood. He did not want to put on any company manners and public faces. He was disgusted when Bö Roos told him that the chief of the Churubusco Studios, which they were interested in purchasing, was laying on an elegant lunch at a private club in Acapulco. Grumbling, he put on a white suit and attended the affair.

Sitting next to him at the table was Esperanza Baur. She was fascinated by this tall gentleman. He was already well known in Mexico. She talked very fast in broken English, which amused him. He replied in broken Spanish, which delighted her. She knew she must not fancy any romantic hopes with this famous movie actor. She was an avid reader of *Photoplay,* perfecting both her English and her Hollywood fantasies by assiduously studying this periodical. She had read, oh, such a heartwarming article about John Wayne a few months before, about his devotion to his wife and children. She had cut out his picture. He looked so young and decent. She believed the stories published in *Photoplay.* She believed in a home and children and romantic love. She also believed in being a Hollywood star.

It was his height which most fascinated her, though.

"When I first see Duke in Mexico," Chata related to Ruth Waterbury, one of the best fan-magazine writers of the period, "where most of the men they are so short, I know it is good for me. I know that, when I, who am not so long, dance with him, his head will be above me which never happened to me before."

On the basis of their first interview, Wayne concluded, he later told a friend, that Chata was a woman "who would be satisfied with the simple things of life—a home, children, family life, a few friends." He did not think he would ever see Esperanza again, but if he ever had met the ideal woman—who combined Latin-American submissiveness to the male with the actress' passion and a dark mystery—it was this Señorita Baur. However, he put Esperanza out of his mind.

But he could not. Was it the same old obsession with Latin-American women? He once tried to analyze this obsession for Will Tusher, a veteran reporter of the Hollywood scene, who described Duke's erotic patterns for *Motion Picture Magazine:*

"I'm a guy who likes girls, all kinds of girls. No nation has a monopoly on beauty. But I consider the women of South and Central America to be unusually warm and lovely. They have a good feeling for family life—and so have I. I've always liked taking vacations in Mexico. I I work so hard when I work. But down there they lose track of time. They know how to relax. Hell—when a guy is on vacation in Mexico, he meets Mexican girls. If I took vacations in Sweden, I'd meet Swedish blondes. I happen to like brunettes. Your Latin-American women respect their husbands. They respect their marriages."

Now it is true that most women of the Latin-American culture are devoted to husbands, children, *cocina,* and church. But John Wayne already possessed one of them.

And he was unhappy.

He was quite miserable with a lady who respected her marriage vows so much she wouldn't grant him a divorce.

How to explain this contradiction? Impossible, really, for, like all of us, Wayne, in one mood, wanted a faithful and submissive spouse, and in another mood, he yearned for a mate who was voluptuous, who drank and laughed crazily, who was a wild animal. He wanted them both in the same body. He thought Esperanza was the one.

Sometimes, when Duke gets more detached about his Latin-American sex obsession, he may observe that all Latin women cannot be grouped into a single category. They are individuals. It's like saying *all* red-headed girls are hot-tempered, he once pointed out. "Actually, all three of the Latin women I've been married to have been entirely different personalities with different temperaments," he says correctly.

He succeeded in abstaining from Esperanza's company during most of the visit to Mexico. He lolled about the beach, drank margaritas, played poker, and went on trips to look over various Mexican investments, such as silver mines.

Several days before returning to Hollywood, Roos gave a formal supper party and dance for the leading people in the Mexican film industry and several political leaders, including Miguel Aleman, then a governor of a state and subsequently president of Mexico. Aleman was a good friend of Roos'. Duke simply had to go. This time it was a formal occasion in the Reforma Hotel, Mexico City.

Once again, by accident, he found himself in propinquity with Esperanza. She was wearing a white silk evening gown cut so low her breasts were displayed to the nipples. She had interesting nipples. She had deep mysterious eyes. Duke looked deep into her eyes and he became infatuated.

There was the dinner, and the wine and speeches. He wanted to be alone with her. Perhaps he should not feel this way. But he could not help it. He was in Mexico. *When a guy is on vacation in Mexico, he meets Mexican girls.*

They danced. They whispered. They strolled arm in arm in the heavily scented summer night while the orchestral rhythms sounded far away and they embraced and kissed. Wayne experienced a great passion.

And Esperanza suspected that the reporter who had written about him in *Photoplay* had not researched the subject as thoroughly as she might have done.

She said she was bored by all the speeches and toasts. She looked up at the moon and said she would rather be riding a horse in the moonlight than having to go back and listen to more speeches. Wayne liked the idea but he pointed out that they were honor-bound to return to their table.

"But," he murmured, "if we can't ride now, let's go ride tomorrow. At sunrise. Yes?"

It sounded like a marvelous idea and they went riding at dawn.

During this meeting he learned that she not only adored riding, but also swimming, fishing, hunting, and the outdoor life. She said she found night life and the social whirl a bore. Communing with nature was what she loved. She also loved a house and a garden and could a "leetle cook."

The romance of Esperanza Baur and John Wayne was

like a movie, after all, wasn't it? The rich, famous, handsome *gringo* falling head-over-heels in love with the sultry Mexican girl of twenty. He was fourteen years older than she. But they were ready to cast their fate to the winds. During the few remaining days, he was with her all the time and quite openly. They were together all night long. They were never apart. And he was even nice to her mother. Mrs. Ceballos was a handsome woman, who looked more like Esperanza's older sister than her mother. She was full of *joie de vivre*. She thought her daughter had made one hell of a good catch. Once Duke asked her, in halting Spanish, whether he wasn't too old for her daughter. She said that a man was only as old as he felt and behaved, and Señor Wayne was a young man, in her estimation, worthy of her daughter.

He screened several of her films and was surprised to find out she was a good actress with a strong presence. He decided to help her career. He told her she was a splendid actress and he would get her a Hollywood contract.

He returned to Los Angeles to discover that Josie was well informed on this latest escapade. He had flaunted Esperanza Baur as he had never previously flaunted a girlfriend. "He didn't try to hide it," Bev Barnett once confided to me, "because he was serious about Chata. Josie was up on it. There'd been some blind items in the columns and the grapevine in Hollywood knew what was going on and it got to her. She didn't like it, but she was willing to accept the situation and close her eyes to it, as she had before, for the children's sake, but it seemed like Duke was through with the marriage. He moved out and took an apartment on Doheny. He told her he wanted a separation and a divorce. She said no. She was adamant, so everything was deadlocked."

For a long time, Josie had tried to find some answer to the broken marriage from priests and from her close friends like Loretta Young. At one time, she had believed that Duke would change after he got older, but she had now given up. He was different when he got back from

Mexico. She wondered if Loretta was right—if a separation was best.

On May 2, 1943, in the Superior Court of the County of Los Angeles, Josephine Saenz Morrison asked for a legal separation, which was granted. They had been married nine years, eleven months and three days. She felt angry for a long time. For two years she did not speak to Duke or allow him into the house. When he had a day with the children, a friend came by to gather them.

She still was against divorce, however. For nineteen months more she delayed, hoping he would change his mind, love her again, return home, and everything would be the way it was when they married in 1933.

During the interregnum, Duke suffered. He was now able to identify with his father's agony during the years his parents had been quarreling. Duke had never been able to resolve the right and the wrong of it then. He had sided more with his mother. Now that he was going through a similar experience he saw his father in a new light. He began to mature emotionally because of his suffering. The maturity reflected itself in his work.

But for some time his physical appearance was against his inner growth. He was still cursed with the look of the perennial juvenile, the dashing young hero, and was to look like this even into his forties.

Yet it was to turn out that his genius was in portraying older men. He did not suspect this. Nor did his agents, nor did the studios, and not even John Ford divined this element in his art.

There are certain actors who are the poets of ripeness —for example, Michel Simon and Jean Gabin, Spencer Tracy, Humphrey Bogart, W. C. Fields, Emil Jannings. There are others born to play young men—John Garfield, Robert Donat, Robert Montgomery, Gerard Phillipe most of all. And it seemed, at first, as if John Wayne was of this type, for he had impersonated romantic raw youths in *Stagecoach* and *The Long Voyage Home,* but youth was not his forte, after all. It was to take some time until Wayne's body and face were worn through, and became the objective correlative of his emotions.

He expressed his heightened awareness of, and deep respect for, his father in two films he made around this time: *Shepherd of the Hills* (1941) and *In Old California* (1942).

*Shepherd of the Hills* is one of Wayne's less celebrated films, though it is one of his better ones. His characterization of a son who has hated his father a long time is one of Wayne's most intensely felt and expressed roles. The father was played by Harry Carey (who had been a father-figure to young Morrison, a man he had always venerated and would continue to do so until Carey died). The son (in the movie) believes that his father deserted his mother, bringing about her death. He lives a life of violence and hatred among the mountain people of the Ozarks. Comes now a strange Christ-like figure with a message of love and forgiveness, and he turns out to be the long-vanished father. Ultimately father and son come to understand and love one another. It is a gentle, sensitive film, beautifully photographed in black and white by Charles Lang and directed by Henry Hathaway, with whom Duke was to make six more films, all superior.

Making *Shepherd of the Hills* became an upsetting experience for Duke. The nightmares came back and he often woke up screaming as if he were back on the homestead in Palmdale, remembering and reexperiencing the rabbits and the rattlesnakes, the shouts and revilings of the parents, the meager rations, the boys who tormented him at school. The fear came back, the fear of being deserted by his parents, the anger at his father, the loneliness and the anxiety. He was tormented by the past—and he felt guilty about the present, being aware that his own children must now be feeling some of the agony he had felt in that time.

The use of his emotions in this picture, and Hathaway's quiet management of the story, produced extremely touching sequences as Wayne's genuine emotions flowed out.

Audiences responded to the film. It touched something deep and buried in all of us. It was popular at the time. It is frequently revived on television nowadays.

While working on this film he found himself truly forgiving his father, as he tried to forgive himself. He tried to accept rage and violence in himself as part of the order of things, as the price of being human. Many of his later roles, mingling bitterness and extreme rage with heroism and love—Tom Dunson in *Red River,* Sergeant Stryker in *Sands of Iwo Jima,* Harry Brittles in *She Wore a Yellow Ribbon*—were learned during this part of his life and come out of this film of Hathaway's, in which Duke could transfer the double emotions of being the son of his father and the father of his sons to the character he was playing, and the characters he would play in the future.

The screenplay of *In Old California* was in a group of a dozen scripts which Yates had submitted for Duke to fulfill his one-picture-a-year commitment to Republic. Duke leaped at it because the lead role was that of a pharmacist! It is the only time he fictionally tried to portray his father as a druggist. Pharmaceutical leading roles don't come up very often. And this is the only druggist Wayne ever played. He was Thomas Craig, young Boston pharmacist, who treks out to California and opens the first drugstore in Sacramento during frontier days. And of course he played Clyde L. Morrison, Doc Morrison. He idealized his portrait and he fixed him forever as the man he remembered from Winterset, Iowa, still strong, still the football player, the kindest and wisest of men, the philosopher and friend to everybody in town. The movie character was an idealistic young man—curing sickness, tending children during an epidemic, struggling against villainy, solving all problems with kindness as well as with guns.

If only the original had been around to see these two pictures. But Doc Morrison had died in 1938 of a heart attack.

# 15

# Esperanza in Hollywood

Once the separation from Mrs. Morrison became a legal fact, Duke had no compunctions about seeing other women. It had been over a year since he had fallen for Esperanza. He had not been in face-to-face contact with her since then. You could not conveniently make phone calls to Mexico in 1942. Absence did not always make his heart grow fonder. Depending on his mood, he was either hopeful of a relationship with her, or else determined to retain his freedom. He had a framed photograph of her on his desk. He thought of her often. Should he use his leverage at Republic and get her a contract so she could come to California and he could make up his mind? In one of his fantasies, he imagined her becoming another Dolores Del Rio, becoming his partner in an acting team. He now knew he liked sharing with a woman who was part of the movie business. He had enjoyed sharing his working life with the scintillating minds of Paulette Goddard and Marlene Dietrich.

In other moods, he shuddered at the idea of marrying an actress. No, she would have to give up her career and become Mrs. Wayne if they ever got married. He wanted more children. He must be the center of her life. Esperanza Wayne as his worshiper!

He would convince himself this was what he wanted even though she had bewitched him, mainly because she was a person in her own right, a woman of fire and independence.

But she was down there and he was up here. On certain

days he would hardly think of her. Ward Bond urged him to remain a bachelor. They went out on double dates. But there was a difference. Bond liked being single, while Wayne had a persistent need for a relationship with one woman. He wanted to be married again. He required the stability of marriage. He did not fancy the swinging life, though Charlie Feldman, like Bond, exhorted him to revel in sexual variety.

Bö Roos pointed out that he couldn't afford a new wife, for he had to take care of the first one and the four children.

Reasonable viewpoints did not assuage Duke's loneliness. He hungered for the companionship of his woman— the one who belonged body and soul to him. It seemed, when his mood careened into a tremulous adolescent love-sickness, that if he once possessed such a divine creature as Esperanza—well, he would be forever faithful to her.

In the second year of separation, he started writing letters. She answered. Chata confided to Ms. Waterbury that their correspondence, besides the usual lyrical references to aching hearts and lonely dreams, also delved into outdoor sports, the art of acting, and the architectural design of houses. Since Wayne, when he put himself to it, could write good letters, she was moved. She answered him in charmingly broken-English style: "We will garden build together in these little house of the mountain."

In one letter, he broached a proposal which sealed their doom. He said he had convinced Yates to give her a screen test if she came to Los Angeles. She would be signed up at Republic. She could remain in the U.S. as long as she was working. Duke expected her to fly to his arms. She had seemed so anxious for a movie career in Hollywood. Suddenly her letters became short, vague, impersonal. There were lengthy delays between his letters and her responses. She did not leap to the bait he dangled. Then her mother wrote and said she was sick. He began conjuring up visions of her as a dying Camille. He had deserted her. He had left her to die!

One night he was dining in Chasen's with a group of

people. Howard Hughes was among them. The two men had met each other at the Hollywood Athletic Club. They became acquaintances. Hughes was the kind of a tall, reckless, determined guy whom Wayne liked. Hughes admired John Wayne as an authentic movie hero. He wanted to produce movies starring John Wayne, which, one has to admit, was not exactly a novel idea in Hollywood in 1943, as there was a severe shortage of leading men.

Wayne got drunk and maudlin in Chasen's. He moaned about his love for Esperanza, her dying, his loneliness. Why was he not with the one person he loved more than anyone else including himself?

He had started a movie about the American volunteers flying against the Japanese in China, a Republic disaster, *Flying Tigers*. He and Hughes discussed aviation pictures. Then Hughes said he had a little plane lying around in Inglewood, and why the hell didn't they just go to Mexico right now? He swore he would get Duke back in time to the studio Monday morning.

"What the hell are we waiting for, *amigo?*" Duke said, and off they flew to Mexico City.

Duke and Esperanza had a thrilling reunion. Wayne did not question her though she seemed to be in good physical condition. Had she been seeing other men? Had she been on a drunk? He didn't ask any questions. He was full of bliss when he held her in his arms again. All his misgivings went away. Before he departed on Monday morning, they decided she would get a visa and come to Hollywood.

She came. She was tested.

Yates was overjoyed to test Wayne's protégée. He paid her transportation and put her up at the Beverly-Wilshire Hotel. She was given a good makeup woman, cameraman, and director. The tests were good. She signed the contract. Yates breathed a sigh of relief. He would not have to feel jealous now.

For Yates had fallen in love with a Czechoslovakian ice-skater. At age sixty-one, he had gone bonkers for the gorgeous blonde, Vera Hruba Ralston. He had made her Republic's leading woman star. She quickly won a deserved reputation as the most stiff and amateurish performer who ever starred in pictures. She had been a big skater in the 1930's, almost as famous as Sonja Henie. Equipped like Esperanza Baur with a faithful mother, she fled Czechoslovakia in 1938 and lived in England, where she tacked "Ralston" onto her name for no particular reason. She appeared in ice shows and came here as the star of a musical revue, *Ice Capades*. She didn't talk much in this show. She skated.

Herbert Yates bought the movie rights to *Ice Capades* and produced it for his studio. And he fell for her—hook, line, and skatekey. In his lover's eyes, she was not only a skater of finesse. She was also a woman with the vocal skill of Grace Moore, the acting talent of Garbo. She was one of the finest actresses who had ever graced a screen.

Yates now knew jealousy. He was jealous of any actor on the lot who said more than "good morning" and "good night" to her. He was torn by jealousy over John Wayne's polite attentions to his adored Vera Hruba (which was was they called her around Republic). Duke may have entertained ideas but he did not go beyond the mental. He did not pursue her. Yates was worried. He was forty years older than Vera Hruba Ralston.

Yates had everybody on the lot spying for him. One of his agents reported Wayne had been visiting her dressing room and helping her learn English. It was the old Harry Cohn syndrome.

So it was good news when John Wayne got this crush on a Mexican girl. Yates knew she had no talent. He figured it was the usual Hollywood routine. But Esperanza did have talent. She could have been some success in films. She did not make any films for Republic or for any other studio. Somehow, John Wayne took up all her time.

A year after Chata came to Hollywood, Josie Saenz Morrison finally made up her mind to sue for divorce. At a hearing in Los Angeles Superior Court on November 25, 1944, she appeared and told of Wayne's "repeated acts of cruel and inhuman treatment," and how he had "inflicted upon plaintiff grievous physical and mental suffering." Her testimony was supported by evidence given by a sister, Mrs. Zoraida Dickinson, and Loretta Young's mother, now remarried and known as Mrs. Gladys Royal Belzer.

Wayne did not contest the action. Mrs. Morrison was granted an interlocutory decree of divorce which would take effect a year later. At this time, Esperanza and Duke began living together under the same roof.

Through counsel, Mrs. Morrison released the following statement to the press:

"Because of my religion I regard divorce as a purely civil action in no way affecting the moral status of a marriage. I am, however reluctantly, accepting the advice of counsel, and am seeking a civil divorce from my husband. I have received permission to do this from the proper authorities of my church. It is the only means of clarifying the position of my children, whose interests are of paramount importance."

*However reluctantly.* She was now thirty-five. Sixteen years ago, she had fallen in love and never changed. The divorce was the end of one life. There was to be no other love in her future. She had looked forward to a future in which she and her husband, growing older, would share the growing up of their children, endure the tribulations of their problems and others, and finally wane into the amenities of old age, with grandchildren around them. It was for a life of holy matrimony, only ended by death, that she had gone against her parents and even her church, and waited for six years to marry Marion Michael Morrison. It was for this dream she had gotten up early in the morning, when Duke was a slave in the Poverty Row sweatshops, and made his breakfast and lived in shabby apartments and been too proud to ask her parents for money. How many mornings, struggling awake, she quietly prepared a breakfast of steak and eggs for Duke and then made him get up, hoping the children would not awaken, struggling to get him conscious while he slept like a dead man after a night of carousing with his friends, pouring cup after scalding cup of coffee into him. It was for this she had endured a reduction in her way of living materially and socially. She had been happy in the years without luxuries when she took his name and they had no money.

She had become a Hollywood wife, a heroic sub-species of the American wife, and one to whom little attention has been paid, even by the scientific students of the Hollywood culture such as Hortense Powdermaker and Leo Rosten. She is worth serious study, the Hollywood wife, study in depth—social, psychological and anthropological.

She will tell you, "Hollywood is a man's town."

And what she may mean is she has no man.

Because to be a Hollywood wife is to be, in effect, without a husband, without a man. The demands of the movie factory are more time- and energy- and emotion-consuming than that of any other American industry.

And the fact that it manufactures a product which may, now and then, partake of artistic beauty, enhances the tensions of moviemakers. Perhaps the craft workers— gaffers, grips, sound men, wardrobe personnel—perhaps they are exempt from the tensions. But producers, writers, directors, cinematographers, and actors know the enslavement of the work.

It is the star who most suffers. For the film projects the star into the consciousness of the nation. He becomes part of our dream life. He becomes therefore larger-than-life.

Of course, if the Hollywood wife's husband is a rich star, then it is misery first class all the way. Acapulco. Hawaii. Paris. London. Rome. The Riviera. Only the facade looked good. Because she did not have a man. He was already committed to his next picture and his anxiety was building up or the studio head had sent over a dozen scripts to read or his agent was phoning with bulletins.

And you could never elude the strangers who loved him. You could never enjoy the privacy of vacations, quiet meals in isolated places. You could not hide. Your face was there for the world to see. You were constantly being bothered by smiling strangers with questions and opinions and pieces of paper to be signed.

The ultimate paradox was that most everybody in the normal world envied the Hollywood wife. And now Josie

was the most unhappy variety of it—the divorced Hollywood wife. But she was a brave woman, and she went
on patiently, and ultimately she arrived at a *modus vivendi*
with Duke and he with her . . .

A property settlement had been agreed on before Mrs.
Morrison's suit for divorce.

"When we split up," he recalls, "I took just one car
and my clothes and Josie got all the rest of it, including
every cent I had saved."

She was awarded the North Highland Avenue mansion
and all its contents, the delicate Louis XVI antiques and
the Aubusson carpets and the porcelain and marble *objets
d'art*. The cash settlement was seventy-five thousand.
Wayne agreed to pay her twenty percent of the first hundred thousand of his earnings and ten percent of everything he earned above this figure to continue as long as
she lived. Individual trust funds were set up for each of
the children. The agreement, as is customary, gave her
custody of the children, with visitation privileges. At the
time of the divorce Michael Anthony was ten, Mary
Antonia was eight, Patrick John was seven, and Melinda
Ann was five.

As time went by, Josie resigned herself to conditions.
She and Duke became friendly again. He often came to
the house, to converse with her and recount some of the
incidents in his career, and share her experiences with
the children.

"I believe I got along better with my children and saw
more of them *after* Josie and I were divorced," Duke once
informed me. "I had the feelin' I actually spent more
time with them, even though I still worked hard. I think
what it was was the fights stopped. I only saw how much
hard feeling had built up after we split, and realized this
had made the children nervous. They accepted the situation.

"Josie was a wonderful mother to them. I know that
at first there were recriminations on her part, which I
don't blame her for, but she forgave me as time went
along, and one thing I've been thankful—she never made
the children hate me. For this I'll always be grateful. I

remember when Toni was eight, she went to a birthday party at a friend's, and some woman started pityin' her sayin', 'How nice that you have a wonderful mother—such a shame about your father.' And little Toni just reared up and answered, 'My daddy's wonderful too.'

"I and Josie got to a point where I could phone her and ask about the children and if I was intendin' to take one or more of them out, well I would first ask her if there was anything planned, as one thing was I didn't want to force them into bein' with me out of a sense of duty.

"We had had our quarrels, bad ones, but when it came to the kids, the quarrels just stopped right there. We remained partners for them. I was part of their life as they were growin' and I was at their wedding receptions and at the ceremonies. I was always there and Josie knew she could call me to be there whether it was somethin' like braces for a kid or glasses or an operation or some trouble in school or a problem of dating.

'Well, Josie and I were blessed with four wonderful children." (At the time he said this, they were twenty, eighteen, seventeen, and fifteen.) This is how John Wayne described his brood at that time: "They're energetic, lively, smart, kinda imaginative—without being rude or impudent. They are all good students—respected by their teachers and friends."

He remembered with pleasure how he began taking them on location, on trips to Catalina for swimming, down to Balboa, sometimes on Ford's yacht for a fishing trip, and when Pat and Mike were older they accompanied him and Ward Bond and Grant Withers on hunting trips. And sometimes he took all four kids on excursions to the Mojave and San Diego and Mexico and northern California and Alaska.

So he had not repeated the destructive pattern of his parents. Uncluttered by matrimonial edginess, the natural tenderness that he felt for Josie and she for him rose up in friendship.

The children of Hollywood stars have a hard time growing up naturally and finding themselves. Largely because Mrs. Morrison was such a good mother and Duke was such a wholehearted loving father, all four Wayne children have lived good productive lives and are emotionally balanced, not suffering from the excesses of luxury and special privileges which come often with being born to the Hollywood purple.

As he prepared to take a new wife, Duke thought often about the breaking up of his first marriage. Later, he was to ascribe it to the demands of his career, but at the time when the divorce became final—December 26, 1945— he believed that was because of temperamental differences and conflicting values that he and Josie were sundered. He believed that Chata was like him in personality and that she shared his interests, both in his work and in sports. Since he could not live alone, since he had to have a wife, he was not going to repeat any of his previous mistakes. He did not discern that he expected her to be about a dozen women in one.

His first mistake was to discourage her acting. It had been her knowledge of moviemaking and the experiences of the industry that had given them a strong bond originally.

Yet no sooner had she arrived in California, taken her test, been signed by Republic than he began finding excuses to deter her from making her way as an actress.

By the time they were married, she was already doomed to the role of Hollywood wife. She was not cut out to play it.

After all, it seems, he did not want her as an actress.

"I don't wish ever for acting again," Chata Wayne said after the nuptials. "But I am glad for Duke that I did act for a while, for it makes me know, without his having to explain anything at all, when he is tired or cross. Then I will either baby him or I just go away and let him gloom by himself."

And Ms. Waterbury let slip, in her perceptive *Photoplay* article, a hint of the emotional unrest in a famous actor's life. She talked of how Wayne often became depressed and that he had "all the temperament of the creative person." However, she reported with considerable relief that Chata (whose name she spelled "Chotta" throughout) "accepts such temperament with a gay serenity. Her amused face says, very clearly, 'This is my husband. This is his home. He is the law and I abide by it—but my eyes can dance just the same.' "

Her face was not always to be amused. Her eyes were not forever doing a fandango. She was subsequently not to find it to her taste to abide by his laws.

Duke's second mistake was to encourage the presence of Chata's mother as a member of the wedding—permanently.

They were married—three weeks after the divorce became final—in the Unity Presbyterian Church of Long Beach on January 18, 1946.

One could have literally quoted (in slight translation) Dr. Johnson's famous epigram on a second marriage: "It was the triumph of *esperanza* over experience."

The church was the one Duke's mother attended. She was now married to Sidney Preen and she lived in Long Beach. Preen was a sewer inspector for the city. He had achieved some fame in the world of municipal sanitation as the inventor of a sewer ball which reamed out clogged sewers efficiently. It was patented. Preen named it in honor of his stepson. It was marketed as the John Wayne Sewer Ball.

The wedding ceremony was performed by the Reverend Johnson Calhoun. The bride was given away by Herbert J. Yates. Yates' radiant smile was remarked upon by all the wedding guests, who thought it so nice that one was joyous for a friend. Why, they said, he looked as radiant as if he were the real father of the bride. The best man was Ward Bond. Bond arrived at the church somewhat incapacitated for his duties. He came on crutches, his leg in a cast. He had been crossing Olympic Boulevard in Beverly Hills and had been struck by an automobile. He had almost lost his leg and it had been saved only by the insistence of Bö Roos that it not be amputated.

The reception, tendered by the Preens, was at the California Country Club in Long Beach.

Señora Ceballos had cried during the ceremony and drunk much vintage champagne and flirted and danced.

She cried even harder when it came time for her to go to Mexico City and for the newlyweds to go on their honeymoon. They had rented a small ranch house at 4735 Tyrone Street, Van Nuys, in the valley. The divorce settlement had just about wiped Duke out for a while, and he and Chata would have to live modestly for a year.

Several days before the leavetaking, Duke came home from work and found his new wife and her mother sobbing and embracing. Both were devasted by the prospect of the separation.

In what might be generously described as a fit of temporary insanity, Duke said he wanted Mrs. Ceballos to live with them. There was one bedroom and a den—but they could convert the den into a guest room for her. He felt like she was one of the family. Mrs. Ceballos, weeping copiously, embraced him and said he was one fine Americano and she would have the *casa* Wayne in beautiful condition when they come from the honeymoon and afterward she clean the house and cook the meals and be as quiet as a little old *ratón*.

Yates, still basking in the glow of his security, paid the expenses of their honeymoon. Howard Hughes arranged space for them on the first civilian flight to Hawaii since the war.

So this time, at last, John Wayne came to Hawaii in style. He told Chata about his youthful misadventure. Now he was a conquering hero with a young bride. There were three glorious weeks of *luna de miel* ahead. There would be long afternoons on the beach of Waikiki as they bronzed their skins in the tropical sunlight. There would be luau feasts outdoors and visits to back-country beaches where the surf was high and brave young men risked their necks on surfboards.

Well, it rained the afternoon they arrived in Honolulu. They were met by a delegation of local movie exhibitors. They were driven to the Royal Hawaiian Hotel, where they occupied the Presidential Suite.

The next morning it was also raining. It rained every day and every night of the three weeks they were on Oahu.

And yet the inclement weather did not impede their happiness. Outfitted with slickers and umbrellas, they walked in the rain, wet palms rubbing sensuously together, wet cheeks rubbing sensuously together. In the rain they went on sightseeing trips to behold pineapple plantations, acres of sugar cane, volcanic mountains and grass shacks, for there were still hundreds of grass shacks on the islands then. They went on sailing trips to the other islands and fished for mullets—in the rain, of course. They were given permission to go to the Pearl Harbor base and witnessed the wrecks of the *Arizona* and *Utah* and the devastation around Hickam Field which was still there and which Duke would remember when he made *In Harm's Way*. They climbed all the way up to the rim of Mauna Loa and saw a volcano in the rain. They went swimming on Waikiki Beach in the rain. A veritable Reverend Davidson and Sadie Thompson, they made love in the suite while the rain beat on the windows and in the rain they visited nightclubs, including the depraved ones on Hotel Street, the ones the servicemen visited, and saw the brothels—from the outside—of Honolulu's red-light district, always in the rain.

Yes, Duke thought, contemplating the bliss of the last three weeks, as they prepared to board a plane for home, yes, she was his kind of woman, yes, they would make a splendid life together, and yes, she seemed to take to his children and he knew the kids would like her when they knew her better, and yes she was a warm and sensual person, tumultuous, adventurous, and he loved doing all kinds of things with her, for, to paraphrase Conrad Aiken, volcano climbing he did with her was more than volcano climbing.

It was so nice to be in love. Movie actors possess the capacity to fall in love again and again and again and always with absolute vehemence and conviction.

Returned in February, Duke was plunged into his labors at the studios. He had completed two films, back to back, with only a day's respite between them, before his marriage: John Ford's *They Were Expendable* for Metro and *Without Reservations* with Claudette Colbert for RKO.

He had been made a producer at Republic. This was how Yates placated his superstar as he watched him being courted by the other studios. James Edward Grant, who now began a long and intimate association with Wayne, was to write the screenplay of the first John Wayne production for Republic. He was also to direct it. It had the working title of *The Gun* and was released as *Angel and the Badman*. Gail Russell, a voluptuous young actress with dark hair and an aura of powerful grace, a Jane Russell type, played a Quaker girl who converts John Wayne, a gunfighter and criminal and killer, to a peaceable life. She may or may not have converted him to other activities as well.

And now as the second Mrs. Wayne and her spouse settled into the new life on Tyrone Street, the carefree Honolulu hours in the rain began receding into the past. Now Duke came home exhausted from the studio, for he not only had to play his part but he had to attend to innumerable petty production details. He came home and had a tumbler of bourbon and ice. He ate a huge steak. He was too tired to converse. Chata had told Ms. Waterbury that when Duke was tired or cross, she would baby him or just "let him gloom by himself." He would gloom for an hour and then go to sleep. They did not go out in the evenings. There were fine nightclubs like Ciro's and Mocambo's on Sunset, and even one or two interesting little places on Ventura Boulevard, but they did not go out at night because Duke was too weary. He gloomed by himself. He even worked on Saturdays and Sundays. Sometimes Jimmy Grant dropped over for story conferences. Sometimes Duke remained until midnight at the studio for conferences with Grant and costume people and set designers.

Sometimes Chata Wayne gloomed by herself. In fact she began to gloom more and more by herself.

And what did they do, Mr. and Mrs. Wayne?

"Mostly Chata reads and I sleep," Duke revealed.

"I am trying to teach heem Spanish," Chata said.

And how were the lessons going?

"Bad, bad, ver' bad," Chata said.

He was too sleepy to learn Spanish. He was too tired to give her consideration and tenderness. He had returned to the factory and its demands. She would have to learn to adapt to her new role as a Hollywood wife. She would have to learn not to be jealous of beautiful women like Gail Russell who saw more of her husband than she did. Jealousy began to eat her up. She heard from some other Hollywood wives whose mates worked at Republic that Duke was showering attentions on Miss Russell, and was frequently alone with her in her dressing room or his. She heard that he had bought her a little car to tool around in. She could not believe these stories. She did not accuse Wayne. She was silent and fumed inside.

Then the filming of *Angel and the Badman* finished and Duke went out with the company of actors and the director, Jimmy Grant, to celebrate, as is customary. Chata was not along. She sat at home and waited. She waited and waited and finally when it was after two in the morning she began making phone calls around and about to locate him. Somebody told her that after the first party had ended there was another party at . . . Miss Russell's home! She then said—in testimony she gave before a Los Angeles Superior Court five years later—that she called Miss Russell. She talked to a servant who told her that Mr. Wayne and Miss Russell had gone to a motel in Studio City (the name of a stretch of the San Fernando Valley, not far from Republic).

This got her very mad. When she heard the front doorbell ring at five in the morning she would not admit the bell-ringer. Duke kicked open the glass panel of the door and let himself in. She charged in and confronted Wayne. She was holding a fully loaded automatic. She threatened to kill him. She said that his vows were as inconstant as the moon. They had not been married a year and already he was betraying her. Her mother became hysterical and clutched the gun, thus preventing the murder of John Wayne. Chata accused him of being drunk and unfaithful. He admitted he was drunk but said he had not been unfaithful.

"I was quite hurt and upset," she testified. She admitted

she had held a loaded gun on Wayne but said she had been scared and thought he was a "robber." She said she had asked him about the rumors that he had given Gail Russell a car, and he said it was nothing—it was just the "down payment" on a car he had given her. Well, but wasn't it strange that a man would spend a whole night with a woman and give her a down payment on a car?

"Oh," she quoted him as saying, "that is nothing to be upset about."

Wayne did not think it was honorable of Mrs. Wayne to drag Gail Russell's name into their imbroglio. "If she'd testified against me," he told a friend, "that would be bad enough, but draggin' in my friends, makin' white look like black, poor Gail Russell. The poor kid went to work for us on a loan-out from Paramount. We paid Paramount a lot of money but Gail only got her contract player's salary. She was workin' for practically nothin.' She did a great job in our picture and we tried to get her some of the loan-out money but those pricks over at Paramount wouldn't give her any. So Jimmy Grant and I, we chipped in five hundred dollars apiece and gave it to her. It was for a down payment on a car. It was open and above-board. Sure I did take Gail home from that party—but her mother and her brother were there."

Wayne's account, under oath, of the evening was as follows. "I offered to drive her home in her car," he testified. "We left the studio and were following some friends in another car . . . We lost them in traffic . . . We went to a cafe in Santa Monica and had something to eat and I ran into some old friends from Glendale and we were there a while . . . Then I took her home . . ."

Frank Belcher, his attorney, asked: "Were there any improprieties between you and Miss Russell?"

Wayne: "Absolutely not."

Belcher: "Were you at a motel any time that night?"

Wayne: "Absolutely not."

Belcher: "What happened when you arrived home?"

Wayne: "I got home about one-thirty A.M. My wife refused to let me in. I could hear her and her mother talking about me loudly. I rang the bell but they wouldn't open

the door. Then I broke a glass panel, reached in, and
opened it myself. Later Chata and her mother, they came
charging out. Chata had a .45 in her hand. She and her
mother were fighting over it. Then things quieted down."

Such was the night life of the gods. A little cafe in
Santa Monica, a chance encounter with some old friends
from Glendale, and he swore he had never gone to any
motel, and all he tried to do was a good deed for a young
actress who was being exploited by Paramount, damn it,
a girl needed decent transportation around Los Angeles,
didn't she?

But Chata was suspicious, heaven knows why. She
formed an intense dislike for Jimmy Grant, whom she
decided to blame for the trouble. Wayne gloomed more
and more by himself, and yet, strange to say, he loved
her intensely, loved her with all the fibers of his being,
as they used to say in the movies, really seriously loved
her, but he gloomed and she gloomed.

Her face was not amused. Her eyes rarely danced. She
took to drink. She drank heavily and when she was drunk
she fought with him. Soon she took lovers. And she drank.

Her attorney, Jerome B. Rosenthal, had described his
client on the first day of the preliminary hearing, as an
innocent frightened Mexican girl who had been brought
into a depraved way of life by a sophisticated actor and
enmeshed in a whiskey-soaked atmosphere.

With more truth than poetry, counselor Rosenthal
cried, "She was swept into a mode of living where life
came from the mouth of a whiskey bottle."

But what was a Hollywood wife to do, after all?

Jeanette Mazurki, former wife of Mike Mazurki, recalls an evening when her ex-husband was working in
*Dakota* with Wayne. The Mazurkis had been swept into
the same "mode of living." Mike Mazurki had been taken
into Duke's little circle. And Mrs. Mazurki remembers the
wives always being in one room and the husbands in
another. She especially recalls an evening when Duke,
Mazurki, Ward Bond, Grant Withers, and Jimmy Grant
were playing poker in Duke's den, and she was sitting
alone with Chata in the living room of the beautiful Colo-

nial house furnished with Spanish antiques and they had
nothing to do but drink and they both got intoxicated.

Chata Wayne drank every night and soon in the daytime.

We shall, for the time being, take our leave of Chata
Wayne and, during the next chapters, follow John Wayne's
progress as a leading man and his coming of age as a
superstar. We shall have to go back several years and
forward several years. It is melancholy to speculate that
even as I and you are deserting Mrs. Wayne, leaving her
to drink alone or with other Hollywood wives, as we
describe Wayne's activities in pictures, so Wayne himself
was compelled to desert to make some of the pictures
described in the succeeding pages.

But now and then we shall return to Chata Wayne—
even as John Wayne did . . . now . . . and . . . then . . .

16

## The Sexual Imperative

Between 1938 and 1947, Duke Wayne became a leading
man. A leading man is not a superstar, because a leading
man operates with a leading lady. Leading man–leading
lady pictures become love-game stories in any genre:
western, farce comedy, suspense mystery. This is as true
of *Double Indemnity, The Thin Man, Destry Rides Again,
To Catch a Thief* as the more poignantly romantic films
such as the Garbo-Taylor *Camille* or the Dietrich-Cooper
*Morocco.*

Wayne became a leading man because many of the
established romantic players were in the armed services:

Cooper, Gable, Robert Taylor, Robert Montgomery, Jimmy Stewart, Tyrone Power, and Henry Fonda.

Consequently Wayne was one of the few available romantic heroes during this period. All situations, even war and death, are dramatically expressed in terms of sexual intrigue in the man-woman film. It is a man and a woman. It is Whitman's *urge and urge and urge, always the procreant urge of the world.* Now the superman role, in films as in Greek tragedy, is a Promethean who transcends human desires to wrestle with the gods. So well, however, had Wayne developed his technique that he could, for instance, wrestle with Claudette Colbert on the level of high comedy in *Without Reservations.*

He played opposite a galaxy of great woman stars— Claire Trevor, Marlene Dietrich, Paulette Goddard, Jean Arthur, Susan Hayward, Claudette Colbert, and Joan Crawford. He played opposite rising stars like Ella Raines, Ann Dvorak, Donna Reed, and Laraine Day.

Wayne played an American flier shot down in Nazi-occupied France in M-G-M's *Reunion in France,* co-starring with Joan Crawford. Jules Dassin directed this film and Joseph L. Mankiewicz produced. There was one splendid scene when Miss Crawford—who works at a Paris couturier's—helps him elude the Gestapo. She takes him to her apartment and hides him until he can contact the French underground. She prepares supper for him. He is tired, unshaven, his clothes dirty, his appearance utterly weary. As she is getting the food on the table, she realizes the look of hunger on his face and she suddenly knows that he has been wandering around in France for many days and probably is famished.

"When did you last eat?" she inquires.

He pauses for two beats and then pensively replies, "Years ago—in Wilkes-Barre." And in the distant look in his eyes, in the quietness of his voice, he projected the memory of innumerable Sunday dinners with a family, pot roast and mashed potatoes and peas and carrots, apple pie and a slice of cheese and coffee, small-town America—in the way he said five words he made it come alive.

But when there was Joan Crawford and John Wayne, there had to be the love-game.

Then producer Frank Ross—also husband of Jean Arthur, one of the most endearing comediennes of the period—asked him to take a fling at high comedy: *Lady Takes a Chance,* an RKO picture. The screenplay was by Robert Ardrey, who subsequently went away from Hollywood and immersed himself in the science of ancient man and wrote a series of fascinating books about our instincts for violence and property.

Ardrey's story for Jean Arthur and Wayne concerned the sexual, rather than the territorial, imperative. She played a bank cashier who yearns for adventure and, dismissing her three Manhattan swains, embarks on a cross-country sightseeing tour on a Greyhound bus. In Oregon, the tourists go to their first rodeo. Wayne, playing a rodeo rider, is sitting on a fierce bronco. He is bucked off and he falls right into Jean Arthur.

She is bruised slightly and rather put out. But then she looks at him closely and it is a case of love at first sight. She straightens out her disheveled clothing and bats her eyelashes, and somewhere from deep inside her diaphragm came that irresistible husky voice, breathing, "Oh . . . hello."

And Wayne is aroused by her. But not romantically. He wants to copulate. And right away. He is not inhibited like her Manhattan beaux. He is strong, rough, daring. He gets her to drink at a local bar and jazz club and then it is right up to his hotel room and he has a bottle and two glasses and the rest of it is her fighting him off and he pursuing her and marvelous dialogue and the bantering game of love is played until he surrenders to her moral standards and marries her.

It is a fine example of high comedy and was a critical and a box-office success, one of the few John Wayne films of which James Agee took notice. He praised Duke and the film. "John Wayne," he wrote in *The Nation*, October 8, 1943, "suggests how sensational he might be in a sufficiently evil story about a Reno gigolo. Besides the unusually frank erotic undertones, there are some good harsh street and rodeo shots, a fine small hotel and a saloon scene which gets down the crowded deafening glamour which unforeseen daylight drunkenness can have, better than I have ever seen it filmed before." And he found in his amorous warfare with Claudette Colbert in *Without Reservations* "kinds of hardness and conceit in [his] relations with women which are a good deal nearer the real thing than movies get." Though he greatly admired Wayne as an erotic realist, Agee never put himself on the record in homage to Wayne as a shooting star.

Strangely enough, though Wayne in this and other films would demonstrate his technical flexibility and his flair for comedy and romantic drama, he was forever defined in terms of the western film—by the public and by the critics.

His range as an actor is indicated by the variety of roles he played during 1944, 1945, and 1946, when he sweated out one film after another, working constantly with hardly an interlude, during the period of his final separation and divorce from Josie and the liaison with Chata. In *The Fighting Seabees* (Republic) he headed up a corps of construction engineers and hardhats building landing strips and fortifications in the Southwest Pacific theater of war. Then he went on to a frontier western, *Tall in the Saddle* (RKO); a San Francisco waterfront whore-and-gambler theme climaxed by the usual San Francisco earthquake sequence, *Flame of the Barbary Coast* (Republic); fighting with the Filipino underground, *Back to Bataan* (RKO); another frontier western, *Dakota* (Republic); and finally to John Ford's *They Were Expendable* (M-G-M), a war movie.

*Tall in the Saddle* was written by his old friend Paul Fix. Ella Raines started her short career as a charming lady in this vehicle. While on location at Lake Sherwood, Wayne was interviewed by New York *Times* correspondent Frank Daugherty. Three years before he had told a UP reporter he never wanted to make another western. Now he had changed his mind. He had apparently resigned himself to his fate. "Mr. Wayne," we were told, "likes westerns and feels he can do better work in the kind of pictures he likes than in the run-of-the-mill program pictures. He says now that he will stick with the westerns until he gets the ones he wants."

*Tall in the Saddle*, ostensibly a western, was basically a variation of the theme of a man and a woman. That was not where his destiny lay. He did not know it at the time. He did not suspect it. He had still another rendezvous on the road to his ultimate city. This time it was in Culver City, in the Thalberg Building, administration headquarters of M-G-M.

He was summoned to a conference in John Ford's office. He had two unreleased films in the can, *Flame of the Barbary Coast* and *Back to Bataan*.

He had just returned from Ojai. He had finished the location sequences for *Dakota*.

He was living then in felicitous infidelity with Esperanza. He got a phone call from John Ford, Lieutenant Commander John Ford, United States Navy. They talked about one thing and another and Duke thought he was phoning from Washington, D.C. Ford said he was home in Los Angeles. He had a temporary office at Metro. He wanted to see Duke tomorrow. He said he was going to start working on a new picture and that he planned to put John Wayne in it.

Duke asked when had Ford been discharged from the Navy.

"I wasn't," Ford snapped. "I've got leave. This is a picture about the United States Navy."

At the conference, Wayne met an interesting and heroic man, the screenwriter of the film, the famous Frank W. Wead, known as "Spig" Wead.

# 17

# Of War, Peace, and Avocadoes

Frank Wead was fifty years old in 1945. He had served in the U.S. Navy aboard a minesweeper in World War I. He became a career officer and was one of the pioneers in naval aviation. He and a team won the Schneider cup for the Navy on a round-the-world flight in international competition in 1922. He had fought during the 1920's for a strong navy and for the development of aircraft carriers. An accident—falling downstairs in his home—in 1927 had left him paralyzed from the neck down. Three years of determined exercises and physical rehabilitation at a San Diego naval hospital had enabled him to walk again—though on crutches—and learn to use his fingers. He and Ford had known each other while Wead was recovering in San Diego. "Spig" Wead was a natural-born story-teller. Ford suggested that he become a writer so as to keep his mind occupied. Wead began writing and selling pulp magazine fiction about aviation and naval combat. Toward 1930, he got into screen-writing and became successful. Over the years he wrote the screenplays for Ford's *Air Mail,* Frank Capra's *Dirigible,* Howard Hawks' *Ceiling Zero,* John Farrow's *Blaze of Noon,* and *Up Periscope.* When the Japanese attacked Pearl Harbor, Lieutenant Commander Wead asked to be put on active duty and he was instrumental in developing a technique of mini-aircraft carriers until our aircraft transport ships were restored to full complement. He had been under fire in the Kwajalein battle in 1944.

Spig Wead was a tall, gaunt, high-strung person who

was a hard drinker and a heavy gambler: a strange incandescent personality who attracted everyone to the fire burning inside him. He was a witty person and a fine raconteur. He became one of the fixtures in the moviecolony high life. He had a reckless, wild streak about him. He was one of the few men to whom Ford deferred. Ford was respectful of the man's pure courage. John Wayne was awed by it.

Wead was in his naval uniform at that conference in Ford's office. So was Robert Montgomery. Montgomery had come back to Hollywood after four years under fire. He had the rank of lieutenant in the Navy. He had commanded a PT boat and taken part in the Guadalcanal battle. He had also served aboard a PT in the recent invasion of Normandy. A round-faced gentle-voiced player of comedies mostly, Montgomery still looked youthful and his voice was still gentle. There was now a hard look in his eyes. And Ford, now Lieutenant Commander Ford, was as tough and hard as any of them. Ford had also seen action in Normandy during the invasion—along with Lieutenant Bulkeley, the greatest of the PT commanders. Ford had made a series of extraordinary documentaries during the war years—*December 7th, The Battle of Midway, We Sail at Midnight*. He had filmed *Midway* while the battle was going on. And he had manned the camera himself. He was shot in both legs during the filming. He lost the sight of his left eye. He won Academy Awards for *Midway* and for *December 7th*.

Wayne was in gray flannel slacks, a brown sports shirt, and a brown hound's-tooth jacket. He had just wrapped up *Dakota*, his first film with Vera Hruba Ralston. He was negotiating with Herbert Yates for a new five-year deal with Republic. He wanted to be a producer.

The three naval officers were on leave from their duties to make the movie version of W. L. White's nonfiction novel about the exploits of Lieutenant John Bulkeley and Lieutenant (j.g.) Robert B. Kelly, *They Were Expendable,* which was about a flotilla of PT boats which had been converted into small attacking vessels and harassed the Japanese battleships and cruisers attacking the Philippines, delaying the conquest of them and permitting the escape of General MacArthur with a small army. At that time, nobody could foresee the ending of the interminable war, and the government was still encouraging the making of patriotic films. The PT story was an inspiring one. The film was to describe the lost battles of Bataan, Cavite Bay, Manila, and Corregidor.

The war still went on. The Nazis were putting up a stiff resistance in their last days. The Japanese were giving ground slowly, island by island.

Wead had written the screenplay based on White's book. Montgomery was to play Bulkeley and Wayne would play Kelly, who was the more flamboyant of the officers, and who has a violent love affair with Donna Reed, a naval nurse in a Manila hospital. However, the names would be changed. Bulkeley became Brinkley and Kelly became Ryan. Nobody asked Kelly how he felt about it. Nobody asked Lieutenant Beulah Greenwalt, the nurse, how she felt about it.

The four men drank and discussed Ford's conception of the film and what he wanted, and Montgomery and Wead were throwing ideas on the table. Wead would make notes now and then. Wayne was quiet. He seemed to be sulking morosely. Ford had a bottle of twenty-five-year-old Hennessey V.S.O.P. and Duke was quietly sipping it and nodding now and then. Ford, who always was aware of all that was taking place around him, saw what was happening. Suddenly Wayne got up. He went to the private bathroom in Ford's office suite. He remained there for a long time.

When he emerged, Montgomery and Wead were gone. Ford had dismissed them. Wayne was red-eyed. He had been weeping. He had run the water loudly and cried. He felt ashamed of himself. He felt disgraced by his civilian clothes. Ford knew he had wanted to be in the service, especially in the Navy. Ford's heart went out to him. He was a soft sentimental Irishman under his mean facade. Ford felt he would cry himself in another minute. Finally he decided to give Duke the cold water treatment.

He shoved him into a chair. Then he yanked him out

of the chair. He stood close to him, eyeball to eyeball, and said, "Listen, you dumb bastard, get the hell out of this office. We got a picture to make. We go to Miami for our locations in three weeks. I expect you to be there. And you can take that fat Mexican broad with you if you want. I'm gonna work your ass off, Marion. We got to make this in three months or less. We got to get this into release in December. Metro is timing it for December seventh.

"And another thing, me boyo, when I ask you to come here for a meeting I expect you to talk up and let me know how you feel about the story."

And he now cursed John Wayne out to the best of his profane ability.

Wayne was shocked out of his self-pity. He knew that Ford loved him. Whom the Ford loveth, he chastiseth. He knew that Ford knew he had done his best to get into the Navy. And he had done the USO tours close to the battle zones.

Oh hell, Ford knew. That was enough.

During the making of *They Were Expendable,* Wayne watched how Ford—who produced as well as directed it—went about handling the small details of a production. Someday, Wayne vowed, he was also going to be a producer and a director. He was going to direct that movie about Sam Houston, Texas, and the Battle of the Alamo. He was going to make that movie about Honor. Someday. After all, he was over forty now. He could not go on playing leading man roles much longer, and he did not want to be one of those old men—and you are old, so the fear goes, in films when you are over forty—who stoops and shuffles about playing character roles and slowly disintegrates. He had seen it happening to Harry Carey—Carey trying to make it again by doing a play with John Garfield on Broadway, *Heavenly Express,* and damn near dying of heart failure while doing it. Duke was going to become a director. Many actors had done it before him. He was going to set up his own production company. He and a young executive, Robert Fellows, had talked about it. Fellows had produced *Back to Bataan*. So Duke was watching Ford's movements.

In Miami, at the Coast Guard naval station, scores of Hollywood special-effects men, carpenters, technicians, strove to re-create the look of Manila and Cavite as it was before December 7, 1941.

There was a cast of seventy principals and about two hundred extras. And even while they were filming the recapitulation of those dark hours of 1941, a huge invading American force of seventeen aircraft carriers and a thousand planes and five hundred ships, and an army of a hundred and fifty thousand men, spearheaded by the Marines, conquered Iwo Jima on March 16, 1945.

When not working in a scene, Wayne stayed close to Ford and studied how he put the pieces together. Sometimes, Wayne went among the stuntmen—there were stunt fliers used in the film—and the special-effects men under the direction of Jim Havens, a former Marine sergeant himself, who was a genius at concocting explosions. They mined the harbor at Miami and set off explosive depth charges to go off as the play-acting PT boats darted among the replicas of Japanese battleships. Planes crashed. Torpedoes went off. Bombs burst in air. Machine guns rattled. Men "died." Men "fought." Ships blew up.

Wayne saw how Ford meticulously planned it all on paper and blueprinted every long sequence for his second units. He knew where every explosion was to take place and where every scene was to fit into the greater whole which he envisioned. He saw his final film even as the seemingly disconnected pieces of footage were being photographed. Most of the time he was editing the film in his brain.

But he always took advantage of a break. One day, there was a large brush fire over on Key Biscayne island, a few miles from the location. There were enormous billows of gray smoke and red flames and sparks. Ford shrieked joyously at the sight. He ordered a second unit to go there at once and film the fire.

"Perfect for the burning of Manila," he chortled.

Wead was told to rewrite a scene. Wead was always

rewriting. Ford liked to have the writer on the set. He liked to make changes. He was improvising all the time. How did he keep it all in his head? He was hot-tempered and violent—and also patient. It was a contradiction, but he had infinite patience and a short temper.

"Ford was always taking unexpected shots, like this one of Manila burning," Wayne remembers. "He would use any situation that developed. If it was raining when the script did not call for rain, he shot in the rain and changed the script. He had this blueprint, sure, but he was always looking to change it."

They finished the location work and came back to Culver City for the interiors, scoring, and final editing to get it ready for the December premiere.

By then we were no longer at war. The Germans had signed the unconditional surrender on May 8. In August the atom bombs fell on Hiroshima and Nagasaki. The treaty with Japan was formally signed aboard the U.S.S. *Missouri* on September 2, 1945.

Would a nation at peace be unwilling to see a war movie? The country was tired of the killing and the uniforms, the basic training, the V-mail, the rations, the shortages of meat and gasoline, the deaths of relatives and friends, the battles, battles, battles.

*They Were Expendable* was a critical success. And Wayne's performance elicited praise for its simplicity and robustness. Some called it the best acting of his career. And the battle scenes were perhaps the most gripping pictures of air and naval action ever put on film. They were as close to the bone as a documentary and they were as cunningly shaped as a work of imagination. The cunning hand of the great artisan was at work, in the scenes of humorous interplay, in the weaving together of personal stories, of love stories, with the photography of men at war, men with women, men without women.

But was the movie too late?

Bosley Crowther thought so. He found it a magnificent movie on every count, but he said, in his New York *Times* review, "if this film had been released last year— or the year before—it would have been a ringing smash.

For then, while the war was still with us, and the wave of victory was yet to break, the national impulse toward avengement, for which it cried out, would have been supremely stirred. Now with the war concluded and the burning thirst for vengeance somewhat cooled, it comes as a cinematic postscript to the martial heat and passion of the last four years." He had found the battle scenes "thrilling and electrifying" and praised the depiction of the "dignity and courage" of American soldiers and sailors in the months of defeat.

And yet the public came to see *They Were Expendable*. There were long lines about the two theaters in Los Angeles which were showing it on first run—Grauman's Egyptian and the Fox Ritz.

Howard Barnes in the New York *Herald Tribune* said that some war pictures might be dated, but not this one, which he said was "more than merely entertaining. It is an abiding testament to the valor that made victory possible."

Among those who were not entertained or honored by the tribute to their valor was Commander Robert Bolling Kelly (USN). He sued M-G-M for fifty thousand dollars, alleging that Wayne's portrayal of Rusty Ryan was a grotesque libel on his reality. He was awarded three thousand dollars by a federal court in Boston.

And former Lieutenant Beulah Greenwalt—now Mrs. Beulah G. Walcher—was displeased by what Donna Reed had been up to, and she did not find the rendition of a supposed love affair with a fictional version of Lieutenant Kelly to be conducive to her peace of mind and she sued, claiming infringement of privacy. She asked M-G-M for four hundred thousand to soothe her nerves. And she collected the sum of two hundred and ninety thousand!

Though peace had broken out, John Ford was not ready to put the Army and Navy in mothballs. Ford had a mystical sense of the romance, beauty, and tragedy of men in combat. He was not about to eschew war films because they were out of fashion. If he had to, he would make historical war films. He would make films about the wars between the Indians and the U.S. Cavalry on the frontier seventy-five years previously. But he would make war films. He believed that the prospect of imminent death while fighting for one's own country engendered great emotions in the characters and in the spectators.

John Wayne, on the other hand, was of another way of thinking. His initial picture as a producer was a film in praise of nonviolence. He would be a proponent of making love, not war.

John Wayne, Pacifist?

Well, yes.

In 1946, he had signed a new five-year contract with Yates. He was to make one high-budget film a year for Republic. He would produce his films. He would continue getting ten percent of the gross, against a guarantee of a hundred and fifty thousand salary per film. And he was free to work for other studios. He signed a five-year contract with RKO-Radio Pictures, which was to be one of the reasons why his friend Howard Hughes set about buying RKO.

Robert Fellows, with whom Wayne was soon to set up an independent production company Wayne-Fellows, introduced him to James Edward Grant. And James Edward Grant, a writer who wanted to be a director, introduced him to the Quaker philosophy. He had an original story and screenplay about a beautiful Quaker girl who converts a western gunfighter from shooting to loving his neighbors.

Wayne did not want to play Quirt Evans. He tried to get Gary Cooper and Randolph Scott but they had other commitments. So he had to do it himself. In the course of making this film, he began leaning on George Colman, head of transportation at Republic. And he became intimate with Jimmy Grant, for Wayne himself always thought in literary terms rather than pictorial terms. Wayne was not what the Germans call an *"augenmensch,"* a person who most intensely experiences reality through his sense of sight. He had to learn about composition and about pictorial values by hard work and by studying paintings in museums and by listening to John Ford.

Wayne was a person who thought in terms of story, in terms of words rather than of pictures. And he loved the words of Jimmy Grant.

Grant, who had not yet learned terseness, had written a lovely and eloquent screenplay, with long block speeches of dialogue between Gail Russell and her Quaker family and the gunfighter, as they debated the philosophies of violence and of peace.

Grant was making his debut as a director.

Wayne found himself in trouble as he tried to pull together the innumerable petty problems of getting a film into production. He had a hot temper like Ford—but he was without the calmness, the patience, the infinite capacity for taking pains (and bearing pain) which a movie producer, a much maligned breed, has to be able to take and to bear. He leaned heavily on Bob Fellows and George Colman to bear much of the administrative burden.

Colman, like Jimmy Grant, became a lifelong friend and worshiper of Wayne, as well as an employee. Colman, who later became an integral part of Wayne's producing organization, was a man ostensibly responsible for transportation, for getting the cameras and cables and klieg lights out to the locations, for arranging hotel rooms and accommodations for the cast and crew, for hiring and firing dozens of employees.

He was more than that. He was a man who could get Wayne anything he needed and get it cheaply. He was a man who got a job done. He was, in Duke's words, a ramrod. For instance, in one Wayne movie, the Mexican government allowed them to shoot some scenes in an enormous granary near Durango. The granary was infested with rats. There was a certain poison which was fatal to these huge Mexican rats. They told Colman he couldn't get it in Mexico. So he ordered every member of the company coming down to fill one suitcase with rat poison. But he still felt he was paying too much. So he began making inquiries around and about until he found somebody in Durango who could mix him the ingredients for the poison in large quantities. He probably saved Batjac Productions all of a hundred dollars. But that was how Colman operated. He died suddenly in 1972, a week after the completion of *The Train Robbers*.

No detail was too small for this man to work over and no problem was too complicated for him to solve. He was an unlettered roughneck Jew from New York, hardboiled, a former Seabee himself, a coarse, cigar-chewing, and absolutely insensitive guy. He stepped on everybody's toes. He was hated by every person who ever worked in a Wayne movie. But he got his job done. Once, while at Republic, Colman had insulted an executive and was about to be fired when Wayne intervened and saved his job. After that, his loyalty to Duke was total. He had the same conception of eternal loyalty and friendship as Duke. He also revered Wayne as a great man. He loved him. If he heard anybody say—or even hint—that Wayne was anti-Semitic, that individual was liable to be fighting with Colman.

Somebody once asked Wayne, "Why do you keep Colman on all your pictures? He makes trouble. He gets everybody mad. He's a son-of-a-bitch."

"I know he's a son-of-a-bitch," grinned Wayne, "but he's *my* son-of-a-bitch."

Duke made only two films in 1946. Besides *Angel and the Badman,* he made *Tycoon* (for RKO) with Laraine Day. He had to hustle to stay even. He did not want to get involved in another movie but he had to have money. Miss Day had just married Leo Durocher. Wayne once told me that Durocher was the most openly jealous husband he ever came up against. The Lip took all the fantasy lovemaking in the movie for authentic expression of lust between his wife and John Wayne. He stood around on the set every day, glowering at Wayne and making remarks to Laraine.

This finally got on Duke's nerves and he ordered the set closed to visitors, the only time that he has ever done this. He does not like a closed set. He loves to have visitors on the sidelines watching him work. But he found that he could not concentrate on his role with the hot-tempered shortstop looking suspiciously at him.

This is the house in which Marion Michael Morrison was born.

Marion, age 14 (rear, third from left), poses with the coaches and members of the Glendale High School track team.

This is how young Morrison looked when he played on the U.S.C. Frosh Squad.

PHOTOPLAY AND MOTION PICTURE MAGAZINE

Morrison, prop man and bit player at Fox, finagled movie jobs for his Sigma Chi brothers in John Ford's *Salute*. Shown with Marion (sitting fifth from left) are members of Howard Jones's great U.S.C. football squad of 1928. A non-Sigma Chi football hero made his debut in *Salute*: Wardell Bond, then a medical student. Bond is seen in the third row left.

Now renamed John Wayne, he got the Fox publicity treatment in 1930 as he posed with co-star Marguerite Churchill of *The Big Trail* and child actor Tommy Clifford. The dog's name was Champion.

Josephine Saenz was a beautiful bride when she married Marion Michael Morrison in 1933. The scene was the gardens of Loretta Young's Bel-Air home. Left to right: best man Louis Gerpheide, Duke, the new Mrs. Wayne, Miss Young, and the bride's father, Dr. Jose Sainte-Saenz.

A rare photograph of Mr. and Mrs. Wayne in their home in 1937 before Duke became rich and famous. This is Michael sitting on Daddy's lap and Toni on Josie's lap.

Josie Saenz Wayne loved parties and dancing and laughter. In these pictures she is shown with Duke, already addicted to those cigarettes, at a post-premiere party in Ciro's and,

UNITED PRESS INTERNATIONAL

on another occasion, with Loretta Young and William Powell at the Brown Derby. Loretta was Josie's dearest friend.

Osa Massen coaching Duke for his role in *The Long Voyage Home*. Miss Massen was Duke's first experience in love, European style.

On the set of *Dakota,* Herbert J. Yates (left) looks on suspiciously as Wayne engages Vera Hruba Ralston in persiflage. Mike Mazurki (right) played many fight scenes with Wayne. Yates, President of Republic Pictures, was a lover and husband of La Ralston.

Wayne, a good chess player, waits for Marlene Dietrich to make her move, on the set of *Pittsburgh* (1942).

Wayne puts his fistprint in the cement of Grauman's Theatre, helped by Sid Grauman. The marines are Pvt. Inga Boberg, and, left to right: Maj. Gordon West, Lt. Col. C. A. Youngdale, Col. J. O. Brauer. The men were at Iwo Jima and the sand in this batch of cement came from there. Wayne's current release was *The Sands of Iwo Jima* (1950).

On location in Ireland for *The Quiet Man*, Duke strolled with his children (left to right): Toni, Patrick, Melinda and Michael (1951). All acted in this picture, making their film debuts. Patrick is still acting and Michael is now president of Batjac Films, which produces most of John Wayne's pictures.

PHOTO © BY DAVID SUTTON

Twenty years later on location in Durango, Mexico. Patrick Wayne is on the left and Michael Wayne is on the right. The film was *Big Jake* (1971).

In 1965, during the shooting of *El Dorado*, John Wayne and Robert Mitchum seem to be enjoying a dash of oedipal complexity. Duke's mother, Mrs. Sidney Preen, lived to be 85. Mother Mitchum's name is Mrs. Hugh Morris.

An actor is known by the directors he keeps and Wayne has kept good company over the years. Here he is with the old master, John Ford, and Jimmy Stewart, on the set of *The Man Who Shot Liberty Valance* (1961).

With Howard Hawks on the set of *Rio Bravo*.

With Edward Dmytryk while making *Back to Bataan*.
Dmytryk was the friendliest of the unfriendly ten.

With Henry Hathaway in Madrid to film
*Circus World*.

With Otto Preminger and Kirk Douglas during
the filming of *In Harm's Way.*

And with himself when he directed *The Alamo,* and William Clothier, who should have won an Academy Award for his superb color cinematography on *The Alamo.*

In 1973, veteran John Sturges directed Wayne in his first cops-and-robbers movie, *McQ*. Wayne tests the new M10 9-mm. gun which he uses in some scenes—a change from his customary Winchesters and Colts. Wayne has a large collection of rare pistols and rifles of the 19th century.

Señora Baur, Wayne and Esperanza Wayne, Duke's second wife, take afternoon tea on the patio of the Encino hacienda in 1947. It was rare for Duke, his wife and his mother-in-law to drink coffee, milk or tea.

On October 28, 1953, Esperanza and John Wayne were divorced. She is wearing a large hat. He is wearing a large grin. Behind him, as he strides by in Superior Court, are business manager Bö Roos and his longtime publicity man Beverly Barnett.

Though divorced, Josie and John remained friends and shared time with their children. This is the Beverly Hills Hotel reception after Toni was married to Don La Cava. Left to right: Josephine Wayne, the groom, the bride, the Duke. The year was 1955.

PHOTOPLAY AND MOTION PICTURE MAGAZINE

UNITED PRESS INTERNATIONAL

Wayne almost burned to death when a stunt fire got out of control during the filming of a circus-tent fire at Aranjuez, Spain, on December 27, 1963, during the filming of *Circus World*.

During a South American holiday, Wayne was guided by
Richard Weldy, center, and he fell in love with Mrs.
Weldy (right). Mrs. Weldy, the former Pilar Pallette, later
married the Duke.

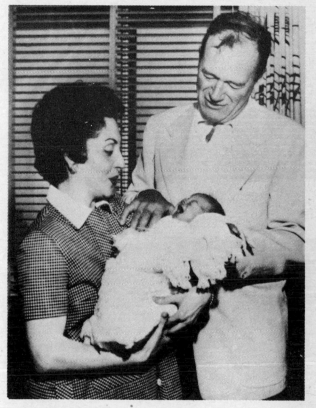

Pilar and John had their first child, Aissa, in April 1956. Aissa was a week old when this picture was taken at St. Joseph's Hospital in Burbank, California.

During his 1966 tour of Vietnam Wayne was caught without his toupee. With Wayne is PFC Richard Jacaruso.

On Father's Day, 1967, the clan gathered at Wayne's estate in Newport Beach, California. Back row, from left: Duke's stepfather, Sidney Preen; Mike Wayne; Pat Wayne; Duke. Middle row, from left: Mrs. Patrick Wayne; Mrs. Carmela Pallette (Duke's mother-in-law); Pilar Wayne; Mrs. Preen (Duke's mother); Toni Wayne La Cava holding son Christopher; Donald La Cava; Mrs. Michael Wayne holding daughter Josephine; Melinda Wayne Munoz; Gregory Munoz holding son Matthew. Front: Mike Wayne's Maria; Duke Wayne's John Ethan; Mark La Cava and sister Brigid La Cava; Mike's Alicia; Duke's Aissa; and Anita La Cava hugging Michael's Teresa.

Politics-Makes-Strange-Bedfellows Department: Wayne and Frank Sinatra, formerly political enemies, join Bob Hope and Dean Martin to support Ronald Reagan in his 1970 campaign for reelection.

WIDE WORLD PHOTOS

Presenter Barbra Streisand kissing Wayne the night he finally got his Oscar for playing Rooster Cogburn in *True Grit*. A few moments later Wayne began weeping with happiness.

And at home, there was more suspicion, as he and Esperanza alternated between episodes of tremendous tenderness and physical ecstasy—a union so intimate that they became like one—and then ferocious interludes in which she screamed at him and he insulted her and they drank heavily and fought and fought and fought.

It was like his two most important films of this period: some fighting and some loving and some fighting and some loving.

They did their loving and their fighting in a beautiful two-story Colonial house in Encino. At that time, Encino was still an undeveloped area of the San Fernando Valley and there were few stores and few habitations and many ranches and large estates. The Clark Gables had a ten-acre spread in Encino and Gable had a stable of horses. And Ford was now living on a ranch in Encino. A real estate agent had showed Duke and Esperanza this beautiful white house with the high pillars and there were five acres of land and rolling hills. It had been originally built by Lum, of the comedy team of Lum'n'Abner, a popular radio comedy duo. There were high brick walls around the property and an electric gate and five bedrooms and an enormous den and servants' quarters and a huge living room, thirty by fifty feet, equipped with a projection booth and a screen that recessed into a wall.

But there was no swimming pool. They were asking three hundred fifty thousand for the house and land and there was no swimming pool. The owner agreed to come down in price to two-fifty since there was no swimming pool. But at the moment John Wayne was in financial trouble. He did not have two hundred and fifty thousand dollars. He spoke often of his personal difficulties to his friend Howard Hughes. Hughes had taken to dropping in informally on Duke's set or going out on location. He liked to sit around and watch and listen. And he enjoyed Duke's company. He asked many questions about how Wayne worked in pictures, and he would remember some scene, say, in *Stagecoach* or *Seven Sinners,* and ask him how Ford or Tay Garnett had concocted it. Hughes had determined to learn how to make pictures rapidly. He was soon going to own a studio and he was going to be the best movie director and producer in the world.

He rarely made appointments with Duke. He would suddenly appear—usually in the afternoon—and sometimes he and Duke would have steaks somewhere and talk about movies and about the problems of life. When Hughes heard about Wayne's financial dilemma he at once loaned him the money for the house. Wayne built a lovely terraced slope leading down to an olympic-sized swimming pool, and there was still enough left over to have the house decorated in Early American style with authentic antiques. He had glass cases in his den, and now for the first time displayed his collection of rare guns and his assorted cups and awards. (There were not too many of these at the time.)

Overcome by the postwar mood of the nation, and his conviction that he had wrought a beautiful film in *Angel and the Badman,* Wayne had forgotten everything he had learned in John Ford's College of Cinema. He had, like most of us, felt the urgency of world peace. He believed in the United Nations. He had voted for Franklin D. Roosevelt in 1944. He thought the world had had enough of violence. He wanted to do what he could to broadcast a message of peace and brotherhood. This was all very well, and even admirable, but films are stories told in terms of physical action and images, and not with words, and they convey emotions and not abstract ideas.

Wayne was to change his values and his abstractions, but whenever he made a film himself he was always victimized by his static approach to a story. As a director, as a producer, he was never able to feel the story and the characters. He knew what he wanted to say and in his haste to say it he did not make a moving picture. He made a succession of stills, slowly flicking over, like the stiff frames of those old penny-machine Mutoscope films, the kind you hand-cranked in amusement parks long ago.

*Angel and the Badman* was a failure and audiences did not come to see it. *Time* magazine was one of the few influential periodicals or newspapers which admired it. *Time* said it was a "genteel western." It praised its phi-

losophy and the leisurely pace of the narration. Actually
it was a slow-moving and rambling film, drowning in
long dialogues, which ran a wearisome two hours and
twenty minutes—though on its second run it was fortunately cut to an hour and thirty-five minutes. *Time*
thought it was so good that the Quakers were treated
with "good humor" and "affectionate respect."

Though the New York *Times* and most critical outlets
were sympathetic to Wayne's message of peace and love,
they were simply unable to recommend such a torpid
exercise. There had been many experiments at that time
in making variations on the traditional western film, and
Alton Cook of the New York *World-Telegram* cynically
observed that here was another experiment which "tries
virtually to dispense with action . . ." He complained
that there were too many closeups of "Wayne grimly
fighting things out with himself. Harry Carey drops around
occasionally as an old marshal spouting corny wisdom in
an owlish manner. Before the picture was started, director and cast apparently went through a short course
on how to be an undertaker."

And Archer Winsten, a discerning critic and a person
whose liberal values inclined him to dote on a pacifist
film, despised it enormously in the New York *Post*. Winsten heaped most of the blame on Jimmy Grant. After
complimenting Republic on trying to make better pictures with good casts and good production qualities, he
wrote, "Unfortunately one item has been neglected by
director James Edward Grant. He has failed to hire a
writer, undertaking the chore himself, and proving once
again how important a good writer can become as soon
as he is absent. The dialogue in this picture frequently
sounds as if it had been written by someone who couldn't
think of what to say next. So he wrote the first thing that
came into his mind. It doesn't make much sense as conversation or as dialogue intended to forward a plot. All it
does is fill the soundtrack and emphasize the fact that
the picture is twice as long as most westerns. It is an
outrageous waste of time, celluloid, and productive ambition. A fundamental plot flaw and the absence of anyone

resembling a writer cause the downfall of *Angel and the Badman.*"

As the reviews piled up, and the adverse reactions of the critics were duplicated by low box-office grosses, John Wayne was discouraged. But he was not defeated. He was used to bad notices. But Grant, making his debut as a director, responsible for his screenplay for Wayne, whom he felt was like a father to him now, was devastated. He was tortured by guilt. He felt completely responsible for what seemed, at the time, like a debacle which would prove an insurmountable setback for Wayne's career and would crush his own career before it got under way. He did not realize that Wayne had already lived through such a devastating experience with *The Big Trail* and that he had learned the world soon forgot failure as it forgot success.

Grant, who had become increasingly addicted to alcohol, had disappeared from home, and Mrs. Grant phoned Wayne late one night and said she was desperately worried. She had not called him sooner because she had hoped Jimmy would return, as he usually did. Now he had been away for several days. She was afraid that he might be sick or worse yet hurt in a car accident. Wayne began looking for him in his usual Sunset Strip haunts and got in contact with his other drinking cronies. He finally succeeded in tracing him to a seedy hotel in Long Beach. He went down there with George Colman. Grant was in bad shape. They got him shaved and cleaned up and tried to get some coffee in him. They took him back to the Athletic Club for a steam-room session and a Scotch douche and Wayne told him, when he recovered some of his senses, that he believed in Grant's talent. He said he didn't give a damn about critics, New York critics or any other critics.

Wayne meant what he said. Grant was his friend. And friendship was not something that he took lightly. From now on, he saw to it that Grant was assigned to every film in which Wayne had some authority. Grant himself never directed another movie. As time went on, he learned how to write simply, directly, and concisely for films,

and learned how to write scenes rather than verbal ex-
plications of emotions, learned how to portray actions
rather than how to talk about them. The good screenwriter does not write words, he writes actions. As a friend
of mine, the writer-director Ernest Lehman, likes to say,
"You have to learn how to write what the critics will call
*director's touches.*"

Michael Wayne recently explained Grant's affinity for
Wayne's acting style as follows:

"Jimmy Grant became my dad's favorite writer. He not
only wrote the screenplays for which he gets credit, but
also did rewriting on many of Dad's pictures for which
he got no credit or money, but he did it as a personal
favor.

"What Jimmy Grant did so well was write crisp dialogue and pack a lot of meaning into it. He would write
one line which would advance the story, reveal the character, and lead to action. He got to write just the kind of
short sentences my dad likes.

"Now I'm not saying that he has to have lines tailored
for him. He believes a character should say lines that fit
him. But any good actor will give the same line his own
reading. You could give, for instance, Gary Cooper,
Robert Mitchum, and my dad the same line—and you'd
have three different readings—and yet all three are western actors.

"I believe this—that Dad can add a personal involvement to any line, written by anybody, a strength to it,
so he is a benefit to any writer, I don't care who. He backs
up a writer.

"Burt Kennedy is another writer whom Dad likes, also
the Ravetches, and Henry Julian Fink. Borden Chase
was a writer who could write perfect dialogue for him.
But he went along with Dudley Nichols, or Frank Nugent,
and he will tell you that the screenplay Marguerite Roberts
wrote for *True Grit* was one of the best in his career."

Wayne learned something from the *Angel and the Badman* fiasco. He would try to eschew introspection and the
subtleties of facial suggestion, all those qualities of symbolism which he connoted by the term "reaction." He

would let his "reactions" show by his "actions." He would leave symbolism to others. He would leave message films to Stanley Kramer and Dore Schary. He would leave the vagaries of subtle dialogue to George Cukor and Alfred Hitchcock. And yet . . . and yet . . . when he had the control, as he did in *The Alamo* and *The Green Berets,* his films would become loquacious and be stalled by the fatal messages. But he did not direct himself too often, which was a good thing.

And he learned something else which had to do with the love-game—the leading man–leading lady pattern. This was not his game any longer. Love should never again and would never again be the prime mover of his films, or, hardly ever—for he was still a workhorse actor who had to take the pictures that were offered to him. Even so, the amatory urges, when they appeared in a story, as in *The Quiet Man,* were not to be imperative. We remember more vividly the fight between Victor Mc-Laglen and Wayne in that movie than the sparring between Maureen O'Hara and Wayne.

However, love and the concomitant hate were still prime movers in his personal life. He and Chata, as he told me once in 1954, were like two volatile chemicals in a jar, and they were always being shaken together and exploding. There was a third chemical—ethyl alcohol. Chata was just one of those persons whom strong drink changes into a violent, aggressive person with a sharp tongue. Duke could drink and be warm and kindly—but when they both drank, and especially when they drank at parties or in groups, she would unconsciously say and do things which aroused his temper and made him explode and do things he would not remember and be ashamed of if he did.

They had gone to Honolulu with Jimmy Grant and his wife in December, 1946, to celebrate the completion of *Angel and the Badman,* which was just as well because there was not much to celebrate when it was released.

"We were at their suite at the Ala Moana Hotel one night," Esperanza Wayne recalled a few years later in court. "Mr. Wayne was intoxicated. Mr. Grant was worse.

They were talking and I was tired. I lay down on a twin bed. Mr. Wayne grabbed my by the foot and dragged me to the floor. I asked him what was the matter. He insulted me. He berated me. I cried. I was upset. My eyes were swollen from crying. We were supposed to go to another party. I couldn't go. Mr. Wayne later apologized and asked me to forgive him. I forgave him and said that if liquor did things like that to him he should not drink so much. He promised never to strike me again and never to swear."

And yet she was by now a compulsive drinker herself, and when she got drunk she would start coming on strong, probably to get his attention, but in ways that antagonized him and brought out the animal in him. It was a difficult situation. They loved each other passionately but they seemingly could not live peacefully together. Yet after each battle, they were physically excited. They were emotionally dependent on each other, and if Chata sometimes betrayed him with other men, which she had begun to do—she always made sure that he found it out, being gone from a party, say, for some hours, and returning with suspicious grass stains on her clothes and a guilty-looking male guest in tow—she thought, as drunken and foolish persons sometimes think, that this technique would stimulate a lover. It did. It stimulated him to rage, blind rage.

Chata remembered another violent episode at the Hotel Del Prado in Mexico City. Wayne was producing *The Bullfighter and the Lady* with Robert Stack. She got drunk. Duke got drunk. They started arguing and finally he lost control and "grabbed me and threw me against the wall and pulled my hair. He kicked me, then dragged me the full length of the corridor. He called me awful names. He punched me in the eye. Next morning my eye was swollen. I had to wear dark glasses to hide it."

On another occasion, at a party at actor John Carroll's, he was drinking too much and she told him to stop drinking and he took umbrage at this and "knocked me down, hit me while I was on the floor, and kicked me. I was completely bruised. I was sore all over. I had to stay in bed."

As Duke remembered it, at the time it was Esperanza's mother who was the bane of their marital existence. She not only drank, shot for shot, with her daughter, but as the ladies got more intoxicated, she would fan the customary grievances of any Hollywood wife into a roaring blaze. She also liked to beat up her daughter. She believed in corporal punishment and harsh discipline. Wayne insists he did not beat up women. He did not believe, as one of Noel Coward's characters did, that women are like gongs and should be struck regularly. It was Mrs. Ceballos who went for the gong theory.

However, in fairness to both sides, it would seem that when they were sufficiently befuddled by tequila, Scotch or bourbon, both Esperanza and Duke lost their judgment, their refinement, and their memory of what had taken place. Persons who regularly consume large quantities of alcoholic beverages are prone to states of amnesia, known as "blackouts," during which they can perform physical actions—such as driving a car for hundreds of miles, beating up a spouse, viciously insulting a spouse, and other things—and have no recollection whatsoever of these actions.

One of the little incidents during the marriage, which is so typical of all marriages in which a small disagreement is the disguise for a deeper rift, is the Adventure of the Avocado Sandwich. On one occasion, they were playing gin rummy together, having a nice evening at home, feeling congenial together. Mrs. Ceballos, by now, had been dispatched home to Mexico, in one of the frequent attempts to bring about a reconciliation and muffle the discords. Wayne said he was hungry. So she got up and went into the kitchen and broiled a steak and made him a steak sandwich. The servants were asleep. It was late at night. All was tranquil in the Encino home. He had his steak and a bottle of beer. She had her favorite sandwich: a guacamole (avocado) on toast. She had a bottle of beer. He said he wanted another sandwich. She went back to the kitchen and saw that some minced avocado still remained in a bowl. So she made him an avocado sandwich. Did she do this deliberately to provoke his temper? Was it an unconscious gesture? Was it an accident? Because she knew that he *detested* avocado in any form. He complained about the guacamole sandwich in no uncertain terms.

"Mr. Wayne does not like avocado," she reported. "I was getting up to get him a different sandwich, but he flew into a rage, slapped me down in the chair, called me vile names, yelled and insulted me in a very loud voice."

## 18

### Fort Apache, Red River, Three Godfathers

In May, 1947, Wayne became forty years old. During this year, in a prodigious outburst of physical and emotional energy, he gave three magnificent performances in three magnificent films: *Fort Apache* and *Three Godfathers,* both directed by Ford, and Howard Hawks' *Red River.* Far from being in the twilight of his career, Duke was at the blaze of noon. His apotheosis as an actor began in 1947. They used to believe in the studios that the box-office life of a star was five years and then, during the 1930's, it was stretched to ten years; a few exceptions, such as Joan Crawford and Gable, went to fifteen and more. Wayne had held on for almost twenty years—but all that had come before was only a prelude to what took place now, and what was to continue to happen until the present.

I do not know how to explain this miracle year, for

his energies were being sapped by the combats at home and the quarrels at Republic. He was dispirited by the reception of his first production, *Angel and the Badman*.

These three films of 1947 were not routine films. They were highly wrought, complex stories, in which he had to satisfy two directors of high standards, and in which he had to convey a range of powerful emotions. They were demanding roles in demanding films.

Yet with an utter indifference to his mental fatigue and his forty-year-old physical exhaustion, he threw himself into these films with the exuberance of a young actor in his prime. Nowadays we are impressed when a star makes one good picture in a year. Even for those days, his achievement stood out. He had acquired a self-discipline and a mastery of movie technique which enabled him to perform miracles.

*Fort Apache* was written by Frank Nugent, a former movie critic, and it was adapted from James Warner Bellah's "Massacre," a *Saturday Evening Post* story. It was shot entirely on location in Monument Valley, on the Monument Valley Navajo Indian reservation. It is about the wars of the U.S. Cavalry against the rebellious tribes, in the period following the Civil War. Henry Fonda plays a demented colonel, determined to slaughter Indians. Wayne was Captain York, a man who knows and respects the Indians, a man of peace and conciliation. Colonel Thursday is a widower. He comes to Fort Apache with his daughter, played by the grown-up Shirley Temple. Miss Temple had recently married John Agar, an Air Force lieutenant, who, after his discharge sought to become a movie actor. He was playing his first role in *Fort Apache*—the West Point-educated young officer whose father is Ward Bond, one of the enlisted men at the fort. Miss Temple and Agar fall in love in the story.

From the first Wayne and Fonda get into strong disagreements about tactics. Fonda, anxious to regain his prestige by bringing the Apaches to heel, sneers at them as "digger" Indians. They have fled over the border, leaving the reservation, and are in Mexico. Wayne tries to convince him that the Apaches are good warriors and are led by Cochise, a superb tactician. He says the Apaches are disgruntled because they have been lied to and exploited by the Indian agent (played by Grant Withers). Wayne cries out against the federal bureaucrats, the corrupt "Indian ring" in Washington.

Fonda tells Wayne to ride over the border and persuade Cochise to bring back his tribesmen.

"If you can assure him of decent treatment, he will lead his tribe back to the reservation," Wayne says. "But you cannot *make* him come back. He has outfought us. He has outgeneraled us. There are not enough troops here to *make* him—but maybe we could persuade him."

Wayne rides out alone, a desperate middle-aged career soldier. He makes an agreement with Cochise. Then Fonda reveals that it is a trick. Wayne was used as a decoy to trap the Apaches, whom the Cavalry will slaughter when they cross into the Territory.

"But I gave my word to Cochise," Wayne says. "Nobody can make me break my word."

And the colonel replies that no honor is involved when dealing with an Indian. And Wayne, in a great moment of nobility, stands stiffly and says in a deadly tone, *"There is to me, sir!"*

And so in the end almost all the U.S. soldiers are slaughtered. They lose the battle. Only Wayne and a few men escape, because Wayne has been punished by being ordered to the rear-guard. Yet the Eastern papers make Fonda a hero, and an oil painting of the battle starring Colonel Thursday hangs in Washington, D.C.

The film ends with Wayne defending the lie—because it is a lie told for the sake of the United States Army, which is greater than any individual and which he has to serve.

With the young Johnny Agar, Mr. Ford followed his usual method of badgering the youngest principal in order to make the others feel more secure. Agar couldn't take it. He was constantly being chastised for his halting delivery, his forgetting words, his awkwardness on a horse, even for breathing, it seemed. At times Ford got really nasty, calling him Mr. Temple. And he didn't spare Miss

Temple, whom he had once directed as a child star in *Wee Willie Winkle* with Victor McLaglen.

After a particularly rough day, Agar became so disgusted and enraged that he went back to his room (he was sharing a room with McLaglen, who played an Army sergeant). He started packing his things and was ready to leave the picture, leave the movies, leave his wife if she would not accompany him. There was a knock on the door. He opened it. There stood John Wayne, asking if he could come in. Duke sized up the situation at once. He had been watching Agar for days and seen that he had finally reached the breaking point.

Agar said, "Mr. Wayne, I'm through. I've had it. I just can't take any more of his insults."

"Now hold on just a minute there," Wayne drawled, as if he were in character. "Mr. Ford insultin' you don't mean he doesn't admire you. He likes you or he wouldn't insult you. Let me tell you what he did when I worked for him in *Mother Machree* and *Stagecoach* and a few other times, Johnny."

And he told him. He explained that it was Mr. Ford's way of getting you to loosen up and how he got a performance out of an untried actor or even a veteran. He said soon Mr. Ford would start bullying him and Fonda, just wait and see. He advised Agar not to trade ripostes with Ford. He should shut his mouth and bear it and try to learn. Agar cooled down.

Wayne ran the next day's lines with him. He also took him out for some sessions of riding and taught him what Jack Padgin and Yakima Canutt had showed him years before.

It was an act of thoughtful generosity to a younger player. Agar subsequently acted in many films starring Wayne. He would do anything for him. "I would go to hell and back for Duke," he told me.

And he saw that nobody worked harder than John Wayne. Duke was among the first to get to the location. He was in his makeup by the time the others began drifting in. He always knew his lines. He always listened to what the director told him.

"I am not sure which I admire most," he says, "John Wayne as a person or John Wayne as a dedicated actor. Let's say he is just about the best human being I have ever known."

Not only was *Fort Apache* remarkable for its favorable attitude toward the Indians and its honest portrait of American military men, of every shade, and for its humorous interludes with the enlisted men, but there were fantastically beautiful scenes of battles and chases and landscapes. It is a classic western. Bosley Crowther praised Wayne for being "powerful as [the] captain, forthright and exquisitely brave."

He was not nominated for an Academy Award for his portrayal of Captain York.

Wayne went through a phase of self-examination when Ford asked him to play a man well on in years. He went through that *crise de l'âme* which most men experience at the threshold of forty. What made this period so painful for Duke was that it was the second year of his marriage. Chata knew that his pride in his masculinity was a weak point in his armor. And she played on his anxieties, arousing his jealousy with every feminine wile and intrigue of which she was capable. At this time, she had begun striding out of the house at the height of an argument. She would get into the car. He would hear the door slam. She would drive away in a burst of speed. She would go to the bars on Ventura or drive into Hollywood and make the Sunset Strip scene. She picked up strangers and bought them drinks and presents and spent nights with them. She frequently went to Las Vegas alone and gambled and had lovers. She embarrassed him and humiliated him in public by flirting outrageously. She tried to seduce every young man she could.

And yet she loved him. She was trying to get him to belong to her. And Duke's oldest friends, like Paul Fix, found her a warm human being, a friendly and amiable person and entertaining to be with. His friends felt that Chata was being exploited by parasites. But she was lonely. Perhaps she knew they were parasites, but she was lonely and she did drink, and sometimes she got lonely drinking alone and she had to have a drinking companion.

Yet she loved Duke and he loved her. Between the fights, between the infidelities and the roaring drunks, there were interludes of great passion and great tenderness. Wayne was madly in love with her and remained madly in love with her. But he was not so much in love with her that he was prepared to make just one picture a year. He wanted her, but on his terms. She had surrendered her acting to possess him. She had forsaken her Mexico for him. And in return she had received loneliness, vast stretches of ennui punctuated by lightning flashes of divine passion, and it was not enough; the lightning was not enough for her.

And she did not give him children. She was unable to bear children. The dream they had of a new family was not fulfilled. He took it as a slur on his manhood. The difference in their ages became another pretext for differences between them. Privately, they both knew he had plenty of machismo. He was one of those fortunate males endowed with an inexhaustible fountain of libido.

And yet . . . and yet . . . why did he make three movies in the second year of their marriage?

He had to. It was his destiny. He would always tell himself that there would be just one more picture and after that he would learn how to live differently, but there was a next movie and a next . . .

He was troubled by his relations with his children. It was important that he have a good relationship with them. He did not want to duplicate his own childhood. He loved them. He wanted above all to be a strong father to his sons. Mike and Pat were different in build and temperament. Pat was growing tall and bony; he resembled his father in the sensitive face and he showed an introspective quality. He read, he was thoughtful, he was artistic. Mike was stocky, tall, inclined to athletics, smiling and gregarious. He got along better with Esperanza than the other children.

The children were another issue in his marriage. Between films, or when he was working at the studios, he would want them visiting or staying for long periods. Chata resented the children. They took more of her man away from her.

But her biggest rival, as it had been Josie's, was the "industry."

And yet, beyond the rationalizations he made about having to grind away at the pictures because he had to support two families and pay his debts, there was the fact that he had become fanatical about his work. He was now in a position where every studio wanted him. He enjoyed his growing power and authority in Hollywood. The 1940's, as William Everson has pointed out, were the decade of the western spectaculars. *Stagecoach* had re-opened the territory and proved the perennial appeal of the western. And when a studio thought of investing a million or more in a western, John Wayne automatically came to mind—it was either him or Gary Cooper.

So the work was there. Wayne worked. And because there was tension at home if the children came to visit, he would take Mike out on his hunting trips and Pat on the fishing trips. As they grew older, he took them, and Toni and Melinda, to stay on location, and ultimately the careers of Mike and Pat blended in with his own.

In 1947, Howard Hawks was fifty years old and he decided that it was high time that he make a western movie. There is not a movie director who does not sooner or later want to prove to himself that he can make a great western. For almost twenty years Hawks had made many kinds of films—from gangster films like *Scarface* and aviation pictures like *The Dawn Patrol* to a series of delicious high comedies of the 1930's: *Twentieth Century, Bringing Up Baby, His Girl Friday, Ball of Fire*. He had recently wrapped up, back to back, two memorable films with Bogart and Bacall: *To Have and Have Not* and *The Big Sleep* for Warners. He had left Warners and formed his own independent production company with agent Charlie Feldman, Monterey Productions.

Back in 1940, Hawks had come close to making a western. He had directed *Scarface* for Howard Hughes.

Then Hughes hired him to direct *The Outlaw* with his new discovery, Jane Russell. *The Outlaw* was another Billy the Kid epic. Persons ambitious to make westerns are always drawn to new interpretations of Billy the Kid, Wyatt Earp, or Roy Bean. A company went on location in New Mexico and Hawks started shooting *The Outlaw*. He worked for two weeks. He had completed two sequences, including a dramatic confrontation between Billy the Kid and an older gunfighter, Doc. Doc, while drunk, tries to get the young killer into a fight by taunting him to make him draw, shooting at his feet and face, trying to make him pull his gun. Billy the Kid likes old Doc. He stands his ground and faces down the old man. They become friends. Billy the Kid, who is the fastest man with a gun around, knows he can draw faster and kill Doc any time he wants, but he chooses not to do so.

At this juncture, Jack Warner beseeched Howard Hawks to make a deal with Warners. He presented him with a generous contract for a seven-year period and a promise of the best properties in the studio, starting with *Sergeant York,* a biographical film about a World War I hero, which was in key with the patriotism sweeping the country. Gary Cooper was signed to play York. Hawks could not resist Warners blandishments. He went to Hughes and said he was unhappy with *The Outlaw* and wanted to go to Warners and make *Sergeant York.*

Hughes was enraged. A commitment was a commitment. There were stormy arguments, but Hawks finally put up a large sum of money to gain his release.

Hughes completed *The Outlaw* himself. *Sergeant York* was a popular movie and Cooper won an Oscar for it. Hughes resented deeply what he considered Howard Hawks' cavalier treatment of him.

But now in 1947 Feldman and Hawks had bought a story by Borden Chase, "The Chisholm Trail," about the first cattle drive from Laredo, Texas, to Abilene, Missouri.

Originally, as Hawks cast the film in his mind, Cooper would play Tom Dunson, an implacable middle-aged Texas rancher, and Cary Grant would plap Cherry Valance, a worldly gambler and pimp and gunfighter who

joins the cattle drive. There was a third important role—
that of the adopted son of Dunson—Matt.

Hawks started having problems right away. Cooper did
not like the total ruthlessness of the role. He wanted Chase
and Charles Schnee—who had collaborated on a fine
screenplay, now titled *Red River*—to mitigate his monomania, as he felt it did not comport with his strong but
amiable screen image. For there was something almost
evil in the part, something on the edge of sadism and insanity—the old rancher literally kills several of the cowboys who interfere with hs ruthless drive up to the North.
Furthermore, Dunson was out of the film a good deal of
the time and did not reappear until the final climactic
confrontation with his son.

Now Copper, of course, trusted Hawks and had worked
with him many times, but he felt he could not do this
role unless the character was changed.

And Cary Grant could not see himself playing the sub-
ordinate role of Cherry Valance unless his part was en-
larged to equal the Dunson part.

In this crisis, Hawks began negotiating for Duke's services. Since Charlie Feldman was Duke's agent as well
as producer of *Red River,* he figured he could count on
Wayne to be enough box-office power so he did not need
to look for another big name to play Cherry Valance. He
signed John Ireland. Then young Montgomery Clift, who
had been turning down one script after another, agreed to
play the son.

Wayne liked the script and liked the role. He did not
want Tom Dunson softened up. He would play a hard
character. He always believed western heroes should be
hard characters anyway, aside from that momentary aber-
ration with Quirt Evans, convert to Quakerism. But he
had not signed. He was finishing *Fort Apache* and was
still on location.

Meanwhile, Hawks had to find his own location site.
He and Feldman and some assistants leased a private
plane and scouted locations from the air. They traveled
fifteen thousand air miles and then, sixty miles south of
Tucson, he came upon a high desert plain, at an elevation

of five thousand feet, which had desert sand and trees and rivers and distant mountain ranges, and other kinds of landscape variations. The place was called Rain Valley. The reason it was called Rain Valley was that it did not rain there very often, and never during June, July, August, and September, when they would be filming. Monterey Productions rented a portion of Rain Valley.

Then Hawks came up with a marvelous idea, he thought. He would get authentic real Arizona cowboys to play themselves in *Red River*. He signed up seventy real cowboys. This got him excited. He felt like Rossellini going out in the streets of Rome and finding men and women to play in his neo-Realist pictures. Why, he was breaking fresh ground. Nobody had ever used so many real cowboys before in one picture. He hired horses by the dozens and a thousand head of cattle; the horses would represent hundreds of horses and the cattle, ten thousand head of cattle to be shown on the screen.

Wayne remembers a meeting he had with Feldman and Hawks at Feldman's patio and swimming pool one Sunday, when he came up from Monument Valley to state some of his objections to *Red River,* for he had some. The setting for the meeting did not impress Duke. "You don't make westerns by sitting around a swimming pool," he once told me. "I could see Howard Hawks and Feldman, well, what they knew about makin' westerns amounted to a pitcher of warm spit.

"They had a budget of just under a million and a half. My own salary was a hundred and fifty thousand and a percentage. I told them, if they can't get United Artists to spend at least two million five, they would never make this picture—they were thinkin' in terms of a blockbuster, you see. Actually *Red River* cost three million and it grossed about ten.

"The next thing I said after I straightened them out on the budget was about these Arizona cowboys. No dice. Absolutely no amateurs. I told them flat out, *I don't go in on this deal unless you get some professional western actors and a dozen trained western stuntmen*. I could see Hawks was payin' attention. I started telling them something of my experiences with westerns and all the location problems, and even Charlie Feldman, who was a hard man to shut up, did, and Hawks followed my lead and by God he learned fast and found out how to make westerns."

The amateurs from Arizona were fired and trained western actors were employed. The budget was increased. Wayne agreed to play Tom Dunson.

Hawks' education in westerns was sometimes painful. He was bitten by a centipede while standing on a sand dune and had to be hospitalized with a swollen leg. His leading lady, Margaret Sheridan, confessed that she was five months' pregnant and began to show a protuberant belly. Hawks had to find a replacement in a hurry, and he pushed Joanne Dru into the part. Since the women were different types, the screenplay had to be rewritten hastily. Then it started raining.

It was not supposed to rain in Rain Valley during the hot months, and it had not rained there in the summer for a hundred years, but perhaps some hostile Navajo medicine-man did not like Howard Hawks. Wayne told Hawks that he should go on filming in the rain. He said he did not mind acting in the rain. He said on a western you worked with the weather and you did not complain about it. The screenplay was rewritten so that among the natural hazards encountered on the cattle drive was a fierce storm. There were awesome shots of dark clouds and rain and splashing drops and puddles of mud and fog-shrouded landscapes. Wayne got a bad cold and Joanne Dru got a touch of influenza, and most of the cast was coughing and sneezing. But they went on shooting, all the time.

And always Wayne was at Hawks' hand, as if he were an assistant director, a writer, suggesting bits of action, remembering a "gag" he and Yak Canutt had done in a Republic quickie, figuring out how to do a stunt, showing Montgomery Clift how to stage a fistfight so it looked real, so they could punch murderously without laying a finger on each other.

Duke and Hawks got into their most serious aesthetic controversy over how Duke was going to project middle age. His face could be wrinkled by a makeup man and his hair grayed. But Hawks did not like the way Duke moved and talked. He said Wayne was altogether too lively for an old man. He assigned Walter Brennan—who was playing Groot, a crusty old man and Dunson's sidekick—to coach Wayne in geriatric mannerisms.

"Well," Duke recalls, "Brennan showed me his idea of an old man walkin' and talkin'. His idea of it was kinda shufflin' and totterin'. And mumblin'. I was supposed to be tough and hard and walk like that? Hell, I was thinkin' about those old cattle guys I knew when I was a kid around Lancaster and there wasn't one of them that didn't stand tall. I played Tom Dunson my own way, standin' tall. Oh yeah, Hawks and I had a few fights along the way, but he accepted me as an expert, which I was, and we did not have any more trouble, and I was always happy to work for Hawks."

There is a scene in *Red River* during which all the men, led by Dunson's own son, Matt, and seconded by Cherry Valance, turn on the old rancher and defy him. They say they are trekking to Abilene on a different route than he has planned for them. Wayne stands alone against them all. He cannot accept their decision. He has to abdicate his leadership—under compulsion.

Rehearsing the action, Hawks told him to cringe—just slightly. They had a big row over this. Wayne refused to cringe.

"Howard," he said, " a guy can kill, he can be mean and vicious—and he could still hold an audience. But let him show a yellow streak and he will lose them. I'm not about to cringe. I agree with the audience."

He mounts his horse and rides away alone, vowing to get revenge and kill the person he loves most, his son.

And finally at the end, when Montgomery Clift and John Ireland have brought the cattle safely through, and Harry Carey, the cattle buyer, has bought the surviving nine thousand head for thirty dollars each, father and son meet on the quiet street for the classic shootout. Except that Clift does not draw his gun. Wayne is angry, for by the rules of the game he cannot shoot an unarmed

man. He attempts to goad his son into drawing. He taunts
him. He sneers at him. He starts shooting around his boots
to get him riled up. But his son stands quietly. And finally
they pummel each other until they are exhausted and
then become reconciled.

*Red River* was booked for national release in August,
1948.

Suddenly a legal problem ensued. Howard Hughes sued,
alleging infringement on *The Outlaw*.

John Keats, one of the biographers of Howard Hughes,
gives the following account of the curious incident:

> "One day I was on the set when a delegation of
> Hughes' attorneys arrived," Hawks said. "In my film
> *Red River,* one of the characters uttered the line,
> 'Draw your gun.' The Hughes men notified me that
> Howard Hughes was filing a lawsuit against me. He
> claimed that 'Draw your gun' had been stolen from
> the script of *The Outlaw*.
>
> "I couldn't believe my ears," Hawks said. "I asked
> the lawyers if Hughes was serious. They assured me
> he was."
>
> Hawks said he burst out laughing when the law-
> yers left, and he laughed again when telegrams began
> to arrive from other directors. PLEASE BE ADVISED
> THAT I OWN THE RIGHTS TO "THEY WENT THATAWAY,"
> one director wired. YOU ARE FORBIDDEN TO USE THE
> LINE "CUT 'EM OFF AT THE PASS," another said. THE
> WORDS "HOWDY, MA'AM" MAY NOT BE USED WITH-
> OUT PERMISSION.
>
> Hawks deleted "Draw your gun" from *Red
> River*'s script.

This is an amusing story but it must be almost entirely
erroneous. It is suspicious even on the face of it, for
Hughes had grown up in the picture business because his
uncle Rupert was an old-time scenario writer. And
Howard himself had been active as a producer and director since 1926. He may have been eccentric, he may
have been indecisive, he may have had megalomania—

but an idiot he was not, certainly not about movies. His second film, *Two Arabian Nights,* had won a director's Oscar for Lewis Milestone. And *Hell's Angels,* which he had directed, was a classic of aviation war films. His production of *Scarface* was a gangster film classic. He was a good friend of Duke Wayne's and had been on his sets and his locations many times, and he had himself directed *The Outlaw,* a full-length western of some quality. In fact, up till 1948 Hughes had had more experience with westerns than Howard Hawks.

It is unlikely that he would take anybody to court for the plagiarism of a "copyrighted" piece of dialogue like "Draw your gun."

The facts of the matter are—as reported by *Variety* and the Los Angeles *Times,* among others—that on August 16, 1948, the Hughes Tool Company, which owned *The Outlaw,* filed a copyright infringement suit in the Federal Court in Dallas, alleging that "the climactic scene from Howard Hughes' *The Outlaw* had been used in Howard Hawks' *Red River.*" The plaintiff named as defendants United Artists, which owned *Red River,* and the Interstate Theater Circuit of Texas, which was booking the film into its chain. Hughes asked the court for an injunction to restrain United Artists from releasing the film until it had deleted the infringing sequence from the final print!

And what was the issue? Was it "Draw your gun"? Was it "Thank you, ma'am"? Was it "They went that-away"?

Not on your Moviola. It was that scene in which, as Hedda Hopper reported in a bylined story in the *Times,* "Billy the Kid resists the efforts of his erstwhile friend Doc to draw him into a duel. Billy refuses to go for his guns even though Doc shoots a few nicks in his ears. *The two are reconciled during the scene.*" [Italics mine.]

Howard Hughes asserted in his complaint that in 1940 he had engaged Hawks to direct two films. From Ben Hecht he had purchased an original story, "The Outlaw." Jules Furthman, one of the most competent of American screenwriters had written the screenplay. Hughes affirmed he owned copyright to the screenplay and the film, which were submitted in evidence.

United Artists, aware that Hughes was on solid ground, did not contest the lawsuit. And Hawks did not demur. Was there not a clear correlation between the confrontation between Billy the Kid and Doc on the one hand, and Matt and Tom Dunson on the other?

Hughes met with two top United Artists executives: Gradwell Sears and Edward Small. They agreed to give Hughes a print of *Red River,* so that Hughes could *personally* excise the infringing sequence from *Red River.* Already delayed by the lawsuit, *Red River* now was an unfinished movie, a movie without an ending, and its ending was part of the design, for it harked back to the prologue in which Tom Dunson, a young man of twenty-five en route to California in a wagon train, becomes hungry for land as he sees the open spaces and decides to make his home in Texas. His fiancée, remaining on the train, is captured by Indians and killed. And this transforms Dunson into a cold-hearted implacable man, until he comes to a meeting of the hearts with his adopted son, whom he had found as an infant, the only survivor of that wagon train of settlers . . . Without the scene of understanding, the hero is to the end a ruthless madman. (And when *Red River* is televised, which happens often, the wagon train prologue is usually cut so that his motivation is gone.) In an interview with the then editor of *Cahiers du Cinema,* Eric Rohmer, Hawks in January, 1963, explained the character Wayne played: "Driven by his ambition, filled with this tremendous greed for his own land, Wayne is a man who has made a terrible mistake and lost the only girl he has ever really loved. Having made this mistake, he is all the more anxious to carry out every plan he makes. He can't admit he is wrong. A man who has made a serious mistake in order to accomplish his goals will never let himself be stopped by little details. He has built an empire which he sees breaking up in pieces. And he will not let any of his cowboys leave the drive or change the direction. He warns them of what is in store for them if they disobey. And they all leave him.

In telling such a story, we were treading on a high thin wire. Would the audience continue to love Wayne or not? *Happily, we had finished with a resolution which made a solid characterization of a man and the public loved Wayne.*" [My translation.]

Hawks asked Wayne to intercede with Hughes. Wayne did so.

He put it this way, "Howard, I'm not asking this favor for Howard Hawks. I know there's bad blood between you and him."

"The son-of-a-bitch walked off my picture," Hughes said. "On a week's notice, he walked off, and then he stole a sequence out of it. I'm not about to take that, Duke."

"I'm asking it for me, personally. We need that sequence. Without it, I come off a hard-hearted bastard. It's going to hurt me as an actor. It means a hell of a lot to me, Howard."

Hughes smiled and put out his hand. "You can have the scene back, Duke," he said. "I guess I've made my point." Then he looked into Duke's eyes. "Why did it take you so long to ask?"

Bosley Crowther complimented Wayne about *Red River:* "This consistently able portrayer of two-fisted, two-gunned outdoor men surpasses himself in this picture . . . a withering job of acting a horse wrangler . . ." he wrote in the New York *Times.* Well, it was not exactly the way one wrote about Laurence Olivier, Ronald Colman, and Fredric March. You did not get respect if you were in the western trade. At best you were patronized. John McCarten in *The New Yorker* could only say it was an "utterly satisfactory cowpunching drama," and Wayne is not singled out in the review. *Time* magazine said it was a "rattling good outdoor adventure movie." Hawks was praised, Montgomery Clift made much of, and Wayne ignored.

And that was the way it was. Wayne was continuing to be taken for granted. He had, with this film, found himself, found his style, found his presence, adapted his personal tensions and emotional struggles to his techniques, and he could use his feelings for his own sons, Pat and Mike, and be the son of his own father, and project it into his characterization. He would give what we now consider one of the greatest performances in any western film, but it was conceived of as "cowpunching" and "horse wrangling" by the crtics of the 1940's.

John Wayne was not nominated for an Academy Award for his performance in *Red River*.

*Red River* was Harry Carey's last picture. On September 21, 1947, he died of heart complications following the bite of a black widow spider. There was an outdoor memorial service in the rehabilitation center for men of the Signal Corps which John Ford had recently set up in Reseda and which was known as the Field Photo Memorial Ranch. The pallbearers were Ford, Fonda, Ward Bond, Spencer Tracy, and Wayne. Wayne read Tennyson's "Crossing the Bar" at the services.

*Red River* was the third movie and the first important picture that Harry Carey Jr. made. They call him Dobie Carey, and had called him that since childhood because his hair was the color of an adobe building. He played a young cowboy in *Red River* who gets killed during the cattle stampede.

Dobie's first dramatic memory of Wayne was in 1939, when *Stagecoach* was released. Duke, already building up a following with his Republic and Monogram five-reelers, had stunned everybody (except the man at *The New Yorker*) with his playing of a desperate young gunfighter. There was an annual rodeo at Saugus. They had chosen the Ringo Kid as the grand marshal of the parade which would open the rodeo. Dobie was home from military school for the weekend.

Duke arrived early in the morning of opening-day ceremonies in a big black Packard twin-six. There was a chauffeur and Josie Saenz Morrison was along. The limousine pulled up at the Carey ranch house. The Waynes weren't staying at the main house of Carey's dude ranch. They were staying with Olive and Harry Carey in the guest wing of the Carey abode. Josie had to help Duke out of the car, that's how smashed Wayne was. His eyes were bleary and his big body was sagging. He weighed a hefty two hundred ten pounds despite his basically slim physique. He slumped in Josie's arms and the chauffeur bore him on one side and Dobie, now eighteen, propped him up on the back, and then they maneuvered him into the house and he flopped on a couch. He looked ridiculous because he was all dressed up for the parade. He had on a pair of beautiful hand-tooled boots and fancy leather trousers and an embroidered shirt and kerchief and a fancy white Stetson that looked to be fifteen or twenty gallons, so to speak. He looked the very opposite of what Harry Carey thought a western hero should look like.

Duke explained to the Carey family that he had not had any sleep. He and Josie had been out celebrating at a party honoring the *Stagecoach* actors. They had been dancing and drinking at the Ambassador Hotel's Cocoanut Grove. The festivities had gone on and on into the dawn, and the Waynes had driven straight to Saugus from there. He had put on the parade regalia for the Hollywood party and had been quite the sensation there, as he danced and clomped in his boots. Wayne has always been an excellent ballroom dancer, even in boots. And Josie loved dancing. He had gotten very drunk as usual, but they had not had an argument.

As he reclined on the couch and rubbed his eyes, Duke told Ollie that he thought a drink would straighten him out. Dobie stared at his hero adoringly. He admired Duke the way Duke had once reverenced his father when he was a lad in Glendale going to the picture show and watching them shoot pictures on Verdugo Boulevard. Ollie Carey, who could bend an elbow herself and was one of those marvelous natural and uninhibited ladies, fetched Wayne a bottle of Old Taylor. He downed the contents of a tumbler and shivered like a big wet collie dog, and then straightened up and grinned. His eyes seemed to clear. His skin came alive. They had a big breakfast of ranch steaks and fried eggs, and Dobie remembered Big Duke just putting away one popover after another and consuming great quantities of black coffee.

By noon, he was human again and was making jokes and telling stories and smoking cigarettes.

Dobie thought Duke and Josie were an affectionate nice married couple. He had no idea of the misery which stained their lives.

The next time he saw Wayne was during the war, when his father had a heart attack in New York. Dobie got leave from the Navy and came up from San Diego. He had no money and he borrowed a few hundred dollars from Duke to get to see his father.

Dobie started going out with Paul Fix's daughter, Marilyn, during the war. They were married in 1944. The Waynes were now legally separated, but Josie and Duke loved the Careys and treated Dobie like a son. They came together once more in the North Highland hacienda to lay on a champagne and buffet wedding reception for the couple—who are still happily married.

That happened to be the type of party which Mr. and Mrs. John Wayne persisted in sharing as host and hostess —wedding receptions. When each of their four children was married in succeeding years, they jointly gave the reception at the Beverly Hills Hotel. And the children were all married at the Roman Catholic Church of the Good Shepherd in Beverly Hills, which is the St. Patrick's Cathedral of elegant Catholicism in the movie colony.

One always gets reports that at these functions Josie Morrison was a light-hearted and delightful hostess. She was a shining success in society, and this image does not comport with the dark picture we get of a pleasure-hating religious fanatic dedicated to casting out all the sins of the flesh. I suppose Josie was, and is, a contradiction in many ways, like all of us, but she was not, I believe, so troubled by warring and contradictory urges and ideas as her husband. He was a battleground of contradictions. One of his favorite poets was Walt Whitman, and he appreciated the lines in which Whitman says:

"Do I contradict myself? Very well then I contradict myself. I am large. I contain multitudes."

After the war Dobie Carey thought he might go into the movies. He got a nice part in a Robert Mitchum movie, *Pursued*. Milton Sperling, the producer, decided to publicize his screen debut with a title reading "And introducing Harry Carey Jr."

Dobie was troubled. He went to Wayne and said, "I don't know what name to use. They want to bill me as Harry Carey Jr., but I think I should use Dobie Carey professionally. I don't want to trade on my father's name."

"I think," Wayne said, "you should let them tag you Harry Carey Jr. Hell—we both know they're buyin' the name, not the actor. You haven't made your mark as an actor. My suggestion is—don't go into the picture business. Find yourself another line of work. You're gonna have a rough go in pictures, Dobie. You just aren't a handsome-lookin' feller. Physically you are not a leading man. What you are is a character actor. There aren't that many parts for young character actors. Incidentally, what did your father-in-law [Paul Fix] tell you when you asked him?"

"He said to ask you," Dobie said.

"Paul's no idiot," Duke said. "My suggestion is you get yourself some little business as a sideline, because you aren't ever going to be workin' steady in pictures, Dobie."

After *Pursued,* Dobie did two more pictures, in each of which there was a title reading "And introducing Harry Carey Jr." It gave some producers and directors a feeling of pride to think they were enabling a young performer to make his debut in their picture, even if he had already made his debut. Then Dobie did *Red River*.

After Harry Carey Sr. died, John Ford, who had loved him deeply and whose very beginnings as a director were linked to Harry Carey's encouraging him to make his first five-reeler, decided to remake a classic western story, Peter B. Kyne's *Three Godfathers*. It was fashioned as a tribute to Harry Carey and also as an expression of Ford's increasing feeling of the truth of revealed religion and of the sacred mission of Jesus Christ.

Carey had made the first movie of the Kyne tale—a pastiche of Bret Harte's *Luck of Roaring Camp*—as a two-reeler in 1916. It was directed by Eddie Le Saint.

(Mr. Le Saint later achieved a brief notoriety by marrying the widow of the escape artist Houdini.) In 1919, it was remade by Ford with Harry Carey again and released as *Marked Men*. William Wyler remade it in 1929 as *Hell's Heroes* and Richard Boleslawski tried it again in 1936.

Ford emphasized the religious symbolism as he contrived to tell the story of three escaping bank robbers, dangerous outlaws, fleeing the law in the Mojave desert and coming upon a burned-out wagon train destroyed by Indians, and a pregnant woman survivor. The three bandits were played by Wayne, Pedro Armendariz, and Harry Carey Jr., who played the Abilene Kid. Incidentally, though McCarten of *The New Yorker* had stated that a pregnant woman was an obligatory character in a western, this was the first pregnant lady who had occurred in any of the twelve westerns which Duke had made since *Stagecoach,* and she did not remain pregnant very long. She gave birth. The three "godfathers" roam across the desert, and finally the only survivor, Wayne, brings the baby to the town of New Jerusalem, Arizona.

That does not sound terribly exciting, but it is a beautiful western with all the qualities of tenderness and humor and pictorial grandeur and action sequences which every Ford western has possessed. And it had three beautifully etched portraits of badmen.

Upon completing the film, Ford proposed to have a main title reading THIS FILM IS DEDICATED TO THE MEMORY OF HARRY CAREY—BRIGHT STAR OF THE EARLY WESTERN SKY. The title would fade out and be replaced by AND INTRODUCING HARRY CAREY JR., A NEW STAR IN THE WESTERN SKY.

This would make the fifth time that Harry Carey Jr. had been introduced, as he had also been "introduced" in *Red River*. He was becoming one of the most introduced actors in the annals of Hollywood.

Dobie still felt guilty about cashing in on his father's reputation. And he didn't like this constantly being introduced. He was like a debutante who keeps coming out, season after season. Some people might get annoyed by this reiteration of his debuts. His pride made him want to do something about it.

So he brought up the problem to Wayne. Should he request Mr. Ford to call him Dobie Carey or be billed as Jr., and what about this business of introducing him once more?

Wayne mulled over the problem. "Don't make any difference now," Duke finally said, "what you use. Dobie, Harry Carey Jr., Joe Blow. Fortunately, Dobie, you have a little talent."

He paused and his eyes narrowed. "As for introducing you, hell, let Mr. Ford have it his way. It gives the Old Man pleasure to do it, makes him feel he's carryin' on a tradition. But I'd still get a little sideline, if I were you —you have an ugly face, Dobie." And he smiled and put his arm around Dobie.

Dobie let John Ford "introduce" him for the fifth time, and retained his correct name of Harry Carey Jr. He has made several score films by now, including many with Wayne.

Young Carey experienced the usual treatment from Ford. "He started ragging me on the first day of work," Dobie recalls. "And it got worse. I thought he was being purposely mean to me because he wanted to show me I couldn't fill my father's shoes. We were filming in Monument Valley. I was sharing a room with Ward Bond. Bond was playing the sheriff. After a day of Mr. Ford's ribbing, I had a night of Ward Bond's ribbing.

"Audie Murphy was what Mr. Ford used against me. At that time Audie Murphy was one of our most decorated heroes and he was playing juvenile roles in many pictures. I'm not sure whether Mr. Ford had tried to get him for the Abilene Kid. But any time I did something he didn't like, Ford would say, 'I should have got Audie Murphy to play this part. You are not giving it any guts.'

"He was constantly throwing Audie Murphy at me. It was Audie Murphy this and Audie Murphy that. I finally had it up to here and I decided to quit. Didn't care if I never worked in movies again the rest of my life. I couldn't take it any more.

"I went and told Duke of my decision. He talked me out of it. He spent a whole Sunday with me. He convinced me that Mr. Ford was trying to get me riled up to get a performance out of me. And he told me that as far as he, Duke, was concerned, I was a good man and worthy to carry my father's name. He saved my life."

*Three Godfathers* was John Ford's first color film. His cinematographer was Winton Hoch. The result was a western masterpiece, largely unappreciated, another John Ford triumph which was either shrugged away or taken for granted, and another John Wayne portrayal which was overlooked. The film made some critics uncomfortable because of its religious theme, and others found it unbelievable. *Time* summed it up as an "unintentional parody on the old-fashioned western."

Yet Crowther of the *Times,* who sometimes seemed to patronize the western genre and, if he were deeply moved, to feel uncomfortable with his emotions, wrote one of the most favorable reviews he ever wrote about any western during his years on that newspaper. It read, in part:

> Mr. Ford's wonderful style in picturing a frontier fable that has the classic mold. . . . John Wayne as the leading badman and ultimate champion of the child is wonderfully raw and ructious . . .

John Wayne was not nominated for an Academy Award for his performance in *Three Godfathers,* nor for equally excellent performances in its successors, *Wake of the Red Witch* and *She Wore a Yellow Ribbon.*

Toward the end of 1948, the New York *Times* finally took notice of the fact that there was something mighty strange taking place in the movie industry, and the name of the phenomenon was John Wayne. There appeared a long feature article by Gladwin Hill, a Los Angeles correspondent. It ran on the first page of the Sunday drama section, under a pejoratively snickering head: TALE OF A HORSE OPERA HOT SHOT.

Hill noted the plethora of new John Wayne films in

release, observing that one could "hardly peek out the door these days without coming into contact with [him] . . . Theater marquees blazon *Fort Apache* and *Red River* . . . The dailies report that John Wayne, having finished *Three Godfathers* and at the moment engrossed in *Wake of the Red Witch,* is about to start work in *She Wore a Yellow Ribbon.* . . . Meanwhile his venerable hit, *Stagecoach,* still pulls them in on the reruns . . . And although Wayne who, it seems like only yesterday was looming out of the sagebrush, is still playing 'juveniles,' a little finger counting establishes that he's been at it for twenty years and for more than one hundred films. What gives? Ask anybody in Hollywood to analyze the ubiquity and professional longevity of such a fixture as Wayne and you'll precipitate about the same mystification as if you asked a New Yorker to account for the existence and persistence of Sixth Avenue or the Chock Full O'Nuts."

Now here, as Mr. Hill writes his essay, Wayne has given two stalwart performances as older men in *Fort Apache* and *Red River.* He has not played a young lover. There has not even been one of those mature and eternally feminine creatures like Maureen O'Hara or Patricia Neal around for him to adore. But he is called a "juvenile" by a competent and usually accurate reporter. Montgomery Clift was the juvenile in one film and John Agar in the other. In the strictest sense of the word, John Wayne had played awfully few juvenile lovers over the past ten years.

Where had Gladwin Hill been all these years when Wayne was engaging in amorous foreplay with Marlene Dietrich, Claudette Colbert, and Jean Arthur? Had he talked to Paulette Goddard?

What, to quote Mr. Hill, gives? Had he been afflicted by that curious blindness which would be suffered by movie critics and movie writers when they came near John Wayne the superman? It was a perennial lapsing, a consistently selective inattention—operating regularly—which simply did not see what was there and was unable to cope with the presence of this great creative force which fitted none of the preconceived patterns of film theory or film criticism.

In 1948, Wayne, who had been lagging in the popularity polls, began spurting again into prominence. In 1948, he had been voted number thirty-three in the prestigious *Motion Picture Herald* poll of exhibitors. In 1949, he vaulted up to fourth place. (Bob Hope was first, Bing Crosby second, and Abbott and Costello were third.) And in 1950, he became *número uno*. In that year, also, the readers of *Photoplay* voted him their favorite male actor, and he got the similar top rank in surveys by *Showman's Trade Review* and *Box-office Magazine*, and in a poll of the Independent Theater Owners of America. Having once made top position in "Fame" (which was what they called the annual rating of the *Motion Picture Herald*, a trade magazine), he remained among the leaders. He was number one in 1951, 1952, 1953 and intermittently among the first five thereafter. In the 1971 "Fame" poll he was again in first place! He set a record unequaled by any other star—twenty-three. The closest to Wayne in frequency of appearances was Gary Cooper (sixteen times) and Clark Gable (twenty-two times).

In 1949 he finally received an Oscar nomination for his Sergeant Stryker in *Sands of Iwo Jima*. He did not win. Broderick Crawford won it for *All the King's Men*. The year before Laurence Olivier had won it for his *Hamlet*. And the year before that Ronald Colman won it for *A Double Life*.

Wayne frequently attended the award ceremonies because friends or persons he knew would ask him to go there to receive their Oscars if they should win. These were actors or directors out of the country or on location. Wayne had already accepted awards for John Ford, Meriam Cooper, Burt Lancaster, Montgomery Clift, and Gary Cooper. He told me once that he felt like the shortstop in a double-play infield combination. He never made the putout but would pick up the ball and throw it to second.

John Ford said you won no prestige, no awards, by making westerns. He said being taken for granted was a cross that Wayne would have to bear. Even the nomination for an Oscar in 1949 had come for a performance in a war movie, probably the best war movie about World War II.

Duke went through many vagaries of self-analysis to explain his treatment at the hands of his peers. He told me once, in words similar to what his admirers Andrew Sarris and Peter Bogdanovich would use fifteen years later when the critical reevaluation of Ford, Hawks, Hathaway, the western film, and John Wayne took place. He said to me at that time, "I guess that I am never chosen because the kind of acting which I do is not considered acting by anybody." He was serious. He did not drop his final g's. He was thoughtful and spoke somberly. "I know that the hardest thing to do in a scene is to do nothing, or seem to do nothing, because doing nothing requires extreme work and discipline. I just stand there —or so it looks to the critics and even people in the Academy of Motion Picture Arts and Sciences. They would say, *Well, it is only John Wayne being John Wayne. He is not acting.* They have an idea that acting is putting on a disguise and being somebody you are not in a kind of blatant way. But, look, when I played Tom Dunson—was I a cattle rancher, a Texan? Or was I a Marine sergeant? Or was it *me* being the captain in *She Wore a Yellow Ribbon?* I was disappointed at not even being nominated for *Yellow Ribbon*. I had played a man sixty years old, which was seventeen years older than I was. I have always believed that this was my best achievement in pictures."

The reporter from the New York *Times* said that one precipitated "mystification" if you inquired around Hollywood for some explanation of John Wayne's long career in films and his rising popularity. The mystification was only among those who equated acting with a rank and overpowering distortion of what was assumed to be the actor's "real," the actor's "genuine" self. It was Ronald Colman miming Othello and a psychopathic killer, and Olivier miming Hamlet, and March vibrating his nervous sensibilities. They were acting, it is true, and there was another kind of acting, as well, a kind of visual presence which was the special glory of the movie actor, the movie personality. This was evident during the silent films but not when the movies began to speak. It *is* acting to stand there. It *is* acting to be there. It *is* acting to be listening. It *is* acting to say and do simple actions in a natural manner.

Now John Ford was not precipitated into any state of bewilderment when asked to explain why John Wayne was starring in so many pictures and why the public liked him.

Said Mr. Ford: "Duke is the best actor in Hollywood, that's all."

# 19

# The Politics of John Wayne

On February 7, 1944, the Motion Picture Alliance for the Preservation of American Ideals was organized at a mass meeting in the grand ballroom of the Beverly-Wilshire Hotel. About fifteen hundred persons, from every craft union and economic stratum of the industry, were present. Sam Wood, the director, was elected president. USAF Colonel Clark Gable and USN Lieutenant Robert Montgomery were in the audience. Among the eminent founding fathers and mothers of the Alliance— as it came to be known—were author Morrie Ryskind, Walt Disney, union leaders Ben Martinez and Roy Brewer, Ward Bond, Donald Crisp, Gary Cooper, King Vidor, Norman Taurog, Victor Fleming, Ginger Rogers, Barbara Stanwyck, John Ford, Mike Frankovitch, Cliff

Lyons, John Lee Mahin, Pat O'Brien, Robert Taylor, William Goetz, Irene Dunne, Dmitri Tiomkin, Cecil B. De Mille, and Adolphe Menjou. Menjou, a noted and gifted actor of sophisticated roles, was a fancy dresser and an even fancier intellectual; his principal pastime was the study of the works of Marx, Lenin, Stalin, Bukharin, and other ideologues of the proletarian revolution. Other actors might while away their time dining with beautiful women on cracked crab and *blanc de blancs* champagne at Mike Romanoff's, but Menjou occupied himself making marginal notes on such esoteric works as Lenin's *Materialism and Empirio-Criticism*. A cadre of comparatively obscure screenwriters were active in the Alliance: Frank Gruber, Borden Chase, James Edward Grant, Richard English, Howard Emmett Rogers and Richard Macauley. Macauley was one of the right-wing firebrands in the Screen Writers' Guild. Macauley was the original on which the character of Blumberg in *What Makes Sammy Run?* was based. Blumberg was the sensitive writer exploited by the villainous Sammy Glick.

For many weeks, Hollywood seethed with rumors that a gang of "Fascists and anti-Semites" were plotting to start a company union. In an industry in which many Jews were studio heads and producers, the anti-Semitic innuendos threatened the Alliance.

At the first meeting, Howard Emmet Rogers denied that MPA was anti-Semitic. He said that the finest anti-Communist fighters in the U.S. were Jewish. He cited Eugene Lyons, David Dubinsky, George Sokolsky, Max Eastman, and Ben Gitlow.

"These Jews are leading the fight against communism," he cried.

Those were rather confusing times for persons in the movie colony and elsewhere. Many people in Hollywood, who had previously been nonpolitical, became involved during the 1930's as a response to the Hitler crimes in Germany. The Hollywood Anti-Nazi League attracted many supporters to the movie industry—studio executives and high-salaried writers and actors. It was said to be Communist-inspired, one of those front organizations—

after all, weren't Stalin and the Soviet Union the most ardent opponents of Hitlerism?

Alas, there came the Nazi-Communist alliance of September, 1939, and here were the Communists and the Nazis jointly invading Poland. Overnight, the Hollywood Anti-Nazi League was dismantled. And now the Hollywood Communists were quoting Molotov's statement that fascism was "a matter of taste." They said sarcastic things about President Roosevelt and Eleanor. They wrote folk songs and put on sketches against the Roosevelts, who were now "warmongers."

France fell. England stood alone. England, the radicals said, was an imperialistic power. So was America.

It was very strange and very confusing. What was a person to believe? Who was a person to trust?

Then the Nazis invaded the Soviet Union in June, 1941. Everything changed. President Roosevelt was a fine person and Eleanor Roosevelt was a noble lady. Dalton Trumbo, who had written a gruesome antiwar novel, *Johnny Got His Gun,* withdrew it from public sale. Trumbo was a dedicated left-winger, a skillful and highly successful screenwriter, and an utterly charming and brilliant gentleman. He had no trouble understanding the processes of historical flow and change, the dialectic of human events, though these shifting patterns eluded less clever minds.

As for minds like Menjou's and Macauley's, they knew all the answers to the somersaults—the Communist conspiracy, working on orders from Moscow. And Moscow wanted to take over the American movie industry. Had not—and Menjou would give you the quote and the textual reference—Lenin himself said, old Ulianov in person, that the cinema was the mightiest tool of propaganda ever devised by the mind of man, and that Communists must use it? Hollywood was a beachhead on which lovers of freedom must make a stand.

The MPA started informally with a small group of anti-Communists who would meet regularly at the home of James Kevin McGuinness, an executive producer at M-G-M. Ward Bond brought Duke to his first meeting.

He remembers Leo McCarey, Menjou, Brewer, Ryskind, Borden Chase, and Sam Wood being there. Duke did not speak. He listened. He was sympathetic. He was in favor of, as he put it to me a few years later, "alerting Hollywood to the danger that a small group of Communists, under Party discipline, would take over the unions and control American movies." He saw the possible takeover of the Screen Writers' Guild as especially ominous, because he had "always believed that a picture begins and ends with a good story and screenplay."

Looking back, he was to see that his politicization took him out of "the narrow self-contained little world in which the sun rises and sets only on pictures." Whatever one may think of his political viewpoint, his values, the Motion Picture Alliance jolted Wayne out of his customary routine. He saw there was a way in which he could feel of value as an American citizen and a part of the world. He owed something to his country. He was in love with the United States of America. He saw his participation as the payment of the debt.

He says he had been aware of radicals in the movies as far back as 1937. At that time, he thought of himself as a liberal and Democrat. He was a Roosevelt voter. He believed in labor unions and in the world community. He believed that freedom in a democracy was a precious gift. John Ford, himself an Irish rebel to the core, was nevertheless anxious about the anti-religious and anti-American quality of some of the Marxian sounds he heard, and he had discussed it with Duke.

Wayne was on the executive board of the Screen Actors Guild during the 1940's and remembers how two of the fellow actors on the board seemed to be following a "line." They talked about the "masses." They fomented dissensions and aroused suspicion of studio heads. They talked about a general strike in the industry. He would attend parties and hear that Russia was the hope of the world. He says "once you get sensitized to it, you'd begin to be aware of cracks at our President, the flag, God, patriotism. A kind of sneering.

"In SAG, the left-wingers would try to pass resolutions

supporting a strike by Harry Bridges' longshoremen's union. Or I would get letters not to go to the Brown Derby or the Hollywood Athletic Club because some Communist-controlled union was pulling an outlaw strike. Some people I knew were going to the Actors Lab, to take classes in acting—and they came back telling how they were trying to indoctrinate them with Communist Party propaganda.

"I didn't attend the first few meetings of the Alliance, because I was making *Back to Bataan,* which Edward Dmytryk was directing for RKO. I had been asked by our State Department to make this movie because it was about the Filipino underground. Our technical adviser was an American colonel, one of the first to get out of the Philippines. He was a religious man and a very sincere patriot. On days when I wasn't on the set, a few men—including Eddie Dmytryk—were ragging him about God, singing the 'Internationale,' and making jokes about patriotism.

"This colonel came to me and asked what was happening. They were driving him up the wall. I went to Eddie Dmytryk and I said, 'What is going on around here? Are you a Communist or what?' I repeated what the colonel told me. He laughed and said, 'Aw, we were just kidding the guy.' Later he was named as a CP member and took the Fifth Amendment and went to jail and finally came out and was a friendly witness and became an anti-Communist himself."

The MPA met monthly in the American Legion auditorium on Highland Avenue. There was a short business meeting, votes were taken on resolutions, and then a well-known anti-Communist would speak on some phase of the Communist "conspiracy." MPA members heard such speakers as J. B. Matthews, Louis Budenz, Victor Riesel and Ralph de Toledano, who had co-authored a book on the Alger Hiss case with Victor Lasky.

Soon liberals became alarmed. They regarded the Alliance as a group of reactionaries, tools of Louis B. Mayer and Jack Warner. They began openly to attack MPA. Among those who organized and spoke at these meetings were Walter Wanger, Dudley Nichols, Marc Connelly and Emmett Lavery. Hollywood gradually divided into two hostile camps. The liberals—joined by some fellow travelers and some Communists—organized the Hollywood Independent Citizens Committee of the Arts, Sciences, and Professions, or HICCASP. A galaxy of stars joined it—Humphrey Bogart, John Garfield, Lauren Bacall, Danny Kaye, Edward G. Robinson, and numerous others. The "trades" took sides. *The Hollywood Reporter* and its publisher Billy Wilkerson were anti-Communist and pro-MPA. *Daily Variety* and weekly *Variety* were also anti-Communist, but took the stand that the MPA was smearing the motion picture industry by flinging loose charges. Who were these "Communists" they were raving about? Why didn't they name names?

On March 15, 1944, when MPA was beginning, *Daily Variety* published a long editorial captioned in huge letters: TIME TO NAME NAMES. They demanded to know the identity of these conspirators. "Lay it on the line," concluded the editorial, "or get off and stay off the line."

Then, in 1947, the House Committee on Un-American Activities began hearings on alleged CP infiltration of the movies. Soon there appeared witnesses and evidence in the form of membership cards and other documents revealing that there were CP cells operating in Los Angeles. Trumbo, Lawson, Lester Cole, Dmytryk, Ring Lardner Jr., Albert Maltz, and the others, who became known as the Unfriendly Ten, were summoned to Washington. (Director Billy Wilder observed that "two of them had talent—and the other eight were just unfriendly.")

Many liberals and some conservatives in Hollywood believed that these accusations were false, or even if true, that an American had as much right to be a Communist as he had to be a Republican or a Democrat. The famous Committee of 100 was hastily put together to defend Hollywood. The celebrities flew to Washington and held press conferences in defense of artistic freedom and against "red-baiting."

To their horror, the "unfriendlies," upon taking the

stand, did not testify that they were innocent. They stood on the First Amendment.

Stars like Bogart and Kaye, who had gone out on the limb, having received assurances that the Unfriendly Ten were unjustly maligned, were disgusted. The committee was disbanded. "They got a billion dollars' worth of stars to defend Hollywood," Ryskin recalls wryly. "And they came to Washington in a burst of publicity and they made speeches and had a lovely fanfare. When the Unfriendly Ten showed their true colors—well, that billion dollars' worth of talent looked like thirty cents."

The Unfriendly Ten went to jail. They served their terms courageously and, except for Dmytryk, they never recanted.

And now came a long parade of "friendly" witnesses, and the naming of names which *Daily Variety* had asked for, and then came the "blacklist."

Now, members of MPA will tell you that their side had been blacklisted for years by "Commies" and "Commie sympathizers." They had been victimized by whispering campaigns. Wayne recalls that in those days if you were active in MPA, people began spreading rumors around town that you had been drunk and disorderly in Chasen's, had been overheard praising Hitler, or expressing hatred of Negroes, and that your wife would get anonymous phone calls stating that you had been seen in San Diego hotels with blondes. Howard Emmett Rogers, Jim McGuinness, Adolphe Menjou were among those who were unemployed—it is claimed—because of the "Commie" blacklist.

Wayne himself never testified before the House Committee. He did not believe in blacklisting. He never blacklisted anybody on productions he controlled at Batjac. All studios had *always* had an informal blacklist on an *ad hoc* basis. Persons derelict in their morals could be refused employment. Persons who antagonized studios could be blacklisted throughout the industry. Harry Carey was blacklisted for many years because he refused to help M-G-M defend its lawsuit with Edwina Booth. (Miss Booth played in *Trader Horn*. On location in Africa she came down with a tropical disease and sued Metro for a small fortune. The Metro executives wanted Carey to take the stand in defense of their contention that Miss Booth was already a mighty sick lady when she got to Africa, and that nobody else had succumbed. He refused to tell any lies, and neither M-G-M nor any other major studio gave him starring roles for years.)

Clark Gable had succeeded Sam Wood as MPA president. Robert Taylor succeeded Gable. In 1948, the executive committee proposed John Wayne as its next president. Wayne demurred, saying that he was frequently away on location. He was honored by their confidence, but he was not sure he was able to carry out the office as he was a bashful public speaker. He had made only one speech at an MPA meeting. It was in 1947 and at Jim McGuinness' request. He does not remember what he said. He was probably so scared of speaking that he got plastered to do it and does not remember his maiden anti-Communist talk. But he never forgot the hatred that little talk engendered.

"I was the victim of a mud-slinging campaign like you wouldn't believe," Wayne told me later. "I was called a drunk, a pervert, a woman-chaser, a lousy B picture western bit player, an unfaithful husband, an uneducated jerk, a tool of the studio heads.

"Well, that just made me determined to become the president of MPA if the members wanted me. Charlie Feldman advised me not to stick my neck out, Bö Roos told me to stay out of it, and Herbert Yates told me, 'Duke, you're a goddam fool. You are crazy to get mixed up in this. It'll put you on the skids in Hollywood.' "

On March 30, 1949, Wayne was inducted as MPA president in a mass rally at the American Legion Hall. In his brief acceptance speech, Wayne took up the question of whether Hollywood should welcome Communists as members of a political party, saying, "We don't want a political party here that any bully boy in a foreign country can make dance to his tune." It is not what you would call a deathless political maxim. The main speaker of the evening was Robert Stripling, former investigator for the House Committee.

During Wayne's three-term tenure as MPA president, the members voted a resolution, proposed by board member Roy Brewer, head of the L.A. division of the IATSE (International Alliance of Theatrical and Stage Employees, AFL-CIO), stating that Los Angeles had the "second largest concentration of Communists" in America, that they represented a "clear and present danger," and that the City of the Angels should register all Communists. Wayne backed this foolish resolution. He also favored a dreary and naïve brochure which the MPA published and which catalogued six elements in a film which proved that it bore surreptitious Marxist propaganda. It was as ridiculous as those charts of literature that V. J. Jerome, Serge Dinamov, John Howard Lawson, and other Marxian votaries would draw up and inflict upon the faithful during the era of "proletarian literature."

Wayne was succeeded as MPA president by Roy Brewer, who served until 1955 and was in turn succeeded by Ward Bond. Bond was intensely patriotic. He thought that the welcome Khrushchev received in Hollywood during his 1954 visit was disgusting. Bond flew the American flag at half-mast in his Encino home on the day that the Soviet dictator toured 20th Century-Fox and was banqueted by Spyros Skouras and Darryl Zanuck.

During this period Wayne immersed himself in some of the literature produced by former Communists. He wanted to enlighten himself. He read the works of Koestler, Krivitsky, Kravchenko, Gouzenko, Gitlow, Bentley, Budenz. He was deeply moved by Whittaker Chambers' *Witness*. He had not read so extensively and so carefully since his student years. He has read *Witness* many times, and he believes it to be one of the most important books ever written by an American. He has memorized long sections of it. He has given it to friends. When one of his daughters became sixteen, she received *Witness* as a birthday present. On one occasion, Duke and I were talking about the famous trial of Alger Hiss on perjury charges. Duke remembered the damning business about the prothonotary warbler in Washington's Rock Creek Park (an obscure but startling confirmation, seemingly, that Chambers had really known Hiss intimately, for he related Hiss' excitement at seeing the rare bird, and in private hearings of the Congressional committee, Hiss confirmed it). Dave Grayson, who was making up Wayne for a scene during this conversation, looked puzzled.

"Haven't you read *Witness?*" Wayne asked.

"No," Grayson replied.

Several days later, a copy of *Witness* was in Grayson's hands—sent by Duke.

From a suspicion of Marxism and communism, Wayne, like some other anti-Communists, moved on to a doubt of the validity of government social programs. Again, he read and discussed books on economics and political science and became what he likes to think of as a "Jeffersonian liberal," though he admits that in the current parlance he is, indeed, a "conservative." He likes to quote Jefferson's maxim: "That government is best which governs least."

Even friendly biographers of Wayne, like Dean Jennings, are so accustomed to accepting the idea of statist government as eternal truth that they can make no sense of Wayne's belief in a free-market economy. They assume he is confused or ignorant. Other biographers, like Thomas Morgan, seem to deliberately provoke Wayne into saying ridiculous things and then collate extracts from his opinions in a dazzling series of non sequiturs which portrays him as an amiable savage. An interesting example of the liberal journalist's difficulty in relating to Wayne's Jeffersonian philosophy appears in a long and accurate transcription of an interview between Richard Warren Lewis, a *Playboy* editor, and Wayne. It was published in April, 1971. Lewis, taking the role of a prosecutor, is sharply cross-examining Wayne about his attitudes toward blacks and Indians. There is some rancorous exchange about the pioneers stealing land from the Indians, and Wayne insists that what happened a century ago "can't be blamed on us today."

> PLAYBOY: Indians today are still being dehumanized on reservations.
>
> WAYNE: I'm quite sure that the concept of a government-run reservation would have an ill effect on anyone. But that seems to be what the socialists are looking for now—to have *everyone* cared for from cradle to grave.

Now it would seem that Wayne had, perhaps quite brilliantly, brought into focus a basic difference of viewpoint, but Lewis did not choose to explore the nature of a socialist society and a government in complete control of all production and distribution. He changed the subject.

Duke was not a vindictive anti-Communist. He believed in the redemption of Marxian sinners. This got him into an imbroglio with Hedda Hopper, the gossip columnist. Miss Hopper was the Madame Defarge of the Alliance. Larry Parks, who had played Al Jolson in *The Jolson Story,* had broken with the Communist Party. He had decided to reveal his experiences among the Hollywood Communists. He was slated to testify before the Un-American Activities Committee in Washington. Several newspapers asked Wayne to comment on advance reports that Parks was going to blow the whistle on his erstwhile comrades. Wayne felt that "young Parks needed our moral support." So Duke told the press that Parks was doing a courageous thing. He was to be "commended as a good patriotic American."

At the next meeting of the Alliance, Miss Hopper took the platform and publicly berated Wayne for being a damn fool in supporting Larry Parks so warmly.

A hot argument took place. Wayne said, "When any member of the Party breaks with them, we must welcome him back into American society. We should give him friendship and help him find work again in our industry."

Yet sometimes he would forget his innate sense of decency and react intolerantly. He despises *High Noon,* for instance. He and Gary Cooper had been close friends for years, but "I resented that scene when the marshal ripped off his badge and threw it on the ground. That was like belittling a medal of honor."

Duke had the presumption to telephone Carl Foreman, author of the screenplay, and ask him to remove his name from the credits! He believed that Cooper would be tainted by the relationship with Foreman, a left-wing activist.

Cooper won the Oscar for his performance in *High Noon* (1952). But to this day, Wayne will not grant that *High Noon* was one of the best westerns of the 1950's.

A curious—and inaccurately reported—episode in Wayne's political annals is the notorious Frank Sinatra–Albert Maltz affair. Sinatra's production company had purchased the movie rights to William Bradford Huie's nonfiction novel *The Execution of Private Slovik*. It was announced as a future production starring Sinatra, and the first announcements, in the form of decorously tasteful advertisements, stated that Albert Maltz would write the screenplay. Contrary to widespread opinion, Wayne never attempted to compel Sinatra to fire Maltz. He did not even care one way or the other. It was the least among his many problems in 1960 and 1961. But a wire-service reporter phoned him and asked him what he thought of Sinatra employing a former member of the Unfriendly Ten as a screenwriter.

Wayne merely said, "I don't think my opinion is too important. Why don't you ask Sinatra's crony—who's going to run our country for the next few years—what *he* thinks of it?"

During the 1960 Presidential campaign, Wayne had strongly supported Nixon, and Sinatra had strongly supported John F. Kennedy.

Because of Sinatra's strong ties to the Kennedy wing of the Democratic Party, a hullaballoo was stirred up which was not of Wayne's making. The hullaballoo prompted Sinatra to delve into Maltz's long and self-sacrificing political activities. Since the movie was about the American armed services, Sinatra feared that the

Maltz screenplay might be anti-American and embarrass the new Administration. He thereupon cancelled the movie.

A few months later, at a benefit for SHARE, a widely supported Hollywood charity for the benefit of handicapped children, the two men had a tense encounter. Wayne had come up to the microphone to give a talk, and as he did so, Sinatra left the stage.

Later, in the wings, Duke said, "Now, Frank, what the hell did you walk away from me for?"

"Well," Sinatra said, "you know why."

"You mean that Albert Maltz thing?"

"Yes."

"Let's talk about it, Frank."

"Some other time, Duke. Duke, we're friends—and I hope we'll do pictures together sometimes. Far's I'm concerned—let's forget the whole thing."

Paradoxically, in the course of human events, Sinatra became a fellow Republican. He supported Ronald Reagan for the California governorship in 1970 and Richard M. Nixon in 1972.

By nature, Wayne is not a political animal. He feels uncomfortable at meetings and committee sessions. He dislikes speechmaking. Nevertheless, he became a staunch conservative Republican as time went on. He has contributed generously of his money and his time in behalf of Eisenhower, Goldwater, and Nixon.

He opened the 1968 Republican convention in Miami with an inspirational speech, in which he spoke of his conviction that "this nation is more than laws and government. It is an outlook, an attitude." He described a conversation with Dean Martin, in which the actor-singer asked him what he wanted for his baby girl when she was born, and he said that he wanted "to see that she gets a good start in life. That she had the values that we had as children, that an articulate few are saying are old-fashioned. And, first of all, I want her to be as grateful as I am. Grateful for every day I spend in the United States of America. I hope she never has to raise her own hand to defend our country, but I want her to respect all those who have to defend their country."

In April, 1972, Wayne went back to the USC campus with Bob Hope. They did a turn at Bovard Auditorium. Hope had for some time been doing personal appearances on the college lecture circuit, and Duke agreed to do the USC gig with Hope. Hope said he would get one of his writers to fix up a monologue for him.

"Hell, no," Duke said, "I'm going to write my own speech."

When Hope saw the speech he told Duke that one didn't say this sort of thing to students nowadays. He suggested some changes. Wayne refused to ameliorate his remarks. When he started talking, Hope cautiously went over to the side of the stage, to get out of the way of the heavy textbooks which he expected would be flung at Wayne.

So Marion Michael Morrison, ex-USC student, arose and sipped a glass of tequila. He told about his resentment of the turbulence created by radical students. He told them that he thought the purpose of a university was to be a quiet place where one learned, where one studied and shared intellectual maturing and socializing pleasures, where one learned about American history and acquired a feeling of responsibility. He said that the younger generation owed respect to the faculty, to the deans, to the administrators, to the trustees, to the buildings and facilities. He expressed, with some feeling, his love for his *alma mater* and told how much USC had done for him. He told the students they were wrong when they wrecked rooms and disrupted classes. He told them the California taxpayers were tired of it. He said the schools were owned by the taxpayers and "we are not going to let you destroy our schools."

At first, there had been some booing and heckling, but as Wayne continued, his honesty won over the students. They began to listen to the reasonableness of his statements. He finished by receiving a standing ovation.

Perhaps there is something about John Wayne's rugged individualism which appeals to some of the radical men and women, the ones who have a personal rebellion against centralized government and bureaucracy, who have gone out to homestead the land and grow organic food and do their own weaving and have not asked Washington, D.C., for handouts. Beyond the slogans and the life-style, are they not secret sharers, after all?

During the 1968 election campaign, a rumor started that Wayne was an admirer of George Wallace and would run as his Vice-President on the American Independent Party ticket.

At this time, Wayne was in Montrose, Colorado, filming *True Grit*. Art Wilde, Paramount's unit publicity man, remembers a dramatic moment.

"I got this call from the editor of the Montrose paper," he says. "United Press just flashed a bulletin from Florida quoting Wallace as saying Duke was going to run with him. If true, this was big news. I had no inkling of anything like this. The Montrose editor wanted me to get a statement from Duke. He said UP was standing by waiting for the quote. It would hit every paper in the country, if true.

"I went out where they had set up for the day's work. They happened to be working on the scene where Duke's horse gets shot, he does a horsefall, the horse falls on him. He wasn't using a double. I hated to bother Duke, because it was a tough scene to play. He had been pushing himself. The high altitude made his breathing difficult. He was sitting in a camp chair and looked real tired when I went over. I told him about this query from the UP and that they wanted a statement."

Wayne's jaw went rigid. His blue eyes narrowed. He arose and towered over the short publicity man.

"You just tell him," snapped Wayne, "that the rumor is bullshit."

"They can't print that, Duke."

"That's my statement. Bullshit."

"Could we maybe figure out something different? Like the only Wallace you are associated with is Hal Wallis?"

"Bullshit."

Wilde passed on Duke's "statement," being sure that

it would be purified. The following day the paper published a denial of the Wallace rumor and a streamer headline on page one:

JOHN WAYNE, WALLACE V.P. CANDIDATE? WAYNE SAYS B——T.

The following day a lead paragraph appeared in Joyce Haber's Los Angeles *Times* column that Hal Wallis was the only "Wallace" in Duke's life. It ended the absurd gossip about Wayne's candidacy and put the whole affair into proper perspective.

When Wayne read the screenplay of *True Grit,* written by veteran screenwriter Marguerite Roberts, he accepted Hal Wallis' offer to play the lead. Before he signed the deal, he got a phone call from somebody who told Wayne that Miss Roberts had been named as a person who had attended meetings of the Communist Party faction in the Screen Writers' Guild about twenty years or more previously.

Wayne blew his stack. He told the informant, in a blaze of profanity, that he did not care what Miss Roberts had done years before, but that the script was a hell of a fine script, and it expressed good American principles, and he would be proud to speak its lines. He did not give a damn what a person had once been or once done. It was what a person was now that counted.

He did not bring up the question with Hal Wallis or Henry Hathaway or discuss it with Miss Roberts.

The years during which Wayne went through the trauma of the Motion Picture Alliance and the anti-Communist crusade were also the years of his separation and divorce from Josie and the romance and marriage to Esperanza.

He emerged from these violent experiences a stronger man in many ways, certainly a wiser and more tolerant man, and one who found in himself new levels of feeling, of love, of rage, and of challenge. And this led, in the 1950's, to significant developments in his artistry. He wrought some of the most intense and most human characterizations during this decade.

On a conscious level, his turning to an examination

of what our country added up to had determined him to make a large-scale historical epic, a film along the lines of such classic westerns as Cruze's *The Covered Wagon* and Ford's *The Iron Horse*.

He knew what he wanted to say and he knew the story he wanted to dramatize. It was the Battle of the Alamo. He would tell it as a story of American heroism in defeat.

And, at last, he would portray Sam Houston.

# 20

## He Divorces Republic Pictures

For a long time, Wayne had been unhappy with Republic Pictures. He made many superb films under its symbol —a rampant eagle—but the eagle had become an albatross around his neck, because Republic still operated on Poverty Row penny-pinching methods even though it now occupied a handsome studio in North Hollywood. In 1951, Wayne formed a production company with Robert Fellows. It first was called Wayne-Fellows and later Batjac Productions. (The "Batjac" was derived from Batjak Trading Company, a fictitious corporation owned by Luther Adler in Wayne's Republic movie *Wake of the Red Witch*. Duke loved the sound—*baaatjaaack* . . . It had the ring of gold coins about it, coins hitting felt-covered poker tables. Batjac . . .)

Determined to make his movie about the Alamo, Wayne was beset by problems with Yates. Already Yates was looking for ways to make his dearly beloved, Vera Hruba Ralston, a co-star of this epic. Wayne rebelled at making pictures with Vera Ralston. She had made twelve pictures for Republic since 1945, and only two showed a profit, the ones with Wayne. At the annual meeting of the stockholders in 1950, a dissident group openly said that Miss Ralston was driving the company into bankruptcy. They demanded an accounting of her pictures. They pleaded with president Yates not to put her into any more pictures.

Yates told his stockholders that Republic would keep on making John Wayne pictures, with or without Ralston. But the future was in television. He said B pictures were finished. He told the stockholders not to worry any more. He set up Hollywood Television Service. He started renting old Republic pictures to television. Wayne's old ones—the real old ones, the ones from the 1930's—found a new audience. They are still being played on many local television stations. (KTLA in Los Angeles, for instance, has a nine A.M. daily showing of 1930's vintage Wayne under the rubric of "The John Wayne Theater." A Tucson, Arizona, station runs a similar program at midnight, which it calls "The Worst of John Wayne.")

Wayne's second flight as a producer was *The Fighting Kentuckian.* This, he insisted recently, had an excellent screenplay by George Waggner, an old friend of Duke's. It was set in the 1820's and concerned a group of exiles from Napoleon's defeated armies who come to Kentucky to settle. Wayne played a Daniel Boone type of Kentucky frontiersman with coonskin hat and squirrel gun.

"Well, it was a damn good story in which we combined sophisticated French men and women with simple frontier people," Wayne was recalling in 1972. "I was producing and starring. I wanted to have some say in who was going to play the French girl. She's the daughter of a French general. I wanted a girl who was French. Simone Simon or Danielle Darrieux, Corinne Calvet. Many were available to us.

"But no. Yates made me use Vera Hruba . . . I don't want to malign her. She didn't have the experience. She didn't have the right accent. She talked with this heavy Czech accent. I was looking for a light Parisian type of speech, which my rough pioneer dialogue would play against. Yates made me cast her. It hurt the picture, because now we had to hire other Czech and Austrian actors to play French characters so her accent would be matched. Hugo Haas played her father. Can you picture him as a general of Napoleon's? He was always playing her father. He played her father in *Dakota*.

"I've always been mad at Yates about this because we lost the chance to make one damn fine movie. Oliver Hardy was in it, by the way. He played a frontiersman.

"Yates was one of the smartest businessmen I ever met. I respected him in many ways, and he liked me. But when it came to the woman he loved—his business brains just went flyin' out the window."

Yates married Miss Ralston in March, 1952. He was seventy-two, she was thirty-one. He died in 1966. Mrs. Yates now lives in elegant retirement in the aristocratic community of Santa Barbara.

*The Fighting Kentuckian* resulted in an important change in Duke's acting. He was getting along in years now. He still insisted on doing his own stunts when he could but he just had to rely on doubles more and more. He had not been able to find a convincing double since Canutt left stunting to become a second-unit director.

Now in this movie there was a scene in which Wayne, courting Miss Ralston, leaves her mansion and encounters a rival entering after the butler had told him that Mademoiselle Fleurette Marchand was not *chez elle*.

"Well," Duke says, "so this rival walks right in like the place belongs to him. I wanted to show how mad I was. I wanted to jump on my horse, which was bare, no saddle, mount him with a jump, and shout to my rival, *Try that, mister* . . . Then I'd ride away. Now it's hard enough to stand flatfooted and straddle a horse with a leap. But try doin' it without saddle and stirrups. Now none of the stuntmen was able to do this, even Jock Mahoney, our chief stuntman. They all said it couldn't be done. No way. Well we had a young stuntman on the set, he was playin' a frontier bit part. Chuck Roberson. He said, *Hell, I can do it*. And he went and did it.

And he's been doublin' me and stuntin' for me ever since."

That was almost twenty-five years ago.

When you see them, side by side, they do not look alike, and yet on films, when Roberson's figure is seen in a long shot, or in a violent piece of action, he is the spitting-image of Wayne. Roberson is very tall and treads with the loping gait of the real cowboy. Roberson happens to be a real cowboy.

Roberson expressed his doubler's credo as follows:

"I ride exactly like Mr. Wayne. Walkin' like him—now that is tough. His movements. I don't know if he walks pigeon-toed or what, but it ain't a normal type of walk. Now I have doubled Gable, Mitchum, Gregory Peck, and never had no trouble walkin' like them. But I have to work hard to get Duke's walk.

"But the ridin'—easy. Duke don't slouch on a horse. Tall in the saddle in his ticket. He don't ride like a real cowboy rides. He has picked up on a couple of bad habits but that is just his way of ridin'. He holds on to the horn. I kin see mebbe why as when he puts his palm on top of the horn it makes him seem even taller, don't it?

"Now Duke, he is one hell of a fine rider, but you gotta realize in real life you kin ride in a way you cain't ride for pictures. I ride a horse different on my ranch than I do in a movie. I ride looser on the ranch. I am a much looser rider than Wayne is. Most guys, real cowboys, are sloppy riders, by which I don't mean bad riders, but sloppy, loose, easy-slouchin' riders. The more you know how to handle a horse, the sloppier it looks to a person don't know nothin' about ridin'. So you cain't ride a horse in pictures like you do on the range."

Wayne himself confirms that "motion-picture riding is rough. You can't fake it. I took a bad fall in *Yellow Ribbon*. I'm leading some horses through an Indian camp. We were riding McClellan saddles—no horns. I was supposed to wave a blue coat and start a ruckus to confuse the Indians. The cinch belt come loose and when I started waving, the saddle worked free, and the horse, he panicked, stiff-legged, and threw me. I hit the ground.

Hit my head. Blacked out. Now there's about fifty horses tear-assing at me. I came out of the blackout to hear the Old Man, Mr. Ford, yelling and there was general hysteria, but a wrangler with guts, he ran out and headed off the stampeding horses, which were within about a few feet of tromping me to death."

It was his frustrations about *The Alamo,* as well as the cinematic couplings with Vera Ralston, that burned up Wayne. He spelled out his grievances in an interview with Bob Thomas of the Associated Press.

"Yates," Wayne said at the time, "will have to make me a darned good offer to get me to do another movie with him. I'm fed up to the teeth with him. I wanted to do the Alamo under my own company, Batjac, and release through Republic. Yates said I would have to give up my company and make the picture for Republic. He said to me, 'You owe it to Republic. We made you.'

"How do you like that? I don't owe them one thing. I've made plenty of money for Republic. I've brought Frank Borzage and John Ford to Republic. And screenwriter Jimmy Grant. Grant wrote *Sands of Iwo Jima*— one of Republic's biggest hits. Not only did he want me to do *Alamo* for his company but he wanted to postpone the starting date and cut the budget. I refused.

"Then the location. We planned to shoot in Panama, not Texas. But Yates deliberately told some folks there I was shooting it in Texas. We could save about two million shooting in Panama, but now the Texans are angry with me. I had to go down there and square it with my Texas friends. I had to find the location in Panama myself."

Duke pointed out that Yates had had trouble with Roy Rogers and Gene Autry—both of whom had left Republic. "The difference is that Yates built them into stars," Wayne said. "He didn't make me a star. No, I'm not going to give up my own production company. I'm looking for some security for my kids. Don't forget I didn't start making big money until the era of high taxes. Right now, I get to keep six cents out of every dollar

I make. That's why I have to get the residual rights of some of my pictures so the money will keep coming in."

On November 11, 1952, Yates wrote a letter to Thomas in which he denied Wayne's allegations. Duke had made "irresponsible" statements because he had been under "great mental strain and personal problems during the past year . . . Duke was employed by Republic on May 11, 1935 . . . I always found Duke a gentleman, a friend, always willing to cooperate and he has beyond any doubt been helpful in establishing the success of Republic . . . At no time have I attempted to take any credit for his success; however, what Republic has spent in publicizing and establishing his name throughout the world must have been a contributing factor to his success. . . ."

It was too late. Wayne returned from Panama. He had found an ideal location on the outskirts of Panama City. It looked like San Antonio of the 1830's. There was a two-mile airstrip already built nearby. He and Yates had started arguing about budgets and locations. Wayne gave him an ultimatum.

"You go through with this, Herb, or I won't be on the lot when you get back."

Yates was going to New York for several weeks. While he was away, Wayne-Fellows Productions moved out of the Republic studios, lock, stock, and *Alamo*. Making *The Alamo* had become an obsession with Wayne. He didn't like Yates' attitude. He was being belittled. *The Quiet Man,* one of Ford's classics, was his last Republic movie.

Wayne was obsessed not just with making *The Alamo* but with making movies. He drove himself like a madman to make one movie after another. In 1950, he told Hedda Hopper that the reason he labored so compulsively was that he had "to have twenty-six hundred a month to take care of my two families. I just have to keep jumping around from Republic to RKO to John Ford's Argosy Productions to make it."

And yet, despite all the advice of Bö Roos, he was careless with his money. He was an incurable big spender

and check-grabber. He was a sucker for a hard-luck
story. He was a soft touch. He was frequently taken in
by con men and hustlers. He was gullible. He was cred-
ulous. He was not a businessman. He has always been wild
and beautiful and extravagantly lunatic about money. It
is one of his most charming traits of character.

Having done with Republic, Wayne entered into two
new tie-ups. One with Howard Hughes, by now boss of
RKO, and the other with Jack Warner. Warner would
bankroll and release the Batjac features. Wayne and Jack
Warner had a good rapport. The mutual admiration remains to this day. Duke still makes films for Warners.
He has complete confidence in Warner. Warner has confidence in Duke's ability to stay within a budget and to
bring a movie in on time.

In 1954, we talked about the first four Batjac films.
Duke said, "Well, we started with *Big Jim McClain*—not
a great movie, but Warners made a thirty percent profit.
They also made money on *Plunder in the Sun, Island in
the Sky,* and *Hondo.*"

Around this time, Esperanza Wayne told a *Time*
interviewer: "My husband is one of the few persons who
is always interest in business. He talks it all of the time.
When he is reading, it is the scripts for the movies. We
have the guests in the house for dinner and always they
talk of the business and all of his time it is like he is
discuss pictures or is plan the pictures."

Republic. RKO. Batjac. Warners. Argosy. Monterey.
Writers. Grant. Hawks. Hughes. Ford. Bob Fellows. Jack
Warner. Arrivals and departures. Airports. Locations in
Monument Valley, Arizona. Moab, Utah. San Diego.
Station wagons. Trucks. Unloading. Bö Roos. Charlie
Feldman.

*Always they talk of the business.*

# 21

# He Divorces Esperanza

And yet he loved her. He loved her and wanted her, but *always they talk of the business*. They fought. They separated. They came together. They shouted. They ran away from each other. They returned to each other.

Esperanza Baur Diaz Ceballos Wayne, called Chata, was a person who could not come to terms with the loneliness of the Hollywood wife. So first there was the alcohol to deaden the pain. Then there was the alcohol and the pills. Then there was the alcohol and the lovers. And *mamacita* was always around, or if she was not, Chata would fly to her. *Mamacita* could drink you a good glass of tequila, believe me. *Mamacita* had become one hell of a rotten bitter bloated old woman. She had a nasty tongue. She did not help the situation. They had moved her out in the third year of the marriage. Duke was getting tired of everybody talking Spanish around him. His wife. The mother-in-law. The servants. Mexicans. He was up to his ass in Mexicans.

It got down to *either she goes or I go* and *we are not living like a man and a wife*.

"What you tellin' me?" she would cry, moaning in a wounded-animal way, and then getting louder as she became worked up into a rage. "What man and wife is this you speak about? When you come to my bed? You go to bed with the pictures, the business."

She hissed and she spat and she threw things. "You

272

make love with John Ford and Jeemy Grant and heem, the other one, the ugly one, Bond, heem, not me you make love. You not love me."

Then came Mexican curses deep from her Aztec soul and he would cringe and proclaim his love and then she would denounce him for shipping her beloved *madre* to Mexico.

Sometimes, Chata would suddenly take off for Mexico City and be away for a month, two months, visiting with Mrs. Ceballos. When Wayne had to make public appearances without her, it gave rise to rumors of marital trouble. It got bad as far back as 1947, in the springtime, which is the season of banquets and awards; Wayne went everywhere alone. And Bev Barnett was constantly assuring Army Archerd of *Daily Variety* and Mike Connolly of the *Reporter* and Parsons and Hopper and Jimmy Fidler and Sid Skolsky that Mrs. Wayne had to be in Mexico because her mother was sick.

In the summer of 1947, he went on location to Monument Valley for *Fort Apache*. Chata impulsively decided she wanted to go. She couldn't. Ford never permitted wives or mistresses or husbands or beaux to go on location. This blazed into a resentment against Duke and Ford.

She went to Mexico and drank with *mamacita*. Wayne finished *Fort Apache*. He came home. They drank. She went to Mexico again. She was lonely. She returned. They quarreled. They drank. She went away again. He went on location to Arizona for *Red River*. They fought. He came back. She came back. He went to San Diego for location sequences on *Sands of Iwo Jima*. She accompanied him. They fought. She complained of nervous tension. She got hives. She got psoriasis. Her sensitive skin erupted when she was emotionally aroused. For Christmas of 1949, Señora Ceballos came to Encino. There were no silent nights and all was not calm and all was not bright. They all three shouted and fought. Chata's skin was terrible now. She went into the Scripps Clinic for several weeks. Duke was making *Jet Pilot, Rio Grande, Operation Pacific, Flying Leathernecks*. She got nerv-

ous and lonely. She said if she went down to see *mamacita*
she would improve. They were involved in a peculiar
*menage à trois* which constantly became a *folie à trois*.

She could not handle the running of the enormous
house. It had twelve rooms and they had to have three
in help, including a cook. Barnett said that during one of
her more than usual phases of nervousness, there had
been twelve different servants in six months. And they
were always Mexicans. Mexican maids, butlers, housekeepers, cooks. Well, this made Duke nervous. His skin
was fine but he developed an ulcer. He had to stop drinking and smoking for a while. This *really* made him
nervous.

A new crew of servants was put on. This time, Wayne
insisted upon one English-speaking servant. He personally hired an affable West Indian black gentleman, J.
Hampton Scott. Scott was a quiet obsequious party who
did his duties well. He did not gossip. He did not complain about the peculiar arrangements. Why sometimes,
when they were between maids and housekeepers, he
would even tidy up their rooms.

J. Hampton Scott was the sort of person who does
not like to throw away interesting objects, even if useless.
He was your classic string-saver. He came upon curious
bits of flotsam and jetsam as he performed his duties.

Once, he chanced upon some fascinating scrawls in
the handwriting of Esperanza Wayne. He added the piece
of paper to his collection of memorabilia. He was a smiling, efficient man. He could not speak a word of Spanish.
This, in Wayne's estimation, made him a first-class employee.

"I believe," Henaghen affirms, "that most of the trouble in the marriage could be traced to Chata's mother.
She was just a crazy broad. And she was also a greedy
broad. She was trying to take Duke for a bundle. She
was getting Duke so mad that he would throw them both
out and settle a million dollars on them. I believe Chata
really loved Duke and that he loved her. But her mother always made sure that there was trouble."

In 1951, alleging that Wayne threatened her life, Chata got a court order barring him from their home. She hired a private detective. He was stationed on the roof. He was armed with a rifle. He was to shoot Wayne on sight.

Wayne was desperate to see Chata. He wanted a reconciliation. He went to court and got a court order allowing him to enter the premises to visit their dog. The dog was a poodle, Pedro, whom Wayne actually detested. But he wanted to get in and see his beloved.

Wayne was nervous about the reunion so he got drunk.

The rooftop *franc tireur* was dozing, so Wayne got in the house. Good old J. Hampton Scott opened the door. He was escorted to his favorite chair. He waited for Scott to bring Pedro—and perhaps Chata, who might be in one of her lovable moods. He became sleepy. He passed out on the chair.

Gradually, he became conscious of familiar clicking sounds, reminiscent of the sounds of certain moments of his films. He forced his eyelids open. He was staring into the barrel of a Winchester. It was Esperanza's private eye doing his duty.

The man was persuaded not to shoot Wayne. Wayne finally went away. He did not see Pedro the poodle or Chata either.

Then Bö Roos, who was on friendly terms with Chata, arranged a reconciliation. She would go to Hawaii with Duke while he was making *Big Jim McClain*. In Honolulu, they would rekindle the fires of true love as they experienced once more the memories of their Hawaiian *luna de miel*.

It did not work out that way. Jimmy Grant was on the scene. He had written the screenplay with Richard English. It was an anti-Communist movie about FBI men tracking down Commie saboteurs and Russian secret agents.

Well it was not raining in Hawaii *and always they talk of the business*. Shooting scenes by day and discussing production problems by night and heavy drinking. One night they went to a party and came back to their bungalow in a rain. A furious row started at the door. She began hitting him. He seized her shawl and threw it in the mud. Then he trampled upon it. Then they went in. He started pounding on the walls and cursing her in language so foul she was ashamed to repeat it.

She returned to Los Angeles. She retained the services of counselor Jerry Giesler. Giesler was famous for securing large divorce settlements. A press conference was called in his office. She denounced columnists who had printed mean stories about her. She said she was just a sick little girl who was "terribly confused." She had loved and trusted John Wayne. He had betrayed her trust. She had so desperately attempted to make the marriage work, but now she knew there was no hope.

"I will definitely file for divorce and then I will tell the true story of what has made our marriage to be broken up," she informed the world.

One of the episodes in her "true story" described Duke returning home late one night. "He had a large black bite on the right side of his neck," she said. Could this have been a love bite inflicted upon him by another woman? she asked him. Oh, no, not at all. True—a woman had bitten him, but it was just for laughs, an innocent prank, he said. Chata said she discovered that Wayne had gone to a stag party. There had been stripteasers around and one of them had made love to her husband and bequeathed him this hickey as a *souvenir d'amour*. Subsequently, Duke testified under oath that this hickey had been inflicted upon him "against my will, without my consent, and without my collusion."

And yet, and yet, and yet, despite it all, through it all, Wayne experienced an irrational and overpowering passion for Chata. He could not understand this emotion and he did not know how to deal with it. It was she who deserted him. He did not want the separations. He always pleaded with her to return.

After one of their arguments, he flew down to Acapulco with Roos and Henaghen, the latter having become a vice-president in charge of publicity and advertising for Batjac. (He had formerly been the Rambling Reporter columnist for the *Hollywood Reporter.)* Wayne had just finished making *Flying Leathernecks* for Hughes. He hoped that Chata would come join him. She did not. He was mad and sulking. He got very drunk every day with Henaghen. Henaghen could drink as much as Duke. One night, Wayne started crying. He expressed his yearnings for Chata. He said he would give his life for her. He could not live without her.

Henaghen was embarrassed to see this handsome, rich, world-famous star, more sexual at forty-five than he had been at twenty, object of the adoration of millions of women, crying over the one woman he did not have. Duke could not get Chata out of his blood.

This time she did not come down to the Los Flamingos Hotel. Once, in this very place, during a brawl, he had thrown a glass of water in her face. She threw a bucket of ice in his face. He doused her face with rubbing alcohol, which temporarily blinded her eyes. I suppose that what happened often was that Esperanza, desperately seeking his attention, would goad him into frenzies of rage. She would rather have rage than be taken for granted. And now and then, as is universal, these frenzies became erotic, and they both grew excited and found themselves making love.

Henaghen decided to go home. He flew to Mexico City. Duke went along. Henaghen told Wayne that he should buy something Mexican and bring it back to his wife and surprise her. He could suddenly return to Los Angeles instead of Acapulco. Henaghen suggested that he bring her a *piñata,* one of those *papier-mâché* hollow animals filled with candy or small favors, usually given to children.

Wayne purchased an enormous donkey *piñata,* almost life-size. It was pink. They dragged it on the plane, drunk and laughing. Esperanza would love it. She would love Duke. Everything would be fine. He arrived home dragging this *piñata* donkey with him. He brought it in and handed it to Chata. She smiled. She suspected it was filled with diamonds and rubies. She tore it open. It was empty.

She was frustrated and mad. She took it out on the *piñata,* ripping it into small pieces. She told Duke that she would shoot him with her automatic if he did not get out of her sight.

He got out of her sight. He went to stay with the Roos family. Lately he had been staying there a lot.

Frank Belcher, Duke's attorney, started negotiating with Jerome Rosenthal of Giesler's staff. Bö Roos worked out a financial settlement. Elvin Skaggs, a private investigator in the San Fernando Valley, was employed to investigate the secret life of Esperanza Wayne. He uncovered some nasty pieces of information.

Wayne did not want to contest the divorce action. He would accept a standard accusation of "mental cruelty." Chata was offered forty thousand a year for two years, and thirty-five thousand a year for the succeeding seven years.

Mrs. Wayne would have nothing to do with this paltry three-hundred-twenty-five-thousand-dollar settlement. She countered with a hair-raising request, which included forty thousand for legal fees and fifty thousand for auditors, appraisers, and private detectives. She wanted a perpetual monthly payment of twelve thousand five hundred seventy-one dollars.

How in the name of Pancho Villa would a simple Mexican girl need so much money to get along?

Fortunately we do not have to wonder, for Chata's counsel supplied a breakdown of how much it costs a Hollywood wife to exist per month:

| | |
|---|---|
| Household maintenance | $1,245.00 |
| Household expenses | 1,938.00 |
| Personal expenses and entertainment | 3,654.00 |
| Auto upkeep, traveling | 948.00 |
| Health and insurance | 1,518.00 |
| Mother's allowance (sic!) | 650.00 |
| Furs, jewelry, personal effects | 499.00 |
| Charities | 1,023.00 |

| Travel fares | 795.00 |
| Telephone | 301.00 |

Chata would not compromise. Wayne, restless, wanted to pay her the goddam twelve thousand five hundred seventy-one dollars a month and get her off his back. But his advisers advised him to go to court. By now, Skaggs had found enough scandal about Esperanza so she would be reluctant to fight. Wayne's sense of propriety, his courtliness, inhibited him from battling with Chata. During one debate at the lawyer's, he told Belcher, "Oh, hell, give her everything she wants. I don't want to haggle over nickels and dimes. I'll make four pictures a year instead of three. But one thing—I don't want to pay one cent to her mother. Get that taken out and then I'll give her what she wants."

*Mamacita* was taken out. Everything seemed to be moving toward a settlement when, one evening, J. Hampton Scott knocked on the Roos door and said he wished to see his former master, Mr. Wayne. Wayne had a private session with Scott. He emerged from the study looking pale and shaken.

Scott told him that he had been following the events of the troubles between his master and his mistress and he felt a poignant sadness at it all. Yet he had long suspected that something was wrong. He had something which he thought might be of some interest to his master in connection with this lawsuit.

"You see, sir," he explained suavely, "I search my conscience a great time to decide on the justice of it."

He handed Duke an envelope, in which was a leaf from a bedside table memorandum pad. He revealed that once, while the master had been in some faraway location, a man named Nicholas Hilton, whose father or uncle operated hostelries, had been a house guest in the Encino compound. Upon tidying up the next afternoon, as was his custom, he chanced upon some interesting compositions by Esperanza Wayne.

The holographic evidence was certainly damning. Chata had written several different name combinations of herself and Nicky Hilton. Ten times she had scribbled "Esperanza Hilton," nine times "Chata Hilton," four times "Mrs. Nick Hilton," and three times "Chata and Nick."

The case went to trial in the Superior Court of the County of Los Angeles in November, 1953. The courtroom was thronged with spectators. Outside were hundreds of sensation seekers and lovers of the lurid, the fantasy lovers, the Hollywood crazies, creatures of Nathanael West's nether world of furnished rooms in cracked stucco buildings, the sad (and crazy) people, the lonely ones, the weak and ugly ones who lived on the dreams of the strong and beautiful people embodied in the shadows on the screen, embodied in the bodies of persons like John Wayne.

Judge Allen W. Ashburn presided. Everybody was there. John Wayne. Opposing counsel. Their assistants. Clerks and bailiffs and witnesses and spectators.

But not Esperanza. By ten-thirty she had still not appeared. Judge Ashburn retired to his chambers. While they were waiting for the tardy Mrs. Wayne, Lloyd Shearer, a veteran writer about show business personalities, sought an audience with Judge Ashburn. This was granted. He prayed judicial permission to bring a tape recorder into the courtroom so that he might get an accurate transcription of the testimony. He had been assigned by *Parade* magazine to write an account of *Wayne vs. Wayne*.

Mr. Shearer said that his tape recorder was almost noiseless. He knew Chata and he knew Duke. He knew they would not mind it. In those days, the tape recorder was still a new journalistic tool. Judge Ashburn was reluctant to grant permission.

He pointed out that then he would have to let radio newsmen in with microphones and TV reporters with cameras and then "this trial will become a circus. It is going to be difficult enough to conduct an ordinary trial and keep order. However, Mr. Shearer, since you know both parties so well, why do you not see if you can get them to come to some reasonable settlement and avoid what is going to be, I am afraid, an extremely messy court trial?"

Shearer—though he was thereby ruining a good story—said he would do everything he could to bring the parties together. He assured Judge Ashburn that there were no child custody problems and "no questions of principle." He said, "I should not think it would be too hard to get Duke and Chata to come to some fair agreement without a trial, Your Honor, because in this situation nothing is involved but money and ego."

Unfortunately, money and ego are the two things chiefly responsible for much of the world's problems. Shearer said he would talk to both parties. He did. *Nothing is involved but money and ego.*

Chata's ego demanded her day in court. She arrived after eleven A.M. She explained her lateness thusly: she had been stopped by a highway patrolman and given a citation for speeding!

Esperanza Wayne looked dazzlingly beautiful. She had repaired the epidermal ravages of psoriasis and alcoholism. She was wearing a dark blue hundred-sixty-five-dollar tailored suit by Hattie Carnegie, a fifteen-ninety-five pinstriped blouse, and twelve-ninety-eight white gloves. Twenty years ago, these were really expensive prices. The *Beverly Hills Citizen News,* from which I gleaned this data, did not make any references to her shoes, hosiery, jewelry, or hat.

Her dark hair was sleekly combed back in a bun. She had gotten heavier during the past ten years, and that spare high-cheekboned Lauren Bacall–Katharine Hepburn look was gone. But she still looked good.

She was sworn in and she testified as to her early life and her falling in love with John Wayne, and revealed that she had lived with him for two years while he was still legally married to Josie.

The court recessed for lunch.

At two-thirty P.M. she resumed testimony and cited twenty-two specific instances of physical cruelty to her, many including acts of brutality. He had beaten her up, she said. He had slapped her and kicked her. He had trampled on clothes and scarves. He had dragged her by the legs and by the "roots of my hair." He had "clobbered" her oh so many many times. She loved the sound of the word "clobber" and used it frequently. And he had been sexually unfaithful. Once she had even discovered him swimming nude on Waikiki Beach with other naked persons. Not only had she not been invited to the oceanic orgy, but on seeing her, Mr. Wayne said, "Why don't you go away and stop spoiling the fun?"

And he was a heavy drinker and a terrible drunk. He always "clobbered," and especially clobbered her when drunk. And one of his favorite pastimes was going to "nude stag parties, from one of which he returned home in the early morning hours . . . very intoxicated and had a large black bite on the right side of his neck."

She told of being clobbered in Encino and Honolulu, in Mexico City and Acapulco, in Dublin and London and New York.

One day, in the crowd massed outside the courthouse, was a girl bearing an enormous sign which read: JOHN WAYNE, YOU CAN CLOBBER ME ANY TIME YOU WANT.

Ward Bond, who stayed close to his old buddy during this period, said, "I was a bachelor for ten years and loved it. Duke could never take that kind of life. He was broken up when he realized his marriage with Chata was on the rocks. He was sick about it. But he never let it show. He wanted them to get together many times. Well, now he's had two marriages fall apart on him. It's made him sensitive and more cautious about women than I've ever seen him before. Oh, I don't doubt he was partly at fault in both cases. It takes two. But Chata's charges really are ridiculous. Duke never hit a woman in his life."

Yet her accusations were supported by several witnesses, including her personal maid, Augustina Roldan. Señora Roldan had personally witnessed the time when Wayne slapped his wife because she served him an avocado sandwich.

John Wayne took the stand on the second day of the trial. He did not look well. He had come down with influenza. He had 102° fever. His blue eyes were glazed over. During his entire testimony, he leaned forward nervously. He did not look at Chata. He frequently rubbed his eyes as if greatly fatigued. Sometimes he played with his USC class ring. He also fiddled with a large pair of gold cufflinks.

The cufflinks were in the shape of a heart!

Had Wayne given his heart to another? Had a new love bestowed these golden hearts? Did it mean he wanted the world to see he remained a steadfast romantic, wearing his heart on his sleeve? But there were two hearts. Was he a two-hearted man?

In Wayne's testimony, he said that Chata "put me in a position where I had to cover up the fact that she wasn't acting like a wife. I had to keep up the public relations for us. It was humiliating to have her get drunk in nightclubs, fall down, cause disturbances at parties. It affected my work."

He insisted upon the innocence of his relations with Gail Russell. He explained the amorous bite. In the first place, it was on his cheek and not on his neck. There had been a party. Just some old friends and this girl was playing the piano and another girl was dancing and some third girl was there, and "suddenly this girl came around me, reached over, and bit me on the cheek."

ATTORNEY BELCHER: What did you do, Mr. Wayne?

WAYNE: I said, "What's the idea?"

BELCHER: What happened then?

WAYNE: Nothing. That broke up the party. I was worried about what to tell my wife.

He categorically denied that he had ever slapped, punched, or otherwise "clobbered" his wife. On the contrary, it was she who had thrown objects at him and threatened to kill him. She had been reckless with his money. She lavished money and gifts on other men. She lost thousands in Las Vegas casinos. She often deserted him "without any reason" to go to Mexico for weeks at a time. She had a habit of "feigning illness and nervousness." She had frequently caused him "grievous mental suffering, embarrassment, and humiliation." She often stayed out all night. While he had been in Honolulu for *Big Jim McClain,* she had entertained a man in their Encino home.

Attorney Belcher identified the man as Nicky Hilton and he put in evidence the damning "Nick and Chata" doodles.

Wayne also testified that Chata's mother was a violent person. She often clobbered her daughter. Then Chata, drunk, blamed him for the black-and-blue marks. In support of this theory came witness James Edward Grant, who deposed that once Chata and her mother were fighting.

"The next day," he testified, "Chata told me, 'That son-of-a-bitch hit me.' I laughed because I thought that was a funny appelation to hang on one's mother. But she told me she meant that Duke, her husband, had hit her.

"So I said, 'If that is so, it is the longest punch thrown in history, because Duke is up in Moab, Utah, making a picture.'"

Chata explained the Nicky Hilton visit as an act of kindness. Hilton was recuperating from an auto accident; he was engaged to Betsy von Furstenberg at the time. He was living at one of his father's hotels.

"He was going to have an anesthetic," Chata said. "If Miss von Furstenberg went with him to the hotel, it would not look nice. So she asked me if she could take advantage of my hospitality. I put him in a guest room and he was there for a week."

And had anything of a lascivious nature occurred between her and Nicky Hilton?

MRS. WAYNE: Absolutely not!

On the third day, the lawyers arrived at a settlement. Wayne agreed to pay her fifty thousand a year for six years, to pay all her current debts (about twenty thousand), and to make an outright cash payment of one hundred and fifty thousand.

Judge Ashburn resumed his place and announced the settlement. He said he was giving *each* of the parties a divorce. He based his decision on the California precedent of *DeBurgh vs. DeBurgh,* in which it was concluded that in cases of mutual recrimination "such as this, the court may grant a divorce to each of the parties."

Esperanza Wayne went home to Mexico City. She went home to live with her mother. Soon she had used up all the money of the cash settlement. She ended up in a little room in a shabby Mexico City hotel. Her mother died. She lived alone toward the end. She ceased going out and did not eat. She rarely left her room. It was reported that she subsisted mainly on brandy.

Sometime in the autumn or winter of 1954, a year after the divorce, Esperanza Baur Diaz Ceballos Wayne died of a heart attack in Mexico City.

Several months before this, Wayne and I were talking about the divorce. He said: "It is a miserable chapter in my life. It's been often said that an actor lives in the lime-light and so he mustn't be surprised when his troubles are made more of than other people's. I guess bad things make bigger news.

"While my trial was going on, Ann Blyth was married. A religious and deeply beautiful ceremony—but it wasn't news.

"The Wayne case was played up. It was an embarrassing ordeal to live through. I think I tried to live in a dignified, respectable way, and twenty-five years of trying to live a decent life was almost ruined. I'm not blaming anybody but me. I think the final settlement was fair. Today I wish we had done it quietly. But we were angry. When people are emotionally upset, harsh things are said on both sides.

"I guess I have been a romantic all my life. A romantic about everything, not just about women. I will have to learn to drop that pedestal a few feet so I can accept women on a more realistic basis.

"Maybe I'm still afraid of women. I am awed by their presence. I feel there is something beautiful about a fine woman. I hope someday to find the woman I can love, to make her happy. I hope she will respect me and love me.

"This trial was just another smear against Hollywood and the picture business. But you go look up the statistics.

You will find we have less divorce and marriage trouble than any community of our size.

"My money situation is bad. I've worked hard as an actor for twenty-five years and my assets and liabilities just about match up. I'm not complaining. I'm living in a good country. I'm doing work I love. My four children are in good shape and I've provided for them.

"Retire? I never want to retire. I know that I am getting too old to be a star. Lately I have been playing character parts more and more." (He considered Tom Dunson in *Red River* and Captain Brittles in *Yellow Ribbon* "character parts.") "But I am soon going to be too old for even the kind of character parts I can play. When the time comes, maybe in five years, I'll stop acting. I am going to be a producer and hope to also direct."

It was impossible for him to foresee that twenty years later, he would still be a star, still be playing the hero, grizzled and wrinkled and fat in the stomach, but playing the hero, the superman, and that there would even be an Academy Award in the future, for, as one looks at his career in retrospect, one sees that his creative achievements had only begun with *Red River*. During the 1950's, and later, he created a series of characters who, in sharpness and ease of execution, in vividness and grandeur, in emotional intensity, revealed that his acting work had attained the noblest quality to which a movie actor can aspire, which placed John Wayne in the pantheon reserved for the rare breed, for Chaplin, for Garbo, for Monroe and Keaton and W. C. Fields and Humphrey Bogart, for the everlastingly shining presences.

## 22

# The Fanatical Hero

Between 1948 and 1959, John Wayne starred in twenty-five pictures. Of these, interestingly enough, only five were westerns. His performances in ten of these rank as among the most powerful of that decade: *Red River, She Wore a Yellow Ribbon, Sands of Iwo Jima, Rio Grande, The Quiet Man, The High and the Mighty, The Searchers, The Wings of Eagles, Rio Bravo, The Horse Soldiers*. And five of these ten can stand comparison with the best movie characterizations of all time: Tom Dunson, Captain Brittles, Sergeant Stryker, Ethan Edwards, and Spig Wead.

In these latter, as well as in other later roles, Wayne projected a new film hero, the fanatic, the madman, the obsessed idealist. The only words he could find to express what he was playing was the phrase "character roles." For he was not a leading man, really, he was not acting out the traditional movie hero. He was creating a new film type, for which there were then no adequate words. He was, in a sense, giving you Captain Ahab hunting the white whale. It is perhaps a uniquely American type: a man utterly disregarding his physical safety and eschewing the normal desires for creature comforts and a regular existence in work and in marriage. A fanatic prepared to sacrifice himself for a large abstraction, be it the U.S. Cavalry or the Marines, the Nation, a Cattle Drive, a Kidnapped Girl. Wayne, as an actor, entered upon an almost mystical plane of behavior and motivation.

The well-known *auteur* theory maintains that the director is the primary creative influence on a movie. In general, this is true. There are exceptions. The exceptions are the superstars. The screen presence of John Wayne is a powerful creative influence on any movie he makes. His presence is so magnetic that it conquers a screen. His entrance changes a movie. His voice, his wrinkled face, his cold eyes, his ironic smile alters and transmutes a screenplay and a director's conscious preparations. Sometimes the *acteur* becomes the *auteur*. The movie expresses his vision of life, and not the author's or the director's. The images Wayne projects transcend the words he speaks, even the actions the director has suggested he take.

From the moment a director casts John Wayne, he has already made a decision about the film. Wayne's personality will sculpture the movie to his needs. He cannot help this.

One should also keep in mind that Wayne, like any superstar, exerts power of choice as to story, cameraman, and director.

Wayne's artistic vision is difficult to put into a neat formula because it is beyond words. It is even beyond the definable tools of the actor, such as his use of his voice and his body, his knowledge of lighting and camera. The vision is expressed in all these ways, but above all, it is in a mysterious emanation of his soul on the screen that Duke communicates his dark knowledge and emotional tonalities to us.

The fascinating thing is how Wayne's morbid pursuits and missions take place in a realistic environment. We are never in a Buñuel or Bergman metaphysical country. In a Wayne movie, deserts are deserts, buttes are buttes, real snows fall, and bullets kill, and the dying is bloody, ugly, often seemingly useless.

Wayne made his own fanatical hero. It started with *Red River*. Director Howard Hawks respected, from the first, Wayne's intuitions about a scene, a sequence. He gave Duke a great range of freedom to move about and express himself as he wished to do. From then on, as he strengthened his powers of dramatic execution, Wayne more and more became a collaborator with his directors, rather than a dutiful object being moved around in a pictorial composition. Even Ford, the dictatorial Ford, came to accept Wayne's genius, though he could not understand how the "big oaf" had become what he had become. There is a continuity of work and achievement in Wayne's movies, from *Red River* onwards, and it does not matter whether he is directed by Ford, Hawks, Hathaway, Allan Dwan, John Farrow, Nicholas Ray, William Wellman.

The fanatical hero shines through in film after film in all his glory and derangement. Sometimes there are streaks of humor to him. Sometimes he is in love with a woman, or he is married, but his sacred mission is always his core. He is a monomaniac. Hence *True Grit,* far from being a parody of the John Wayne hero, is an interesting variation of his great theme, which is, essentially, that a man fulfills himself only when he loses himself in a great adventure that is of little or no *personal* profit to himself.

In *True Grit,* Marshal Cogburn is an Ahab—a drunken, unruly, uncouth Ahab but an Ahab. He has the assistance of a girl Ahab. The chase is a passionate pursuit and the whale is her father's murderer. These two stand against the sane community, the nonfanatics, who certainly are in favor of law-and-order. But the sane people are not about to pause in their daily life and go on some lunatic mission in uncharted Indian territory, without warm beds and good food, just to arrest and shoot some outlaws. Now Cogburn, fanatic though he is, lonely though his life may be, solaces himself with whiskey, as does Spig Wead. Even Dunson, Stryker and Brittles reveal slight flaws of weakness. But Ethan Edwards is pure madness. Neither alcohol nor woman's love, neither creature comforts nor the work of the day, nothing that is of interest to sane human beings, is in this man who is a consummation of the fanatical hero. *The Searchers* is one of those chillingly beautiful films. Its images are unforgettable, lingering in the memory like moments of all the most exquisite films we have known. Wayne himself thinks his achievement in this film is his best work and I think that it is also. Yet drunken Cogburn is related to monomaniac Edwards. Seen in this context, Wayne's acting in *True Grit* assumes more resonances and one sees many interesting aspects to it.

Two men—Howard Hughes and Spig Wead—made a profound impact upon Wayne. Out of his experiences with them, he got the raw material for his fanatical heroes. Hughes and Wayne had an affinity from their first meeting. Duke admired the courage and absolutism of Hughes. Hughes admired the passion and art of Duke. It was in their films that the admirations were joined together. *Jet Pilot* was the RKO film Hughes personally produced. It was a wild and extravagant gesture. John Wayne was playing Hughes. He was an American test-pilot involved in an espionage drama with a Russian test-pilot, a woman, played by young Janet Leigh. Josef von Sternberg, in the twilight of his career, was hired to direct this picture, which was the first mistake. It was two films, neither of which Sternberg was capable of doing, even at his best. One was a comedy, a pastiche of *Ninotchka,* a flippant sex-comedy about the conversion of a stern lady Communist to the capitalistic blandishments of love and material objects and, oh yes, freedom. This should have been written by Billy Wilder and directed by Ernst Lubitsch.

The other was a film about the beauty of flight, the exuberance of experiencing supersonic flight. This was a film for William Wellman to direct. It did not have to be written.

Wayne completed most of his *Jet Pilot* sequences in 1949 and early 1950. But the film went on and on and on, costing almost four million to complete, because producer Hughes wanted it to have the most beautiful sequences of flight and aerial combat which had ever been photographed. He sent camera crews to fourteen air bases with the cooperation of the Air Force. Captain Charles Yeager actually piloted a supersonic plane, the X-1, for the first time in this film. Chuck Yeager was a technical adviser on the film.

Sternberg had nothing to do with the aerial sequences. They took sixteen months. There were a hundred and fifty thousand feet of exposed film, from which Hughes eventually cut a 148-minute film, which was recut further.

Cinematographer William Clothier was responsible for the great aerial sequences. He had been a second assistant

cameraman before World War II. Then he had enlisted in
the U.S. Air Force. He headed a film unit and served in
the U.S.A.F. six years, filming aerial combat in the European theater. After the war, he became a specialist in
aerial photography. He was often employed as a second
unit cameraman in war pictures. He also worked on westerns. He was first assistant cameraman on *Fort Apache*. He
became, after 1951, Wayne's favorite cameraman. Together they have made a score of pictures, including some
of his finest. Anyway, in late 1949, Clothier got a call from
an RKO executive asking him to go up to San Francisco
for three days. They wanted to know if you could shoot
film out of a jet airplane and he said, hell yes, he had been
doing it for years.

So he began shooting footage at Travis Air Force Base.
He developed a technique of shooting from one plane, in
supersonic flight, and getting good shots of other equally
high-speed planes. He worked a week at Travis and came
back to look at the rushes of his film. He went to the
Goldwyn Studios one evening. He sat in a projection room.
Howard Hughes entered and sat down. They projected two
reels of Clothier's photography.

Hughes arose and shook Clothier's hand. "Don't shoot
anything," he said, "unless you have clouds that good or
better."

Most of Clothier's footage had been shot against a background of fantastically gorgeous cumulus cloud formations

"Yes, Mr. Hughes," Clothier said.

He did not know it then but he was the fifth cameraman
to be hired—and the first one whose photography satisfied
Hughes' idea of what aerial combat sequences should look
like.

After that, Clothier worked on the picture fifteen months
more, often filming at speeds of over five hundred mph.
Together with Yeager, Clothier blueprinted the sketches of
how the planes would be located in the air and what they
would do.

And always he made sure there were clouds. "Unless
I had beautiful clouds I wouldn't shoot," Clothier recently

told me. "Sometimes I would have arguments with the front office, but I said Mr. Hughes says he wants clouds and I will give him clouds. Every foot I made had beautiful clouds. Now Duke never was up in the air. We shot around him in these aerial sequences and then went into the studio and shot it in process, using my aerial sequences as background and having closeups of Duke in a plane. It looked real."

Clouds or no clouds, Hughes was unable to edit the movie. He loved every frame. Years went by. It wasn't until 1957 that *Jet Pilot* was finally released. It had been cut and recut and cut again, by other hands, and was finally an hour and forty minutes long, though Hughes desired a film as long as von Stroheim's original eight-hour version of *Greed*. Most of the thrilling aerial photography of jet planes maneuvering and shooting each other down had to be cut. The film got disastrous reviews and was quickly withdrawn.

In 1952, Duke returned from Ireland, where he had made *The Quiet Man*. Events with Chata were entering their last agonizing phase. He was an enervated and unhappy person. Howard Hughes proposed to put a private plane at his disposal and send him on a South American goodwill tour for RKO. Was this the act of a good friend who wants to help somebody get his mind off his troubles?

Noah Dietrich, business manager of Hughes' enterprises, has another interpretation.

In his biography of Hughes, Dietrich writes:

Howard feared that Wayne would make another movie that would reach the screens before *Jet Pilot*. So Howard devised an intricate scheme which would keep Wayne away from alien cameras. He proposed a goodwill trip of South America, to be paid for by RKO. Glen Odekirk flew Wayne in a PBY and they visited major capitals and stopped to fish and hunt along the way. Wayne had a great vacation but he didn't realize that it was simply designed to keep him from working for other producers.

Hughes may have been crazy. But he was not stupid. He knew that Wayne had commitments with other studios. He knew that Wayne made at least two pictures a year and that a few weeks in South America would hardly be enough time to keep him out of the clutches of other producers.

It was, I believe, the kindness of a friend—and it had unexpected results for Wayne, this foray to South America, which we will recount in the next chapter.

Duke's next film for Hughes was *The Conqueror*. He was working on the preliminary stages of the role of Genghis Khan the first time I met him, back in 1954.

*"The Conqueror,"* he said then, "is a western in some ways. The way the screenplay reads, it is a cowboy picture and that is how I am going to play Genghis Khan. I see him as a gunfighter."

One time we were at Western Costume Company. It is so named, not because it specializes in garb for cowboy pictures, but because it is located on Western Avenue, near Melrose. Wayne was being fitted for his Mongolian wardrobe. He was trying on Genghis Khan helmets, the kind with a spike on the crown and flaps over the ears. He had started growing his Charlie Chan moustache. He was on a stringent diet, as he was to be a slender Genghis Khan. He was taking Dexedrine tablets four times a day to kill his appetite.

"You know what I've been living on the last month?" he said. "Hard-boiled eggs, spinach, green salads, cottage cheese. I'm allowed a steak or lamb chops once a day. The worst of it is no liquor."

Wayne's definition of "liquor" was hard liquor—brandy or bourbon. He did not classify champagne as "liquor" and he drank much of it. He had also acquired a taste for Guinness stout while in Ireland. He consumed splits of Guinness now and then.

His dimensions posed some difficulty for the fitters— a 46 chest, a 37 waist, and a 17 collar. The fitters scurried about, bringing him costumes and helmets and boots. Present at the fitting was a lean gentleman with a thin moustache. He was introduced to me as Howard Hughes.

I knew him only as a famous aviator and producer who had discovered Jean Harlow and made *Hell's Angels* and went to New York's Stork Club wearing sneakers. I came to regret that I did not trouble to interview him about John Wayne but it simply did not occur to me at that time. Mr. Hughes sat in an antique Morris chair and observed the fitting with unsmiling detachment. After an hour, he got up, whispered something to Wayne, and then departed quietly.

On another day, I was with Duke on Soundstage 7 of the old RKO lot when he was taking a fencing lesson with Fred Kavens. It was the first of many lessons. He had never fenced before but the action in *The Conqueror* called for swordplay. Up till then, the only swords he had used were cavalry sabers, but he never chopped or killed with them. He waved one aloft as he cried, "Charge!" to his cavalry.

Soundstage 7 was deserted. The huge shedlike building was damp and drafts blew through it. On one side there was a beach set from *The Big Rainbow*.

Kavens was a slim chap in black velvet slacks and a black blouse. He moved like a lithe panther. Wayne, slim and looking about twenty-five as the result of his diet, towered over the fencing expert. He was also clad in black pants, sneakers and a black blouse. They dueled back and forth for hours. Wayne was wearing a mask. You could see huge beads of sweat rolling down his forehead behind the mask, rolling into his eyes. He never took the mask off to wipe his eyes. He worked at this unfamiliar exercise patiently, listening to Kaven's criticism, trying to change his positions and thrusts. He had a bad habit of moving his feet too soon.

Kavens was speeding up his commands. "Right cheek cut . . . Left cheek cut . . . Parry . . . Cut . . . Riposte . . . Moulinée . . . Cut . . . Parry . . . Riposte . . ."

If *Jet Pilot* would have benefited by the light touch of a Wilder or the aerial dramatics of a Wellman, *Genghis Khan* required a director with a historical sense, ideally a D. W. Griffith or an Eisenstein or at least a Cecil B. De Mille. Dick Powell, an engaging actor and personality, was making his debut as a director. He was unable to bring the past to life.

*The Conqueror* was a debacle. Critics hooted it down and audiences laughed at it.

*But Howard Hughes loved it!*

It was the last film which he personally produced. By the time it was released he had sold RKO to General Teleradio for twenty-five million. For this amount, they bought a library of seven hundred thirty-eight RKO films, and the studio on Gower Street, including all the buildings and equipment.

Several years later, Hughes decided that he wanted to own two of these seven hundred thirty-eight pictures. He wanted them so badly that he paid twelve million for them! Just for these two.

They were *Jet Pilot* and *The Conqueror*.

He has never leased them for showing on television. He has never allowed them to play in John Wayne retrospectives in theaters. They are his personal monument, his Taj Mahal.

One imagines the isolated Howard Hughes, in his lonely grandeur, shuttling about the earth, escaping from reporters and other invaders of his privacy, in a Las Vegas penthouse, in a Grand Bahamas suite, in a Managua residence, in London, in New York, wherever, always accompanied by the octagon-shaped cans in which film is stored, carrying with him these most precious perhaps of all his possessions, the prints of *The Conqueror* and *Jet Pilot*. And when existence grows tedious for him, he perhaps requests one of his Mormon bodyguards to set up a projector and lower a screen so that he may once again regard himself in some ideal form, escaping his problems in the fantasies of a John Wayne movie, and in so doing, paradoxically enough, he is doing what millions of his fellow tasies of a John Wayne movie, and in so doing, paradoxi-citizens have been doing for years. Eugene O'Neill often screened his prints of *The Long Voyage Home,* seeing himself young once again, personified in the body of John Wayne.

The other influence on Wayne was that of Frank "Spig"

Wead, who wrote *They Were Expendable*. In *The Wings of Eagles* (1957), Ford and Wayne collaborated again on this biographical movie. More than any of the seventeen films these two giants created, the Spig Wead story is their least known and most unappreciated masterpiece. It confused the critics. Its strident militaristic attitude angered some reviewers. Audiences were unable to sympathize with a hero who turned away from his wife and his children because he followed a vision of service to his country, the U.S. Navy, and naval aviation. He is, as his wife, played by Maureen O'Hara, remarks bitterly, "Star Spangled Wead." He loves her. He loves his two daughters. Yet he cannot come to terms with existence and live a normal family life. His mission takes him away from these human concerns.

Like Hughes, Spig Wead was a flier, the first Navy officer to prove the validity of carrier-based bombers and pursuit planes. He is portrayed by Wayne as a hard-drinking, hard-living, belligerent, brave, and somewhat eccentric man, hovering, as all Ahabs hover, on the brink of schizophrenia. Lieutenant Commander Wead and his wife would separate and then be drawn together and then separate. His life took a tragic turn when he fell down a flight of stairs *at home* and suffered a spinal injury so severe as to cripple him the rest of his life.

In a long and painfully elaborated sequence, Wayne shows us the fanatic slowly learning to recover the use of his limbs by exercises and therapy, in a naval hospital. As happened in Wead's life, he came to be a magazine fiction writer and a screenwriter through his naval friendship with John Ford.

Wead seems to have been one of those persons of infinite charm and mystery who fascinated persons who met him. Ford loved him and Wayne looked up to him as an incomparable hero. In the film, Ward Bond, wearing dark glasses and a broad brimmed fedora and miming the gestures and arrogance of Ford, gave a delightful impersonation of the Old Man.

When Wead becomes a successful movie writer and we see him in his lovely hillside Beverly Hills mansion with its swimming pool and terrace of white wrought-iron chairs and tables, he is still alone, still pursuing his solitary visions, though now they are of writing films and plays about aviation, still alone without the woman he loves, without his daughters. *The Wings of Eagles* speaks of self-immolating visionaries, for Wead's dedication to his art is as life-excluding as his dedication to the U.S. Naval Air Force.

The movie is therefore also the biography of John Ford and John Wayne.

*The Wings of Eagles,* like many of Wayne's fanatical hero pictures, did not have a conventional resolution, a simplistic happy ending. You wanted this strange brave gifted man to take this passionate life-loving brilliant educated intelligent woman in his arms and be embraced by her. It was hard to accept that he could not do it. For when they attempt, once more, to come together, the Japanese attack Pearl Harbor and our aircraft carriers are destroyed. Spig Wead, crippled, walking on canes, demands to be put on active duty. He invents a technique of baby aircraft carriers. He takes part in the Battle of Kwajalein, and the film ends with his returning to the mainland from Hawaii by himself. There is no woman to meet him there where he is landing. The fanatical hero must go his own way by himself, pursuing his secret dreams, sacrificing himself to his visions, crazy, brave, resolute, Prometheus bringing fire, Ahab seeking revenge, and women and children, though you love them deeply, are distracting elements to be evaded so that one may do one's duty.

Ford and Wayne climaxed their joint examination of the fanatical hero in *The Searchers,* as overlooked in its time as *The Wings of Eagles.* Now considered a masterpiece by the revisionist critics, it was either patronized or ignored at the time. John McCarten's review in *The New Yorker* for June 9, 1956, is a curious example of how we are all prisoners of our sensibilities, which are defined by our time and place much more than we would like to admit. Here follows his full review—in its entirety. Complete.

In "The Searchers" John Ford and his celebrated road company headed by fearless John Wayne are back—chasing around Texas, fighting Indians, fighting each other and fighting time. The thing has to do with the search for a couple of maidens some nasty Comanches have abducted shortly after the Civil War, and it certainly contains plenty of action. Besides Mr. Wayne, we have Ward Bond, John Qualen, Olive Carey and practically all the rest of that old Ford gang of ours.

In Ethan Edwards, Duke's mastery of film technique is combined with his personal sufferings and his experiences of human weakness to crystallize in a sublime portrait of a man who has gone berserk. He pursues a heroic quest, but he loses his humanity in the pursuit. He is doomed to his loneliness. When he has brought back one of the lost children to the family, we last see him, framed in the doorway, saying good-bye, then receding slowly down the road. A Chaplin fadeout was no more moving.

# 23

# The Peruvian Appointment

Pilar Weldy, née Palette, was a ravishing woman of twenty-two in 1951. A native of Peru, she spoke English and was well educated. She stood five feet three inches tall, weighed one hundred pounds soaking wet; her eyes were large and black, her hair long and lustrously black, her complexion milky white, and her neck unusually long and sinuous. She possessed an intriguing Gioconda smile and came from an upper-class family. Her father was a senator.

If there were a special group of craftsmen in heaven whose special assignment it was to create women calculated to enrapture the soul of John Wayne, they would certainly have put together this particular creature from Lima, Peru. He had an appointment with a romantic destiny, though he could not have envisaged it. For at this time, she was married to Richard Weldy, a public relations executive with Pan-American Grace Airways, or Panagra. Weldy was tall, handsome, and American. Miss Palette had been a Panagra stewardess when she fell in love with Weldy. Their marriage had come upon uneasy times. They were not living together and she had begun a small career in Peruvian movies.

Wayne was enjoying Howard Hughes' gift of a South American holiday. He had hunted, fished, and drunk in Argentina, Brazil and Chile. Then fate brought him to Peru, to Lima, where he was guided by Dick Weldy. They became good friends, sharing among other interests, the bitterness of being unhappily married to women whom they loved. Weldy described his spouse as a hot-tempered, domineering, self-centered bitch. Duke was convinced that she was as bad as his own lady. Both men swore that if they ever got divorced they would never, never marry again.

Wayne went out frequently while in Lima, as Weldy arranged dates with Panagra stewardesses and other agreeable companions. Duke was having a good time. He wined the *señoritas* and romanced them with amorous flippancy, as he had done in comedies with Jean Arthur and Claudette Colbert. Some incidents in his hectic Peruvian adventures were described by an Associated Press stringer in Lima who wrote under the pseudonym of Manuel Negri in the scandal magazine *Confidential* of November, 1956. One episode involved a Chilean "cutie," Cecilia Sanchez, a Panagra hostess. (The *Confidential* prose style was male chauvinist pig. Women were known by the epithets of "cutie," "babe," or "doll." When the "cuties," "dolls," and "babes" became fractious they were "vixens" or "minxes." Prostitutes were "rental wenches.")

Señorita Sanchez and her date, Señor Wayne, it seems, had been drunkenly brawling in the Negro-Negro, a cabaret, and had been thrown out of the joint. Later, Duke was locked out of her apartment. He pounded on her door until the police came.

With Dick Weldy, he had repaired to Rosita's, a high-class bordello in the San Ysidro suburb of Lima. Here, Duke had hired a "rental wench" and taken her to his suite at the Crillon Hotel. During the night there was a downpour. The lovers, it was alleged, were so swept up in their passions that they were unaware that rain was leaking through the roof into the penthouse suite. They awakened the next afternoon to find that they were ankle-deep in water.

But life wasn't all "cuties" and "rental wenches" in Peru. Wayne was there on a mission for RKO. A formal dinner was given in his honor by RKO, Panagra, and the mayor of Lima. Wayne spoke about *Jet Pilot* and Howard Hughes. He toasted Eduard Movius and the future of the Peruvian movie business.

Movius was the Jack Warner of the Peruvian film industry. He had seated his country's finest actress next to the guest of honor.

She was, of course, Mrs. Pilar Palette Weldy!

Well, if it wasn't Acapulco and Mexico City all over again and meeting Esperanza Baur at a reception.

You flee from one Latin-American "vixen" back there in Encino—and, dammit, here you are sitting beside another one. He did not know he had an appointment in Lima. He did not know that he might make the same mistake a third time. He knew about this one, this Pilar Weldy, oh he had learned a lot about her, how she was a hard-boiled mean domineering broad. He was not having any, thank you. And she was not bowled over by him. The name "Juan Juayne" meant little to her for she had not seen any of his films. When he stood up later and they shook hands, she was awed by his "height, his width, and his strength . . . I felt as if I had been hit with a telephone pole."

But she knew what these strong big American *gringos* were really like. Spoiled children. So they made small talk and she smiled and laughed a musical laugh, but he was not falling for any of it, not him.

She went out on location to work.

Of course, it was inevitable that Movius would invite Wayne to watch a Peruvian movie being shot. He went a few hundred miles into the interior and watched them filming *Sabotage in the Jungle,* out in Tingo Maria. He watched them for two days. He remembered a scene in which Pilar danced barefoot before a fire in a night setup. Well, he sure would have made a play for her, but, thanks, thanks just the same, I just happen to be going to Bagdad, see.

So he went back to his Bagdad, which happened to be Hollywood, and made *Trouble Along the Way* with Charles Coburn. Coburn was one of his fellow activists in the Motion Picture Alliance. Coburn was probably the best poker player among the MPA members. There was a faction of poker-playing fanatics in the MPA, which included Ryskind, Wayne, Ward Bond, Ford, and Coburn. They played table stakes and they played hard. Any time you beat Wayne in any game of skill you can consider yourself damn good, and Charlie Coburn often beat him. I have seen Wayne play poker and also played a little with him. I can assure you that he gives a convincing performance at the gaming table.

But now the gloomy desperation descended upon Duke once more. The South American vacation had not changed him. When he played poker with the boys it was clear that his heart was not in it. His bluffs were transparent. Ryskind and Coburn did not have the heart to take away his money but they took it anyway. He was sunk in deepest melancholy, day after day; his drinking did not alleviate the mood but only enhanced its hopelessness. He did his day's work. He went to Burbank, he went to the Warner lot, and he played the scenes. Then he went home. He went home alone. Often he did not eat. He sat and drank in the darkness and reminisced moodily about the misfortunes of his accursed life and how he had been mistreated by all the women he had ever known.

At the studio, Duke was having his troubles with *Trouble Along the Way*. Melville Shavelson and Jack Rose had written the screenplay about a former football player who has become an alcoholic. To raise money for an impoverished college, its rector hires this man, an alumnus, as a coach. The former "gridiron great" (as they are, I believe, known in sporting circles) starts to build winning teams for this obscure Catholic college. Soon they are beating Fordham and Notre Dame. Most of the picture was about the "gridiron great's" ingenious schemes to sneak professional players onto his roster and hustle athletic equipment. He also has a romance going with a social worker.

Shavelson wanted Wayne for his star. He took the screenplay to Steve Trilling, a Warner Brothers executive producer. Trilling liked it. He sent it to Duke.

One day, Shavelson picked up his phone and he heard the familiar vibrato of Wayne's voice saying, "I just had to let you know how anxious I am to make this picture. I like the plot. For years I've been looking for a good football story. Nobody ever asked me to play a football player before. That's what I was when I went to USC."

(It had somehow slipped Wayne's mind that away back in 1931 he had played a football player in Columbia's *Maker of Men,* or *Cohn's Revenge*.)

Shavelson said he was delighted with Wayne's reaction. Shavelson was going to produce.

Then Wayne murmured a murmur which sent chills through Shavelson. Duke said that the screenplay needed a little polishing and he knew just the man for the polish job—James Edward Grant, "who has kind of a good feelin' for my way of talkin'."

Since this was Shavelson's first try at producing, he had no intention of permitting Jimmy Grant, who was rated a good action writer but no comedy wordsmith, to lay a typewriter on the script. He persuaded Duke that Grant was not required. From the first day of shooting, Shavelson and Wayne were butting heads. Wayne insisted on making changes in his own speeches. Grant was secretly rewriting the dialogue. Duke also wanted changes in other actors' speeches. Shavelson was desperate. He believed that Jimmy Grant's clandestine revisions were killing the gags. He figured out a clever strategem. He would have *two* scripts! One would be for Wayne to take home for Grant's revisions and the real script, which they would actually be shooting. When Wayne was in a scene, then they kept to the lines he wanted, but when he was between takes, Shavelson used the real script. But the producer did not know that Wayne studies a script, memorizes it, and also gets to know the lines of every actor.

Two days out, Duke discovered Shavelson's trick. He denounced him. They fought constantly.

Michael Curtiz directed *Trouble Along the Way*. An amusing incident took place, involving an "established" minor character. To assist Curtiz in getting technical football details correct, a former USC All-American had been hired as the assistant director. There was a scene in which Wayne, playing Steve Williams, the coach, was supposed to show a student how to take out a blocker. The A.D. thought that instead of merely demonstrating, the "coach" should actually throw himself into the action.

"In this scene," the A.D. said, "I think that Mr. Wayne should take out the guard."

"What?" asked Curtiz.

"We should take him out."

Curtiz, a foreigner famous for his fractured English and good-natured bursts of hysteria, was aghast. "My ears are not believing this," he shouted. "Take him out? Fire him? Impossible. He is established in every scene. Hey, Duke, what's your opinion as a person, not as a star, forget star, as a person knowing this football, what do you think?"

Wayne deadpanned a shrug. "I think he's right. We should take out the guard."

Curtiz had a fit. He demanded that somebody get the producer on the set. Shavelson arrived and Curtiz said that these lunatics wanted him to fire an actor who had appeared in every football scene they had shot and it made absolutely no sense. Shavelson saw what was afoot and he began to explain.

Have you ever tried to explain to a crazy Hungarian who knows nothing about football, and wants to know nothing about football, what "taking out" an opponent implies?

Curtiz calmed down, and they went ahead with the scene. The actor playing the blocker decided to be smart. When Duke hit him, just playing it lightly for the camera, the man (who was a college football player, as it happened) stood his ground and sneered. Which got Wayne mad, and he went at him with a full body block and brought him down, smeared the hell out of him.

It was a splendid take. But Duke had also smeared his shoulder, the old rotten shoulder. It was an expensive revenge. His right arm was paralyzed. He couldn't even pick up a comb to straighten his hair. The next day they were doing a key scene in which Wayne has to lose his temper and throw a ball through a church window. He couldn't hold the ball in his right hand. He became left-handed and threw it that way. For the rest of the picture he worked left-handed. Nobody, strangely enough, noticed the sinister change in his movements—perhaps because film acting is so much centered on the face and the eyes. Neither Charles Coburn nor Donna Reed nor director Curtiz remarked on the switch or asked why. Recently, I mentioned this episode to Shavelson and he said that he had never noticed it either, though he had studied the daily rushes and seen the film many times during the process of editing and scoring it and screening it. Shavelson and Wayne were enemies. Shavelson swore he would never cast Wayne in any movie he ever made if he was the last movie star on earth.

Wayne felt the same way about Shavelson, doubled and redoubled. Now he had excruciating shoulder pains on top of his emotional malaise. He was so miserable, he rarely answered the phone. He didn't go out. He became an apathetic hermit, full of self-pity. To get him out of the house, Bob Fellows dragged him out to a party one night.

Wayne secluded himself in a corner. He looked glum, until he saw somebody familiar. Somebody small and female and dark-haired and Latin-American. The old Latin-American syndrome asserted itself! He could not remember who she was, but he knew he had seen her before.

He roused himself out of the spiritual torpor and slouched over. "Hello," he said, "I think we've met before."

"I am not sure," she replied. "What is your name?"

This tickled him. The idea that any inhabitant of the planet Earth would have to ask his name amused him.

"John Wayne," he said, feeling in such moments that he was an impostor, that it was really Marion Michael Morrison.

"Oh, you're in the movies, yes?"

"Yes."

"But I do not think that we have met, Mr. Wayne. My name is Pilar Palette. I am from Peru."

Then it came back. That wife of Dick Weldy's, that's who she was.

"Yeah," he said, "we sure did meet. You were making a picture out in Tingo Maria. *Sabotage in the Jungle.*"

"Yes," she said, clearly not remembering his visit to the location.

That ended the conversation, and Wayne scuttled right back to Bagdad and melancholy.

But he did not remain there for more than five or six days. They had taken a break on the soundstage of *Trouble Along the Way.* He went out for a brisk stroll. While strolling, he sharply turned a corner on the lot and collided head-on with Señora Weldy, who was sharply turning the same corner from the opposing end. It was just like in a Frank Capra picture. They both laughed. She assured him she had not been hurt or bruised in any way. He felt guilty. The next day was Thanksgiving. He had planned to dine alone. He was so misanthropic at this time he wasn't even seeing his children.

On the spur of the moment, he asked her, if she were free, to join him for a Thanksgiving repast, though he personally did not think he had anything to be thankful for. She accepted. He took her to the Tail o'the Cock on Ventura Boulevard. She had a marvelous dinner of cracked crab, roast turkey, baked sweet potatoes, string-beans, and mince pie. He ordered white wine for her and a good red Bordeaux for himself. His repartee had loosened up considerably since the recent party. He regaled her with tales of his misadventures in the movie business. She was fascinated. He took her home and they said good night.

He did not intend to see her again. He believed he was too old for her. He had already struck out twice in the marital game. He did not wish to go to bat again. Yet he was grateful for her charming company. She had somehow gotten him out of his black mood. He began to feel an interest in life stirring again. He thought it would be nice, though—even if he wasn't ever going to see her again, which he wasn't—to send her a token of his esteem. His infallible brain cells fed him the memory that while resting between setups on that jungle location in Peru, she had strummed a guitar and sung folk songs.

"The following day," Pilar says, "a large box came to the hotel for me. It was a stunning and beautiful gift from Duke—a handsome guitar."

And now she had to express her gratitude for the guitar. She invited him to a screening of *Sabotage in the Jungle* at Warners. She and some American actors had been dubbing the English soundtrack for it. So he took her to a romantic seafood restaurant, Jack's at the Beach, and God had provided an unusually sensual sunset for them. Then they went to the screening. She loved to recount how Wayne did not say a word about her acting. All he would say was that the jungle photography was marvelous.

They now began going out together and soon became an item in the gossip columns. He was reported dining with her in Macayo's, a new Santa Monica hot spot. Usually they met at the homes of friends, for they had to be discreet since she was still legally married.

Slowly, the torch he carried for Esperanza began to glimmer and die away.

She returned to Peru.

He made *Island in the Sky* and *Hondo*.

And they wrote letters.

"One day," reported Henaghen in an account in *Motion Picture Magazine,* "John Wayne woke up in the morning and he realized he wasn't in love with Esperanza any more, and he knew he had fallen in love with Pilar."

In February, 1954, she returned to Los Angeles. He resumed his courtship. By now he was divorced. Chata had gone back to Mexico. He was again living in the Encino mansion.

They had dinner there. J. Hampton Scott, that intrepid straightener of rooms and loyal servant, waited on them. They dined by candlelight. It was rare roast beef, they had, and a bottle of Chateau Latour 1947.

And then he said, "Pilar, you know how I feel about you. I want you to marry me. Will you?"

She looked at him over a glass of wine.

J. Hampton Scott hovered apprehensively around. One can imagine that another Latin-American chatelaine was not exactly his dream.

"I'll have to think it over," she said.

Mr. Scott sighed. In relief?

She paused. She played the love scene as well as Claudette Colbert or Maureen O'Hara. She took four beats, six beats, eight beats. Then:

"I have thought it over. The answer is—yes."

Duke asked Scott to bring out some champagne and they sipped a Dom Perignon.

He then inquired if she liked the house and the estate.

"If you don't think you could be happy here, I'll sell it and buy a home wherever you like."

"I could be very happy here with you," she said.

He finished *The High and the Mighty* and *The Conqueror*. He was to go to Hawaii to make *The Sea Chase*. She went along. Her own divorce was now being processed. His decree would not be final until November.

It was his kindness and strength and thoughtfulness which had won her love. In 1954, speaking with Will Tusher, she said of Wayne:

"He is the most tender man I have ever known. Sometimes he goes to extremes in being considerate with me. For example, when I had yellow jaundice last year, I felt fine all the time—but he was worried about me constantly. And he telephones all the time, even when he's working on a picture. And last Christmas, he trimmed the tree himself. He bought me all sorts of lovely presents and he wrapped them himself."

*He wrapped them himself!* How loving of Wayne to have chosen the presents and clumsily wrapped them with his big fingers and how beautiful of her to have been aware of the joyousness of this action!

For he could have given her name to his faithful and efficient secretary, Mary St. John, and dispatched her to Bullock's or Robinson's to buy six presents for Pilar. But he had taken the care to select the presents and he had wanted to wrap them.

*He telephones all the time—even when he's working on a picture.* She knew very well that his pictures were the core of his reality. She never was in opposition to them. And she worked strenuously to be a part of his acting, even to traveling to locations, many of which were primitive. She was a partner, in the sense in which none of his wives had been before, and this is not necessarily because they were less women, but partially because Duke Wayne had not been emotionally mature enough to enter into a complete partnership with a woman before. It had taken him a long time to grow up in the area of interpersonal sexuality but finally he had arrived at an emotional strength in which he was able to venture there without inward fears and reluctances.

On October 25, her birthday, they were still in Honolulu. He did not bring her a gift. Not even flowers. He did not speak of her birthday. He had forgotten it! She was unhappy. She was angry.

"I went to my room early," she recalled, "took my makeup off, and was getting into bed when New Year's Eve broke loose. Everybody in the company, from stars to prop men, banged on my door. An orchestra played

'Happy Birthday' and there was champagne, a cake, and presents. And I looked like a ghost."

*The Sea Chase* was completed on October 30. On November 1, 1954, they were married at sunset on the lawn of the home of William Hill, a territorial senator. His residence was on a cliff overlooking Keakoa Bay. Against a background of a first-rate tropical sunset—a composition of vermilion and maize and lavender and pearl gray—they were declared man and wife. Director John Farrow gave the bride away. Mary St. John was the matron of honor.

As the skies darkened, the Hawaiians lighted torches. Then they sang old Hawaiian songs and danced fertility dances.

In the morning Mr. and Mrs. Wayne flew back to Los Angeles. She would always say, smiling, that some people from the state got married in California and went to Hawaii for the honeymoon. "But we got married in Hawaii and flew home to California for our honeymoon," she said.

And she would laugh her musical laugh. And they laughed together. And the honeymoon lasted twenty years as each contributed to the counterpoint of sharing from separate sensibilities. Yes, there was heavy weather sometimes but it seemed that they would survive everything to grow old and ever more content together. And then, on November 19, 1973, a trial separation was announced.

Yet it was only a year or so ago that, watching Duke as he described the building of a tennis court on their place in Newport Beach, you felt you knew how strong was his love. Pilar had taken up tennis and the court was for her.

"My wife loves it," he said, and you have to imagine for yourself that with the words *my wife* there was a melodic line below like Mozart's *Là ci darem la mano*. "She just *loves* it . . . She took it up about three, four years ago, and now, if she doesn't play tennis every day, it is a wasted day. No, I don't play tennis. I think I'll take some lessons in tennis."

Upon settling into her new home in Encino, Mrs.

Wayne made several changes. The first was the discharge of J. Hampton Scott, a lamentable event but one which is understandable from a new wife's viewpoint. Scott received a generous settlement but he must have felt that his loyalty had been poorly rewarded.

Pilar staffed the establishment with three Peruvian servants. Wayne was back to being surrounded by Spanish accents and Spanish vocabularies. But the servants were under strict orders never to serve the master avocado in any way, shape, or form. When in doubt, they were to give him steaks—for even breakfast, lunch, and dinner.

She also altered the decorations of the house. She disposed of Chata's heavy imported Spanish antiques. Some of Duke's friends used to say that the home had been more like a "museum" than a home. They had said similar things about Josie's taste in antiques and Aubusson carpeting. Admittedly these men did not have sophisticated tastes.

Pilar liked the style of the house, an American Colonial of fieldstone and white frame. She wanted to carry out its feeling in the interior. Avery Rennick, a decorator, handled the contract, and commissioned custom-made reproductions of Early American furniture for every room. The living room had been a little ballroom—fifty by thirty feet. She had it broken up by an archway. A fieldstone fireplace was built for the living room and another one for Duke's den.

The bed in the master bedroom was made vast, but of Early American vastness. There were to be no canopied couches with rococo cherubs. James Hoffman described it in *Photoplay* as "an Early American settle bed built on the foundation of a tremendous Old English bench on which Yorkshire farmers had smoked more than two hundred hams at a time. It had been really modernized: arm rests on the sides which could be raised and lowered; a cigarette compartment for him; a pull-down book rack; a control panel for television, radio, several telephone lines—by just flicking a switch you could turn on the lights downstairs or even open the front gate; and a slide-out backgammon tray fitted into the headboard."

The third Mrs. Wayne was a Roman Catholic. A priest came to bless each room of the newly decorated house. When he finally arrived at the master chamber and beheld this massive contraption, he gasped.

"It is like a football field," Pilar remarked gayly.

"Then," reported the man from *Photoplay,* "the priest prayed that God would bring joy and fertility to all who lived in this house."

In 1956, Richard Weldy emerged from his Hispano-American obscurity into the limelight for a brief moment. In September, *Confidential* appeared with the story about Pilar Weldy and her former husband and how, allegedly, Duke had stolen her away from her spouse. It was a nasty article with slurs on Weldy's *machismo.* The publisher of *Confidential* was a plump sleek man, Robert Harrison. He and his managing editor, A. P. Govoni, had gone to Ciudad Trujillo in the Dominican Republic to gather material for a series of articles on the amatory secrets and unnatural virility of Porfirio Rubirosa. While researching Rubirosa's libido, Harrison decided to visit a resort in the Jarabacoa Mountains of that region.

By a coincidence, Weldy, who had been so cruelly maligned in *Confidential,* also happened to be in the Jarabacoa Mountains. He was later to claim that he had gone to the Dominican Republic to fulfill an order from several American zoos for "a rare type of ferret, a weasel type animal that digs in the dirt for its prey."

Harrison, Govoni, and a woman companion—a night-club singer—were trudging around in the mountains looking for game, and there is Weldy, also on safari, looking for these weasels, and who does he happen to run into but Harrison.

According to his story, Weldy was so surprised to see Harrison in the Jarabacoa Mountains that he dropped his rifle. It accidentally went off and shot Harrison. Harrison was badly wounded and lost much blood until the bearers could get him to a hospital.

The news of Harrison's shooting and extreme suffering

brought joy to the hearts of innumerable celebrities all over the world whose private lives he had made public, whom he had photographed in embarrassing situations with telephoto cameras, on whose amorous habits he had hired private detectives to report. At the time of his wounding, he had twelve million dollars in libel suits hanging over his head. Wayne did not sue him for libel, though he too had been libeled. Someday he hoped to meet Harrison and then he would show him a thing or two about hitting and punching.

An Associated Press reporter called Wayne in Hollywood. He told him that Robert Harrison had been shot by Dick Weldy and that the former was seriously injured but alive. Asked his reaction to this event, Duke replied, "Dick Weldy is one hell of a nice guy, but I deplore the fact that he is such a bad shot."

Pilar and Duke had been embarrassed by the *Confidential* story, a cruel account replete with nasty innuendos. But with Pilar, Duke was able to laugh at the pain. In this marriage, he found a new dimension of shared amusement at the pleasures of existence—but also at its frustrations. With her, he could sublimate his rage. Even when disaster struck they could laugh together.

In February, 1958, Wayne was on location in Kyoto, Japan, making *The Townsend Harris Story,* released as *The Barbarian and the Geisha,* directed by John Huston, his first picture on the 20th Century-Fox contract. It was a full-length biographical epic about the American diplomat who came to Japan in 1856 and opened its doors to the West. Huston and Wayne did not get along. Wayne still writhes when he speaks of how slowly and lackadaisically Huston directed his scenes. He believes that Huston was fascinated by petty irrelevant details and shots. He told how Huston shot a lengthy and interminably boring opening sequence in Townsend Harris' cabin in the Navy ship bringing him to the Orient. He is convinced that Huston is one of the most overrated *metteurs en scène* in Hollywood. We got into a heavy argument one morning when I maintained Huston was a brilliant director. He said he couldn't think of one good picture he had ever done. He watched me when he said this since he knew perfectly well that he was mistaken. I, of course, at once cited *The Maltese Falcon* and *The Treasure of the Sierra Madre*. And Duke insisted—with no basis except the fact that he disliked Huston and felt he had been artistically mistreated by him—that these pictures had succeeded because of Huston's father, because Walter Huston had been in both these films and had assisted his son. So I said how about *The Asphalt Jungle*, and Duke changed the subject.

What made the first weeks of work on *Townsend Harris* even more tedious was that Pilar was not with him. She was at home in Encino with their little baby. Though they had now been married four years, he was still passionately in love with her. He had an insatiable craving for her company and her comments on the day's happenings. She had resolved, from the first, that she would not be a Hollywood wife. She had determined to be a participant in his movies, a true marital partner, and she would go on location when he went on location. She had gone on location to every film since they were married. She had even made a long trip out to the Sahara Desert to be with her husband when he made Henry Hathaway's *Legend of the Lost*, a fabulous entertainment in which Wayne projected a sort of Clark Gable panache as Sophia Loren's lover.

Pilar planned to take Aissa and join Wayne in Kyoto after the first month's shooting.

One evening, she was asleep in the mammoth Early American settle bed when she was aroused by Blackie barking and scratching at her face. Blackie was a dachshund. He had leaped on the bed and began nipping her when he failed to arouse her. She sleeps deeply. Stirring awake, she saw the room was full of smoke. She smelled a fire. She raced to the crib and seized Aissa. She ran downstairs and picked up the fire extinguisher. She opened the windows. She did not know where the fire was. She tried to work the fire extinguisher with one hand, holding the infant with the other. She could not work it. She roused the servants. The flames seemed to be upstairs.

They all went outside. She phoned the Encino fire department. Before she went out, though, she took an old U.S. Cavalry hat which Wayne had worn in all the John Ford U.S. Cavalry pictures, such as *Rio Grande*. She stood outside, cradling the child, watching in horror as the flames spurted outside the windows of the second floor, and the entire upstairs rooms burned away by the time the firemen arrived. Everything—including her clothes and his clothes and the Early American settle bed—went up in flames.

Ward Bond and his wife and Jim and Fran Henaghen came over at once. They got her some underwear, sweaters and slacks. When she went to stay with the Bonds her composure finally cracked a little. She started crying and wanted Duke. They could not get to him on the phone. He was out of the hotel, out on location. A doctor came and gave her a shot to make her sleep.

Ward kept on phoning Duke all night until he finally got through. He told him of the events and of Blackie's heroism and assured him that Pilar and Aissa were fine but that all her clothes had burned and she literally had nothing to wear. She had been put to sleep but would speak to him later.

Duke and Pilar had often engaged in teasing ripostes when she would say—having a closet full of dresses—that she had nothing to wear when they were getting ready for a social event. And now it was literal. He at once signed a check, leaving the amount blank, and sent it by airmail, special delivery to his wife. He enclosed a note:
FOR THE GIRL WHO REALLY HAS NOTHING TO WEAR.

He had to get some sleep to be ready for tomorrow's shooting and another argument with Huston. He polished off a bottle of Scotch and fell into a restless sleep. A bellman roused him with two telegrams. One read:
HOW DO YOU LIKE ONE-STORY HOUSES? LOVE. PILAR.
The second:
I GUESS I AM A PERUVIAN NATIONAL HERO BUT ALL I DID WAS WAKE UP MY MOMMY AND SAY "GET ME OUT OF THIS HOUSE" SINCERELY YOURS BLACKIE.

Across the Pacific, he shared the wonder of the kind

of love he had found with her, for she had, in the words of Maurice Chevalier's song, brought a new kind of love to him. Perhaps his other wives could have given him this as well and perhaps he had not been ready for it previously. Now he could get into areas of tenderness and expressions of delicate feelings which he had never explored within himself before.

Finally they spoke on the phone. The second floor was devastated but downstairs it was fine. She was fine. The servants had not been hurt. Then Aissa got on the phone and made small sounds. In the background, he heard Blackie yapping.

Pilar said, "He wants some attention, too. He wants you to see the medal on his neck. It says 'To Blackie— for bravery above and beyond duty.' He knows we're talking about him. He's wagging his tail."

"Give him all the steaks he can eat, darlin'."

Mrs. Wayne assured him that Blackie would be put on a John Wayne diet of prime strip steaks.

Her final bulletin imparted the happy information that she had already spoken to Avery Rennick and he had promised her that he would scour Yorkshire and other remote counties of England until he found a similar contraption out of which he would have another gargantuan bed made.

This was reassuring to the philoprogenitive Mr. Wayne.

Pilar is a woman of strength and perception, as well as wit and tender affection, and he would need all of her strength and all of her trust in him to sustain him during the years that preceded the making of *The Alamo*.

# 24

## Remembering the Alamo

ALAMO, THE (Span.=cottonwood), a building in San
Antonio, Texas, erected in 1744 as a mission, in 1793
converted to a fort, and in 1836, in the war for Texas
independence, the scene of a desperate resistance by
about 150 Texans, under Col. William B. Travis, to
a besieging army of 4,000 Mexicans under the command of Santa Anna. The siege ended on March 6 in
a hand-to-hand encounter which resulted in the complete annihilation of the Texans. When but six of the
latter remained alive, among them the famous David
Crockett, they surrendered upon the promise that
their lives would be spared, but were slain at Santa
Anna's orders. Col. James Bowie, another Texan
hero, was killed while lying ill on his bed. "Remember
the Alamo" became the war cry of the Texans in subsequent encounters, and the date is still com-
memorated in San Antonio.

*—The Columbia Encyclopedia*

At about a quarter of eight on the morning of September
22, 1959, three hundred twenty-one persons were gathered in a courtyard before an accurate and beautifully
contrived reproduction of the Alamo, the old mission
which had become a fortress. The old mission and the
whole town of San Antonio de Bexar had been labor-
iously reconstructed on several hundred acres of a ranch
outside of Brackettville, Texas. The sun was already bak-
ing the white buildings. The persons assembled were the
cast, the principals, and the technical crew of a colossal

film which was about to start its first day's shooting. There was John Wayne and Richard Widmark, who would play Bowie, and the young Laurence Harvey, who had recently triumphed as the amorous opportunist in *Room at the Top,* who would impersonate Colonel Travis. Wayne would play Davy Crockett. One of his Tennessee coonskin-hatted companions would be taken off by the redoubtable Chill Wills, a bluff hearty character actor in westerns. Michael Wayne, eldest son of the Duke, who was also directing and producing *The Alamo,* was there, his head bowed along with all the other bowed heads. For several years he had worked around the Batjac office. Now he was ready to be an associate producer and he cut his eyeteeth on this one. Mike Wayne was to mature ten years' worth during the next eighty-three days of filming. There were stuntmen and second-unit directors and cameraman William Clothier, and assistant cameramen and juicers, grips, prop men, script girls, heroines, makeup men, makeup women, costumers, and still there would be thousands and thousands of Mexicans and Texans to be employed as extras in the battle scenes.

The first day's shooting began in a strange fashion. It began with a prayer. Never, *Variety* said, quoting "veteran film men," had a movie been blessed by a priest—not even those religious films based on Old Testament and New Testament sources. The priest was a hearty thirty-five-year-old *padre* from San Antonio—the real San Antonio—the one with a population of 587,000 which was a hundred miles away. He was Father Peter Rogers, of the Order of Mary Immaculate, and he was attached to St. Mary's Catholic Church. He had taken an interest in the movie and in the town being built to its 1836 dimension on the J. T. "Happy" Shahan ranch. He had become a good friend of Mike Wayne and Bill Clothier and had persuaded Duke, who was an agnostic, that it would be fitting to ask God's blessing and guidance for a movie about a building and the men who had died within it, for the Alamo had once been a religious building when the Spanish friars had come to carry their message to Wayne's old antagonists, the Apaches of Southwestern America. Well, somewhat reluctantly, Wayne agreed and Father Rogers had driven several hours to get here in time.

And now, his soutane waving in a pleasant breeze, his crucifix dangling by his side, he looked at the men, arranged about him, many in their costumes, some on horses, some carrying flintlock rifles, some in coonskin caps, two Mexican actors riding a cart pulled by a pair of oxen, everybody bareheaded, bowing their heads and he said:

"O, Almighty God, centuries ago Thou raised a magnificent mission—a harbor, for all, of peace and freedom. This was the Alamo. Today we ask Thy blessing, Thy help, and Thy protection as once again history is relived in this production.

"We ask Thee this so that the film *The Alamo* will not only be the world's outstanding production, but will also be a tribute to the spirit of the men who first built it, who lived in it, who died in it. We ask these things in the name of Our Lord, Jesus Christ, who lives and reigns, world without end. Amen."

*Amen, amen, amen,* they all echoed, and even Duke, that hardy skeptic, was seen to move his lips.

Then they set up the lights and the reflectors—for klieg lights are used even on the most beautiful days of sunshine to emphasize the faces which otherwise might be washed out—and director Wayne lined up a crowd scene on the plaza and called for the cast of extras to move about and Clothier directed his camera operator and the assistant director screamed *Quiet everybody* and for the Mexicans *Silencio* and Wayne cried *Action* and *Speak* and then the camera was rolling, they were shooting in 70 mm., Todd-AO process, and this was an establishing scene . . .

It had taken John Wayne almost ten years to realize his dream. It had taken two years to construct this replica of San Antonio and the Alamo mission. They started building it in 1957. John Wayne was fifty years old in 1957.

"At the age of fifty," George Orwell has said, "every man has the face that he deserves." It was the face he had had before he was born, to paraphrase the Zen paradox. It was a face that had been sculptured by adversity and by pain. It was a noble face, wrinkled and weatherbeaten and hard, and the eyebrows were thick over narrow eyes imbedded deeply with surrounding crosshatches of wrinkles and the nose was a Roman nose and the jaw had become stronger and the mouth was heroic and there was still a lean look in his face. It was a face that had weathered all loneliness and, what was even more complicated, all fulfillment, and like Ulysses in the poem of Tennyson's, it was a face whose deep blue eyes looked beyond, looked to the next voyage, the next adventure.

But its nobility, its heroism, was not a quality that had been accomplished once and for all. The face had to be forever renewed, over and over again, every day. And he pursued his quest of *The Alamo* with a single-minded obsession and an unwillingness to bow to obstacles that was in the style of his fanatic heroes—Dunson, Stryker, Ethan Edwards.

He was determined to produce *The Alamo* and he was determined to direct it himself. He was told he was mad and reckless and foolish. He had sundered his long relationship with Herb Yates and Republic because of *The Alamo*. Because of it he had fought with his business manager, Bö Roos, who believed it was financially unwise, and he had parted with Roos. His partner, Robert Fellows, opposed the venture as being unrealistic unless they hired a famous director. Even John Ford advised him not to produce and direct *The Alamo*. Wayne was too old. He would have to play a major role as an actor. He had no experience in directing and hardly knew too much about production. It was a complex project which would be very expensive—at least five million. Eventually it went into production budgeted at eight million and cost over twelve million to get in the can. And so he and Bob Fellows came to a parting of the ways.

Where would he get the money? Howard Hughes, a

Texan with plenty of money, was now out of the movies.
Universal said they would be interested if Frank Lloyd,
John Ford, or Hawks were directing. Wayne said no
deal. Jack Warner, a friend and business associate whose
judgment Duke respected, pleaded with him not to do it.
Warners would be happy to coproduce *The Alamo* with
Batjac—provided Raoul Walsh, Mervyn LeRoy, Henry
Hathaway, or Ford was director. And 20th Century-Fox,
with whom he had a three-picture deal, scoffed at the idea
of Wayne directing a spectacle movie. Paramount, where
Batjac now leased quarters, would coproduce it provided
that Cecil B. De Mille or Henry Hathaway or . . .

And John Wayne just shook his stubborn head and
said, "No." And "No." And "No." To agents, to lawyers,
to friends, to movie executives. To his son Michael. To
almost everybody. You could as easily have dissuaded
Captain Ahab from seeking the white whale as John
Wayne from directing *The Alamo*.

The obsession had seized him during the late 1940's,
part of the patriotic zeal engendered by the anti-Communist crusade.

During one of his Mexican holidays with Esperanza,
he and Jimmy Grant had begun conversing about Santa
Anna and the Texas war of independence. They had had
no film in mind. They were talking about American history. Duke loves American history. But something was
started in his mind. It began taking root and growing,
until it became an all-compelling obsession, over which
he had no longer any control. Later, he would explain
the obsession, and as always when persons speak of great
forces that are gripping them, their words come out in
a way that makes them sound fatuous. But Wayne deeply
believed what he said.

He would say, "This picture is America. I hope that
seeing the Battle of the Alamo will remind Americans
that liberty and freedom don't come cheap. This picture,
well, I guess making it has made me feel useful to my
country. I think it's important that foreign countries
know about this aspect of the American struggle for
freedom. I hope our present generation of Americans,

our children, will get a sense of our glorious past, and appreciate the struggle our ancestors made for the precious freedoms which we now enjoy—and sometimes just kind of take for granted."

Does this have the counterfeit ring of false patriotic coin? Is it one of your July Fourth speeches? Hypocrisy? Wayne meant it. He proved it by committing everything he owned in the world materially to this movie. As the costs ran way over the budget, he mortgaged his house, his two cars and station wagon, an expensive cooperative apartment he owned at New York's Hampshire House, borrowed money on his personal notes. He would say, "I have everything I own in this picture—except my necktie."

In the end he was sustained by his own vision and Pilar's love. She believed in him completely and adored him, and therefore she gave him her strength, her humor, and her companionship during the frustrating years preceding that September morning in Brackettville.

He did not put everything else aside to concentrate on *The Alamo* during the 1950's. With one part of him he was making two films a year, many of them long and difficult works, many of them made on hazardous locations, while with the other part he was assembling the capital and the forces to mount his own battle of the Alamo. It would be, if you will forgive the reuse of the analogy, as if the captain of the *Pequod* had, during that long voyage, been simultaneously organizing a fleet of herring fishermen and opening a seafood restaurant in Boston. Looking back at these years, when Wayne should have been getting sere and yellow, it is almost impossible to comprehend how he brought it all off.

Besides Pilar, there was also James Edward Grant to sustain him. Grant was a year older than Duke, and standing alongside of him, he appeared to be even smaller than he was. He was five feet five inches tall. He had a mischievous Irish face. He was slender and wiry and quick of wit. He could have been played by Barry Fitzgerald. He wore eyeglasses and his hair was cut short. He was one of those hard-boiled newspapermen who had come into the motion-picture industry after talking pictures. Along with Ben Hecht, Herman Mankiewicz, Jules Furthman, Kubec Glasmon, Charlie MacArthur and many others, he had brought the quality of tabloid journalism into pictures—fast, breezy gangsters and gun molls; American slang, sex, and scandals. A native of Chicago, Grant had left college to work for the Chicago *Herald-American*. He covered sports and crime. He became an authority on racketeers. He wrote a syndicated column about organized crime. "It's a Racket. It's a Racket" was used in two hundred papers.

Grant wrote his first novel, *Whipsaw,* when he was twenty-seven. M-G-M purchased it and Irving Thalberg brought Grant to Hollywood, where he wrote the screenplay for it. The picture starred Spencer Tracy and Myrna Loy. Soon Grant was making two thousand dollars a week and buying sports cars and a huge house and estate on Benedict Canyon and polo ponies and a yacht. He began to drink more and more. But he was one of the most successful screenwriters in the business and wrote over seventy screenplays, including *She's No Lady, Boomtown, Johnny Eager, Belle of the Yukon, The Great John L.*

He and Wayne had entered into a relationship which is rare in movies: an intimacy between a writer and a star which became a fusion as much as it was a collaboration. They had done *Angel and the Badman* and *Sands of Iwo Jima.* Wayne loved Jimmy. Jimmy loved Wayne. But there was some angry animal scourging Grant's insides and he was in the grip of the alcoholic's disease, so that he was compelled to drink in order to assuage the pains of living and then the remedy became a terribly wracking destructive thing. Grant was nearly destroyed in the process, as the bottle became his be-all and end-all.

Perhaps it was his creative frustration, for many of these wild, exuberant men who brought excitement to the movies were compulsive, self-destructive drinkers, just like Grant—Mankiewicz was a conspicuous example; so was Charlie MacArthur, so were many others. Grant loved to write books and magazine articles. He had written many

*Saturday Evening Post* articles on sports and crime. He was a literary man and not really a dramatic writer. Perhaps this was the unhappiness he tried to drown in the bottle. We don't know. We do know that sometime in 1956, much to Duke's surprise, Grant began attending meetings of Alcoholics Anonymous. He had been proselytized by a Cy Malis, now dead, a former baseball player and later a movie actor, who had reformed his life and who made many converts among movie actors and writers. Several of the actors mentioned in this book, and others who are not, were brought into a life of sobriety by Grant in turn. Grant changed his life completely. He had always been an idealist and a man of religious inclinations. Now he cast aside an interest in material possessions and became a serene and sweet-tempered human being concerned with other people. He had probably been as hard a drinker as anybody in the John Ford-John Wayne *cénacle* of drinkers and nobody could believe the metamorphosis.

Grant not only wrote the script of *The Alamo* but he went down to Texas and remained there during the entire filming, rewriting old pages and writing new scenes. And he did not take a single drink.

Reminiscing about this, Tom Kane, who has been story editor of Batjac Productions since it started, told me one day, when it was almost noon, "By now, Jimmy Grant, when he was drinking, would have already drunk his first bottle of bourbon." He had been good for three, sometimes four bottles a day until he began attending AA meetings in the small clubhouse on Radford Street in North Hollywood, near the old Republic studio.

A famous actor—not Wayne—who knew Jimmy Grant prior to his change and who himself was brought to his first AA meeting by Grant, told me, "I have never seen AA affect a man as it did Jimmy. When he was drinking, he was a noisy overbearing brash Irishman. When he became sober and changed his ways, he became the total opposite. Now he was soft-speaking. He was kind. He was considerate of your feelings. Hell, he became an all-around decent guy. But I think Duke missed his drinking company. It's hard to be around a guy who isn't drinking when drinking is still an important part of your life."

Those speeches about loyalty and God in *The Alamo,* which amused some of the sophisticated reviewers by what struck them as their transparent Hollywood fakery, were not that at all. They were expressions of Jimmy Grant's genuine feelings and beliefs and not pasted on the script to gull the small-town audiences. But who would believe that?

Grant signed aboard Duke Wayne's obsession and he became obsessed by the making of *The Alamo* himself. He read a hundred books on Texas history and on the battle. He searched in the Texas libraries and in collections for old records and diaries and journals. He employed a San Antonio graduate student in history to do more research for him. About three years of researching and thinking went into his script, which was as accurate historically and psychologically as any historical epic film has ever been. Lon Tinkle, book editor of the Dallas *Times Herald,* and author of *Thirteen Days to Glory,* a book about the Alamo resistance, found the script and the film to be accurate, as did the eminent J. Frank Dobie, the Texas historian and scholar and professor. There would be those who would find *The Alamo* a fantasy, a lie, but to my knowledge they never cited any specific errors.

While Grant was writing his screenplay, Wayne had hired a fine art director, Alfred Ybarra. Since 1952(!) Ybarra had been "almost totally occupied . . . with the research, design and construction of the reproduction of the Alamo, and its adjacent community, San Antonio de Bexar . . ."

There was still no releasing company and no capital and no production. Wayne was not discouraged. He had sent Henaghen out on various missions to Dallas and Fort Worth and Houston. Between pictures, Henaghen and Wayne would try to persuade oil millionaires to invest money in this project for the greater glory of Texas. I don't know why they should have had such a hard time. Perhaps the potential backers had qualms about whether this movie would redound to the glory of Texas if it were directed by John Wayne. Now if it were John Ford . . . or Howard Hawks . . .

Then there was something else. Wayne did not want to play a big role. He wanted to do a cameo. He wanted to play his old dream of Sam Houston. Finally, United Artists, late in 1956, said they would risk two and a half million on two conditions. One—that Batjac put up an equal sum. Two—that Wayne play a starring role, a lead. He was too old for Bowie or Travis. So he would have to impersonate David Crockett. He finally acceded. He went out and raised the two million five. In 1957, they began rearing a reproduction of San Antonio and the mission as it was in 1836. Eventually, more capital had to be secured. The McCullough brothers, I. J. and O. J., came up with three million and Clint Murchison ponied up another two million, and a consortium of other Texans came up with more millions.

It was an expensive movie. It was the most costly movie ever filmed until that time.

Wayne, in the grip of his obsession, leaped over all the obstacles in his way. His energy was more than human. He was functioning as two persons—the producer of *The Alamo* and the star of *Rio Bravo,* a fascinating Howard Hawks western, in which he co-starred with Dean Martin, and *The Horse Soldiers,* John Ford's Civil War film about the conflict between a fanatic Union Army colonel of cavalry—done by Wayne—and William Holden's Army doctor. Wayne was outstanding in both pictures. Both roles were physically and emotionally demanding. It staggers the imagination to realize that this man was in his early fifties and was giving all that he had of body and spirit to the daily work on these films—and at the same time, on the weekends and in the evenings and when he was between takes, approving contracts and designs, dispatching emissaries to Dallas and Houston to raise more money, dispatching emissaries to Brackettville, talking to Mike Wayne and Jimmy Grant and production supervisor Nate Edwards and art director Ybarra constantly, from the location in Louisiana.

Going to his Baton Rouge motel room, at night, he would gulp down a pot of coffee while studying estimate sheets for *The Alamo,* making notes on Jimmy Grant's script, blocking out scenes, visualizing points of action in his mind's eye, telephoning agents to get the men he wanted for the leading roles. Richard Boone would, after all, be Sam Houston. Jimmy Grant promised to write a new screenplay, a biography of General Houston, which Duke would play in a year or two. And Duke was so delighted when Richard Widmark agreed to play Bowie that he took a one-page advertisement in the *Hollywood Reporter,* crying: "WELCOME ABOARD, DICK." The next time he saw Widmark in Hollywood, before they all were transported to Brackettville, Widmark looked at him in a surly fashion and said, "You tell your press agent, or advertising man, that I didn't like that ad. *The name is Richard.*"

Wayne stared him down. He lighted a cigarette. He waited for his resentment to simmer down. Then he replied, "If I ever take another ad, I'll remember that, *Richard.*"

Meanwhile down in Brackettville (pop. 1,858), one hundred twenty miles from San Antonio, not far from the Mexican border, they were building a complete city and mission. Ybarra and his staff had researched in the dusty archives and collected old drawings of the city, old plans, sketches, verbal descriptions. They claim that these were faithfully followed. Mexican workmen—they are extremely gifted in making and laying bricks—were employed to make genuine adobe bricks out of river mud. Twelve million bricks were made and three-dimensional buildings were put up. These were not the customary false fronts seen on the Hollywood back lots. These were real buildings with real rooms and walls and ceilings. And they had imported Spanish tile for El Alamo and made a beautiful reproduction of the mission. Several dozens of small and large adobe buildings were put up on the two hundred thousand square feet of land they had leased from "Happy" Shahan. Batjac employed four hundred plasterers, bricklayers, carpenters, electricians, and other construction union craftsmen to make a city.

The indefatigable George Colman was there with his transportation crew of sixty to get jobs done on time or sooner, his men driving trailer rigs, bringing electrical equipment, cables and lights, and boxes of supplies. He did everything. Wherever there was an insoluble problem, they would come to Colman and Colman would do it. His loyalty to Duke was fantastic. He had been in some serious trouble with his union, the Teamsters, and was suspended and in the process of being expelled. Wayne stepped in and saved him by putting up some money to take care of a financial responsibility which Colman was alleged to have neglected.

Had he lost his union card, his career in movies was over. Duke got him reinstated and in good standing. Colman would have gone to hell and back for him.

To house and feed the cast of crew and principals— some three hundred—there would have to be water and lighting. There would also have to be provision made for thousands of extras for the big battle scenes. They had to be fed and housed. On the rolling range of the Shahan property, miracles were happening. The ground was leveled by bulldozers. More than ten miles of electric and phone cables were installed underground. Fourteen miles of heavy-duty gravel-and-tar roads were made. A river was needed for some sequences. So another crew, well-diggers they were, went around with a dowser and dug six deep wells producing twenty-five thousand gallons of artesian water every day. The water was filtered and piped to every part of the location. The mind reels! Five miles of sewage lines were put down to drain off the wastes of the modern toilet facilities. The electricians put in seventy-five thousand dollars' worth of small portable air-conditioners on each interior set and in the dressing rooms of the cast. A million square feet of lumber, forty miles of reinforced construction steel, a hundred twenty-five thousand square feet of concrete flooring, thirty thousand square feet of Spanish tile roofing. The adding machine trembles. The accountants weep. What—an air strip so planes can land! Four thousand feet of strip? They are crazy. The accountants scream to Edwards and he mangles a cigar between his teeth and says, "That's what John Wayne wants and that's what he's getting."

John Wayne wanted decent toilets for the actors and crew. He didn't want the usual portable johns. So they had to lay the sewage pipes. John Wayne wanted his dailies processed fast and returned so he could study them so he wanted a landing strip to send the dailies to a film lab in Dallas and get them back the next morning. *But do we have to have an airfield, for God's sake?* Now there is John Wayne, playing Colonel Marlowe and being ordered about by Ford down in Louisiana, and when he wants to catch his breath, between setups, there is another long distance call from Brackettville or from U.A. in Hollywood. *Yeah, you're fuckin' right we need an airfield.*

And stockades for the horses? So much money for these expensive corrals? *My God, Duke, we ain't gonna go inna the cattle raising business!* The adding machine clicks. The costs mount and mount and mount. Mike is on the phone. Jim Henaghen is on the phone. Wayne is trying to remember his lines for tomorrow. *We gotta raise more money.* The corrals covered five hundred acres. And the horses were one hell of a problem. John Wayne wanted fifteen hundred horses and five hundred mules. *Duke—it is a waste of money. You can make two hundred horses look like ten thousand.* Look at Howard Hawks. He used a thousand head of cattle and made them look like ten thousand in *Red River.* John Wayne got all the horses he wanted. But it was a problem. The experienced horses, the ones who could do the tricks and bow their front legs and help a stuntman in a horsefall, the real veteran Screen Actors Guild horses, were all signed up for the television programs because it was the time when westerns were popular on television with eighteen regularly scheduled weekly shows, including the two spectaculars *Gunsmoke* and *Bonanza.* So Bill Jones, head wrangler, went out to find saddle horses, traveling more than thirty-five thousand miles through the Southwest, buying horses, like Duke Wayne rounding up horses for Maximilian's army in *The Undefeated,* crazy, it was. Getting three hundred seventy-five rare Texas longhorn steers. Hiring about seven thousand Mexican and Texan extras. Advertisements like these appeared. WANTED 300 MALES. MEXICAN OR LATIN DESCENT. FINE FACIAL FEATURES. AT LEAST SIX FEET TALL, WELL BUILT, CONFIDENT. MUST BE ABLE TO RIDE WELL UNDER TRYING CIRCUMSTANCES. THOROUGHLY FAMILIAR WITH HORSES.

WANTED TEN YOUNG FEMALES, GOOD LOOKING, FLIRTATIOUS MANNER.

WANTED FORTY MALES UNKEMPT IN APPEARANCE. MUST BE EXPERT HORSEMEN AND FAMILIAR WITH THE HANDLING OF RIFLES.

They were placarding the employment offices in Eagle Pass, Laredo, Del Rio, San Antone, and Uvalde.

WANTED TWELVE TO EIGHTEEN MEXICAN WOMEN. LONG BLACK HAIR. MUST WEIGH OVER 160 POUNDS.

Numbers, numbers, statistics, each representing a detail of the production, a small cog in an enormous contraption, fantastic numbers. Four thousand rifles. Four thousand pistols. Sixty cannon. A thousand and one costumes.

Speaking of all this, a New York *Times* correspondent filing a story from Brackettville, stated that "few Hollywood films, even the great Biblical spectacles, have had such extensive preparations for production."

I have secured my figures from the longest press release in the history of Hollywood press releases. It was written and released by Russell Birdwell Associates prior to the world premiere of *The Alamo.* It is not a press release. It is a book. A book of a hundred eighty-four pages!

Before one foot of film was exposed, over two million dollars had already been spent.

Then Father Rogers gave the benediction and the sound of the clapboard was heard: THE ALAMO. TAKE ONE.

It was a high moment, a beautiful and sweet fulfillment of a dream for Marion Michael Morrison, though the glorious moment, like all glorious moments, soon was dissolved in the sweat and stench and physical exertion of the daily labors of making the film. But that first day, that first warm and windy morning in September, 1959, after the prayer had been intoned, standing beside the camera, watching the principals and extras milling in the square, leaning into the action from his distance, Wayne felt a completeness inside. He was where he wanted to be. He wanted to be no place but where he was at this moment, doing what he was doing at this moment, with this photographer, with this screenwriter, with these actors, with his wife, waiting for him in the nearby Old Fort Clark Ranch and Hotel.

It was to the southwest country that he had come as a young man thirty years previously, young and uneasy, to play his first starring role for Raoul Walsh in *The Big Trail,* a raw youth, more fearful and apprehensive than exuberant, and they had made that one in Fox Grandeur, a 70 mm. process, and he had wanted to shoot this one of his also in 70 mm., in the new Todd-AO wide-screen process. He had come a long way, a long way, from that time, he had walked a long and lonely trail sometimes, and now he was the best damn actor in the western form, and he knew it, and now he was going to prove to John Ford and himself that he would be able to direct a film, and he had chosen a large canvas for his great challenge, El Alamo, the cottonwood mission, the last stand, the courage despite failure.

On the set, he was in complete control. He knew his script so well, and he knew what he wanted so precisely, that he was never seen to refer back to his script, never asked the script girl to check a reading, never showed any signs of self-doubt or anxiety. Like most actors who direct, he made his suggestions as much by showing them, by demonstrating a move or an attitude, as by a verbal suggestion. He brought out a superb performance from Laurence Harvey. He and Widmark were in a continual state of tension, and yet somehow it was not reflected on the film. He was fast. He was competent.

He worked himself and he worked his cast. He exposed five hundred sixty thousand feet of film, which was cut to two hundred thousand in the final cut—a running time of three hours and twelve minutes. Toward the end, during the last few weeks of filming, there were as many as twenty-seven camera setups in a single day. He had determined to complete the film by December 20 because there were indications that heavy rains would come toward the end of the year.

Director Wayne wrapped up *The Alamo* on December 15, 1959. Bill Clothier and second-unit director Cliff Lyons remained behind until December 23 for some action shots.

Duke was in perpetual motion during the filming. He could not stand still. A lighted cigarette always dangling from his lips, he would leap about and help the prop men rearrange pieces of furniture, show some Mexican extras how he wanted them to mount horses, tell Linda Cristal how to stand and look at Davy Crockett, push lights, pull cables, restless, exuberant, almost insane, smoking, smoking, smoking, inhaling, exhaling, going beyond his customary three packs a day, to four packs, six packs, coughing frequently, spitting out phlegm. At five P.M., when they broke, he would drink coffee and have a sandwich as he watched yesterday's rushes, and had meetings with Mike Wayne or Russell Birdwell who was planning one of the most extensive publicity campaigns ever conceived for a film.

Birdwell, a thin, high-strung master of ballyhoo, had been the virtuoso of the campaigns for *Gone With the Wind* and *The Outlaw*. Originally, he had been hired by Jim Henaghen as a consultant. In October, Duke and Henaghen had a dispute about money. Jim felt he deserved an extra hundred thousand as a finder's fee for raising three million Texas dollars for the production. Henaghen resigned. The dispute later went to arbitration. Birdwell and his organization were now put in full charge of the publicity. Birdwell, a verbal visionary, says that he was influenced by Wayne's tremulous and deeply felt sense of patriotism about this movie. His campaign was based on Wayne's own ideas and philosophy.

Wayne's fingers were in every phase of the production. He would finally get back to his quarters late at night and talk a little while with Pilar and take a hot bath and then go over his notes for the next day's shooting. He would flop into bed around midnight and sleep a few hours. It was a restless, uneasy sleep. Around four he would arise and start drinking coffee, and the next two hours were agony because his heavy smoking had corrupted his lungs. He coughed and hacked and seemed to be tearing himself apart with these seizures. Pilar was concerned about the coughing but he would not see a doctor and he would not take any cough medicines. He had now reached a stage where he was chain-smoking, compulsively lighting one cigarette after another.

"So maybe it's six months off the end of my life," he said to reporter Dean Jennings, "but they're not going to kill me."

In the third week of filming, John Ford arrived in Brackettville. He was between films. He came to see how his protégé was getting along, to watch, to observe, to help if his help was wanted. Yet once he was on the location he instinctively took over. He began to tell the actors what to do. He began giving orders to Bill Clothier. Suddenly there was tension on the set. They were all watching the situation. Would Wayne defer to the Old Man? If he did, his authority would be diminished. And yet while Wayne could not send the Old Man packing, there had to be one ruling power on a movie. There could only be one director. If he had wanted John Ford to direct *The Alamo,* Batjac would have signed him and they could have had *The Alamo* into production ten years before with Universal or Warners or 20th Century-Fox.

After several days of Ford's domineering, Wayne saw a way out of the dilemma. He went to Ford and requested him to do some second-unit work as a favor to him. This was the only means he could conceive to get Ford away from the main action. After some objections, Ford consented. He was given a second-unit cameraman, all the extras he wanted, and all the technicians required. Wayne told him to shoot as many feet of film as he needed. He was to do scenes of river crossings.

"I don't care what it costs," he confided to his associates, "but I am not going to let him feel rejected. I'd rather spend a million dollars than hurt his feelings."

When *The Alamo* was released and its scenes of battles and soldiers storming the Alamo and dying and killing were praised for the impact and drama, there were rumors around Hollywood that these sequences—both inside and outside the Alamo—had not been directed by Wayne. There had been ghost directors. There had been John Ford and there had been Cliff Lyons, a veteran stuntman and one of the most competent second-unit directors in the business.

Not one foot of the film that Ford shot was ever used in the picture. Had John Ford lurked in the background secretly calling the shots? Erskine Johnson, a syndicated Hollywood columnist, investigated the nasty gossip. He put the question to Ford, who was on location for *Two Rode Together*. Ford was at great pains to "minimize the help he gave long-time pal Wayne. [He] told me: 'I was the coach—on third base.' "

In 1966, Ford was again queried by Bogdanovich on his clandestine part in the making of *The Alamo,* and again he denied it. "I was merely down there on vacation and Duke said, 'Do you mind going out and getting a shot of so-and-so?' And I did. We got some wonderful scenes —guys swimming rivers, that sort of thing—but they were all cut out."

Nevertheless, among the confirmed Wayne deprecators, the opinion still lingers to this day that Wayne did not direct the action sequences, the battles of *The Alamo.* Their theory was given credence when Ford said publicly and was so quoted: *"The Alamo* is the greatest picture I've ever seen. It will last forever, run forever, for all peoples, all families everywhere."

Those in the anti-Wayne group who accepted the idea that Ford had not directed *The Alamo* adopted the Cliff Lyons theory.

Clothier, ordinarily a person of imperturbable serenity, still gets irritated when it is mildly suggested that perhaps Ford or Lyons was the "real" director. Clothier was there. He was lighting the setups. He saw Duke sweating and striving, day after day. He saw Duke lose weight. Wayne lost about thirty pounds during the filming.

"*The Alamo* in its entirety is Wayne's movie," he told me, with some feeling. "His idea. His directing. Santa Anna's army approaching the Alamo was Duke. Everything was Duke's—except the horsefalls. Cliff Lyons directed the horsefalls. For instance, when Santa Anna's army comes charging up to the Alamo and Laurence Harvey says, 'Hold your fire,' and then they fire and a hell of a mess of horses falling and men falling, Cliff directed that. These are typical second-unit operations, which on a Ford or a Hawks picture would always be done by the second-unit director. We had about twenty, twenty-five stuntmen. We put down beds of sand, about two feet of sand, so nobody would be hurt in the falls. That's what Cliff did—working with the stuntmen. Horsefalls in the sand. Horses, eight or ten horses and riders, right over the camera, Duke directed that scene. Duke directed horses jumping through cannon fire, rifle fire, all the close-ups of the principals, Duke did that, why John Ford wasn't even around, and Cliff Lyons was just standing by, when those sixteen horses and riders leap over the wall of the fortress—hell, dammit to hell, John Wayne directed that. Placed the men. Told me how to light it. Told me the effect he wanted. Told the stuntmen how to move and when to move. John Wayne directed *The Alamo*. All the way. Could have been one of the best directors in Hollywood, if God had not made him a star."

Filming completed, Wayne collaborated with the editor in the cutting, and with Clothier in balancing the color as they worked on the work print, day after day. He worked with Dmitri Tiomkin, who scored the film and wrote the music for its theme, to a lyric by Paul Webster. There was much cutting to do and much editing. George Stevens, famed not only for the quality of his pictures but for the meticulousness with which he edits and assembles the final cut, saw *The Alamo* at a screening, and put himself on record with these words:

"When the roll call of the great ones is made, *The Alamo* will be among those few by which the films of the future will be measured. There are images in *The Alamo* that will haunt you for a lifetime: a glorious restoration in film of the historic Alamo epic . . . it is a modern classic."

Spyros Skouras, then president of 20th Century, who had started as an exhibitor, said that its box-office potential was vast and saw it as grossing twenty-five million domestic in its first year of release.

And now Birdwell began beating the drums, so well and so thunderously that the Harvard *Lampoon,* in making its annual awards, bestowed its "Along the Mohawk Award" on *The Alamo* as "the film with the most drummed-up publicity campaign."

Three months before the release of the film, in the July 4, 1960 issue of *Life* magazine, there appeared a three-page foldout, under the cover. Two pages were a painting of the mission, with a cannon and some cannonballs in the foreground. On the last page was a long dissertation on the significance of the Alamo, seen in the perspective of the 1960 Presidential campaign. The Democratic and Republician parties were soon to convene.

THERE WERE NO GHOSTWRITERS AT THE ALAMO, proclaimed the advertisement, which was signed by Birdwell, Wayne, and Grant. It cost two hundred thousand dollars for the single insertion. It was a formidable *coup de publicité.* The text of the peculiar movie advertisement argued that political candidates in our time were puppets. A political party would nominate a candidate for President. But, queried the advertisement, "Who has written his speeches? Who—or what board of ghostwriting strategists—has fashioned the phrases, molded the thoughts, designed the delivery, authored the image, staged the presentation, put the political show on the road to win the large number of votes? Who is the actor reading the script?"

American political leaders were disparagingly compared to the Alamo defenders. There were inspiring quotations from Crockett, Bowie, and Travis.

"There were no ghostwriters at the Alamo. Only men."

The advertisement, breaking on the July Fourth weekend, splashed on the national consciousness. It certainly impressed *The Alamo* on the public's mind. The high-powered ballyhoo which launched *The Alamo* made many

Amercans feel an antipathy toward the film even before they saw it. Some persons thought it was in poor taste to link a movie to a political campaign. Others thought it was absurd for John Wayne to wave the flag to sell tickets. Obviously, the argument was specious. There were no ghostwriters at the Alamo. Neither were there cameramen, directors, screenwriters, or national magazines like *Life*.

It was a superior historical film. Those great sequences of battles—which take up about an hour of the film's time—with the defenders preparing their last-ditch stand, and Santa Anna's army riding in grandeur, with the classical intercutting and shorter cuts as the tempo of the confrontation comes closer, the assault of the bastion, the hand-to-hand battles, all were magnificent and reasonably true to the history books, as were all the characters and events delineated.

It is, as Ford and Stevens said, one of the classic historical epics of American film, and can be put in the same category as *The Covered Wagon* and *The Iron Horse,* though it obviously did not achieve the eminence of *Birth of a Nation* or *Gone With the Wind.*

Considering the widespread resentment, it was well received, on the whole, but not with the appreciation it should have gotten. *Time* praised the film and the "gorgeously gory fracas at the finish." It even went out of its way to rave about Wayne's Davy Crockett, saying that Wayne "demonstrates once again his superiority over the rest of Hollywood's strong silent types in portraying the unaccommodated man, the natural ignobleman, invested with the authority of size and the dignity of slow wits."

But at the hands of those other two national arbiters of movies, the New York *Times* and *The New Yorker,* the film did not fare well. Bosley Crowther liked the battle scenes but said the film was "burdened" with endless and boring scenes of tedious dialogue. He said it was just "another beleaguered blockhouse western."

Brendan Gill was now reviewing movies for the West 43rd Street magazine. He was no more enamored of John Wayne than John McCarten had been. But at least he did not slough off the film.

He wrote a serious and quite devastating attack on the picture. You could see that he had experienced the same resentment most of us had experienced because of the obnoxious flag-waving campaign. The opening guns of Gill's attack tell the story of his brilliant critique:

Not like "The Alamo"? What am I—some sort of un-American nut or something? For here is a telling of one of the great American stories, and if I accuse John Wayne, who produced and directed it and plays one of the leading roles, and his associate producer, James Edward Grant, who wrote the screenplay, of having turned a splendid chapter of our past into sentimental and preposterous flapdoodle, I'm apt to be accused in turn of deliberately downgrading Davy Crockett, Jim Bowie, and all the other brave men who died in that heroic fiasco . . .

Grant had the misfortune of writing screenplays which were so literary that the speeches called attention to themselves, and, consequently, when critics disliked one of his films they would frequently seize upon the script and make Grant the scapegoat. Brendan Gill singled out Grant by name as he found the screenplay lacking in authentic speech and convincing human motivation. Usually screenwriters are ignored by the critics. They are rarely praised if a movie is good—and rarely ridiculed if a movie is bad. It was the curse of Grant's life that when he wrote a good script, like *Sands of Iwo Jima,* nobody was aware —and when he wrote one that they did not like, they vented their dislike upon him.

Now *The Alamo* was popular with audiences, but it was not a blockbuster movie. And it had to be to make back its investment and the extra millions which had been expended on the promotion campaign.

What can we say of Wayne as a director? Considering that he was making his debut, he scored a triumph in every direction. *The Alamo* is certainly not a flawless picture. Yet Wayne proved that he could successfully control a complicated and many-sided story, peopled by diverse characters, moving in separate rhythms to a shattering climax of blood and gore and courage. He had to project characters who were subtle and he did so. There was a running conflict between Colonel Travis, a foppish marti- net, young and arrogant, and Colonel Bowie, bitter, alco- holic, reckless, and older, and he painted the characters of both men beautifully. His own role, Davy Crockett, was out of his style, but even so he did it smoothly. He had to be—as the original Crockett was—the hard-drink- ing, lecherous, vulgar, uncouth Kentucky frontiersman, but he also had to suggest the man who served in Con- gress several times and had a natural poetry in his writing and his feeling. In the film, Crockett is the force uniting the opposing rivals of the free-wheeling frontier fighters brought into Texas by Crockett to fight for freedom and the regular army forces of Travis—in which the neurotic Bowie, sharply etched by Widmark, is a strange com- ponent.

Wayne as a director conducted the sections of his or- chestra with finesse and with dash. Yes, the first two hours of the film did move slowly, establishing the lines of conflict between the Alamo defenders, but it was this preparation which made the final tragedy a poignant ex- perience. Wayne showed himself to be a master in his handling of groups and crowds. There was a wild drinking scene in which the newly arrived Kentucky mountaineers and the regular army soldiers get drunk together and start fighting with one another. The riot and revelry as well as the brawling was staged and pictured with clarity and excitement in Wayne's work. There was a tender birthday party for the daughter of an aide of Colonel Travis'. The child was played by four-year-old Aissa Wayne, who made her movie debut in the role. If we can speak of a "John Wayne directorial touch"—and this is rather diffi- cult, for he has directed only two films—it would be in the sentimentality of the birthday party, for as he grew older, he began to feel and to project excessively the ten- derness of an aging man for children. Some of his most illuminating acting has been as the guide and protector and companion of younger persons—*True Grit* and *The*

*Cowboys* being examples of this Waynesian paternal quality. And the romance with Linda Cristal, I thought, was dashingly done by Wayne as an actor and by Wayne as a director. Here again there is an authentic Waynesian touch—the delicate passions of older men and older women toward one another, reflecting the depth of his new-found peace and concupiscence with Pilar.

Of course, the battle scenes, occupying the final hour of the film, were simply stupendous. In a great collaboration with Clothier, they moved the camera in so closely you became part of the action. Dick Williams, the movie critic of the Los Angeles *Mirror,* now defunct, described the stimulating effect of these sequences as follows: "The battle, fought between the small one-hundred-eigthy-five-man force of Col. William Barrett Travis and the attacking army of eight thousand men under Mexico's General Santa Anna, takes up much of the ninety-nine-minute second half of the production.

"The action rises on a furious, undiminishing crescendo throughout the give-no-quarter battle and includes some of the most remarkable battle photography ever put on celluloid.

"One of the reasons it is so lifelike, that one seems to be looking through an open window on actual history in the making, is that the camera moves in close on much of the hand-to-hand action. The varying patterns of battle are kept remarkably in focus.

"The seething turmoil involving men, horses and cannon was photographed by William H. Clothier in one of the major cinematography accomplishments of the year."

There is a side to Wayne's character which helps him recreate the past as he did in this picture. Wayne has a curiously warped sense of time, in which past, present and future seem to flow in a continuum changelessly.

"Duke doesn't live in the past," Tom Kane says. "Time stands still for him. I remember when we were planning *Chisum,* there was a question came up of who we could cast as Billy the Kid." (*Chisum,* a 1970 picture, concerned a New Mexico cattle baron played by Wayne and a redoubtable villain, done by Forrest Tucker, who got burned alive at home at the end of a fierce knockdown and drag out fight with Duke. A subplot involved a meeting between Billy the Kid and Sheriff Pat Garrett.) "Well, we were sitting around in Duke's office and he said, 'How about Ben Johnson for Billy the Kid?' Ben had not yet won that Oscar for *Last Picture Show*. Anyway, there was a big silence."

Duke looked around the room. "What did I do?" he asked. "Did I say something wrong?"

Finally Mike Wayne said, "Ben Johnson is much too old to play Billy the Kid. Hell, he's about fifty years old."

Wayne furrowed his brow and glared at Mike. "The hell he is," he growled. "What are you talking about? Fifty? When did he make *Three Godfathers?*"

Then he was silent, doing mental arithmetic, recalling Ben as a supporting actor, a young man in his twenties. Finally, Wayne sighed and muttered, "Guess he is too old for it . . ."

While a sense of existence as a timeless flow may hamper one in casting, it is valuable in filming history, because one tends to seek out the changeless elements in human nature under the disguise of period objects and clothes and phrases.

By the end of December, 1960, *The Alamo* having been out several months, Hollywood was beginning to seethe with the annual fever of the Academy Awards. First, the Academy members in each category would nominate five nominees, and then, in the next round of balloting the favorites would be selected. As is customary, the studios, the stars, the producers, the various personalities began advertising in the trade papers, vaunting their accomplishments. Special screenings of films were scheduled. There was intense campaigning. Masterminded by Russell Birdwell, *The Alamo* at first took out full-page ads in *Daily Variety* and the *Reporter* which were self-seeking, and yet in good taste by the standards of the annual Oscar madness. They were no better and no worse than the usual Oscar puffery.

The nominees were named in February, 1961. *The Alamo* was named as one of the five pictures, its rivals being *Elmer Gantry, The Apartment, The Sundowners,* and *Sons and Lovers.* There had been other good pictures that year—*Exodus, Never on Sunday,* Laurence Olivier's *The Entertainer,* and one of Hitchcock's most enthralling murder stories, *Psycho.*

Wayne himself was not nominated as director or actor. Chill Wills got a nomination for Best Supporting Actor, Dmitri Tiomkin for his score, and Bill Clothier for his color cinematography.

Now the Oscar campaigning entered its second and more furious phase. It was believed in Hollywood that *The Alamo* was very likely to win Best Picture, that Chill Wills, who had given one of his amiable roistering down-home characterizations as The Beekeeper, would get Best Supporting Actor, and that Tiomkin and Clothier looked like sure bets. In fact, Clothier's cinematography was so superlative that he was considered to be a sure thing.

Then John Wayne made a serious error of judgment. Blinded by his own love of America, his own conviction that *The Alamo* was a noble statement of Americanism and that it had a genuine value above and beyond its quality as a movie, he permitted a campaign to be developed which sought to suggest that a vote for *The Alamo* was a vote for the United States. There were advertisements for *The Alamo* which cried WHAT WILL OSCAR SAY THIS YEAR TO THE WORLD? and another one which suggested that those who voted for *The Alamo* to win were patriotic Americans.

Wayne compounded the mistake when he gave interviews. He had been to London, Paris, and Rome on publicity campaigns for *The Alamo* which had opened to capacity crowds in Europe. In Rome, he had gone to an audience with the Pope. He had filled his pockets with medals of St. Christopher, St. Jude, St. Genesius, and other saintly personalities of value to believers so that Pope John XXIII could bless them. Wayne told Birdwell, who accompanied him, that he did not believe in the dogmas of the Roman Catholic church but that his children did and that all his wives had, and he thought that perhaps his one chance of entering the gates of Heaven was the metallurgical one.

However, his medals did not prevent him from making a fool of himself. Duke should have known better than anybody else that no person likes to have his arm twisted. He and his associates were engaging in psychological arm-twisting.

He arrived at International Airport in L.A. on March 12, from London, and a *Variety* interviewer asked him about how *The Alamo* stood in the race for an Academy Award.

Standing toe to toe with the reporter, Wayne threw back his shoulders and said grimly, "This is not the first time *The Alamo* has been the underdog. We need defenders today just as they did one hundred twenty-five years ago this month."

He believed it sincerely. He lacked the objectivity to see that this equation of a movie with a heroic battle rubbed people the wrong way.

In Europe he had contracted influenza. He had to cut short his trip.

He had gone through a terrible and lengthy journey to get to the place finally where *The Alamo* was up for an Oscar. He was physically and mentally at the end of his tether. He was overwhelmed by debts and everything he owned was hypothecated for money he had raised for *The Alamo*. But what is the good of knowing all this? *After such knowledge, what forgiveness?*

Dick Williams—who had written a long and admiring review of *The Alamo*—now expressed his resentment in his column in the *Mirror,* complaining of the high-pressure campaign, and pointing out that "the implication is unmistakable. Oscar voters are being appealed to on a patriotic basis. The impression is left that one's proud sense of Americanism may be suspected if one does not vote for *The Alamo*."

This impelled Birdwell to take out an advertisement criticizing Williams. John Wayne wrote an angry letter to the Los Angeles *Times* objecting to the criticism of the publicity campaign for *The Alamo*.

Then Chill Wills got into the action. Wills was a *compadre* of a well-known Hollywood personality, W. S. Wojchiechowicz, who was known as Bow Wow; whenever the trade papers had occasion to mention his real name it was a linotyper's nightmare. Bow Wow was a tall, handsome, muscular, athletic gentleman, who was one of Sheilah Graham's husbands. Can one imagine a more vivid contrast to the gentle, soft F. Scott Fitzgerald than this Bow Wow? Bow Wow was operating a small scale public relations company. Chill Wills was his client as well as his bosom companion. Bow Wow was masterminding Chill's campaign against his Best Supporting Actor rivals—Peter Ustinov *(Spartacus),* Sal Mineo *(Exodus),* Peter Falk *(Murder, Inc.),* and Jack Kruschen, who had portrayed the kindly doctor in *The Apartment.*

As Gladwin Hill, Hollywood correspondent of the New York *Times,* remarked in a dispatch, Chill's "propaganda campaign . . . outbirded Mr. Birdwell's." His full-page ads were horrifying displays of vanity and bad taste. He almost seemed to be mooching for votes. One of his ads showed the stars he had supported during his career. Another one was full of testimonials from famous Texans. And a third was a two-page spread in which he listed—by name—hundreds of actors and actresses, members of the Academy, and then, in large letters, replete with spurious sportsmanship, he stated: WIN, LOSE OR DRAW, YOU'RE STILL MY COUSINS AND I LOVE YOU ALL.

This rural fakery got on Groucho Marx's nerves. He took out a page ad and it said: DEAR MR. WILLS, I AM DELIGHTED TO BE YOUR COUSIN BUT I AM VOTING FOR SAL MINEO.

Now *Exodus* entered the battle with huge advertisements. Their advertisements advised the voters to Judge the Picture—Not the Ads.

Wayne countered with more advertisements quoting the praise his picture had received from George Stevens and John Ford.

Then Chill's campaign touched an all-time nadir in Oscar advertising. Bow Wow got up an advertisement which showed a picture of the Alamo mission and, in the foreground, the principals and supporting players, and on it was the message:

"We of *The Alamo* cast are praying—harder than the real Texans prayed for their lives in the Alamo—for Chill Wills to win the Oscar . . . Cousin Chill's acting was great. —Your Alamo Cousins."

*Daily Variety* rejected the ad but the *Reporter* published it. Its gaucherie was so consummate that it turned the movie colony against the film, against Tiomkin's music, against Clothier's magnificent camera work.

Birdwell remembers meeting with Wayne the day that Chill's advertisement hit the fan. There was a pall of gloom over everyone present. They had all heard the slogan making the rounds of movie circles: FORGET THE ALAMO.

"We felt," Birdwell recalls, "as if someone had taken a bucket of fecal matter and thrown it over a beautiful red rose."

Should they ignore Chill's ad? They decided they had better answer it. And so Duke took out an unprecedented one-page ad in the *Reporter* and *Variety* for March 27, 1961. It said:

I wish to state that the Chill Wills ad published in the *Hollywood Reporter,* of which we had no advance knowledge, in which he wrote, or permitted to be written, that "We of The Alamo cast are praying—harder than the real Texans prayed for their lives in the Alamo—for Chill Wills to win the Oscar" is an untrue and reprehensible claim.

No one in the Batjac organization or in the Russell Birdwell office has been a party to his trade paper advertising.

I refrain from using stronger language because I am sure his intentions were not as bad as his taste.

JOHN WAYNE

The final yelp was emitted by Bow Wow Wojchie-chowicz. He took a chaste advertisement in the trades:

Notice: John Wayne. Chill Wills was in no way responsible for the "Alamo" ad which appeared in the *Reporter* Friday. Chill Wills did not know anything whatsoever about this ad and when he saw it he was madder than John Wayne and Russell Birdwell together. I informed John Wayne and Birdwell after the ad appeared that I was fully responsible.

W. S. WOJCHIECHOWICZ

Like the original mission, *The Alamo* fell in the battle. *The Apartment* won the Oscar as best picture, so Oscar told the world that lasciviousness flourished in our corporations, a theme which perhaps made capitalism more attractive to foreign audiences. As for poor Chill Wills— his cousins deserted him and so did Sal Mineo's *mispochah*. It was Peter Ustinov, an Englishman without a single cousin, who captured the laurel wreath, or statuette to be precise.

And all the others went down to defeat. Clothier lost out to Russell Metty's *Spartacus* in the best color category and the Tiomkin-Webster team lost to *Never on Sunday* for best song and to *Exodus* for best scoring.

The only survivors of the massacre were the sound technicians, who were unnamed. *The Alamo* received the award for Best Sound. It went to a congeries of companies—the Samuel Goldwyn Studio Sound Department and Todd-AO Sound Department.

And in Houston, Texas, Sakowitz', an elegant department store, received an interesting proposition from Batjac, which illustrates how desperate for money Wayne was at this period. Would Sakowitz' like to sell a city? What did Sakowitz' think of putting up for sale the entire reproduction of San Antonio de Bexar—all thirty-six of the adobe buildings and the mission? Sakowitz' agreed to take the merchandise on consignment and offered it for sale at an asking price of three million.

Now you would think that here is an ideal present to give your teen-age son or daughter, if you are one of these fabulously wealthy Texans we have learned to revere.

You would have thought that Sakowitz' would have been deluged with offers.

I recently got in touch with Sakowitz' to find out who now owned the Alamo replica. I received a brief reply from Buddy McGregor, director of public relations for Sakowitz', who informed me that the property had never been sold. It was taken over by J. T. "Happy" Shahan, owner of the Shahan ranch on which the Brackettville version of San Antonio had been raised up at such great expense. It is now open as a tourist attraction. Mr. Shahan made a direct deal with Batjac for the property. He did not have to pay anywhere near three million for it. More like two hundred fifty thousand. At this price it was not hard for "Happy" Shahan to be happy.

Not long ago I asked John Wayne what he now thought of that flamboyant advertising for *The Alamo*.

He chewed a slug of tobacco. He spit it out. He looked at me with that hound-dog sadness he sometimes gets on his face and said, rather morosely but pithily, "It hurt us."

As if John Wayne did not have enough troubles in April of 1961, he was suddenly shafted by a man he considered one of his friends: Darryl Francis Zanuck.

Zanuck had exiled himself to Paris after a power struggle at 20th Century-Fox. Introspecting over his problems, Zanuck contemplated the specter of all the stars who were becoming corporate entities and setting up production firms and usurping the power of men like himself. He looked upon Marlon Brando and his Pennebaker Productions, Kirk Douglas' Bryan Productions, Burt Lancaster and his Hecht-Hill-Lancaster, Wayne and his Batjac. Asked to comment on Hollywood today by a Paris-based wire service correspondent, Zanuck unloosed a blast, blaming actors for the woes of the movie business.

"Actors are now directing, writing and producing," he said. "Actors have taken over Hollywood completely together with their agents. They want approval of scripts, stars, still pictures. The producer hasn't a chance to exercise authority. I'm sure on the pictures Jerry Wald has made he doesn't even own twenty-five percent. He had to give it all away. What the hell—I'm not going to work for actors. I've got a great affection for Duke Wayne, but what right has he to write, direct and produce a motion picture? What right has Kirk Douglas got? Or Widmark? Or Brando with *One-Eyed Jacks,* which he's still shooting after all this time . . . Everyone is becoming a corporation with their own managers, own agents, own lawyers. You can't deal with individuals any more. You can't work as I used to, assigning one man to a story. Everyone has a percentage of everything. As a result they end up with nothing. Look at poor old Duke Wayne. He's never going to see a nickel. He put all his money into finishing *The Alamo*."

Wayne called a press conference and he lashed back at Zanuck and Hollywood producers who went to foreign countries and made "runaway" pictures. There were no ghost-writers at this particular personal fortress. Wayne was speaking his own mind and in his own words.

"So," sneered Wayne, "Darryl Zanuck has decided to stop working for actors, has he, and is shedding crocodile tears for poor old Duke Wayne and his *Alamo*. Please inform him that as far as old Duke and his picture is concerned—which was made by the way, in the United States—it has made just under two million in three months in thirteen theaters in America and has ten thousand more play dates to go. It's breaking records in such places as Tokyo, London, Paris, and Rome . . ." He said that Douglas, Lancaster, Brando, and Widmark did not need his defense. He praised them highly. He said that he loved Hollywood and did not plan to run away to Europe like a coward. He concludes by stating that he was "proud to be a member of the group of hard-working dedicated men and women who are giving us a new and spirited industry."

Zanuck's attack on him, the patronizing kick, was a final crushing blow which plunged him into the worst attack of depression he had ever experienced. He had always known black moods of melancholia. This time he faced a profound crisis of the soul. At great cost to his spirit and his body, he had succeeded in capturing a difficult prize, in killing his own white whale, in finally getting on film the story of the Alamo, and it had seemed to turn into a heap of dross under his eyes. A series of personal misfortunes and the death of several close friends coming around this time sealed his sense of the futility of existence. Was not the world a rank unweeded garden? Yes, he had found a new life, a satisfying love, with his woman, and he had started a new family, and yet it was not enough. A sadness gnawed at him. A feeling of emptiness. A terrible despair that simply would not go away.

John Wayne had come face to face with the vanity of human wishes. He now had to come to terms with his own mortality and the sure and certain knowledge that he was going to die because he was a human being.

25

## The Longest Night

Grant Withers was the first to go. He went in the spring of 1959. Wayne had known him and loved him for thirty years. He had shared many an escapade with him. They had roistered together and acted together. Withers was one of John Ford's little band of character actors. A huge hulking man, he was full of wild laughter and amusing japeries. As the years went on the laughter died. He became a helpless victim of his compulsion to drink whiskey, as so many of Wayne's companions became. He had gone through five disastrous marriages, including the one to Loretta Young in 1930, when she was under twenty-one and the nuptials had been annulled by her mother. His life was a record of arrests for drunken driving, car accidents, and wife-beating. It was a painful existence.

For years Wayne had taken care of him. When Jimmy

Grant sobered up, he argued with Duke about giving Withers money. Jimmy once figured out that Duke had given Withers over seventy thousand dollars. He argued that Withers' only possible chance for salvation lay in his being thrown on his own completely. This might make him so desperate that he would come to that state of defeat which was the only means by which a confirmed alcoholic changed his lifetime habits. Grant had dragged Withers to meetings of Alcoholics Anonymous, had attempted to imbue him with the vision of the "Higher Power" and the famous twelve steps. Withers, though he made many trials of the sober life, was unable to persist.

Wayne had always found it incomprehensible that other men could not drink as he could drink. One of the four men whom he most admired was Winston Churchill. (The others were, as I've said, Houston, and also Lincoln and Douglas MacArthur. For a long time, he has fantasized a movie in which he plays Douglas MacArthur and he has talked about this with several screenwriters. The Sam Houston project was another ideal. And the most extravagant of all would be to portray Lincoln and Churchill before he dies.) Churchill, like Wayne, was born with an immense capacity for absorbing quantities of alcohol without any destructive effects. Some men are able to metabolize ethyl alcohol in formidable amounts without damaging their livers, kidneys, pancreas, and hearts. Wayne hoped that someday Withers would learn how to drink like a man. He therefore paid his rent and gave him money for sustenance, which Withers spent on vodka and on pills, to which he had also become addicted.

Yes, it was a sad and painful story. And it was well-nigh unbearable for Duke to see his old friend getting bloated, flabby and peculiarly deranged, as he grew more besotted. No matter how much he drank, no matter how fatigued his body was, Duke Wayne was able to do his work on the set and to fulfill his family responsibilities. Why couldn't Grant Withers do the same? Duke just didn't understand it. But he would not let Withers go hungry or thirsty.

In his last years, Withers was reduced to playing bit parts in low-budget melodramas—*White Squaw, Hell's Crossroads, I, Mobster*. He was in the dregs of the movie business.

On March 27, Grant Withers wrote a note to his "friends." He asked them "to forgive me for letting you down. It's better this way."

Then he swallowed a bottle of sleeping pills and finished a quart of vodka and laid down to his eternal sleep.

Ward Bond was the second to go. He went in the winter of 1960, not long after the world premiere of *The Alamo*. Bond had finally achieved stardom in 1957 after thirty years of a career as one of the great character actors in Hollywood. He was the star of NBC's *Wagon Train*. Around the time Duke married Pilar, Bond had married Mary Lou May. The former Miss May was a secretary at Bö Roos' company, Beverly Management, and she was a friend of Pilar and Duke. Duke was Ward's best man. The last episode of *Wagon Train* he made was directed by John Ford. It was Ford's only television drama, and in it—under the amusing pseudonym of Michael Morris —Duke played the cameo role of General Sherman. It is Wayne's only dramatic appearance on television. The plot concerned an alcoholic army doctor at the Battle of Shiloh, the worst defeat of the Union armies.

On November 5, Bond had flown to Dallas. He planned to see the Los Angeles Rams play the Dallas Cowboys. He was taking a shower in his motel room when he was stricken with a heart attack and passed away within a few hours.

He was fifty-five years old when he died.

The *Wagon Train* episode was shown posthumously on November 23, 1960.

Services for Bond were held at the Field Photo center in Reseda. Wayne, his voice breaking, his eyes suffused with tears, spoke the eulogy:

"We were the closest of friends, from schooldays right on through. This is just the way Ward would have wanted it—to look out on the faces of good friends. He was a wonderful, generous, big-hearted man." He looked at

Mary Bond and murmured, "I want you to know that our hearts go out to you."

They buried Ward Bond but they could not bury the memories which Wayne carried in his soul—for now there was nobody left to share them with—memories of the carefree days at USC and football training and the Trojan games and working for John Ford. All the times they had gone on location together. All the heartbreak and fights they had had and hunting for quail in Hemet, California, and getting drunk and punching at each other and breaking up a joint. Marriages and divorces and double-dating. Joining in the crusade to save our country from the menace of the Hollywood Communists—the interminable meetings, political discussions, and lectures. He was the closest friend whom Wayne had ever had.

He could not accept Bond's death. He could not accept Grant Withers' suicide. He could not come to terms with the presence of death, which was slowly proliferating in his own body now, at this moment. He could not grasp the reality of growing old, maybe because he had always looked and lived twenty years younger than other men. And he did not have anybody with whom really to drink now, because Jimmy Grant was sober. John Ford had stopped drinking also. Bev Barnett never liked to drink anyway, and Jim Henaghen and he were no longer friends.

Bev Barnett was the third to go. He went in the spring of 1961. He was a shy, soft-spoken little man, who was hard of hearing. He wore a hearing aid. Beverly Barnett did not resemble the flamboyant Hollywood press-agent type. He was a publicist addicted to understatement and hard facts. The releases or data which he gave to the reporters and columnists over the phone were always the truth. He just did not lie. He never lied to Wayne or hustled him. Duke knew he could get a completely honest and undistorted opinion on everything—including Duke's last film—from Bev Barnett. Barnett had an instinct for public relations, and it was he who had guided Wayne through the difficult years of the late 1940's and 1950's when, at times, Wayne the patriotic crusader threatened to submerge Wayne the artist. Beyond everything else, Wayne felt a deep love for Bev Barnett.

Coming at a time of physical enervation and the defeat he had suffered at the hands of the critics and his peers of the Academy of Motion Picture Arts and Sciences, convinced that he was not understood, he felt insulted and injured by life. It all seemed so useless and so empty now—yes, even his work. He found a certain solace in the tenderness of his wife's arms and in watching the little children, Aissa and John Ethan. Yet there was an emptiness in him so profound, and an agony so piercing, that not even quarts of bourbon could fill the vacuum and quench the agony.

Jimmy Grant and John Ford, who, in different ways, had come to some reckoning with old age, disease, and death, were persons who gave him some strength during this dark time, which lasted about five years. Some of Jimmy Grant's faith in a Higher Power and in the justness of God's Will, one of the tenets of Alcoholics Anonymous, seeped into Wayne, though he found it almost impossible to get down on his knees and pray, for his reason could not accept these concepts. Ford, who had become a deeply mystical Irish Catholic, assured Wayne of the presence of God.

But acceptance came very slowly to Wayne. Even when Pilar became interested in the ideas of Mary Baker Eddy and began reading *Science and Health with Key to the Scriptures,* and its homilies about God being kindly and loving, Wayne resisted the conception that there could possibly be any purpose, relating to Universal Harmony, in the deaths of Withers and Bond and Barnett, or in his face of wrinkles and his legs' weaknesses and his balding head and this terrible coughing which tore him apart in the early morning.

Toward the end of 1961, it seemed as if everything went to pieces all at once. *The Alamo* was not the triumph it should have been. He could only meet the payments to the banks and his other creditors by making more and more and more pictures. A Trivoli Shrimp Company of Panama, in which he had invested much capital, went bankrupt. His real estate holdings and other investments were going down in value, and therefore he had to raise additional security for his loans. It had all been in vain, hadn't it?—he was now fifty-four years old and getting poorer and older and wearier.

Under the title of "The Woes of Box-Office King John Wayne," there appeared in 1962 in *The Saturday Evening Post* an account of the trials, tribulations and melancholy of Duke. It was written by the late Dean Jennings, one of the most competent reporters in the Hollywood press corps. His story reflected the attitudes of Hollywood toward John Wayne.

And it could be summed up in a phrase: "He was finished."

Jennings limned Wayne's financial distress and his personal grievances at the death of his friends. He delved at some length into Wayne's activities as an anti-Communist and he explored, somewhat disdainfully, Wayne's economic and social opinions. He painted a portrait of a washed-up human being, whose notions were peculiar, erratic, and slightly deranged, and who was, as he had been during his long career, just a good cowboy actor doomed to go on playing hackneyed parts in routine pictures in order to pay his creditors and support his family. Except in terms of boy-office success, Wayne's career had been an artistic failure and his future held a promise of nothing significant or beautiful, it seemed to Jennings. He wrote:

John Wayne is still tenaciously playing herioc leads in action pictures because he desperately needs the money. And he still swashbuckles in uniforms and other manly costumes, albeit a little short of breath, because he knows that director Raoul Walsh, who discovered him more than thirty years ago, spoke the hard truth when he said, "Anytime you put guys like Duke in civilian clothes, they're dog meat."

Such singleness of purpose, while limiting artistic achievement and ruling out such honors as Academy Awards for acting, has given Wayne a sort of immortality. He has been paid as much as $666,000 a pic-

ture, and his 161 films have grossed about
$350,000,000, a record that Hollywood historians
expect to stand for all time.

Of course Jennings was grievously mistaken, and in a
few years the same *Saturday Evening Post* would publish
a lovely tribute to Wayne by Joan Didion. But what is
interesting to me about the Dean Jennings article is that
it reveals, in striking fashion, that John Wayne had become an Invisible Man, even to the eyes of a sharp reporter. For instance, Jennings wrote that "Wayne maintains his own film producing company, Batjac Productions, and keeps a full staff on salary there, even though
the company has made only one movie—*The Alamo*—in
its eight years of existence."

Well, in 1962, Batjac had been in existence for eleven
years and it had made six major films with Wayne, including *Big McClain, Hondo, Island in the Sky, The High
and the Mighty, Blood Alley* (with Lauren Bacall), and
*Legend of the Lost.* Batjac had also made two films without Duke—Robert Stack in *The Bullfighter and the Lady*
and Robert Mitchum in *Track of the Cat.*

There's a Father Brown detective story by G. K. Chesterton in which the murderer is a mailman whom nobody
identifies because he is taken for granted, being a daily
presence. He has become invisible. Something of the sort
had happened with John Wayne. Not only were his great
achievements as an actor invisible to the naked eye, but
even such simple facts as a highly efficient and functioning
independent producing company also became invisible.
Did not Dean Jennings know about these eight Batjac
films? Did not Jennings have any awareness of the mastery
of acting and human emotions which Wayne had portrayed
in his magnificent classics of the 1950's? Was it not possible for him to see that this man was gaining stature
technically and enlarging himself emotionally and that
there were possibly more artistic achievements ahead for
him?

One of the most infuriating things in writing about
John Wayne is this paradoxical invisibility of one who is

a superstar, who plays in film after film after film, who is directed by great directors and appears frequently with other stars. Andrew Sarris and Peter Bogdanovich and William Everson, the men who have been important in changing our ideas on the western and on John Wayne, have expressed their annoyance at this invisibility, at John Wayne's being taken for granted. Perhaps it is the very continuity and quality of his work which has made him invisible, as the daily rounds of the mailman made him invisible in Chesterton's story.

But it turned out that for Wayne, the decade of the 1960's was not to be a period of stultifying hack miming and routine swashbuckling in second-rate action pictures. It was to be a fascinating, colorful, and hyperactive ten years. It began with a delicious revenge on Darryl Zanuck.

Zanuck was preparing his spectacular filming of the invasion of Europe in 1945, *The Longest Day*. There were many American soldiers and officers to be portrayed. And who did he want to play the role of one of the leading American officers? Why, none other than John Wayne, poor old Duke Wayne, whom he had so recently scorned. Poor old Duke had now become to him wonderful manly Wayne. He telephoned Wayne and started to tell him there was a good part for him in the movie.

Wayne informed Zanuck that he could take his good part and his movie and shove them. Not a man to be easily discouraged, Zanuck insisted that he had been misquoted and that he had always admired Duke and knew that Batjac was a fine organization. He appealed to Wayne's well-known sense of patriotism. He could have his choice of playing any outstanding American general. How about Mark Clark? Patton? Gavin?

Wayne said no, no, and no. He cursed Zanuck. He spent a fortune of Zanuck's transatlantic phone money cursing him. Zanuck ignored the insults, and then said, how about a small cameo role? Ever since Mike Todd in 1955 had persuaded stars like Dietrich, Charles Boyer, and Sinatra to play extra roles in *Around the World in 80 Days,* producers had been hiring stars to play little roles, which were known as "cameos" and for which they

were paid outrageously low salaries but were assured they
would derive prestige.

Zanuck told Wayne how much prestige there was in
doing a cameo in *The Longest Day*. It would be the veritable redemption of his reputation. He was hustling Duke
for all he was worth. Well, poor old Duke Wayne said
that he might be willing to talk a deal, but he would want
a quarter of a million dollars for the cameo and not one
*franc* less.

Zanuck pleaded, spoke of patriotic duties and their old
friendship, but Wayne was adamant. He was enjoying
himself. He had not felt this buoyant since he had refused
to make *The Gunfighter* for Harry Cohn. He was sure
that Zanuck would not pay him two hundred fifty thousand dollars for a few days' work. Meanwhile he was
basking in one of his most shining moments in Hollywood.

Zanuck did indeed pay him this salary, and he went to
Europe and was before the camera four days.

With great dash and verve, he played Lieutenant Colonel Benjamin Vandevoort, who leads a battalion of para-
troopers on a descent into Normandy. He fractures his
ankles while landing and nevertheless bravely marches at
the head of his soldiers, hobbling and stumbling and using
a rifle as his crutch. Crowther in the New York *Times*
praised his realism and "notably rugged" portrayal ahead
of any of the other leading players and cameoists, including such notables as Robert Ryan, Mitchum, Fonda,
Richard Burton, Jean-Louis Barrault, Madeline Renaud,
as well as Irina Demich, who was Zanuck's current *aven-
ture*.

"Poor old Zanuck," Wayne recently remarked, a broad
grin on his face, "I shouldn't have been that rotten I guess.
The other cameos, they were gettin' maybe twenty-five
thousand the most. I always liked that son-of-a-bitch. A
good chess player. A good poker player. Loves pictures.
Good studio boss. A real gambler. My idea of the kind of
guy Hollywood needs. We need more Zanucks. But I was
goddam mad at his attack on me. I didn't like being pitied
by him or anybody. But you know it was nice that when

I got over there on location, old Zanuck was decent to me. He was so pleasant I kinda wished I hadn't charged him that much money. That has to be the most expensive interview a movie producer ever gave. Should teach us all to keep our mouths shut more often. What the hell, I needed the money at the time. Furthermore, I didn't think Zanuck would give me the quarter of a mil."

He did need hard cash badly and now Paramount came to his rescue. They would pay him six hundred thousand a movie for ten movies. This was about a hundred and fifty thousand less than his current price. But they would give him the six million *in advance* and in a lump sum. They had made him an irresistible offer. He accepted. He was now able to settle the most pressing bank notes, as well as other debts in connection with the shrimp company failure and the flop of a whiskey importing company—another one of his capers into international finance. He was slowly but surely settling up his obligations and, by dint of hard work, he would begin accumulating a new fortune.

There were other cameos during the 1960's. Ford asked him to once again impersonate General William Tecumseh Sherman in the Civil War sequence of the M-G-M-Cinerama epic *How the West Was Won* (1962). Hathaway, Ford, and George Marshall divided up the directorial labors. Ford chose the Northern defeat at Shiloh for his contribution. Wayne painted an unforgettable full-length portrait of an unshaven, cigar-chewing, drunken, cursing, sweating human being, a man of rage and brilliance, a soldier, a human being in a dirty uniform. He was seen arguing vehemently with a discouraged, equally drunken and unkempt General Ulysses S. Grant.

He was satisfied to receive a twenty-five-thousand-dollar fee for his six days' shooting on this sequence.

He had already had a trial run as General Sherman on the *Wagon Train* episode. Television audiences seeing that familiar face gasped and shouted, "Hey—there's John Wayne." That was why they had billed him as "Morris."

But should a superstar play a cameo role? Or a historical personage?

The question of whether one's involvement in a movie is dissipated by seeing familiar faces is an interesting one, and it was raised by Crowther in his analysis of George Stevens' life of Christ, *The Greatest Story Ever Told*. Except for Christ, who was played by Max von Sydow, the leading players were familiar faces in cameo roles—the faces of Shelley Winters, Ed Wynn, Charlton Heston, Sidney Poitier, and Wayne as a Roman centurion.

As much as he had approved of Wayne in *The Longest Day* Crowther despised him in *The Greatest Story*. His contention was that the "pop-ups of familiar faces in so-called cameo roles" is a distraction.

"Most shattering and distasteful of these intrusions," he wrote, "are the appearances of Carrol Baker and John Wayne in the deeply solemn and generally fitting enactment of the scene of Jesus carrying the cross to Calvary. Suddenly, at a most affecting moment, the plum-cheeked Miss Baker appears as a woman of the streets [Veronica] to wipe the sweat from Jesus' face. And right at a point of piercing anguish, up pops the brawny Mr. Wayne in the costume of a Roman centurion. Inevitably, viewers whisper, 'That's John Wayne.' "

I'm not sure that such a reaction is all bad. It may enhance a Biblical story, or a historical narrative of one's country, if one recognizes the people playing roles, for these events have the quality of community experiences. Thus Jewish children put on Purim plays in synagogues and know perfectly well that Esther is played by the girl whose father is an electrical contractor and Ahaseurus is the kid who wants to be a rock musician. Christian children play Nativity pageants and know that the Three Wise Men are being played by three stupid youths. In such films as *The Greatest Story,* the actors represent the community, the entire audience, in a way that they do not in other films.

Wayne's next cameo was that of a two-star American general in *Cast a Giant Shadow* (1966). General Randolph was a composite of Patton and Maxwell Taylor. On this movie there hangs a strange tale.

In 1964, Melville Shavelson was plagued by a curious

problem. Shavelson had made many of his pictures—which included some Bob Hope comedies and the Gable-Loren *It Started in Naples*—for Paramount. He had an office at Paramount. He had his own production company, Llenroc Productions. If you think that's a strange name, you can figure it out. Shavelson is a graduate of Cornell, class of 1937. Shavelson had never made a serious dramatic movie. Though not a Zionist, he had been stirred by the Israeli war of independence. He had recently purchased the film rights to *Cast a Giant Shadow,* a biography of Colonel David "Mickey" Marcus, an American officer who had fought for Israel. Shavelson was filled with enthusiasm for the movie he visualized. All his life he had been writing and directing frivolous comedies with flippant dialogue. Now at last—it is the old Stanley Kramer syndrome—he was going to make a movie with "social significance." He would make a great film about a great man. He was sure that he could secure Kirk Douglas to play Colonel Marcus. Douglas looked right and he was also known to be an admirer of Israel.

Upon Shavelson's broaching his new project to the Paramount front office, he was told, by one of the highest-ranking executives, who was himself Jewish, that "nobody wants to see a picture about some goddamn crazy Jewish colonel."

He suggested that Shavelson go home to his abode near the northern extreme of Laurel Canyon and invent a frivolous tale about a man and a woman, a Doris Day type of picture, with singing in it.

Shavelson was angry. He wrote a short précis of the novel and made an outline of his plan for converting the book into a spectacular film. His agent carried the material to various studios. It was rejected by M-G-M, Columbia, 20th Century-Fox, Warners, Universal, and United Artists. Now these studios were largely owned or controlled by Jewish persons, or numbered Jews among the executives.

What was going on here? Could it be—as he had heard —that after *Exodus,* the Arab bloc was putting pressure on Hollywood and threatened to expropriate every American-owned theater in the Islamic countries if more pro-Israel pictures were made?

But perhaps, like Shavelson himself, these producers were half-ashamed of being Jewish. He had always felt self-conscious about his Jewish origins. He had only begun openly identifying himself as an American Jew since the birth of Israel. He asked himself how he could convince the studios that his film was essentially not about Jews as such but about people struggling for independence and freedom.

"Well," opines Shavelson, "I was up against something I call Schwartzism. Schwartzism is a Hollywood game. Any time somebody becomes famous, people right away ask, 'I wonder what his *real* name was before he was Leslie Howard, Tony Curtis, Kirk Douglas.'" He calls the game "Schwartzism," after Bernie Schwartz, which is Tony Curtis' real name.

"I had to find an actor about whom the canard of Schwartzism was impossible," Shavelson recalls. He believed that if he could locate one such creature, he might be able to get a production under way. Of course, there are innumerable non-Schwartz stars and superstars, but about most of them there lingered wisps of suspicion as to the provenance.

"Suddenly," he says, "I knew that there was one star nobody could pull Schwartzism on me. He was the Fourth of July, the American flag, sourdough bread, the winning of the West, Washington, Lincoln, Jefferson, the Constitution. John Wayne.

"If God were to print a million photographs of Jewishness, he could use Wayne as the negative. Forgive the wisecrack, it is a habit. You see, at that point I'd heard all the usual talk about Wayne's being anti-Semitic and reactionary. Well, I never picked up any feelings of racial prejudice in him when we worked on *Trouble Along the Way*. But we weren't on speaking terms when that one was completed. Then *It Started in Naples* was released a few years later. John Wayne wrote me a nice letter about the picture and Sophia Loren and Gable. It was unexpected. Well, I figured he was letting bygones be bygones. I would go see the Duke."

He confronted Wayne in his new offices, the Batjac suite, on the second floor of the De Mille Building at Paramount. Duke listened as Shavelson told the story. He did not move a muscle. When Shavelson told how Colonel Marcus died in battle, while lighting a cigarette like Stryker in *Iwo Jima,* Wayne couldn't hold himself down any more. He got up. He pounded his desk. "Goddammit, Shavelson, that's the most beautiful story I ever heard, and it's an American story," he cried.

"Well . . . I . . . that is . . ." Shavelson said.

There was this enormous man, striding in his office, shouting, "Everybody's knockin' the United States these days, claimin' we're sending in troops all over the world to hurt little countries where we have no right to be. They kinda forget who we are and what we have done. Hell, we *need* to remind the whole world how we helped this little country of Israel get its independence and how a goddam *American* army officer gave his life for it."

"You know, of course, that Mickey Marcus is Jewish . . ."

"Don't hand me that bullshit," Wayne said. "Jesus Christ was Jewish, at least he started out Jewish. And furthermore, Mickey Marcus went to West Point. Don't you see that? Colonel Marcus was a West Pointer, goddammit, man, a West Pointer."

Then Shavelson committed a *faux pas.* "You could say that the battle for Jerusalem was the Jewish Alamo."

Duke grimaced.

"Never mind the Alamo," he growled, lighting his fourth cigarette in the last twenty minutes. "Now what's the problem? I'm too old to play Mickey Marcus and besides I don't think I could pass for Jewish."

"What I hoped, Duke, was that you'd agree to do a cameo in it so I can get this off the ground."

Wayne agreed. He also volunteered to make it a Batjac coproduction if he liked the first thirty pages of the screenplay.

He did like the first thirty pages. Batjac joined Llenroc. Now the Mirisch Brothers, who released through United Artists, sat up and took notice. Eventually Kirk Douglas got into the deal. So it became a Llenroc-Batjac-Mirisch-Bryna production.

Several years and several John Wayne pictures later, *Cast a Giant Shadow* went into production in Israel. The World War II battle sequences were filmed in Cincecittà studios in Rome. Wayne and Frank Sinatra, who was also doing a cameo, figured in these scenes. They finally were joined in a movie. Duke filmed four days in Rome. Shavelson was awed by Wayne's energy, for he had come out of a hospital a year before after major surgery, and he had completed a movie in Mexico, and he was, after all, a somewhat older man. But he was making the rounds of the nightclubs with Sinatra and the other swingers and roistering half the night. And he came to the set punctually "and knew all his lines and blasted anybody who was late. A professional through and through. And we didn't have script problems this time. He said he liked the script and he played it like it was written. He is an honorable man. He kept his word down the line."

Shavelson likes to quote a remark he overheard a prop man make about Duke one day in Rome:

*John Wayne is the same man in the morning that he was when he went to bed last night.*

Between *The Alamo* and *Cast a Giant Shadow*, Wayne starred in seven major films. All of them were made on location—to Africa for *Hatari!*, to Northern California for *North to Alaska*, to Hawaii for *Donovan's Reef*, to Utah for *The Man Who Shot Liberty Valance*, to Arizona and Mexico for *The Comancheros* and *McClintock*, to Spain for *Circus World*.

Spiritually and physically exhausted though he was, he performed at the height of intensity. He was dying of a fatal disease. He did not stop working. He labored with the perseverance of an animal in a yoke, of a brute peasant. He had promises to keep and debts to pay. Nobody knew about the faltering of his body, except Pilar. He did not go whining to John Ford. He did not ask for special privileges. His last two films with Ford—*Donovan's Reef* and *Liberty Valance*—were comparable to Beethoven's later quartets. They were soft, transcendent statements about the violent era in his middle age. The new school of critics, the British writer John Baxter for instance, now see these two films as the culmination and the conclusion of the Wayne-Ford partnership.

*Circus World,* which was directed by Hathaway, who had also done *North to Alaska,* almost killed Wayne. There was first a protracted delay because Frank Capra, the first director hired by Paramount, quarreled with screenwriter Jimmy Grant. Wayne says Capra wasted six months "because he was secretly writing a different script which did not fit my character. He cost me a million dollars. I deeply resent the rotten things this son-of-a-bitch said about Jimmy Grant and me in his autobiography. I know he had to justify being fired by Paramount by blaming me and Grant. He could not see that by making this character, Matt Masters, be one of his so-called 'little people' he would have ruined the picture."

Matt Masters was an American cowboy and circus owner who is traveling around Europe with his circus. The climax is a fire during which the big tent burns. A panic. Fleeing. Animals break out of cages. It proved to be one of the neatest action sequences Hathaway ever put on film. Shooting it took five days, during which artificial fires and real fires were being set and quenched and set again.

Of necessity, Wayne had to be constantly eating smoke. That morning cough had become an accepted part of his existence. It was a smoker's cough, all right, he would live with it. He was still smoking five, six packs a day, inhaling, exhaling, coughing, spitting, hacking, chain-smoking.

But the inhalation of smoke for the tent-burning sequence in *Circus World* aggravated his already diseased lungs. His previous cough became more violent, and the expectorations he brought up were now greenish and blackish.

The action called for Wayne—in attempting to control the raging fire and keep it away from the caged animals and the bulk of the spectators—to set up a fire barrier by chopping down seats and poles. Wayne had to work close to the flames, which were real. He wore fireproof underclothes and a fireman's helmet inside his hat. He was chopping away at seats as the fire roared behind him one day. The camera was turning.

Suddenly, the fire got out of control. Wayne did not see it. His back was to the blaze. He was furiously chopping. He felt the heat as fragments of wood and burning fiber flew around him. He saw the fire getting closer. He did not see any gaffers or grips there. He did not see Hathaway. He did not see the cameraman and his operator.

It was a case of *sauve qui peut*.

They had all run away, helter-skelter, to escape the blaze and everyone had assumed that Wayne would also flee. But Wayne went on playing his scene. He does not stop until he hears the word "Cut."

And he had not heard the word "Cut."

Finally he threw his ax into the blaze. He went to the hotel and took a shower.

He was mad at Hathaway and everybody else. He sulked for several days. They could not understand his remaining on the set. They could not see that he was a man so absorbed in his work that he had been impervious to the instinct of animal panic which seizes any of us in a fire.

He had eaten much smoke in a concentrated form, perhaps it was like smoking ten thousand cigarettes in these five days. He did not feel the same after they finished the sequence, he did not feel right, he never was to feel completely right again, for this probably speeded up the deadly process of metastasizing.

His great body and his powerful lungs were still able to withstand the enemy. He completed *Circus World*. He had begun coughing all night. The floor by his bed was littered with paper tissues in the morning. Even the Spanish brandy he loved did not soothe his lungs. A Madrid physician prescribed a codein syrup to use so as not to cough during the filming. Sometimes there were traces of blood in the sputum. He was very angry at this situation for it prevented him from working as hard as he liked to work.

When he came home, Pilar was more concerned than ever about his condition. There had been advance reports in the papers about a soon-to-be-released report of the Surgeon General of the U.S. regarding the baleful results of heavy smoking. There would be emphysema and lung cancer predictably as one got older. Now Mrs. Wayne began to nag her husband to go to the Scripps Clinic to get the complete physical examination which he was supposed to get each year but which he had been evading for the past two years.

And he said he would go *mañana* and she said *hoy* and he said *mañana*. And finally he said, well, after he finished doing the location work in Hawaii for Otto Preminger on *In Harm's Way* he would, he swore it, go to the Scripps Clinic . . .

Navy Captain Rockwell Torrey of this film, commander of a cruiser berthed in Pearl Harbor before the Japanese attack, was a strong character. But the screenplay didn't demand strenuous physical feats, for which Duke was grateful. He would not have to stretch his slender physical resources.

One of the loveliest motifs of *In Harm's Way* is the intense affair of the middle-aged heart between Wayne and Patricia Neal, playing a naval nurse. Wayne spoke of how Miss Neal had matured as an actress and a woman since they had acted opposite one another in a similar dynamics in *Operation Pacific*. As his own acting had been enhanced by the pains of his living, so had hers. She had become a very beautiful woman, in appearance and dignity. She had become an actress of wide range and deep feelings.

His compatability with Preminger was more unexpected. Wayne respected a director who knew his craft and who exerted an authority based on his knowledge. Preminger said he had rarely worked with a movie star who had so intuitive a sense of the camera eye as Wayne. So he accommodated himself to Wayne's genius. Wayne knew how and where to place himself for maximum effect and he knew how to act and react. Preminger found him to be less ego-ridden than any star he had known. He therefore gave him a wide latitude. It was pleasurable to be entangled with an actor who seemed unconcerned about anybody stealing his scene.

Once when he suggested that Miss Neal stand in such a way as to get the camera more effectively on her, she ventured to express the possibility that she would steal the scene from him.

"Well, Pat, if you can steal a scene from me, by God, you're entitled to it," he said, with a slow grin, and the most loving of voices, for he had found her to have grown into a complete professional herself, and he knew that any scene in which she was manifest was a scene not stolen but rightfully earned.

During the making of *In Harm's Way,* everyone on the set was certain that sooner or later Wayne and Preminger would meet in a head-on collision. Preminger is an iron-fisted director, as tough and domineering as Ford. He had crossed swords with Frank Sinatra, Lee J. Cobb, and Marilyn Monroe. He was famous for his harsh language and his Prussian general tactics.

Besides the usual tensions between a star's ego and a director's ego, there were violent political differences. Preminger, like almost all the personnel on the location, was a liberal and a supporter of President Johnson. Duke was one of Senator Goldwater's most ardent financial and moral backers. So if Wayne and Preminger did not get into a fight about the movie, they would certainly get into a bitter political debate. Like many who judge Wayne from a distance, Preminger had assumed that because he was a political conservative, he was probably a rude, unlettered primitive. Max Slater, who has worked on many of Preminger's pictures as his casting director and dialogue coach, was startled to find Duke an urbane and civilized person. He could not believe that Duke loved playing chess and played it well. Slater had been assigned to run lines with Wayne. He started out being suspicious of Duke and came to love him. They played hours of chess together, while waiting for the next camera setup. He also found Duke's retentive memory something of a phenomenon.

Why—John Wayne had even read many books and could converse sensitively about them. Mark Rydell, who directed Wayne's superb 1972 film *The Cowboys,* is also a liberal, and he also was pleasantly surprised by Wayne's sensitivity. He still recalls a moment when Roscoe Lee Browne, the black actor who co-starred in *The Cowboys,* got into a conversation with Wayne about British and American poetry. Browne has published poetry himself. Both actors started comparing—and quoting—their favorite verses. That day they all gathered around the two men and listened to poetry for almost an hour.

Preminger would say to Slater that Wayne was a marvelous actor and he could not understand how such an intelligent man could vote for Goldwater in the forthcoming election. What professional discipline he had!

He came for makeup at seven A.M. He did not leave until he was dismissed. Once, he remained even when he *was* dismissed. Preminger had become aware that he had a bad cough. Wayne said he had a cold, just a little flu. Did he have any fever? Oh, just a little notch or two above normal, but, hell, it was nothing at all, Otto, nothing at all. Preminger said he did not need him for the afternoon's work. He should go home and get into bed.

Preminger was shooting one of the important dramatic sequences of the story, a meeting between Wayne, and his son, played by Brandon de Wilde. The two have not seen each other for a long time. Wayne, divorced from the boy's mother, a Boston snob, is furious because the boy has wangled a soft assignment as a public relations officer in the Navy instead of seeking combat duty. The sequence was one of those beautiful father and son encounters which Wayne has played so touchingly since *Red River,* often with a surrogate son, and in *The Cowboys* he had fourteen filial surrogates. The sequence is a crucial one for the story. It was shot outdoors at night. There were many takes and retakes. The men were shot in two-shots. After Preminger had taken them together from many angles, he wanted to get some reaction shots, in which Wayne is off-camera, while his voice is heard and de Wilde's face is in closeup, reacting. The reaction shots would be combined with the two-shots, later, in the cutting room. It is a fairly routine cinematic device and is often done by having an assistant director or dialogue director read the lines of the unseen person while the actor being photographed speaks or listens. Often a star goes to his dressing room during such takes. Wayne rarely, if ever, does so, as he believes it helps the honesty of the scene if he plays it off-camera himself.

Wayne refuses to go back to the hotel. Slater said he would be happy to do the scene with de Wilde. Wayne refused. He remained until the day's shooting was completed.

"There are certain people, certain actors," Slater says, "that when you meet them you are disappointed. Perhaps they are shorter than they looked on the screen, maybe they are less powerful or less interesting. But Wayne— he was taller and more majestic than I had expected. He did not have any of the usual tricks of a star's temperament. If a take was spoiled he always had it that it was his fault, even if it might have been the lighting or another actor. And he never argued with Preminger. He took correction and direction. He listened to Otto's suggestions and followed them. But we all knew this was temporary— sooner or later comes the blowup. But Wayne did not even argue politics. Though he was being constantly ragged by Kirk Douglas and Preminger.

"One day, I thought—*now finally it's coming.*"

They were shooting a scene with Wayne and Patricia Neal. Miss Neal is a naval nurse in her late thirties. Wayne meets her while he is recovering from injuries sustained in battle. They have a September–September relationship. Just as he became a master of expressing love between father and son, Duke became a virtuoso of romantic love between a middle-aged man and a middle-aged woman. And in Miss Neal he found a marvelous foil—she played the nurse and lover in a sensual, sophisticated counterpoint. The night before he is to depart on the secret mission (Operation Skyhook), he comes to her bungalow and she serves him dinner by candlelight. They have food, wine, love, talk, cigarettes and love and intimacy.

This sequence, though entirely composed of interior takes, was not photographed on a three-walled soundstage with ample space around and above, but in the cramped confines of an actual bungalow on Oahu. Preminger rented several such actual homes for various scenes. To cram a camera, sound equipment, and lights into a small bungalow is a problem, and a giant like Wayne makes even a spacious soundstage appear to be crowded.

Furthermore, any scene during which the actors dine presents a supply problem to the prop department. On the stage, stagehands prepare one meal if there is a collation during a play. In a film, sometimes three or more identical meals have to be made ready in case there are retakes. Nurse Maggie Haines was serving steaks to her lover, Captain Rockwell Torrey. Every retake demanded fresh, uneaten, broiled steaks.

And there was the question of her cigarettes.

Now such details as cigarettes, steaks, bottles of wine, handkerchiefs, and the other flotsam and jetsam of living are of small concern to an actor except when he is pouring wine or lighting a cigarette in an actual scene. Otherwise the whole atmosphere of properties is not in his awareness. His interest centers on whether he is getting his share of closeups and how he should phrase his lines, and whether the lines come trippingly to his tongue and how he ought to place his body and whether his best angle is being photographed and, if he is one of the new breed, whether he is being sufficiently motivated on the emotional plane to do the scene with conviction.

The rendezvous between the lovers was going badly—cinematically, not sexually—and there were many retakes and variations on the setups. They were having a hard time. Suddenly Wayne stepped out of character and approached Preminger, who was standing to one side, several feet from the camera.

"Mr. Preminger," Wayne said loudly. A silence fell

upon the actors and crew. "You mind if I make a suggestion?"

An alligator smile froze on Preminger's face.

Here it was.

"But, of course, Duke," Preminger replied urbanely, bobbing his bald head. "We want to make you com-pletely happy. Is there somesing the matter?"

"I think about these cigarettes now," Duke said softly, "I think Pat should be carryin' a pack, not have them in a case, and maybe have the matches, see, tucked into the pack, like I've seen some ladies do, nurses . . ."

Then he sat down in one of the chairs on the set. He lighted a cigarette and inhaled it and was racked by a cough.

Preminger's face said, *Is that all you are suggesting? You do not want the screenplay rewritten? You do not want to fire Patricia Neal?* He followed Duke's suggestion about cigarettes and other ideas the star had about the steak dinner.

Slater now became conscious of the extent to which Duke was fascinated by the hand props and the set decorations, the lamps and chairs and tables and silverware and handkerchiefs and cigarettes. Never had he seen an actor be so interested in props—it seemed to be a pure interest in properties, and unrelated to his own specific action with a chair and table or using a pack of cigarettes. He noticed how frequently Wayne socialized with the property men and threw ideas their way, small changes in the arrangements of an officer's cabin aboard ship, and the ideas were good because of Wayne's great knowledge of nautical matters. It seemed to Slater as if Wayne had appointed himself an unpaid member of the prop gang— and they accepted him as one of their own.

Curious about this, Slater mentioned it to one of Wayne's group, a man in charge of transportation on the film. This man told him that Wayne started out as a property man!

And he still was a prop man deep down.

He retired after the day's work. He was so exhausted now that he went right home to the suite at the newly opened Ilikai Hotel on Waikiki Beach. Leaving the children home, Pilar had come to be with him. He went to sleep as soon as he had dinner. He was aware that any exertion, even to cross to the bathroom, made him feel exhausted. It was harder to breathe, and he became aware of a strong, and increasingly painful, pressure around his chest.

Upon returning home, he still resisted going to the clinic, but they were all at him now, Mrs. Wayne and Jack Ford, Mike Wayne and Pat and the daughters and his brother, who still used the Morrison cognomen, Bob Morrison. He would wait until after the election, he said, he had to get votes for Goldwater and help win the war in Vietnam. No. Pilar was firm. Well, after he went down to make The *Sons of Katie Elder* for Hathaway in Mexico he . . .

No. No. No.

And finally he drove down to La Jolla by himself and was there in the clinic for five days.

## 26

## The Big C

He seated himself in the Pontiac station wagon for the return. It was an old car with a venerable body. But the engine was still strong, a special engine, custom job, three-fifty hp. A raised roof over the driver's cab, six inches taller than standard, custom job, GM customized to Duke's measurements, enabling him to slide in without bumping his head.

Driving out of the parking area of Scripps, he headed north on California 101, the beautiful, the winding Pacific

Coast Highway. It was for him a road well traveled. And now, he had the feeling that he would be cruising it for the last time. The five days in the clinic were done. He had been X-rayed and X-rayed, blood sampled, checked and rechecked, auscultated and thumped, orifices probed, all units examined, his sleeping studied and his food intake studied.

He had been told, at last, that a growth existed in his left lung. It had to be removed quickly. Well, was it cancer? Ah, now, they would know better when they took the biopsy. *But it is cancer?* Well, he had better go home and make arrangements to go to the hospital and get the surgery. *But is it cancer, Doc?* They never tell you straight out. They hate to tell you. Maybe they don't know. Perhaps it was. Perhaps it was not. The tumor seemed to be a small one, and, *shrug shrug,* the recovery rate, you know, it gets better, but one should not postpone surgery. *Thank you very much.*

*Goodbye now, John, and we'll be seeing you next year.*

But he was thinking there would not be a 1965 for him. That was the way he had to be. He would accept it. He would not take down the Winchester .73, an authentic piece of a past era, one of his gun collection, and go looking for Death in the streets of Laredo to gun him down. He had come to some sort of terms with the universe, because of the dying of friends and the alterations in James Edward Grant and John Ford, *in la sua volontade es nostra pace,* and hell what he wanted right now was a cigarette. Stupid to have thrown away that pack in the clinic. Stupid gesture. He was going to die anyway and he might as well go out coughing. No, maybe there was a chance. Just for the hell of it, he would never smoke another cigarette, live or die. Fingers trembling on the steering wheel, sweat coming out on his arms, he felt twitches all over his skin. He drove very slowly, contemplating his family, his wife, all his children, his first wife and his second wife and his third wife, as men do in last moments, riding an airplane that seems doomed or in a battle, remembering them all, but thoughts of a smoke got in there, remembering sensations of tearing open cellophane, unfolding tinfoil, plucking out the first one, coffin nails they used to call 'em, sticking it between his lips, scratching match on fingernail, inhaling inhaling deeply, killing himself slowly over all those years—well, maybe he was living on borrowed time and should have died often before. The time the horse threw him making *She Wore a Yellow Ribbon*. Got to have a puff. Stop and buy a pack. A spasm of coughing which choked him. No, he wouldn't buy a pack. Cruising through Carlsbad and Oceanside. The ocean rolling in to the beaches on his left side. The fog was almost lifted and the sun was coming out. Further up, in the Newport Beach basin, his yacht *The Wild Goose* was anchored.

Slowly, the station wagon cruised in and out of the small coastal towns, towns he knew like the back of his liver-spotted gnarled hands, strong large hands. Well he would not ever go out on that ship again. He had just bought it and had it refitted like a proper rich man's yacht, that old minesweeper. So what the hell? He had had a good long ride on the merry-go-round and had himself plenty of brass rings. Wish he could know whether Goldwater would win the election. Wish they would end this no-win policy in Vietnam. Help the South Vietnamese win their independence. Never to make another movie. Not to sit on the patio with Pilar and sip Dom Perignon. Not to play with Aissa and John Ethan. Not to watch his daughters and his sons by Josie and to play with the children of his children. Well, he had gone around the carousel a time or two and it had been very good most of the time, and he was fifty-seven, so what the hell, he would stop and buy a pack of cigarettes. He laughed to himself and drove very slowly, more slowly than he usually drove, about thirty-five, forty m.p.h., he wasn't in a rush to get home and have to tell Pilar and he wasn't going to lie because they both had an idea it would be something bad, there was too much in the papers about smoking and lung cancer, smoking and emphysema and heart failure.

He had been living on borrowed time. Could have cashed in his chips on *Hatari!* Time that bull rhinoceros charged the Land Rover he was riding in. Damn near catapulted him into what should have been a fatal accident. And then there was Barcelona. Could have burned to death in that tent fire. Making *McClintock* he took a fall off a roof, just a stunt, an easy stunt, didn't break the fall properly, hurt his spine, ruptured a disc. God had been telling him the same thing the past few years. Time's about up, buddy boy. *Donovan's Reef*—that fight scene with Lee Marvin—breaking his back again while taking a fall.

His body seeemed to be failing him. What was the use of living if he couldn't do horsefalls or roll off a roof? No life to be coughing all night, all day. Only thing was he had more pictures in him. That feeling you get driving out to the location early in the morning when the sun is up but not straight overhead, the good light of the morning, perfect for filming, the good feeling of talking to the makeup man and putting on the costume, looking over the setup, trading ripostes with Hathaway, Hawks, the Old Man Himself, Jack Ford. Too had about that picture he was supposed to do with Dean Martin.

Hell, what difference would it make to God if he had one damn cigarette. Then he had a brilliant idea. He would stop and have a little drink every time he felt the urge for a cigarette. Plenty of nice little bars along the way. He stopped in one and had a Martell's V.S.O.P. and soda. Thought about the state of his finances. He felt good about that. Batjac was doing fine. Mike sure was taking hold like the man he was. He was president of Batjac. And Donald La Cava, his son-in-law, was a sagacious businessman. He was secretary and v.p. Frank Belcher was treasurer. He had gotten into some good real estate investments and land deals and Batjac now owned many of the coproductions outright and was profiting from television deals. *The Alamo* was starting to pay off. Outside of film properties Batjac owned, the other holdings were worth over ten million. From being on the verge of total wipeout four years before, he, and his associates, had pulled out of it beautifully. There was a twenty-four-thousand-acre cattle ranch in Arizona and prize bulls and some cotton plantations and oil wells.

It took a full-time staff of fourteen to hold down the fort at Batjac. Zanuck and that galoot from *The Saturday Evening Post* and the others had written "poor old Duke Wayne" off prematurely.

Passing Newport now, and he stopped for another dollop of brandy and went on, past the channel and that long peninsula with well-formed calf like a woman's lovely leg. One of the beaches was Balboa, where he had courted Josephine Saenz, where he maimed his right shoulder body-surfing. In the Newport marina was that 136-footer, his own boat which he loved so much. And he did not stop to walk its deck for one last time. He did not have an appointment in Balboa or in Newport. This time, sure enough, the appointment was finally in Samarra. Had taken Death a long time to catch him. At a small café overlooking the harbor, he had another belt or two, and by now he was getting smashed so he was going to drive easy because it was against his principles to drive while drunk. He was a fanatic on the subject . . .

Finally, after a long, slow, slightly intoxicated journey, Duke Wayne came home. He told Pilar the facts in the case. She did not break down.

In a few months, they would have been married ten years.

He did not think they would be celebrating the anniversary together.

Dr. John C. Jones would perform the surgery. He had operated on counselor Belcher for abdominal cancer once.

On September 16, 1964, Wayne was admitted to Good Samaritan Hospital, which is known as Good Sam.

The following morning a malignant growth, about the size "of a baby's fist," was removed from his left lung. Two ribs on the left side of the cage and the entire left lung itself were removed.

The operation had been completely successful.

That night, however, complications developed. Edema took place. His body puffed out. He was swollen all over. Pilar who came to visit him said that he resembled Sidney Greenstreet. His neck had swollen so much that he could not swallow. He had to return to the operating room for more surgery.

"While I was in the intensive care unit," he revealed later, "I began coughing and coughed so much I ruptured certain tissues. I developed an abscess, so fluid accumulated in the right lung. They took me back to the operating room. It was the second operation in five days. They took out some of my right lung."

While Wayne was still in the hospital, James Bacon, veteran movie editor of the L.A. *Herald-Examiner* who had known Duke for twenty years, came to see him. Duke had now been in the hospital for three weeks. The movie colony seethed with rumors that Wayne had had, variously, heart attack, cancer, pneumonia, and that he was either dying or had already died, and that the truth was being concealed from the public. Batjac had issued a vague statement about Wayne being in Good Sam for "respiratory complications."

Bacon was the first to publish the news that John Wayne was alive and recovering and that he had had a "chest tumor" removed. Bacon reported him as being in lively condition.

Then Earl Wilson, a syndicated columnist one of whose outlets was the *Herald-Examiner,* published the fact that Wayne had suffered from a cancerous growth which had been removed.

Cancer. The Big C.

"I was sure the whole *Giant Shadow* project was finished," Mel Shavelson remembers. "Strange thing is, I stopped worrying about the movie. I was worried about Duke. I'd gotten to love and admire this big guy during the time we were partners. The important thing was whether the sheriff would survive the shot in the back. Whether the Good Guy on the white horse would outsmart the black hat cattle rustlers and outlaws, who got him ambushed. Cancer will never be the same after its encounter with Duke. He shattered the myth that cancer is invincible."

He was discharged from the hospital on October 8, 1964.

He was told he must rest for six months. He rested for three weeks, at home. Pilar nursed him. He had a twenty-inch scar running from his left armpit down over his chest. Until it healed he was in great pain. But what he wanted most was to smoke a cigarette. He would ask Pilar to please make him a cigarette sandwich. But he would not smoke again, ever again.

It was unbelievable to his doctors how he rallied, how the color came flushing into his face and his muscles got tone back. He could walk more and more. His lusty appetite came back. So, after three weeks they went on *The Wild Goose* for a cruise down the Mexican coast as far as Mazatlán. Wayne was beginning to drink again. He did a little fishing. He felt good. He thought about how his life had been saved. He thought about God. There had been many requests for interviews to discuss his cancer and he had been told by others that it was "a bad image" and that he should shun publicity on this subject. But he concluded that he could help other people if he told about himself and that going to the Scripps Clinic had saved his life.

On December 29, 1964, he called a press conference at his home. He recited the events of his smoking, the examination, the operation. He did not spare any details about the excision of lungs and his edema. And he answered questions.

"Yes, I am cured," he said.

"I am going to Mexico to make *The Sons of Katie Elder* next month.

"They told me to withhold my cancer operation from the public because it would hurt my image.

"Here's what I believe. Isn't there a good image in John Wayne beating cancer? Sure, I licked the Big C.

"But I did not do it myself. I had good surgeons and a good team and a good hospital.

"Yes, and I prayed to God."

It was the first time he had ever acknowledged that he now had come to believe in a Supreme Being and that he had entered into a spiritual relationship with God. Pilar Palette's interest in Christian Science had grown stronger and she also had prayed. Wayne began sharing her faith and eventually they would attend Sunday services at a Christian Science church in Newport . . .

His final message at that press conference was: "My doctors tell me I was saved by early detection. Movie image or no movie image, I think I should tell my story so that other people won't be afraid of cancer and will see a doctor so they can be saved by a checkup."

Now the whole world knew about superman's conquest of the fatal cancer. He was doubly admired by his audiences. Medical men were happy that this disease was being openly faced and that Wayne's recovery would give hope to others. Dr. Charles W. Mayo was one of many physicians who commended Wayne for his courage in speaking out and for the good example he set to other persons who required medical checkups . . .

Publicly, the medical profession hailed Wayne for his frankness. Privately, many of them, especially specialists and researchers into carcinomas, were anxious to study the lab reports and all the data and experiences of the surgeons and doctors and anesthetists involved in both operations. For John Wayne had not merely had an operation and pulled through and now lived a quiet life in a wheelchair. He was riding horses in Mexico for a movie. He was working hard. He was knocking back a fifth of Souza's *Conmemorativo* tequila a day.

Doctors and surgeons were bedeviled by suffering people, with possible cancers, who wanted "John Wayne's operation," so they could lead vigorous lives. They had seen Wayne interviewed on television. They beheld his radiant health. And, would you believe it, he had now fathered a third child—a daughter. Yes they wanted the "John Wayne Cancer Operation," just the way he had had it. They wanted to have virility and potency just like John Wayne.

Those cancer specialists and university researchers who sought empirical data on the "John Wayne Operation" ran into a stone wall when they went to Good Sam.

They could not study the pathology reports.

The entire file on John Wayne is closed to everyone—including the medical profession!

This procedure is a justifiable protection of a person's privacy. It is a decision made by Wayne's family and his doctors. Good Sam cannot go against these wishes.

For many years newsmagazine reporters, Hollywood correspondents, gossip columnists have tried to examine the John Wayne sealed papers. They are better protected than the Pentagon papers were.

Dr. X, a leading internist in Beverly Hills, told me: "In view of the fact that Wayne's operation for lung cancer received much publicity, I believe it would assist scientific research into cancer treatment to open these files to qualified scientists."

Dr. X has several patients in the film business, among whom are some who know Wayne. Dr. X says he knows that Wayne and his family were told that he had a carcinoma of the lung.

"Yet the question which bothers me is this damn pathology report. What kind of a cell was it? Was it a small cell, a nodule, or a larger oat cell, or a squamous, deadlier than the oat, or an adano-carcinol cell, the worst. Now a patient doesn't usually ride horses after a lung removal. I, and other physicians here in Los Angeles, have a difficult time with certain patients. You have to tell them they just are not John Wayne and do not have his sturdy constitution.

"But I certainly would like to see the pathology report.

"I am not satisfied in my own mind as to the exact nature of his growth."

Is it possible, then, that John Wayne really did not have lung cancer? That he has two fine lungs in his chest cavity? That perhaps the entire "operation" was a figment of the press-agent imagination, one of those bizarre Hollywood hoaxes?

No. This hypothesis makes no sense because why would there have been a curtain of ambiguity about the operation until the press conference of December 29?

Another interesting theory is that the operation was

minor surgery for the removal of a nodule, and, through a clerical error, the wrong biopsy report, the mislabeled X-rays, were shown to the family, and once having made a mistake, the pretense was continued.

Under this supposition, Wayne still has two good lungs—as in Hypothesis I—*but he does not know it.*

But is it not highly improbable that a man with two lungs would not know he has two lungs? And is it possible that all the nurses, assistants, doctors, interns, and administrators at Good Sam could have been entangled in a conspiracy of this nature?

But then why does the medical staff of Good Sam and the operating surgeon not release the file on John Wayne to medical scientists researching carcinoma?

This brings me to my third hypothesis.

And this reason would be that the John Wayne case is a complete and utter anomaly, which would make no sense in the generalized categories of science. John Wayne's recovery is unique and miraculous in the light of his pathology, the severity of the two operations, and the length of time during which he had smoked, as well as the quantity of tars and nicotines absorbed into his lungs and bloodstream.

Therefore the case of John Wayne, Patient, has no value to cancer researchers. There is only one John Wayne and he did not experience cancer as you and I might experience the disease. Truly, he seems to inhabit a dimension of being, as Churchill and Stravinsky and Picasso and Chaplin, peopled by supernormal creatures.

Consequently—though Dr. X may not agree with my Third Hypothesis—only this, it seems to me, can explain how John Wayne, being fifty-seven years old, possessed of less than one lung, inhabiting an old body, could go on to make sixteen difficult movies after the operations, all of them on location, most of them requiring travel to far places, and strenuous physical exertions. He could do it for he exists on another plane.

He had lost forty pounds since the operation and his right shoulder was still bad from the old body-surfing injury, and the spinal disc was ruptured, and he went down to Durango, Mexico, to make *The Sons of Katie Elder*.

It was his first location in Durango. He liked it very much. He was to come back to Durango again and again.

It was wild country and high country where it was hard breathing for him. He caught a bad cold. He had to chew tobacco, which he hated. He got tired easily. He had an oxygen inhaling machine now, in his camper on the location, and another one in his bedroom. He rode horses and swam a cold stream for one sequence. He was content. He had come to accept God's plan and his simple *locus* in the universe. He was doing well what he had learned to do well. He was *el tramposo* of *Nuestra Señora* of Durango.

After two months of shooting exteriors, they came to the Churubusco Studios in Mexico City.

And here came Joan Didion, and her husband, John Gregory Dunne. Ms. Didion was on assignment from the *Saturday Evening Post*. She is a slight slender lady, about as tall as Pilar Wayne, and equally introspective. Her eyes were sensitive and restless.

Twenty-two years ago, as a very young girl, she had seen a Wayne film and had spun fantasies of romance with John Wayne in the bend of the river where the cottonwoods grow. Now she was married to a good writer and her brother-in-law was a movie producer.

And in those twenty-two years, Duke had experienced two wives and three children more, and forty-nine pictures—my God, *forty-nine*—and some of them had achieved a level of beauty.

Ms. Didion had felt a special sort of sadness upon hearing of Wayne's illness. Had her hero finally been defeated?

She rejoiced in a headline quoting him: I LICKED THE BIG C.

It pleased her to think of "his reducing those outlaw cells to the level of any other outlaws."

As she watched Wayne working on the set, doing what he had learned to do, jiving with Hathaway and Dean

Martin, playing scenes, some of the fantasy in her memory was dissipated by the sight of the juggler at his labors.

One evening she and her husband and Mr. and Mrs. Wayne went out to a restaurant in Chapultepec Park. For a while it was like "an evening anywhere. We had a lot of drinks and I lost the sense that the face across the table was in certain ways more familiar than my husband's."

It seemed as if she had lost a lovely secret dream of her girlhood which she had locked in a private place for twenty-two years.

Then three musicians came and softly played music from old Wayne pictures. He raised his glass to Pilar and looked at her in a certain way. Watching him, Ms. Didion recovered her fantasy and put it back in its hiding place.

He came back to Durango to make *The War Wagon* with Kirk Douglas.

On February 19, 1966, James Edward Grant passed away after an illness of six months. He died of cancer.

The author of *The War Wagon,* a tall lean handsome gentleman, Clair Huffaker, became a part of Duke's entourage, and for a while it seemed as if he would become Duke's friend and literary adviser but they parted company after *The Hellfighters.* Wellman directed *The War Wagon* and Hawks made *El Dorado* with Duke.

"Howard Hawks is a poor judge of horseflesh," Wayne once told me. "He has bought more bad horses than anybody else that ever made westerns. He was always buying horses on their looks not their quality. He didn't know a good horse from a bad one. He gave me a terrible horse to ride in *El Dorado.* A spotted black mare. He said it had won blue ribbons. Some dealer had put one over on him. Hawks does not know, and never did, how to buy horses but he fancied himself quite a judge of horseflesh."

*El Dorado* was the last movie he owed Paramount on that six-million-dollar deal. Now if they wanted him, Paramount would have to pay one million as a fee and thirty-five percent of the net profit, including any sales to television. Well, the Paramount executives did not think they would ever want John Wayne for anything any more and they were not too sure he would live out 1966.

He had become a good friend of Dean Martin. Dean Martin had started a television show, on NBC. He would like Duke to be a guest star. Wayne hated television. It was not his medium. He felt uncomfortable when he did publicity appearances on talk shows. He pleaded with Dean and said he would do anything for a friend but it was hard for him to do television shows. No, he would not go on this program.

Dean Martin supplicated him.

Wayne gave up. He would do the guest shot.


## 27

## The Last Hip, Hip, Hurrah

In 1968, after twenty-six years of service, Bosley Crowther, distinguished movie critic of the New York *Times,* retired and was succeeded by Renata Adler. She wrote sensitive, and often intricately thought-out, observations on new pictures, but she was not one to kick up a storm. Nobody, consequently, was prepared for the savagery of her attack on John Wayne's latest film, *The Green Berets,* when it opened at the Rivoli Theater on June 19. It was an attack unparalleled in its expression of personal bitterness. While Crowther, and his predecessors, had often ridiculed bad films, they had never been so condemnatory. Overnight, Miss Adler became notorious. Everybody was talking about her polemic that day.

"*The Green Berets,*" her review began, "is a film so

unspeakable, so stupid, so rotten and false in every detail
that it passes through being fun, through being funny,
through being camp, through everything, and becomes an
invitation to grieve, not for our soldiers or for Vietnam
(the film could not be more false or do a greater dis-
service to either of them) but for what has happened to
the fantasy-making apparatus in the country. Simplicities
of the right, simplicities of the left, but this one is beyond
the possible. It is vile and insane. On top of that, it is
dull."

In this fashion, the review went on for several hundred
words, as Ms. Adler pitilessly dissected the film, with a
meticulous eye to details and specific imagery.

Ten days later, in her longer Sunday *feuilleton*, Ms.
Adler expanded her original diatribe into a longer massacre.

Nobody could accuse Ms. Adler of being anti-American or pro-Communist. It is true that she was opposed
to our armed intervention in the Vietnam war. She was
opposed to violence. But it had been clear during her
tenure as a reviewer that she did not approve of Communist violence. She had disparaged a slew of anti-
American, pro-Viet Cong and pro-Hanoi pictures which
had been coming out. (Like her *New Yorker* colleague,
Pauline Kael, Ms. Adler was politically sophisticated and
was never deceived by Communist dogmas masquerading
as idealism.)

Ms. Adler had spoken from her heart and her mind.
She found *The Green Berets* bad art, bad propaganda, a
movie unworthy of decent men and women. On the
whole, what she said about the movie was just, though it
was not America's "fantasy-making apparatus" which had
broken down, it was just John Wayne's.

And yet, though it is a failure, it was a necessary failure for Wayne. He did not plan to make a banal and
ugly film. For him, it was a significant spiritual action.
But it was all wrong—wrong from the start—wrong in
its intentions and in its execution—and John Wayne was,
from the standpoint of his own development and creative

imagination, too late to play the hero of the movie and too confused to be its director.

Having said all this, one must yet stand amazed at a man with the strength and madness to conceive of this movie and the determination to make it against even stronger opposition than his *Alamo* project had aroused.

In the summer of 1964, George Chandler, board member of the Screen Actors Guild and head of the Hollywood Overseas Committee, was asked, by the Defense Department, to organize groups of movie and television stars to tour the combat zones. Chandler began organizing groups of singers, comedians. It took him weeks to get his units into high gear. By the time he got around to asking Wayne, Duke was in Good Sam recuperating from his operations. Pilar brought him Chandler's letter. His reply, in part, was, "I had a little battle of my own, but the minute the doctor says I'm ready, you're going to hear from me."

Chandler heard from him. He heard that Wayne had to make a movie in Mexico. Then he heard again. He was making a movie in Italy. Then he was making another movie in Mexico. In 1966, he was ready. And over he went, accompanied by Paul Keyes, who was then the head writer of *The Dean Martin Show,* on which Wayne had appeared as a guest star, displaying a flippant and slightly fey side of himself to which audiences were unaccustomed.

Keyes had helped break down Wayne's inhibitions about television and soon Keyes, who became a producer and head writer on *Laugh-In,* got Duke on that one, doing ludicrous gags; ultimately Wayne got to like the medium. He has appeared with Lucille Ball, Red Skelton and Bob Hope—and proved himself to be a capable farceur—a talent he had intermittently displayed in several pictures like *McClintock* or *Without Reservations.*

Anyway, Wayne wanted Keyes to travel with him to help him work out gags and wisecracks for some of the personal appearances, though he did not want to play from a stage to huge audiences as Bob Hope did, for he knew he was not the kind of experienced raconteur who could hold a live mass audience. He did hope to appear before small informal groups and, most of all, according to Keyes, "to get close to the men who were in combat, go to war zones, go into hospitals. He told them never to make advance announcements of his appearances at any camp, so if he were rerouted, nobody would be disappointed."

Keyes was awed by the tirelessness of John Wayne. For three weeks he was awed. He says, still shaking his head in wonderment, "He kept going from six o'clock in the morning until ten or eleven at night. I was forty-two years old at the time. I had two lungs. I was in good condition. I could not keep up with him. He had in him some peculiar drive which is beyond my understanding. And, on his orders, we went as close to the firing line as we could go. He went by plane—helicopter—boat."

Wayne went down into the holds of ships where the heat was 145°F. He talked to the sailors down below. He was airlifted to aircraft carrier decks by ropes dangling from helicopters. Once, at Chu Lai, while conversing with men of the 7th Marine Regiment, he was almost killed by bullets from Viet Cong sharpshooters. The shots came out of the surrounding jungle. He did not run.

"I remember one day at Pleiku," Keyes says. "We were going over in a chopper. They radioed us to get out fast as an attack was in progress. Duke said the hell with that. He was landing. We did. They were attacking. Duke stepped out. He walked around the area. He introduced himself. You can imagine a GI's feeling when that hand clasped his shoulder. Suddenly he heard a familiar voice saying just simple things like, *Hello, I'm John Wayne, and I want you to know a lot of folks back home sure appreciate what you are doing.*

"Some of them, I guess damn near all of them, they had loved him since they were little, they remembered him as Sergeant Stryker in *Sands of Iwo Jima,* they had grown up on Wayne pictures, and there's Stryker in person.

"Some of them just started crying. They couldn't believe it was really him. And Duke would start blubbering too.

"This is what he wanted to do. He hated putting on a regular show with some patter and prepared gags. Sometimes I gave him lines that fitted a situation at an army base. Most of the time it was just his walking around and shaking hands with strangers."

In the course of the trip, Wayne came down with a severe eye inflammation. He had to be treated in a hospital. He was put in the Third Field Hospital. The only empty bed was in a neuropsychiatric ward. Duke noticed a patient in the next bed who was in a bad way. Most of the time the man lay quietly, hardly moving. Once, Wayne noticed that his eyes were looking around. He looked depressed. Duke got out of bed and went over and said, "I'm John Wayne. Your doctor tells me you're doing fine. You're going to pull out of this. Your country is proud of you, son."

The wounded soldier started laughing uncontrollably. Wayne went out to get a nurse. When she came in, the soldier whispered to her, "That guy is *really* crazy. Guess what? He thinks he's John Wayne, can you beat that?"

By the time his tour ended, Wayne had to make a movie about Vietnam, because "I owe it to them." He could not be dissuaded from this. Every major studio had avoided making a film about Vietnam because it was an "unpopular war." Wayne, through Batjac, bought the best-selling nonfiction novel by Robin Moore, which purported to be an accurate account of the valorous deeds of the American special forces divisions, though it was written in a dramatic form, comprising a series of episodes.

Wayne was advised that he was making a mistake. He had elicited much sympathy, even from his political foes, by his courage and honesty during his cancer operation. Now, he would stir up old hatreds if he did this movie. He would be called a superhawk and a right-wing reactionary. Furthermore, Wayne himself did not believe in a large land war on the Asian continent. He respected the judgment of one of his heroes, General MacArthur, on this question. He had opposed the election of Johnson in 1964. He opposed the sending of an army of five hundred thousand to Vietnam. He did not like what he called "Johnson's no-win policy." He stood with Senator Goldwater, and the predominant thinking of the Army, Navy, and Air Forces, that North Vietnam's military supply lines and arms factories should be bombed, and that Haiphong harbor should be blockaded. Nevertheless, President Johnson was his President. And the men in Vietnam were fellow Americans who were doing their duty as good citizens. It was a time when more and more educated persons, especially influential intellectuals in the press, television, and the academy, were turning against Johnson and the endless war. American flags were being burned. Draft riots and anti-war protests were universal in the colleges.

Wayne felt he had to take a stand against that.

And he could not forget what he had seen in Vietnam. He was haunted by the vision of the American Marine, the man in combat boots, lonely, frightened, confused, and yet courageous, doing what had to be done, fighting an ambiguous war, sitting in bunkers surrounded by jungles out of which machine-gun fire would suddenly burst, a damp mist-laden atmosphere of heat and stink, dead and wounded, men in field hospitals, and so, no matter how logical were the objections, from a business standpoint or publicity angle, he would always growl, staring stubbornly into space, "I owe this picture to them."

On a level of his animal emotions, he was not making a propaganda movie. He wanted to express his sense of man's bravery in fighting a war whose purposes he does not comprehend, who is living by the code of the military, who is rendering a service to his community by following the orders he is given.

Wayne was going to impart a meaning to these sacrifices in the only way he knew how, in the way he—when Ford directed him—had done in *They Were Expendable*. One's devotion to the Army, to America, to the country, and to God transcended defeat or victory,

for man could only find validity in his existence by serving institutions greater than himself.

But, unfortunately, on the conscious level, there was
an ideologist inside of Wayne, which was aesthetically
at odds with the deep emotional kinship he felt with our
fighting men in the Vietnam quagmire. The ideologist
was the one who studied the books about the war, who
discussed military tactics with John Ford, with his military
friends, and with Senator Goldwater.

The "Communist conspiracy" was not mere babbling
to amuse guests at his dinner table. He deeply believed
in its reality. He deeply believed that those who were
followers of the Viet Cong were part of a movement
which traduced our country and its institutions and consequently destroyed the structure which made our lives
bearable. He would not be persuaded by the changes in
the party line following the death of Stalin. To him,
Khrushchev was Stalin with another face and the Yugo-
slavian heresy and the Maoist deviation were all variations on the same evil motif. He thought the intervention in Vietnam, which he saw as a powerful nation going
to the aid of a small country beset by the "Communist
conspiracy," was a just and noble action, even though he
disapproved of the strategy of the mass army and the
curious unwillingness to fight this strange and undeclared
war.

He did not make *The Green Berets* for money. He
made it to tell the world, as he tried to tell them when
he put his prestige behind *Cast a Giant Shadow,* that our
American republic believed in freedom and that freedom
was indivisible anywhere on the planet. He would say, to
the press, that he was not making a political statement
but that this was a film for "entertainment purposes"
and that he hoped it would make money. But he had
deferred his salary to induce Warner Brothers to get into
the production as Batjac's partner. Jack Warner, as patriotic an American as Wayne, felt the same sense of a
cause.

Some interviewers goaded Wayne into making statements which, when taken out of context or misinter-

preted, would make him appear to be a bellicose and sadistic man, a superhawk, who gloried in the shedding of blood. Nobody who had ever had any knowledge of Wayne would ever believe this for it was not how he lived. When he was given time to express himself, he would give a sensible account of his intellectual position, and though one might disagree with it, it was not an insane viewpoint. Bob Thomas, of the AP, went to Fort Benning, Georgia, where the exterior sequences were made. He began by asking Wayne why he was risking his money and his reputation on making a favorable film about an unpopular war.

"What the hell war hasn't been unpopular?" Wayne shot back. "Nobody's enjoying this war but it happens to be damned necessary. If we hadn't gone into Vietnam, Indonesia wouldn't have been encouraged to beat the Communists. Ever since the Soviet Revolution of 1917, the Communists haven't compromised once in the family of nations. They're out to destroy us, and logic should tell us that this Vietnam war is the only right course. *Besides—we gave our word.*"

He compared, bitterly, the lackadaisical cooperation from the Pentagon on *Green Berets*—though they had approved and encouraged his movie and many promises had been made—to the movies he made in World War II when the studios could stage battle scenes with mobs of extras played by real soldiers and sailors.

"For a number of years," Wayne said, "we established a good picture of America throughout the world with those pictures. But they don't seem to think of that nowadays. Oh, we got good treatment at Fort Benning—within the letter of the law. We could use the Army's equipment if it wasn't tied up in training. We could shoot in areas but only if they were not being used by troops. And the soldiers were not available to us—unless they could get a two- or three-day pass. And we paid them regular pay as if they were Hollywood extras."

No, it was not like the old days when Roosevelt was in the White House, and Marshall, Eisenhower, and Mac-Arthur were cooperating with the movie makers. Now there were new times when senators and congressmen criticized the war and American correspondents in Vietnam were sending back gloomy dispatches about the endless war.

Asked what he thought of the so-called antiwar movement, Wayne said that they were an "articulate minority who attract more attention than their numbers warrant. You always see the same names . . . I suppose the so-called liberal will find some way to get at me. They did it with *The Alamo* when they misquoted me as saying that anyone who didn't go to see that movie was unpatriotic. If they can hit me on *The Alamo,* they sure as hell will do it on *The Green Berets.*"

Those who worked on the movie or visited him on the location were incredulous at his power and tenaciousness. Those few who were close to him, like his family, knew how great a cost he had to pay in order to fulfill his determination to direct *The Green Berets.*

The weather was damp and sometimes cold. There were heavy rains during the weeks of shooting. His conjunctivitis was bothering him again and he worked with one eye closed many times. His aging body was racked by pain in the back and the legs. He had lost his appetite. He was torn by spasms of coughing. Breathing was hard and sometimes almost impossible except when he used the oxygen. There were times when he seemed gaunt and worn out, a living corpse, a being who had already died, in effect, and was simply pure spirit expressing itself.

They had gotten behind in the shooting schedule, for, once again, Wayne was director, star, reviser of the script, and corrector of lighting, props, stunts, of everything. So he shot by day and by night. He worked some days for a stretch of fourteen hours, resembling in the shadows of the make-believe Vietnamese jungles and rice paddies, a Rembrandtlike ghost, like his General Sherman character, a raincoat over his shoulders, unshaven, his green beret worn at a jaunty angle, chewing tobacco and spitting it out, standing on windswept and dusty hills to envision a composition of men in battle, men in silhouette on a hill, a few trees, this shot, and that shot,

alone and crazy, barking out directions to his extras,
telling that veteran cinematographer Winton Hoch the
mood he wanted, a lonely and bizarre figure, playing
some eternally repeated lunatic fugue as he stalked back
and forth, back and forth, contemplating his inner visions, in a world of his own, beyond Jack Warner, beyond profit and loss, friends and enemies, children, and
wife, a lonely genius, cutting another piece of tobacco,
crying *Action,* crying *Cut,* crying *Print it.*

Later, in the office, attending to the little details, making changes in the script, talking to Raymond St. Jacques
and David Janssen about their roles, making decisions,
drinking much coffee, he was like a man possessed by a
demon which had him in its grasp. How could he have
summoned up the physical and moral strength to go on
like this, for over three months, in the condition in which
he was? For him, it is likely, *The Green Berets* would be
the ultimate expression of the dream he had followed since
his childhood, long before Vietnam, long before Ford and
Spig Wead, when his grandfather had told him Civil War
stories as he searched for the concealed pints of bourbon
in the sagebrush, stories of the cavalry and the damned
Confederate rebels, the fantasies he had spun rounding
the bend from Lancaster to Palmdale, riding the old horse,
outwitting the fear he had known growing up, and having
smelled the same fear among the young men at Chu Lai
and in the hospitals. Courage was not being without fear.
It was being with the fear and doing the right thing just
the same.

Possessed by his monomania, Wayne did not seem to
experience fatigue. He wore out the younger actors and
the crew. He was on the phone demanding help from the
Army, telephoning generals and senators in Washington,
thundering to Jack Warner in Hollywood, fighting. He
fell back on his technical assistant, Major Jerrold B.
Dodds, a Green Beret officer. To Joan Barthel, preparing
an article on Wayne for the New York *Times Sunday
Magazine,* Major Dodds told how it was with him: "I
have a simple feeling. I do what I'm told. You don't hear
many GI's who go along with protest. We may not be

as successful as we'd like to be, but we're doing something we believe in, and I just think it's worth fighting there than somewhere else."

Major Dodds, and the hard gemlike clarity of his sense of duty, was lost in the film. It should have been there. It was what the film was about but it was lost. Wayne, as the director, was steering in the direction of his ideology, and he lost the film. That is one reason why *The Green Berets* was a failure. Another reason is that he was trying to make a victorious and arrogant movie. Perhaps this is why Ms. Barthel fell into the illusion of thinking of him as "the man who, from *Fort Apache* to Bataan, has never lost a war."

This sentence in her text was thought to be so apropos that it was repeated as a caption to a layout of two stills of Wayne in two films. Well, I suppose this is just another variant of the Invisible Wayne.

For which man was it who never lost a war in the movies? It must have been another actor. It was not John Wayne. He was losing, always losing. He must have lost more battles than the Italian armies. *Fort Apache*—Cochise and the Apaches won that one. *They Were Expendable, In Harm's Way, Back to Bataan*—losing, always losing. *Sands of Iwo Jima*—dead from a sniper's bullet. And it was only recently that Wayne had lost another war. He had perished in the Alamo with Widmark and Harvey. General Houston, alias Richard Boone, had won that war. And how gallantly were the Mexican soldiers and Santa Anna portrayed in *The Alamo*. Director Wayne of *Green Berets* forgot what *Alamo* director Wayne had practiced—a respect for the nobility of the enemy, especially when he is beating you. Wayne had gotten much criticism from Texans who did not like his dignified portrayal of Santa Anna and the Mexican soldiers. There were outcries and denunciations that he had been too "liberal" in his favorable portrait of Mexican fighters. To these sons and daughters of the Texas revolution, Santa Anna was still "cruel and perfidious" and his was a miserable rabble of an army. Wayne had answered his opponents by declaring that he knew Mexicans and they were a strong and brave people and Santa Anna's army had been a good one.

Had he been as open-minded toward the Viet Cong as he was to Apaches, Comanches and Mexicans, there would have been a more interesting film. But he could not be. His ideology was riding him. Someday the Vietnam war may provide the framework for a John Ford, in the next century, a canvas of lost battles and lost wars and brave frightened men doing their duty because, like Major Dodds, "I do what I'm told."

At making a propaganda picture, Wayne was as boring as the Russians or the Communist-front French directors with their North Vietnamese propaganda pictures. In *Green Berets,* he condescended to the enemy. Penelope Gilliatt, in her penetrating analysis of the banality of *The Green Berets* in *The New Yorker,* made a cutting analogy between Wayne's conception of his role and a British nanny. (Ms. Gilliatt hated the film but she was not as nauseated by it as Ms. Adler.) Ms. Gilliatt wrote:

> The archetypal nanny figure is authoritarian, proselytizing, both Spartan and greedy, and conservative through to her bootheels. She is also often kindly, faithful and impossible to budge . . . I don't know who was responsible for the upbringing of the people who created *The Green Berets* but the film has the real touch of Nanny's fist. Vietnam is treated as if it were a little savage, in dire need of moral upbringing and probably infected with lice . . .

Just about the way Henry Fonda thought of the Apaches in *Fort Apache.* John Wayne could not change his attitude.

The film suggested a smug condescension toward the Vietnamese people which I know that Wayne does not feel for we have talked about this. I have heard him express fervent admiration for the tenacity, courage, fighting ability and brains of both North Vietnamese and South Vietnamese. He is very proud of having been with the

Montagnards and of having made many friends among the Vietnamese people.

But, once again, this genuine emotion which he felt as a sensitive man, just as his sensitive artistic side responded so intensely to the soldiers, these were choked by his compulsion to make propaganda. The role he played was not that of an officer troubled by moral as well as military problems, as are some of the officers in Robin Moore's book, but an arrogant, priggish and unconvincing stuffed shirt.

Wayne did play a strong and honest part in the making of this movie but it was not on the screen. It was when he was standing in the Georgia rain and the chillness, scrawling changes on the script, losing himself in the art of getting it all together for the strips of film, forgetting his old age and his broken body, contemplating the secret visions of compositional beauty which were his own, only for himself . . .

The theme of the foreign correspondent, played by Janssen, who comes to Vietnam as an antiwar radical-liberal and is converted to a proponent of the war, was so utterly untrue to history and to Moore's book that the movie had to break down. One can imagine a story about a battalion of Green Berets who are trapped and killed off one by one, and a news reporter, finally picking up a gun, and dying with his brothers, all of them hoping that it is all for some greater good about which they know very little. But that was not the movie we saw. And I had to agree with her opinions, when Renata Adler wrote:

What is sick, what is an outrage and a travesty, is that while it is meant to be an argument against war opposition—while it keeps reiterating its own line at every step, much as soap operas keep recapitulating their lots—it seems so totally impervious to any of the questions that it raises. It is so full of its own caricature of patriotism that it cannot even find the right things to falsify. No acting, no direction, no writing, no authenticity, of course. But it is

worse. It is completely incommunicado, out of touch.
It trips something that would outrage any human
sensibility, like mines, at every step and staggers on.

Yet Wayne believed, and still does, that *Green Berets*
was a true and honest movie. Sometimes his remarks seem
to suggest that he thinks it has no partisan political content. He talks about those "radic-lib" Eastern critics "reviewing the war instead of the picture," ignoring the obvious fact that it is his version of the war which is on
the line, and that this is not simply a vivid rendition of
the human condition, comparable to Renoir's *Grand
Illusion* or the Ford-Wayne series of U.S. Cavalry films.

He told Roger Ebert of the Chicago *Sun-Times,* "That
little clique back there in the East has taken great personal
satisfaction in reviewing my politics instead of my pictures.
And they've drawn up a caricature of me. Which doesn't
bother me: their opinions don't matter to the people who
go to the movies."

I am sure it did bother him. He wanted to be loved and
understood by the New York *Times, The New Yorker,*
the Los Angeles *Times* as well as the Dallas *Times-Herald,*
the Indianapolis *News* and the *National Review.* Though
he detested the political and social attitudes of that most
successful and famous of so-called underground papers
*The Village Voice,* which he felt stood for acceptance of
mind-bending drugs, sexual promiscuity, gay liberation,
Marxism and all that, he had to admit that they certainly
had one damn smart movie reviewer in this Andrew Sarris.

Indeed it is one of those inexplicable paradoxes that
Wayne was to find the most understanding and love of
his entire gallery of portraits among the young critics, the
new revisionists, the ones who saw beneath the skin, Sarris
and Bogdanovich and William Paul, Richard Corliss,
Richard Kraft, whose essays and reviews were published in
journals which were at the opposite side of Wayne's politics.

Now it would be easy to say that liberals despised
Wayne more than radicals, and that radical extremists of

every stripe feel affinities despite their ideologies. I do not think this is true. I think that these young movie critics were able to look at a John Wayne movie, whether it was a western, a military film, a Howard Hawks or Henry Hathaway entertainment, and see it, free from all the prejudices against westerns, against "action-adventure" movies, which older audiences and critics had.

They were able to experience *Rio Lobo* or *North to Alaska* as pure film. They shrugged off Wayne's ideology, just as he shrugged off theirs. Perhaps some of them even admired a man who walked the way he talked, for there was a salty quality in this man, a certain grandeur of character, and a defiant loneliness to which they also responded. But, in the end, I believe that what mattered to Sarris and Corliss and Kraft and the others was the genuineness of Wayne's achievement on the screen.

Wayne, though he might speak disdainfully of the Oscar, felt badly that he had not received it, for it was the symbol of being respected by his fellows in the movie industry, and he loved the industry.

After *Green Berets,* he was certain that he would always be denied the golden symbol because of his politics. He told the L.A. *Times'* Wayne Warga once, "I'm not hurt and I'm not angry. I'm aware that I'm unpopular in the industry because my political philosophy is different from the prevailing attitude. But I don't reply when they gang up on me, because I think political street fighting is unprofessional.

"Yes, I sometimes feel lost. But my convictions are my own and I'm entitled to them."

Still, he was hurt and he was angry. He was hurt and angered by the ridicule of *The Alamo* and the disgust at *Green Berets.* He often felt alone. But he would not have changed his statements just to win popularity. He had made *The Green Berets* as a matter of conscience. That was that.

Now, his head critically bloodied but spiritually unbowed, he was urged by everyone, especially Pilar, to be done with his unappreciated movies, and come home to

peace and the luxury of children, family, of feudal property. There were those twenty-four thousand acres of land
in Standfield, Arizona, its forty thousand cattle, its thirty-
five hundred acres of cotton. There was *The Wild Goose*
on which to cruise Alaskan waters in August and Mexican
waters in January. There were journeys to be made to
all the places in this world. There were the children, and
now the grandchildren, to be with and to enjoy. Now
Pilar and John had three children, Aissa, John Ethan, and
Marisa, who had been born in 1967.

And Michael Wayne had married Gretchen and they
had begat Alicia, Teresa, Maria, Josephine, and Christopher.

And Antonia Wayne had married Donald La Cava, and
they had begat Anita, Mark, Bridget, Christopher, Peter
and Kevin.

And Patrick Wayne had married Peggy Hunt and they
had begat Michael and Melanie.

And Melinda Wayne had married Gregory Munoz and
they had begat Matthew and Laura.

And now that Pilar and Duke lived in Newport Beach,
they would live by the ocean and the children would come,
and their children. Duke would learn tennis, and even
golf perhaps. Was it not a more peaceful existence than
this all-consuming labor of another movie? He would not
have to be reviewed and be misunderstood by liberal
critics. He would not be called a "superhawk" and other
surly names. He certainly could forget the hope of ever
turning public opinion around and getting good reviews
or winning an Oscar.

Yeah, it sure did appear that the reservoir of good will
he had finally managed to amass in Hollywood, mostly as
a result of surviving and those two operations—all that
had been thrown away by this Vietnam movie which
people hated. If, in 1962, it had seemed to the astute
Dean Jennings that Wayne could never hope to achieve
artistic distinction in films and win an Academy Award,
now, seven years later, it looked even more hopeless. An
influential portion of the voters in the movie industry were

strongly opposed to him. They agreed with every word of Renata Adler's review.

There is a final observation to be made on how Wayne's maturity as an actor also had a profound relationship on the failure of *Green Berets*. For it is possible that even though his patriotic ideology overwhelmed whatever potential life was in this movie, yet, had Wayne been at a different stage of his life it might have been, if not more aesthetically harmonious, at least more true to itself, more alive and exciting.

The role of Major Kirby demanded the hero-fanatic, the ferociousness and monomania of Stryker, Dunson, Ethan Edwards.

But Wayne was now at a point of growth which had taken him into aspects of reconciliation, acceptance and avuncular serenity. This, unfortunately for *Green Berets,* had the *pukka sahib* touches which seemed like a manifestation of white superiority and American neo-colonialism, which outraged Ms. Adler and reminded Ms. Gilliatt of the eternal British nanny.

Underlying this appearance of nannyism was the reality of more and more protective tenderness. The tenderness, increasingly present in his soul since his love for Pilar, had come to take over his personality and hence his acting technique. It seeped into every corner of his soul and body. She had softened his ruthlessness and his harshness. The experiences of the last ten years, the death of beloved friends, his own brush with the Angel of Death, had slowly made him more God-intoxicated. He had begun praying and accepting our world as a whole.

He had become a different person.

Therefore he could not bring what the role needed to his *Green Berets* major. And this was the last time he would ever attempt to impersonate Captain Ahab.

Now he entered the fifth decade of his cinema career. He was not irising out. He was to embark upon a new series of characterizations, some aspects of which would be familiar, which became more patriarchal and protective. He was to be an old man now—but one who could still shoot as fast as a young man and ride his horse as well. He would strive to vanquish land-grabbers, murderers, cutthroats, outlaws, robbers.

He would remain in the service of humanity—the mythic Promethean figure which the true western hero is.

He would fight to protect the weak and succor the helpless.

As he opened a new room in his gallery, the first portrait which he hung was that of Reuben J. Cogburn.

# 28

# A Last Chapter Which Is Not

It was said by many persons who read *True Grit,* by Charles Portis, that he based the character of Rooster Cogburn on John Wayne. Duke wanted to play him as soon as he read the book in galley proofs. Batjac went as high as three hundred thousand. Hal Wallis, a veteran independent producer releasing through Paramount, went to five hundred thousand and also acquired Portis' first novel, *Norwood*. Wallis signed up Wayne for a million dollars and thirty-five percent of the gross. He put together a successful combination. Hathaway to direct. Lucien Ballard, perhaps our best American colorist, as good as Henri Decae, to be cinematographer. Marguerite Roberts to write the screen version.

In autumn of 1968, up they all went to the Colorado mountains to collaborate on a masterpiece. *True Grit* became a triumph, one of those rare occasions when all the elements necessary to the making of film fall into place and are synthesized into a harmonious entity.

Wayne's characterization of a drunken swaggering kindly and courageous U.S. Marshal was so good and so clearly a product of his acting imagination that many eyes, to whom he had been invisible, now saw him clearly. It was now apparent that here was a virtuoso of the limited space which the camera eye records. Here was an artist who knew how to move within its parameters and calculate to exactitude how to arrange his moves and flickerings of the eye.

He emerged as a superhuman presence on the screen.

Henry Hathaway's first fling with Duke went back thirty years to *The Shepherd of the Hills.* He had always been able to evoke from Wayne amiable and amusing aspects of character, though he also inspired the angry and violent when it was necessary. The comical side of Wayne's many-sided character always came through more charmingly in a Hathaway picture than in a Ford or a Hawks picture. In recent years they had been to the Sahara to make the one with Sophia Loren, to northern California for *North to Alaska,* to Barcelona for *Circus World.* It was he who had coaxed Wayne into a brilliant performance when he came back from the dead in 1965 and went to Durango to make *The Sons of Katie Elder.*

He not only loved Duke as a man. He cherished his precious gift. He determined to make *True Grit* the best western of his life. He would also make it an instrument worthy of this musician. He worked softly and gently with Wayne. He did not ever chide him. He rarely corrected him or even made suggestions. He knew that Wayne was almost invariably right as to body placement, though on readings he might suggest nuances. Wayne often praises Hathaway's sensitivity and kindness as a director.

Ms. Roberts' screenplay was a rich and inventive piece of work, which developed the original novel into a superb scenario. Duke told me once that it was the best screenplay which he had ever read.

Ballard's camera work was in the great tradition of the western, revealing the wild landscape and changing terrains with the sensibility of a great *paysagiste.*

Hathaway's prime interest was always the telling of the story. He was a story teller, as were all the veterans who had come of age during the late silent movie period. He was a story teller of images and actions and only secondarily of dialogue. Images.

The image of Marshal Cogburn, our first meeting him, bringing in a van of prisoners to the courthouse jail.

Image of him lying drunk on a cot in the back room of the Chinese grocer.

Image of him shooting the rat.

Image of him tilting a jug of bourbon to his lips with a swing of his arm.

Action shots of his amused antagonism toward the fourteen-year-old Mattie, played by Kim Darby, trying to get him to go into Indian Territory and capture her father's murderer and offering him fifty dollars.

Action sequences of the pursuit of the criminals and the ambush of the men in the cabin by the river.

Image of him getting drunk and falling off the horse and making believe he planned to make camp at the site where he fell.

And the longest speech in the picture, his monologue about his old life, the wife he had once, running out on him with a lover, his never wanting to settle down, being alone, cherishing independence and fearful of a woman's desire for order and domestic cleanliness.

Beyond the words, Wayne conveyed in vocal intonations and sombre gestures the contradictions of the character who craves a woman's arms and love and comprehension—and flinches from her power, wanting to remain cantankerous and filthy and loving his whiskey more than his woman, but still missing the amenities of marriage.

"I guess that scene in *True Grit* is about the best scene I ever did," he says.

And then, at the climax, the most satisfying shootout he had ever done. Not on a western street, but in the open meadow, in a haze of autumnal fantasy, a grove of aspens, birches, maples, leaves fading to golden-yellow and vermilion, as old Marshal Cogburn bestrides his horse, riding tall in the saddle, challenging the four bandits, vowing to kill them or see them hanged in Fort Smith, and the leader sneering, "Bold talk for a one-eyed fat man," and Duke putting his horse to the gallop crying, "Fill your hand, you son-of-a-bitch," *this being the only time he had ever spoken profanely in a movie,* mouthing the reins while he hefts a Winchester in one hand, a pistol in the other, comes out shooting, kills them all, his horse shot from under him, he takes a horsefall, the horse lands on his body.

The closing sequence—which Ms. Roberts had invented as she had for many pages of her screenplay—in winter in the family cemetery on a hill. Snow and leafless trees. Mattie and Cogburn are saying goodbye. She says that because he has no family of his own, she'd be honored if he would be buried in her family plot.

Wayne allows as how this would be fine and he will not let her see how deeply moved he is, but he mounts his horse and leaps a fence, to prove he isn't ready for the grave, and he cries out, "Come and see a fat old man some time."

So only one year after the disastrous premiere of *Green Berets, True Grit* opened in New York, on July 3, 1969 at Radio City Music Hall. Would Renata Adler have loved it? We will never know as Vincent Canby was the new critic of the *Times*. Canby wrote that he never thought he would take John Wayne seriously again after the debacle of the Vietnam picture, but he did now. He praised the film as a "major entertainment," and he lavished extravagant compliments on Duke and on Ms. Roberts, Mr. Ballard and Mr. Hathaway. It was a triumph for all of them and was the best role of Wayne's long career.

In December, Canby chose *True Grit* as one of the ten best films of 1969.

And noble words were composed by the John the Baptist of the new movie criticism, Andrew Sarris in *The Village Voice* (August 21, 1969). He wrote:

And there is talk of an Oscar for Wayne after forty years of movie acting and after thirty years of damn good movie acting. Wayne's performances for John Ford alone are worth all the Oscars passed out to the likes of George Arliss, Warner Baxter, Lionel Barrymore, Paul Lukas, Broderick Crawford, Jose Ferrer, Ernest Borgnine, Yul Brynner and David Niven.

Indeed, Wayne's performances in *The Searchers, Wings of Eagles* and *The Man Who Shot Liberty Valance* are among the most full-bodied and large-souled creations of the cinema; and not too far behind are the characterizations in *She Wore a Yellow Ribbon, They Were Expendable, Fort Apache, Rio Grande, Three Godfathers, The Quiet Man, The Horse Soldiers, Donovan's Reef, Stagecoach* and *The Long Voyage Home.*

And that is only the Ford oeuvre.

*Rio Bravo, El Dorado* and *Red River* for Hawks are almost on the same level as the Fords, and *Hatari!* is not too far behind. Then there are the merely nice movies like *Reap the Wild Wind* (with Paulette Goddard), *The Spoilers* (with Marlene Dietrich), *The Lady Takes a Chance* (with Jean Arthur), *Tall in the Saddle* (with Ella Raines), *Wake of the Red Witch* (with Gail Russell), *The High and the Mighty.*

Finally, there are the leisurely Hathaway movies—*Shepherd of the Hills . . . North to Alaska . . . The Sons of Katie Elder . . .*

No one has suggested that his acting range extends to Restoration fops and Elizabethan fools. But it would be a mistake to assume that all that he can play or has played is the conventional western gun-fighter. There is more of Christian submission than pagan hubris in the Duke's western persona. Relatively "liberal" types like Henry Fonda and Paul Newman have been considerably more conspicuous than Wayne in the matter of flaunting virility and swaggering about with six shooters at the ready. Newman, in particular, exploits the western to express his own anarchic spirit. Wayne embodies the brutal implacable order of the West, less with personal flair than with archetypical endurance. He is more likely to outlast his opponents than to outdraw them, and ever since *Stagecoach* he has never hesitated to use the rifle, an instrument more efficient, if less phallic, than the six shooter.

Ironically, Wayne has become a legend by not being legendary. He has dominated the screen even when he has not been written in as the dominant character.

Having completed *True Grit* at the end of 1968, Wayne took a holiday with his family and then, in 1969, he made *The Undefeated* (with Rock Hudson) in Texas and returned to Durango to make *Chisum*. In January 1970, he was on location in Old Tucson, Arizona. Old Tucson is a small town deliberately built as a setting for western films. Here he was making *Rio Lobo* with his old compadres Howard Hawks and Bill Clothier. It was a post-Civil War story about Wayne, as Colonel McNally, a Union officer, and his long pursuit of some traitors who leaked information about a gold shipment to Confederate spies. Of it, Roger Greenspun would say in the *Times* that "it is close enough to greatness to stand above everything else so far in the current season" and William Paul in *The Village Voice* would speak of its "graceful simplicity and directness of visual style."

He was filming in Old Tucson when the news came that he had been nominated for an Academy Award as Best Actor. His competitors were Richard Burton, Dustin Hoffman, Peter O'Toole, and Jon Voight—a pretty impressive line-up.

On April 13, which was a Monday, he flew to Los Angeles in his plane. He was accompanied by Dave Grapson, his makeup man. They went on shooting in Arizona. Hawks worked on scenes in which Wayne did not appear.

At the L.A. airport, they were met by a limousine and driven to the Beverly Hills Hotel. Pilar was awaiting him in one of the small bungalows in the tropical area behind the hotel. Burton and Elizabeth Taylor had a nearby bungalow. There was an exuberant reunion and much drinking of champagne.

On Tuesday morning, Miss Taylor and Wayne—who were taking part in some of the ceremonials of Oscar night—departed early in separate cars. Wayne and Grayson drove down to the Dorothy Chandler Pavilion. Wayne was outwardly calm. He seemed pensive and almost withdrawn. He was being fatalistic about it, or trying to be. He did not believe that he would win the balloting.

At the Pavilion, he was made up and rehearsed for the television program. There were to be the usual dazzling performances of songs and dances and specially made films—including a fine tribute to Cary Grant and Fred Astaire. There would be songs and production numbers, interspersed with the innumerable awards. Elizabeth Taylor would be wearing her million-dollar diamond pendant.

They rehearsed in the morning and in the afternoon. Pilar came about two o'clock. He got excited when he saw her and swept her off her feet and they embraced a long time.

They went back to the hotel. They returned that night. All the children were there. Wayne went back to the dressing room and was made up. He did some of his early appearances and then came back to sit next to Pilar.

Then the moment came when Barbra Streisand opened the envelope and announced, "And for best performance by a male actor, the award goes to John Wayne."

And he shambled up to the stage, his cheeks blushing and his eyes wet with tears, and he made his little speech, including the famous line, "If I'd known what I know now, I'd have put a patch on my eye thirty-five years ago."

They all got to their feet and cheered and wept and shouted bravo. In that moment, all of Hollywood was united, loving this man who loved their industry, who loved the studios and the making of movies, voicing their appreciation of his fidelity to their craft, and forgetting old antagonisms and political hatreds.

And later that night, in one of the private salons of the Beverly Hills Hotel there was a marvelous party which went on all night and in which Wayne proved that he could still drink as much as Richard Burton.

The next morning, early on this Wednesday, Wayne flew back to Old Tucson. He had a picture to complete.

When he arrived on the set, everybody's back was turned.

At a signal from Hawks, they all whirled about, facing him. And every one of them, from Hawks and Clothier, right on down to the lowliest of bit players and crew members, was wearing a patch over the left eye. Even Duke's horse was sporting a patch over one eye!

So Wayne had to have another good cry. But then he went back to work. And he made *Rio Lobo*.

And then he played old Jake in *Big Jake*.

And then he played Will Andersen in *The Cowboys*.

And now it was clear, as he entered upon the fifth decade of his life as a motion picture actor, and the sixty-sixth year of his age, that he was a superb artist, and he had been weaving a great tapestry for us, peopled by many characters and many scenes, of multicolored threads, of nuances and subtle tones, as well as bravados and fortissimo crimsons, of love and of hate, of insanity and rage, of tenderness and of pity, of kindness and of self-sacrifice, of courage in the face of adversity, some of which he had brought on himself.

There was his relationship with John Ford, the longest and most enduring relationship between a star and a director in the history of the movies, during which both men had ripened and expressed this ripeness in a series of immortal films, and these were on the tapestry. So were the figures he made with the others, Hathaway and Walsh and Hawks, and Andrew McLaglen, Burt Kennedy, Allan Dwan, Mark Rydell. And many ladies were to be seen—Maureen O'Hara and Ann Rutherford and Jennifer Jones and Marlene Dietrich and Patricia Neal and Ann-Margret, ladies of all moods and personalities. And there were other men with him, Harry Carey Sr. and Jr. and Mitchum and Canutt and Roberson and Dean Martin and Kirk Douglas and Rock Hudson and Ward Bond.

And then he made *The Train Robbers*.

And then he made *Cahill, U.S. Marshal*.

And then he made *McQ*.

And then, in March, 1974, the phone rang, echoing through his villa overlooking the Pacific at Newport Beach. He took it on the veranda. It was Hal Wallis, calling from his cottage on the Universal Studio lot. Would Duke be interested in putting on his eyepatch once more in a sequel to *True Grit*? Wayne said he loved the *Grit* character. You had to love a character who'd won you an Oscar after forty years in pictures.

"I'm interested but first I'd like to see the story," he said.

Wallis had a story outline written by a young writer from Texas named Martin Julien. Wayne had never heard of him. Neither had anybody else. Some people said that "Martin Julien" was a *nom du cinema* for somebody else, but Wallis insisted that there really was such a person.

Wallis sent over Julien's story. Wayne read it. He liked it. "I'll do it," he said.

Julien now began hammering out a thirty-five-page treatment. As he worked, the character of the woman, Eula Goodnight—a purse-lipped puritanical schoolteacher, daughter of a frontier preacher, who was against smokin' and drinkin' and cussin' and all the other pastimes in which the reprobate Rooster Cogburn indulged—began taking on larger proportions. Her role was suddenly equal to Rooster's.

The role now called for a star who had the authority, the magnetism, to equal Wayne's. The more Hal Wallis thought about it, the more he was convinced that Katharine Hepburn would be perfect for the part. True, she had rarely played rugged ladies, and not since *The*

*African Queen* had she crossed dialogue with a whiskey-drinking upholder of vice. But that film had been a triumph for her and for Bogart. And Wallis' new project had all the makings of a western plains *African Queen*. Suddenly Wallis recalled something Hepburn had said, back in 1956, after she'd seen *The Searchers*. She had been deeply touched by Wayne's portrayal of the revenge-obsessed hero, and one day she'd said to Wallis, who was producing *The Rainmaker* (in which she co-starred with Burt Lancaster), "Someday I'd like to do a picture with John Wayne. He is a fine actor. Nobody appreciates his talent. Why don't you produce a picture with the two of us?"

Now, eighteen years later, perhaps the moment had come. So he phoned Hepburn, who lives on the George Cukor compound in the Hollywood Hills above Sunset when she is in residence in Los Angeles. She was intrigued. Yes, she was interested, definitely. She read the treatment and then the first draft of the screenplay. Several months of discussions followed during which Hepburn and Wayne never met face to face. Wallis was going from one to another, acting the go-between, the diplomat. Several times a week he went down to Newport for long conferences with Duke.

Then Wayne had to go to London to make *Brannigan*, a cops-and-robbers movie about a Chicago detective and Scotland Yard. And Katharine Hepburn went to London that same summer of '74 to make a television special with Sir Laurence Olivier.

Wayne was filming a scene in Piccadilly Circus one afternoon when a tall and angular lady, beautifully garbed in Edwardian costume, hurtled through the mob of onlookers, brandishing her parasol. It was Katharine Hepburn, fresh from working in TV's *Love Among the Ruins*. Without any warning, she had decided to meet the man she regarded as a great actor. She went up to him. They looked at one another. He grinned. She smiled.

"Kate," he said.

"Duke," she said.

He placed his arms around her waist. He raised her off the ground. He embraced her in mid-air. He set her down. They kissed.

"I was born to be your leading lady," she was heard to tell him.

Those who were present that afternoon say that his eyes misted over.

And so, after *Brannigan* and *Love Among The Ruins,* they all journeyed up to Bend, Oregon, to start location shooting on *Rooster Cogburn.* It was August 15, 1974. Hal Wallis was there too—every day. He is a producer cast in the iron mould of the old school. He does not sit behind a desk. He is out on the firing line. He remained in Oregon throughout the three months of shooting, in hot weather and cold.

There they were, three giants. Hepburn and Wayne and Wallis. Wallis has produced maybe two hundred films, maybe more. *Little Caesar. The Maltese Falcon. Sergeant York. Casablanca. Yankee Doodle Dandy. True Grit. Becket. Anne of the Thousand Days.* His fusing of Wayne and Hepburn in *Rooster Cogburn* was a bold statement by the old Hollywood. It was what the star system used to mean and still means.

During the filming, the two stars rarely used doubles. Hepburn was not a great horsewoman but she did her own riding. "She doesn't really know how to ride but dammit, when she's on a horse she's such a fine actress she makes you believe she's the best damn horsewoman alive." Her strength and ability to endure impressed Wayne, who is quite an endurer himself. She had recently undergone hip surgery. It did not deter her from putting in a long day of riding and acting and then going swimming in the ice-cold Rogue River before dinner. And she could not believe the way he could remain up till two A.M., drinking his tequila and playing cards, and still be there at seven A.M. for makeup the next morning with the power to do his day's work.

She said he was like a giant redwood tree.

He said she was like a forest of them.

So Katharine Hepburn became another figure in the majestic tapestry of John Wayne's life.

In 1975, it was evident that the tapestry was far from finished. John Wayne was weaving new figures for it. Only the end of his life would close the work of his life.

# ACKNOWLEDGMENTS

This book could not have been written without the help of innumerable men and women who have known John Wayne over the years—agents, friends, business managers, fellow actors, stuntmen, cameramen, directors. Since the director is the shaping force in cinema art, I am especially appreciative of the time and insights granted to me by the late John Ford, Raoul Walsh, Mark Rydell, Howard Hawks, Melville Shavelson, and Burt Kennedy. Norman Lear, who directed *Cold Turkey* on location in Winterset, Iowa, gave me a vivid picture of Wayne's home town as it is today. Jim Henaghen, close friend and associate of Wayne for many years, is a fine raconteur and he shared many tall tales, and short tales, about Duke with me. Michael Wayne, president of Batjac Productions and Wayne's oldest son, helped me to understand the family background. He also gave me some incisive observations on the realities of film production. William Clothier, one of the great camera artists in film history, spoke of his problems as a cinematographer with humor and charm and sensitivity. Al Kingston, now a literary agent, was an invaluable source of data on Wayne's early years in serials and B pictures as was Stanley Scheuer. Morrie Ryskind was kind enough to reminisce about the origin of the Motion Picture Alliance for the Preservation of American Ideals.

And there are many others, especially John Agar, Russell Birdwell, Vera Brinn, the late George Colman, Jack Casey of the Warner Brothers Publicity Department, Mrs. Olive Carey, widow of Harry Carey, and also her son, Harry Carey, Jr., Paul Fix, Dave Grayson, Clair Huffaker, Bob Jensen,

Ben Johnson, Tom Kane, Cliff Lyons, Jeannette Mazurki, Ann-Margret, Chuck Roberson, Bö Roos, Lynn Spencer, Dave Sutton, Max Slater, Lloyd H. Smith, Rod Taylor and Cecil Zaun.

Paul Meyers, librarian of the Lincoln Center for the Performing Arts, graciously extended the courtesy of the library to me as I searched for old reviews and news items.

To Mildred Simpson, librarian, and the staff of the Library of the Academy of Motion Picture Arts and Sciences, I am deeply grateful for their assiduousness, their patience, their knowing where to find just the right fragment of information I needed at one time or another. There is more, much more, to the Motion Picture Academy than the annual Oscar awards, and this magnificent library is one of them.

In preparing this book, I have consulted hundreds of newspaper articles, reviews, essays and so forth. The back numbers of *Photoplay* and *Motion Picture Magazine* have been useful. Contrary to accepted opinion, these fan magazines frequently published well-researched and well-written articles, especially during the 1940's and 1950's.

I am most grateful to my friend Bob Thomas, the veteran Hollywood correspondent and author of biographies of Harry Cohn and Irving Thalberg, for generously lending me his extensive files on Wayne. To another friend, Arthur Knight, the distinguished film historian, critic and University of Southern California cinema professor, I am grateful for steering me to sources and making me feel like I belonged when I was a newcomer to the Hollywood scene.

For help in gathering photographs for this book, I am most appreciative of the kindness of Bernadette Carozza, editor, and Linda Breiter, photo editor, of the magazines *Photoplay* and *Motion Picture*. I am indebted to Milton Luboviski of the Larry Edmunds Bookshop and his henchmen, Claude Plum and Jonathan Benair, for their patience with me as I sorted through thousands of stills and newspictures of Wayne.

William K. Everson, scholar, filmographer and cinephile, almost single-handedly restored the western to critical interest by his articles in *Films in Review* and two books, *The Western, from Silents to Cinerama,* written with George N. Fenin (Orion Press, N.Y. 1962), and *Pictorial History of the West-*

*ern* (Citadel Press, N.Y. 1969). I constantly referred to Peter Bogdanovich's elegant monograph on John Ford (University of California Press, Berkeley, 1968). John Baxter's *The Cinema of John Ford* (A. Zwemmer, London, 1971) is good on the affinity between Ford and Wayne. There are two previous biographies of Wayne: *Duke,* by Mike Tomkies, a British journalist (Henry Regnery, Chicago, 1971), and *The John Wayne Story,* by George Carpozi, Jr., American newspaperman and a prolific writer of books about show business personalities (Arlington House, New Rochelle, 1972).

The critical writings of Bogdanovich and Andrew Sarris had much to do with lifting the taboos against the western film and the western hero in high-culture circles. Andrew Sarris' writings on American films, directors and actors in *Film Culture* and *The Village Voice* bristled with knowledge and enthusiasm. Bogdanovich's essay on Wayne in the June 1972 issue of *Esquire* was a gallant tribute. One hopes that someday Bogdanovich will realize his ambition to make a western starring Wayne, Henry Fonda, and James Stewart. Joan Didion's essay on Wayne, "A Love Song," which appears in her collection of pieces *Slouching Towards Bethlehem* (Farrar, Strauss & Giroux, N.Y., 1968), is interesting because she emphasized the sexual appeal of Wayne's acting. Curiously enough, James Agee, film critic of *The Nation,* was also impressed by this quality in Wayne. Wayne's romanticism was rarely perceived by other writers.

The filmography has become part of the biographical ritual these days. I do not append one here because John Wayne admirers are fortunate in having access to an excellent and reasonably accurate one: *The Films of John Wayne* by Mark Ricci, Boris Zmijewsky and Steve Zmijewsky (Citadel Press, N.Y., 1970). This book includes every film Wayne made up to *Rio Lobo.* He has since made *The Million Dollar Kidnap, The Cowboys, The Train Robbers, Cahill, U.S. Marshal* and *McQ.* I believe *Rio Lobo* and *The Cowboys* to be important figures in the Wayne tapestry.

# BIOGRAPHY

# 1979

The Paul Conrad cartoon that morning in the Los Angeles *Times,* a week after John Wayne's cancerous stomach was removed during 9 hours of surgery at the UCLA Medical Center, showed an angry horse pawing furiously, throwing clods of earth and dust, while a hatless cowboy rode him. The cowboy's right arm was stretched out to balance himself. His booted legs drove spurs into the bronco. On the bronco's flank was lettered THE BIG "C."

It was one of Conrad's finest works, simple and powerful. I studied the expression on the broncobuster's face. Wayne looked serene and smiling, secure in the faith of his horsemanship. Leaping over a political gulf, lifetime liberal Conrad was paying his personal tribute to a great man's will to live, to his *élan vital.* It was interesting that Conrad had pictured death as a horse rather than a horseman, rather than as one of the four apolocyptic horsemen. Any of us can learn to ride a horse.

Wayne had been riding the death bronco since 1964, as we have seen, since he was operated on for lung cancer at Good Samaritan Hospital. They took out his left lung and some of his right. He was fifty-five years old.

That was the time to call it quits.

He had already made 134 films. For fifteen years he had been one of the top ten box-office champions. He had made such classics as *Stagecoach, The Long Voyage Home, Fort Apache, Red River, Sands of Iwo Jima, The Quiet Man, The Searchers, Wings of Eagles* and *The Man Who Shot Liberty Valance.*

He could have lived out his life sprawled on a deck chair on the terrace of his Newport Beach home, taking the sun, taking his ease, living peacefully the way his third (and now estranged) wife, Pilar, wanted him to live. To live out his autumnal years as a patriarch, taking care of himself the way an old man who has just survived a hazardous operation—and in his age bracket he was given about a twenty percent chance of recovery—is supposed to.

But he did not. On the contrary, he lived life more avidly than before. Having come close to losing it, having gotten a last-minute reprieve from the governor, he was not about to vegetate in the sun. He fathered more children. He ate and drank and made love and movies like a young man of thirty-five. Between the lung cancer and the stomach cancer, between ages fifty-five and seventy-one, he made eighteen more films, including *The Shootist* (1976) with Lauren Bacall, in which he played an elderly gunfighter dying of cancer.

And these eighteen films were not photographed in the safe confines of a studio, they were filmed on location in rugged terrain and in conditions of extreme heat and extreme cold. He made *The Sons of Katie Elder* and *Rio Lobo* and *The Cowboys* and he finally won his first Oscar in 1970 as best actor for *True Grit.*

In 1971, he was filming *The Train Robbers* with Ann-Margaret, Rod Taylor and Bobby Vinton. He was on location in Torréon, Mexico, and I went down there for a couple of weeks. The company was sequestered in a fine old hotel in town, about forty miles from the actual shooting site, which was out in a desert of magnificent sand dunes. The year before I had watched Howard Hawks directing Wayne in *Rio Lobo,* and over the years—I have been a researcher into the life and deeds of Duke Wayne since 1955—I have also watched him working under the direction of John Ford and Henry Hathaway. I have seen him at work in sound stages and in the open air. But now he was sixty-three. He had to be a little tired out, a little exhausted, a little run-down. He had passed the "five year deadline" for cancer, and he was in good condition, though he was troubled by spasms of diverticulitus.

But what the hell was this man doing in a Mexican desert?

He was on location from early morning until they broke at five. Then he was driven back to the hotel in a van. He slept in a bed on the van on the way home. Then he got together with the company for an evening of drinking and dining and roistering. Rod Taylor, who must be twenty years younger than Wayne, would go drink-for-drink with him until the hotel closed the dining room. And if Wayne was hung over, you could not see it the next morning. He was always the first one down to the coffee shop for breakfast. There, he and I would talk quietly over the same breakfast every day—bacon and eggs, orange juice, rolls and coffee, except I would have three strips of bacon and one egg and one roll, and he would put away a dozen rashers of bacon and six eggs and four rolls and several mugs of coffee.

We talked movies and politics and women and poker and alcohol. And then, gradually, other members of the cast and crew would sleepily slither in and have a fast cup of coffee. Then, finally, Wayne and I and

Dave Grayson, his makeup man, would board the van and drive an hour to the rolling dunes—the lonely, deserted, godforsaken dunes—in the blazing sun, made fiercer by its reflection off the sand.

Now picture the one-lunged guy of sixty-three out there in an average heat of between 90 and 110 degrees, day after day, making a picture with Ann-Margaret. When they were preparing the next set-up he did not siesta under an umbrella. He played poker with me and several other suckers, beating me out of a few hundred pesos every day.

He always knew his own lines. He knew everybody else's lines. He directed the other actors. For a long, long time, Wayne has been the uncredited codirector of every film he has been in, except those he made under John Ford. He was terrified to the last of Ford (as I was) and would not venture to disagree with anything the old man told him to do.

Well, I watched this man working so damned hard all day, roistering at night, putting away maybe a fifth of Sauza Commemorativo tequila at night, and then striding into the coffee shop the next morning, joining me in the same complaint: The bacon was always overcooked, almost crumbling to bits. But he was always happy to see the cook and the waiters. He was always happy to see the cast. He was always happy to drive out to the location. He did not bitch or get angry.

Oh, he was pissed off about political issues. He was furious because the U.S. was not bombing Haiphong harbor. That kind of thing. But in the immediacies of everyday life, in what he was doing and living, he seemed to relish everything, the simple ordinary things, the fried eggs over easy and the toasted rolls and the wonderful Mexican coffee. And he relished every moment he was working.

I had been nerving myself for several days to confront him with the question of his health. And I wanted to ask him about death and the fear of death. Finally, one morning I asked him whether his doctor knew about the strenuous pace at which he was working, and he growled, "None of his damn business."

I paused. I lighted a cigarette. I inhaled the smoke. "You dumb bastard," he said. "You're killing yourself with those things." I shrugged. He had had a terrible time kicking cigarettes. He had for several years been chewing tobacco and spewing brown spit on the ground and now he was smoking cigarillos, little cigars, limiting himself to five a day, not inhaling them.

"Aren't you afraid of killing yourself?" I asked him finally.

He set down his coffee. "We are all under sentence of death," he said gravely. Then he smiled his crooked smile. "Bet you don't know who said that."

I shook my head.

"Whittaker Chambers," he said.

I understood, or thought I understood. At some point in 1964, he had come to accept death as a fact of life, as a built-in condition of existence. He had come to that idea expressed in *Julius Caesar:* "It seems to me most strange that men should fear death seeing that it is a necessary thing which comes when it will come."

But by the time we were conversing in Torréon, Mexico, in 1971, I believe that Wayne was already moving beyond this reconciliation with existence into another attitude, and this attitude is expressed in one of Carlos Castaneda's quotations from don Juan: "You must make friends with your death. He is always standing there at your left shoulder."

The Duke was making friends with death. So he was not afraid. You can't be afraid of one of your best friends.

I suspect he began entering into this new dimension around 1970. Up till then, except when he was relaxing with his cronies on hunting and sailing trips, he presented a stiff and humorless face to his public, and he was a rather grim personification of an ultraconservative, militaristic, tightlipped reactionary. Now he started laughing. He started being amused at himself and his attitudes. Why, he even backed President Carter on the question of the Panama Canal treaty. He broke with his old friend and political ally, Ronald Regan. He knew Panama well and Panamanians, and he thought it would be a very fine thing to give the Panama Canal back to the Panamanians.

Last September at a Century Plaza testimonial dinner held to honor him and to raise money for the purchase of a 577-acre Boy Scout encampment near Lake Arrowhead to be called the John Wayne Outpost Camp, he shared the podium with former president Gerald Ford. Merv Griffin was master of ceremonies. Merv quipped, "Your lifestyle has changed a little, Duke. It's no thrill to see you having Ovaltine with your dinner."

"I still drink red wine," murmured Duke.

"Right, Duke," Griffin said.

"Yeah, as far right as you can go," Wayne riposted.

And Jimmy Stewart delivered a sentimental tribute to his old friend, to which Wayne replied, "If I could pick any man to be my brother, Jimmy, I'd sure pick someone like you—RICH!"

Now this was not the hobgoblin John Wayne, the fanatical anti-Communist and witch hunter and right wing zealot usually pictured in magazines and newspapers.

We had a glimpse of his changing personality when he started being the butt of gags on the old *Laugh-In*. He once even made a cameo appearance garbed in a ridiculous rabbit costume from toe to rabbit ears. He was the Easter Bunny! And, his remarking, when he received the Academy Award statuette from Barbra Streisand in April 1970, "If I'd known what I know now, I'd have put a patch on my eye thirty-five years ago."

True, this is not a quip worthy of Oscar Wilde or George Bernard Shaw—no, not even S.J. Perelman or

Neil Simon. But it was his own joke and he was laughing with death, looking over his left shoulder and knowing it was nice to win an Oscar—but it was also nice to wake up in the morning and look over your left shoulder and say good morning to death and not feel too bad about it. Wayne was looking around at all the men in dinner jackets in the Dorothy Chandler Pavilion that night and all the beautiful women in their evening gowns and seeing with a different vision. He had, to quote Eliot on Webster, started seeing "the skull beneath the skin." And he thought it was rather amusing, after all.

A year ago, last March, in 1978, cardiologists discovered he had a defective mitral valve. He went to Massachusetts General Hospital. He underwent open-heart surgery. The defective valve was removed, and a new mitral valve from a healthy pig was installed in its place. The operation took three hours. He was in intensive care for five days. When he emerged, Dr. Roman de Sanctis, chief of cardiology at Mass General, asked him how he felt.

"When I woke up this morning and saw it was raining," Wayne cracked, "I found myself wanting to roll in the mud."

Later, Dr. de Sanctis told reporters, "I've seen Mr. Wayne in many pictures and he looks tough on the screen. But I didn't appreciate how tough he really is until I saw him in the hospital and examined him after the operation."

After a couple of weeks in the hospital, he got bored. So Patrick Wayne flew him home to Newport Beach. By July, he was sailing the *Wild Goose* to Catalina with his grandchildren.

His last public appearance before his stomach-cancer operation was at the International Room of the Beverly Hilton Hotel on December 13, 1978, when the Los Angeles Advertising Club awarded him a plaque in honor of the Great Western Savings and Loan campaign, which produced, it is estimated, almost $250,000,000 in additional deposits. In television commercials, newspaper and magazine splurges and on billboards, one beheld the smiling and weatherbeaten visage of John Wayne, in western costume, against a background of California mountains or California farmland, and he would tell us why he had decided "to put in with this outfit." I have been a depositor at Great Western for many years—prior to the John Wayne campaign. My reasons are cultural. In its stupendously startling main office on La Cienega Boulevard and Wilshire—an oval shaped, all glass building which resembles a skyscraper from outer space—Great Western offers free to its depositors the finest lending library and reading facilities to be found in the entire United States, with free reservations, free copies of the New York *Times* Book Review available, all the magazines and newspapers in an ambiance of good lighting and comfortable armchairs and friendly librarians. The Great Western's branch at La Cienega and Wilshire is where booklovers put their savings. Anyway, the Ad Club's luncheon was the kickoff for the annual drive, in conjunction with the Marine Corps, known as Toys for Tots. The Marine Corps presented Wayne with a World War I Marine helmet. Ad Club president Harry Spitzer gave Wayne a plaque and hailed the Great Western campaign as an "ideal blending of product and personality."

In accepting the award, Wayne (who had been suffering great pains in his abdominal region for weeks) grinned and said, "I'm happy you guys in the advertising business think well of my commercials. But the way my luck has been running lately, I'm surprised I didn't wind up making commercials for Ford Pintos and Firestone 500s . . . I've got a feeling the real reason you guys are gathered here today is to make an old actor happy—and if I meet an old actor on my way home, I'll tell him all about you."

And then Don Moorhead, general manager of KMET, who was in charge of entertainment at the banquet, also saluted Wayne, thanking him for helping us win the war against Japan because "if we had lost that war, we would today be driving Japanese automobiles, taking pictures of our loved ones with Japanese cameras, and watching programs on Japanese television sets."

And John Wayne was sitting there laughing his head off, knowing he was going into the hospital—though he did not know how bad it was. And if he *had* known, it would not have made any difference.

Wayne's most enchanting gambit these last ten years was his invasion of Harvard in January 1974. The editors of the *Harvard Lampoon* dared him to première his movie *McQ*—a hard-hitting, law-and-order picture about a San Francisco cop—in Cambridge and to submit to a confrontation with Harvard students. If he did, he would receive the *Lampoon's* Brass Balls award.

He loved the way the challenge was phrased: "So you think you're tough? You've never dared set foot in the wilderness of Harvard." They challenged him to outgun the liberal and radical Harvard underclassmen.

"We here," the Harvards sneered, "call the supposedly unbeatable John Wayne the biggest fraud in history."

Wayne replied by telegram that he accepted the challenge, though he regretted to note "a weakness in your breeding."

He agreed to visit the *Lampoon's* office on Bow Street at high noon. He agreed to meet the editors and later, at a mass meeting, to answer all questions thrown at him.

He rode down Brattle Street in Cambridge in an armored personnel carrier, brandishing an M15 rifle, while students threw snowballs at him. Later, inside the Harvard Square Theatre, jammed to capacity with 1,600 students, he faced the enemy. The questions came fast.

Question: "Is it true that since you've lost weight, your horse's hernia has cleared up?"

"No. He died and we canned him—which is what you've been eating at the Harvard Club."

Another question: "Do you look at yourself as the fulfillment of the American dream?"

"I don't look at myself any more than I have to."

One girl asked if the session was being taped, and Duke said, "Well, if it is, I hope the guy taping it is a Democrat because if he's a Republican, you would lose it."

When asked his opinion of the women's liberation movement, he responded, "I think women have a right to work anywhere they want to." Then he looked up and waited for several beats. "As long as they have dinner ready, when we want it."

Remember, all this repartee was fast and sharp and unrehearsed and no gag writers were feeding John Wayne the punch lines. He won over the students that afternoon as he has won over every hostile interviewer and journalist who has confronted him since 1970. It is interesting that the man once so suspicious of, and truculent with, the press, now delighted in interviews and was utterly relaxed.

The Wayne home is in a guarded Irvine Company compound of several score houses overlooking Balboa and the marina, an area of $250,000 and up homes. He resided alone, since his separation from Pilar Wayne, in a ten-room, one-story white ranch house with a pool and a patio. There are elephant statues around the pool. His terrace looks down on Newport Harbor and the Balboa peninsula. He usually wore desert boots, pastel-colored slacks and Lacoste polo shirts when he received visitors. He had three servants and several secretaries headed by the exuberant thirtyish brunette, Pat Stacy, with whom he has been romantically linked. He has twenty-one grandchildren and loved to receive them.

He was a gracious host. He took visitors through the house and showed off his gun collection and his Remington paintings and sculptures and all his awards, and he talked about his plans for future movies and for the new Great Western commercials.

He was asked recently whether he was planning to retire.

"Retire?" he said. "What the hell would I retire to? What would I do? Work is the only thing I know. And as long as I can keep my dignity I'm going to go on making movies. I've got this story about an old geezer, Beau John. Too damn late to go with it this year, we've got to get the script finished. But next year—for sure!"

When he made the sequel to *True Grit*, he played opposite Katharine Hepburn who, Hal Wallis once told me, had been dreaming of playing opposite him for a long time. Persons who think of Wayne only in terms of his reactionary stereotype, rather than the quality of his acting and the tone of his films, forget that he has been a sensitive actor and has portrayed the tender and even passionate aspects of a man-woman relationship with dignity and charm. He has even played bantering love comedies opposite Jean Arthur and Claudette Colbert.

Yet the stereotype of Wayne, the bloodthirsty Indian killer and crazed superpatriot will not go away—except among the passionate critics and admirers of the western, such as Andrew Sarris and Peter Bogdanovitch, both of whom have written about Wayne as one of the most skillful and subtle movie *actors* of our time.

But the two loveliest tributes to Wayne were by women: Joan Didion's in the *Saturday Evening Post* around 1963 and, more recently, from Molly Haskell, film-critic wife of Sarris and author of a study of women in cinema, *From Reverence to Rape,* an equally admiring essay in the July 1976 issue of the *Ladies Home Journal*. And both of these writers—in fact, all four of them, counting the men—had to get past that psychological barrier of hating to admire an actor whose political positions and whose defense of the Vietnam intervention were so galling to them.

It was hard, especially during the 1960s, to be able

to see Wayne's artistry on film apart from his political positions. Then, too, there was his strong anti-Communist stance during the 1940s and 50s, during the era of red scares and red hunts and blacklisting. He was, God knows, a fervent member of the Motion Picture Alliance for the Preservation of American Ideals. The wounds of that time are still not healed. There are many men and women, the injured ones, still walking wounded in Hollywood.

Having known Wayne, I know he was not a bigot— and never a savage, revengeful person. He stuck his neck out many times for the wrong reasons, but when the chips were down he never let an individual's political past influence his decision, as in the example of Marguerite Roberts and her screenplay of *True Grit,* which I've cited in a previous chapter.

Haskell describes a scene she watched being filmed at the Burbank Studios by director Don Siegel on *The Shootist.* Since Wayne has for a long time dominated the screenplays, as well as shared in the directing of his films, we can be sure that this scene is a true expression of his amiable attitude toward death, especially his own death. The scene takes place in a barbershop in Carson City, Nevada, in 1900, and the picture is almost ended as is the hero's life, the hero being John Bernard Books, legendary gunfighter with a terminal cancer. To underscore, with an obvious irony, the autobiographical tone of the film, it opened with a montage of clips from a dozen Wayne westerns, showing him gradually getting older and older, as if they were newsreel clips of shootouts and Indian wars which are being assembled for a documentary on the life of John Bernard Books. Well, as old Books is getting lathered up and shaved, the town undertaker, Beckum, played by an incredibly morose and lively and charmingly sinister John Carradine, approaches the hero and starts making a deal for his corpse. He says he will provide a handsome silk-lined casket and put the gunfighter's body on display for a week. He will provide a handsome funeral and a marble headstone and perpetual maintenance. And it will not cost John Bernard Books one dime. But Wayne is suspicious. He suspects that Carradine will soak the public to view the corpse and when the excitement dies down he will just dump him in a hole somewhere. Furthermore, he doesn't want to just give away his dead body. He haggles with Carradine and they arrive at a price of fifty dollars for the corpse and an elegant funeral and headstone and the mortician agrees and starts to slouch away but Wayne tells him to fork over that fifty dollars before he goes.

"Books, you are a hard man to do business with," Carradine says.

"I'm still alive," Wayne says.

Molly Haskell reported that "the way he says it, in that rich, familiar baritone, the low, husky drawl rising ruefully at the end, says it all. It's a comic moment. Wayne, talking to me a few moments later, will insist on the humor. But if it's so funny, why do I have tears in my eyes?"

(I'll tell you why, Mrs. Sarris, because you are still so young and so beautiful, and there is no reason you should look over your left shoulder and make friends with your death, but she is there walking behind you all the time, and she was there that afternoon on the soundstage in Burbank and some time in the future you may come to know her and laugh with her and somebody else, who is younger than you, will weep and not know why you are laughing.)

Getting back to Katharine Hepburn. Hepburn, who is herself one of the champion suvivors and craftsmen of all time, once confided what it was like to be in the presence of John Wayne and to play scenes with him and to be in contact with his life force. She confessed that when the action called for her to lean against him— and she said she did this as often as possible, even when the script did not demand such close contact—she was "thrilled beyond words for it was like leaning against a strong tree."

She described him in what you might call female-chauvinist-sow language. "Well," she said, "he has great legs and tight buttocks, a real great seat and small, sensitive feet . . . He carries his huge frame lightly, like a feather . . . He has a very fine light walk." She said he was one damn exciting guy physically.

She also talked about his sense of humor and his laughter on the set and his awesome sense of responsibility in his work. And she said, finally, that he was a "simple and decent man," rather like Humphrey Bogart. She did not speak of Spencer Tracy, but I have a feeling that in her mind John Wayne had a largeness of soul like Tracy.

John Wayne was discharged from the UCLA Medical Center and was home sitting on his terrace watching the boats. He was able to eat meat again and he played backgammon and chess with a few close friends and talked about his next movie and his next Great Western commercial. He was not living the past. He was living in the present. He was planning for the future. At the Academy Awards ceremony on April 9, he presented the Oscar for Best Picture won by *The Deer Hunter*.

His condition worsened, and he returned to the UCLA Medical Center on May 2. He died at 5:30 P.M. (Pacific Daylight Time) on Monday, June 11.

You can be sure that John Wayne went gently into the good night and that he did not rage against the dying of the light.

> He made friends with his death.
> He made friends with his life.

M.Z.

June 12, 1979
West Hollywood, California

# ABOUT THE AUTHOR

MAURICE ZOLOTOW, whose biographies of actors and actresses have won him a unique place among American writers, devoted three years to the research and writing of this life of John Wayne. Critics have called the book one of the most revealing in-depth portraits of one of the all-time great movie stars.

Zolotow has written over five hundred profiles of stage, television and movie personalities for *The New York Times, Saturday Evening Post, TV Guide, Playboy, McCall's, Cosmopolitan* and other national magazines. His biography of Marilyn Monroe was the first and among the most intimate studies of the woman. His book about the Lunts, *Stagestruck: The Romance of Alfred Lunt and Lynn Fontanne,* was a national best seller for six months.

A bachelor, Zolotow lives in Hollywood just minutes away from most of the major studios and the Academy of Motion Picture Arts and Sciences Library, where he spends many hours poring over newspaper clippings about his subjects—when he isn't with them at their homes and at Beverly Hills watering holes.